The Cooper's Wife Is Missing

The Trials of Bridget Cleary

JOAN HOFF

MARIAN YEATES

BASIC
BOOKS

A Member of the Perseus Books Group

A Cataloging-in-Publication record for this book is available from the Library of
Congress.
ISBN 0-465-03088-2

Design by Heather Hutchison

The paper used in this publication meets the requirements of the American National Standard for Permanence of Paper for Printed Library Materials Z39.48-
1984.

10   9   8   7   6   5   4   3   2   1

The Cooper's Wife
Is Missing

Contents

Are you a witch?
*   Are you a fairy?*
Are you the wife
*   Of Michael Cleary?*

—Children's rhyme
occasionally still heard
in South Tipp

1

Christmas in Clonmel

"Adeste Fideles"

The place was Clonmel, located on the River Suir in the south of County Tipperary, Ireland—that long-suffering, long-disloyal domain of Queen Victoria's grand and growing empire, where if the stout-hearted, stout-loving men of South Tipperary had their way, there'd be few tears if the Queen, her empire, and the royal family, too, for that matter, were suddenly to sink beneath the icy waves of the North Atlantic.

The year was 1894, and what was sinking, instead, was Prime Minister William Gladstone's political career, fallen to age and Tory imperialism, dashing all hopes for passage of a Home Rule Bill that would grant Ireland a measure of autonomy. In 1893, Gladstone's Second Home Rule Bill cleared the House of Commons but in 1894 had no chance of slipping past the House of

Lords, whose members had their eyes fixed on expanding Victoria's holdings rather than giving them away. Late in the summer, Gladstone fled London complaining of gout and leaving his Liberal government in the weak hands of Lord Archibald Philip Primrose, 5th Earl of Rosebery.

And now it was Christmas in Clonmel, the season of peace, goodwill toward men, and for all the colonial commotion elsewhere in the world, the *Nationalist and Tipperary Advertiser* reported in its first issue of 1895 that the holiday passed with "remarkable sobriety and peacefulness." The worldwide agricultural depression, which was causing grief in America and elsewhere, had little effect in Clonmel, for here depression was a staple. In recognition that purses were slim, managers of the Exhibition House offered winter goods at the "very lowest prices," made possible by their ability to pay "Ready Money" to suppliers, while James Byrne offered budget-minded housewives a large selection of "Room Papers" for covering parlor walls. Likewise David Atkins's Posting and Coach-Building establishment announced coaches for hire at the lowest rates, with funeral requisites if need be.[1]

The police responded to fewer holiday disturbances than in previous years. On Christmas morn there were scattered incidents of unruliness in the "welkin ring" of "darkest Clonmel" as thirsty souls meandered from pub to pub, but even in the rowdiest section of town, order prevailed. In outlying districts, fewer incidents of "roughness" were reported, although a certain Mrs. Miller took the "family jug" to her poor husband's head, exacerbating his hangover more than police thought necessary. Charges were not pressed, for the assault left but a small lump. At the Templemore Petty Sessions, Johanna Tearchy was hauled before the bar for heaping "abusive language" upon the head of her neighbor,

John Bowe. Mrs. Tearchy was fined and ordered to use "good language" in the future so as not to threaten public order.

Authorities in the Bansha district, southwest of Clonmel, reported but one assault, two trespasses, and one dispute involving a watercourse. Otherwise, the district was calm, prompting officials to declare, "It speaks well for the good conduct of the people of the village and district that there would be but few charges of drunkenness against them especially after the Christmas season." In the Templemore district, police received reports of "wild and abusive behavior" at the gaming establishment of Patrick Guider. The police responded and found a game in progress; however, no arrests were made, since Guider and his gaming men used neither cards nor money, so technically were not in violation of the law. As Mr. Guider politely explained, the fellows were playing for a pig's head, and meaning no disrespect to His Honor the Constable, the pig's head was meant as a "Christmas exhibition of good feeling toward the police." The Head Constable was not amused, but recognizing that he had been outwitted, sent the boys home, they no doubt heaving with laughter all the way.

Even the "wren boys" exhibited something less than their usual passion for the traditional St. Stephen's Day hunt for the elusive wren, believed anciently to be the cleverest of birds. At gatherings around the county, rollicking gangs set off through the countryside, "with the whack on the drum and a small drop of rum," in search of the tiny wren. The birds survived, but Daniel Murphy suffered a good whack to the head, and several days later appeared in court, draped in bandages, charging Daniel Greede and John Barleycorn with assault. The judge listened patiently as plaintiff and defendants hurled charges and countercharges, then sentenced the whole lot to serve twelve months of "good behaviour."

In keeping with the season's spirit, women from the upper levels of Tipperary society performed their duties for the hordes of needy, while husbands dissipated their passions at the racetrack. Mrs. Charles J. Boland, mistress of the county workhouse, served a festive holiday dinner to inmates, hoping to brighten their spirits as much as possible "under the circumstances." In a similar gesture, Mrs. Richard Bagwell, the wife of Clonmel's leading citizen and largest landowner, distributed gifts to residents of the male hospital, supplemented by a pint of stout from a certain Dr. William Crean, who will play a part later in our story.[2] At Lord and Lady Buckley's Galtee Castle, Christmas brought "varied degrees of joy and sorrow" to the estate's tenants and laborers. From far and near the estate's poorest residents flocked to the castle, where Lady Buckley graciously attended to "their wants" and, "with ready hand and sympathetic word," distributed the usual store of blankets, boots, clothes, and meat. Special attention was paid to the young scholars at the estate school who received fine gifts for achievement and good attendance.

In rebellious South Tipperary, nonattendance at school was often an indicator that trouble was brewing in the countryside. During the bloody Land War of the 1880s, tenants' rights associations organized boycotts against schools that enrolled the children of so-called emergency men, farmers brought in by landlords to manage farms taken from evicted tenants. In 1887, the village of Cloneen was the site of a particularly troublesome school boycott. In February of that year, headmaster Michael O'Brien complained to officials in Dublin that attendance was "irregular" owing to the presence of two students named Kennedy and Hogan, whose fathers worked for the local land corporation. The parents of these "obnoxious" children, according to O'Brien, were greatly "disliked" because of their association with the land corporation, and as a consequence, other parents in the area would not allow their children to associate with them. By September 1887, after the offending students had been withdrawn, school attendance returned to normal levels.[3] Even though school boycotts were less common after the Land War subsided, the threat of fresh eruptions continued throughout the 1890s.

In Carrick-on-Suir, Clonmel's sister city to the east, observers noted that Christmastide was becoming more "prosaic" than in years past, and marked with less "hilarity and sentiment." Citizens celebrated in a "proper way" and their enjoyment was no less real when unaccompanied by the "exuberant gaiety and gushing sentiment" that some felt a necessary companion to the season. Celebrations in Cashel, Clonmel's neighbor to the west, were both pious and commercial. Observers described the colorful shop windows decorated with cards, beautiful gifts, and sweet things of all description. On Christmas morning, immense crowds gathered at Cashel's cathedral to hear the dean deliver a sermon on the birth of Christ, after which the Temperance Society band performed a choice musical program. In keeping with the spirit of the season, the convent's orphan children received a sumptuous meal of pudding, sweet bread, and tea.

Throughout the county, people went about their business peacefully. At Clonmel's railway station, crowds of travelers gathered on their journeys to and from the outlying villages within Clonmel's orbit of influence. Among the inbound passengers were numbers of country people who came late in the afternoon to attend traditional Christmas Eve Mass, an "old practice" among them, which suggested to watchful clerics that the spirit of "true" religion was active among them, despite newspaper accounts and police reports of lingering pagan superstitions and stories about fairies in the countryside. These silent, rudely clad figures filled the pews at St. Mary's Cathedral, bent their knees, bowed their heads, and reaffirmed their allegiance to God and Church, if not the Queen. These were Ireland's faithful, her sullen masses, who came to town that Christmas Eve, knelt at the rail, and received the wafer as the choir sang "Adeste Fideles."

Authorities were relieved that all was calm among remnants of the "indomitable Irishry," which was what William Butler Yeats called Ireland's rural peasantry. In the years before the Great Famine, which began in the 1840s, this class of laboring poor was "indomitable" in the sense that they comprised most of the population, produced nearly all the economic wealth, and provided the manpower for political uprisings. Fifty years later male farmworkers had dwindled from half the male population to less than a third. This fast-disappearing class, also known as "the old Irishry," was most resistant to change and, not incidentally, the class that most honored the ancient fairy faith.[4]

By century's end, this "old religion" had been driven underground, but hints of its continuing practice occasionally surfaced, as in June 1894, when Clonmel's *Nationalist* reported that ghosts and apparitions were sighted by a group of boys in Ballinacurra, near Carrick-on-Suir. News of the event caused a great stir throughout the area, prompting the *Nationalist* to distance its readership from such nonsense:

> Public talk is no longer solely engrossed with tales and stories of ghosts, hobgoblins, banshees and bibes, and a general feeling of scepticism in spirits, other than earthly ones, has taken hold of the larger proportion of the people and of those who in the first flush of the story were credulous of the opinion that ghosts sometimes do appear.[5]

Eruptions from the "Otherworld" of the fairies were unwelcome in the Nationalist camp because those seeking Ireland's independence could ill afford the embarrassment that these incidents incurred. Intelligence of this sort was promptly relayed to London, where Unionist politicians made good use of the news, implicitly asking: How could anyone seriously consider granting political independence to a nation whose populace still believed in fairies?

While the fairies made good political propaganda, the persistence of pagan beliefs among the peasantry disrupted the orderly administration of justice. Authorities were especially troubled by reports of burnings in the countryside, associated with ancient beliefs about changelings—mortal spirits taken by the fairies and replaced by alien spirits from the Otherworld. This peculiar form of death by fire, particularly of children persisted in the Irish countryside late into the century as indicated by a random sampling of the Fethard district death registries from the mid-1860s to the 1890s. For example, it was common to find entries like these: "John Rocke, 12 months, child of a tradesman, accidently scalded, died 13 December 1877; Anne Hanly, 2 years, child of farmer, accidently burned on the abdomen, died 13 April 1879; Patrick Dannell, 3 years, child of a labourer, accidental burning, died 10 November 1879." In these and other numerous cases, the local coroners almost always cited the cause of death from burning as "accidental," rather than as infanticide or fairy-induced.[6]

Open fires were common in rural cabins, and most deaths were indeed accidental, but some were most assuredly not. To believers, it was a known fact that changelings feared fire more than anything else, and after herbs and incantations had been tried, only burning could drive away the alien spirit in possession of a loved one's body. Young women and small children were favored targets for fairy abduction, according to newspaper accounts in England, Ireland, and the United States in the spring of 1895.[7] Little did anyone suspect that another shocking event was about to disturb the tranquillity of Christmas in Clonmel.

The waning of boycotts, protests, and pagan primitivism left the Queen's enforcers little to do. At Her Royal Majesty's Royal Barracks, the Highlander Regiment celebrated New Year's Eve with a traditional Scottish meal of "bannocks o' barley," after which the oldest soldier of the regiment dressed up like Father Time and at midnight knocked loudly at the door, seeking admittance. "Who goes there?" shouted the sentry. "It is Father Time," the old soldier replied, "bearing with him the New Year, 1895." Those inside entreated Father Time to enter, declaring "all is well." And indeed, all seemed well—for the moment.

The holiday season's calm encouraged the county's Corporation Board to recommend that the tax for extra policemen be eliminated, saving the county nearly a thousand pounds a year. The tax was a large expense, the board contended, for which there was "not necessity . . . now that things have smoothened down." Even though the Corporation felt confident that peace would prevail, British authorities took no chances in volatile County Tipperary. A small notice in the *Nationalist*, dated January 16, disclosed that the Highlander Regiment of British Army regulars, stationed in Clonmel for some years, departed in the night by train, to be promptly replaced by a fresh regiment from India.

The caution was necessary given Tipperary's bellicose history. The gallant sons of Ireland's "premier" county were known for their hatred of the English, their passion for nationalism, and their eagerness to fight. The fighting spirit of South Tipp was akin to the famous Wheaten terriers of Carrick-on-Suir, touted as the best fighting dogs in all of Ireland, if not the world. The vicious "Carrick dog" began his fighting career at nine days old, feared nothing, and took particular delight in demolishing opponents thrice his size, which led the envious to call him a cannibal, but this was not strictly true, since, although he would happily devour any dog within a mile radius, he left his own breed alone. Wary visitors knew of the dog's reputation and its particular fondness for Clonmel canines, so no sensible Clonmel man would dare walk his dog down New Street unless, of course, he wished to leave town alone. The reputation of the Carrick dog was so widespread and well deserved that the phrase "Carrick, I dread you" arose in reference to South Tipp's fierce canine.[8]

Like the Carrick dog, Clonmel's fighting spirit was well documented in Irish history. For over a century, Clonmel was the administrative, military, and commercial center of Tipperary's South Riding district. The town's name comes from the Irish *Cluain meala* (meadow of honey), because of the lush pastures flanking the wooded banks of the River Suir. To the northeast, a mountain, Slievenamon, rises above the river, woods, and meadows, forming a majestic backdrop for the town. Because of its long history of political resistance and agrarian unrest, the British maintained a garrison of six hundred in the town's central barracks, the size attesting to Clonmel's reputation as picturesque but violent—six hundred soldiers for just nine thousand inhabitants.[9]

And then there were the town's legendary and eccentric heroes. Such a one was the good King Brian Boru, who fought the Danes at the Battle of the Boulick in the twelfth century. While the Danes massed a fearsome force at Peddar's Field, King Brian decided to take the afternoon off and fish for salmon. No sooner had he flung his "crooked pin" into the water than the genie of the Boulick Sthrame emerged from the river and asked King Brian what the commotion was all about. "Was it a regatta to celebrate the Queen's birthday?" he asked. No, Brian responded, it was just the Danes come to invade; thinking quickly, Brian promised to make him a Duke if he would drown the Danes. The genie agreed, and shortly the river began to flood with a current so swift and a torrent so violent that it lifted the Danes from their camp at Peddar's Field and swept them into Thomas Osborne's Bridge, leaving a gigantic crack. Nowadays when the rains come, they say the river is fixing to drown more Danes.[10] And the English, too, for that matter.

A more recent local favorite was Hugh Dubh O'Neill, hero of the famous Siege of Clonmel. When the Puritan Roundheads invaded Ireland in 1641, the two powerful families of the district, the Butlers and Kildares, joined forces under O'Neill's command to hold off Oliver Cromwell at Clonmel's fortress. During the months-long siege, Hugh smuggled in twelve hundred troops to reinforce the royal garrison and had them waiting when Cromwell's men stormed the breach in the town's fortifications. Just as the Puritan forces were about to attack, O'Neill jumped up on the wall:

> *Then up he speaks unto his chiefs:*
> *"Ere yet this town we leave,*
> *We'll make a stand for fatherland*
> *Will cause the foe to grieve.*
> *The breach that yawns so widely now*
> *Will serve our purpose well;*
> *Before we go we'll make the foe*
> *Remember 'Rare Clonmel'!"*

Cromwell lost two thousand men in the attempt, and the town held out for another two months before O'Neill took flight. Eventually the fortress fell to the Roundheads, but the siege of Clonmel proved to be the toughest encountered anywhere in Ireland.[11]

After Cromwell left, the sons of Tipperary continued the fight against English landlords who had stolen more land from the Irish and had sent in soldiers to protect their ill-gotten property rights. A subculture of violence emerged in the late eighteenth century when bands of tenant farmers and agricultural laborers—known as hillside men, ribbon men, moonlighters, or Whiteboys—terrorized landlords and lackeys alike. After the Great Famine, violence flared again in the Land War of the 1880s, when bands of "summer soldiers" terrorized the countryside. Political agitators led the way, but the solid core of resistance lay with the country people, those tough, roughly civilized rural peasants who fought at a moment's notice when landlords raised, or "racked," their rents to levels calculated to drive them from the land. In the period between 1874 and 1881, landlords conveniently racked their rents just as agricultural prices fell, resulting in over 10,000 evictions and a huge increase in rural violence—more than 2,500 incidents in 1880 alone.[12] Some of the worst of this violence took place in County Tipperary, particularly around Clonmel. Though Tipperary's "summer soldiers" were armed only with pitchforks, they fought like Carrick dogs to save their homes.

If Clonmel was known for its peculiar combination of beauty and toughness, the region was also notable for its fertility. In the prosperous pre-Famine decade of the 1830s, the town was the thriving commercial center of South Tipperary, as well as the major terminus for the distribution of grain, butter, bacon, and spirits. Its burgeoning population of 18,000 made it the county's largest town. At its peak, Clonmel's packing houses slaughtered over 30,000 pigs, most of which went down river in barrel-laden barges and thence to England. Its huge, factory-like grain mills employed hundreds and annually produced over 300,000 barrels of flour. The barrel industry alone employed a small army of cutters and coopers. At the town's quays along the River Suir, a flotilla of barges waited to lavish the bounty of Ireland's premier county on English tables.[13]

By the mid-1840s, Clonmel, along with the rest of Ireland, was devastated by the Great Potato Famine, and within the space of a few years, half the town's residents were gone—either dead from starvation or emigrated. As a result of this holocaust, Clonmel lost its grain, meat, and dairy industries, and much of its commerce. After the Famine, the once flourishing town withered, prompting many to echo Billy Heffernan, the tenant laborer in Charles Kickham's novel *Knocknagow*, who observed, "There's nothin' doing there."[14] By the 1860s, Clonmel had recovered somewhat, only to be knocked down again by a worldwide agricultural depression that lasted two decades. More children were born, but most of these left, so by 1893 the population still stood at a meager 8,810.[15]

Fifty years after the Famine, although local industries had not fully recovered, Clonmel was becoming a modern town, with a condensed milk factory, breweries, manufacturing establishments that produced boots and carriages, a tannery, flour mills, a gasworks, gaslit streetlamps, sewage connections, telephone and telegraph services, and access to clean water, supplied from a central town pump, links to the railway system, a new cemetery, and a new Town Hall on Parnell Street. There were still grinding poverty, disease-ridden children, and countless pubs, and in the Irishtown shanties, there was talk of trade unions, nationalism, land reform, government informers, and warring political factions.[16]

Even in the mid-1890s, the Great Famine continued to haunt "the indomitable Irishry." Memories of the grotesquely bloated bodies of children, dead mothers lying by the road with nursing children clinging to their breasts, corpses heaped in the lanes with grass-stained mouths, and entire families walling themselves inside their mud huts to die together with a modicum of dignity—these images would not go away.[17]

The Famine had created a state of almost universal despair, and secular and cleric authorities leapt at the opportunity to tighten their grip on the weakened population and pushed ahead with their respective reforms. Landlords ordered more evictions to consolidate their holdings, abandoning any pretense of their traditional precapitalist paternalism and further alienating the remaining tenant farmers and rural laborers.[18] The English colonial government in Dublin expanded the system of National Schools, instituted before the Famine, which systematically eliminated instruction in Irish language and culture.[19] The second oldest of these National Schools, by the way, was established in 1832 in Cloneen, a village near Clonmel.

Meanwhile, in the 1840s and 1850s, the Catholic Church pressed ahead with its "devotional revolution," which imposed ecclesiastical reforms from Rome like regular attendance at Mass and frequent taking of Holy Communion, while a dramatic increase in the number of priests allowed the Church to wage all-out war against the lingering elements of paganism practiced at weddings, wakes, and seasonal festivals. The remnants of "old Irishry" who survived the Famine actually were slightly better off, as cottage size, education, and diet marginally improved in the last quarter of the nineteenth century. This diminished class also became the mainstay of political organizations and their middle-class Anglo-Irish leaders. Tenants' and rural laborers' participation in tenants' rights organizations made political protest more effective and channeled random, rural violence into acceptable outlets, such as organized rent boycotts and competitive sports.[20]

The preference for civilized sport over random violence was celebrated by the astonishing 1886 victory of the Clonmel Rowing Club. In the early 1880s the club had made a name for itself in Irish rowing competitions, but then had hit a bad patch. In the spring of 1886, the club's young bloods were brimming with energy and ready to reclaim the town's lost honor at the summer regattas. At stake was the coveted Leahy Cup, which would become the town's permanent property should their boys win for a second year. Meanwhile, the Dublin team, determined that the cup should not retire to Clonmel, sported a first-class shell, while the Cork Harbour Club sent their four top men. To match these, Clonmel rowed their "tub," which as every oarsman knew could not possibly compete with the Dublin shell. So confident were the Dublin and Cork crews that they bet their own money, five to one, that Clonmel would lose.

When the gun went off, the three boats shot across the water, all three teams pulling hard, with the Dublin and Cork shells slightly ahead. Midpoint in the race, exhausted Cork fell back, leaving Clonmel and Dublin battling for position. In the final sprint, the Clonmel tub gamely responded to its captain's command and flashed across the finish line nearly a length ahead of Dublin. When the conquering heroes returned home, they were greeted with the town's anthem:

> For, 'tis O Rare Clonmel, my boys!
> It's O Rare Clonmel!
> The first in the field and the last to yield
> Are the boys of Rare Clonmel.

The following year, the team's captain left for the west of Ireland, and the Clonmel Rowing Club faded from history, but the glorification of the rowing boys as sports heroes indicated that "rare Clonmel" was growing more modern.[21] To the purveyors of progress in Clonmel and other cities in Ireland, the poorest of rural peasantry threatened the modern social order because they instinctively realized there was no place for them in a modern Ireland. Thus, they retreated to fairy-ridden superstitions more stubbornly than ever—much to the consternation of both Nationalists and Unionists, who preferred political fisticuffs to flights of fairy fantasy.

If Clonmel's townspeople and countryside were quiet through the Christmas season of 1894, politicians of the major political factions in England and Ireland were at each others' throats. With the British government in the hands of Lord Rosebery, an empire-first Liberal more interested in European diplomacy and imperial defense than political reform in Ireland, the Unionists bided their time, knowing they could exploit a major split in the Irish Party and return to power. Meanwhile Nationalists tried desperately to keep their Irish Parliamentary Party afloat in order to reintroduce another Home Rule Bill, Ireland's best hope for ousting the English. To thwart reunification of the Nationalist movement, the English administration and their Unionist allies did everything in their power to keep the Irish factions fighting, and whenever and wherever possible, to pillory the Irish with centuries-old invective. This strategy, elevated to an art form during the Victorian era of British colonialism, was used to demonstrate that the "drinking, wrangling, quarreling, fighting, ravishing" Irish were incapable of governing themselves and that England was the only nation able to rule such a backward, indolent, endemically violent people.[22]

Irish Nationalists were not blind to Unionist tactics. During the holiday season of 1894–1895 Church-sponsored Nationalists in Clonmel mounted a lively campaign to elect a moderate candidate for the National Council of the Irish National Federation (INF) with the hope that a moderate would win the support of the anti-Church, Fenian Nationalists who remained loyal to the memory of the Irish Parliamentary Party's fallen leader, Charles Stewart Parnell. Following the death of Parnell in 1891, the INF was organized to help reunite the Irish Parliamentary Party in the wake of the disastrous split that had divided the party into Parnellite (secular, Fenian) and anti-Parnellite (Church-sponsored) factions.

One of the prime movers of the INF was the testy Archbishop of Cashel, Thomas William Croke, who governed the Catholic faithful from "The Palace, Thurles." For years, Archbishop Croke had steadfastly supported Parnell in his fanatic drive to win Home Rule for Ireland, even when it meant disobeying papal dictates. Croke's support for Parnell was unwavering through the worst of times until 1889, when Parnell's adulterous affair with Kate O'Shea was exposed. The ensuing scandal obliged Croke and other Church officials to withdraw their support for Parnell, an action that led to the schism in the Nationalist movement. To heal the wounds within the Nationalist movement and help shore up the tottering Liberal government in London, INF officials in County Tipperary put forward the congenial figure of Nicholas Kickham Shee, the INF's candidate for its National Council. Mr. Shee was the cousin of the late, much loved, much revered Fenian poet/patriot of Tipperary, Charles J. Kickham. The invocation of his sterling name was ample recommendation for Parnellite and anti-Parnellite alike.[23]

And so it was that Christmas in Clonmel passed peacefully. Politicians stormed but the countryside remained quiet, and for the moment, all was calm in County Tipperary. The country people sang "Adeste Fideles" at Christmas Eve Mass; the wren boys chased their birds; inmates of the men's hospital downed pints of Christmas stout; and the regiment from India settled into their new quarters at the Royal Barracks. Good order prevailed throughout the season, and for this, everyone gave thanks.

From "The Palace, Thurles"

One of those thankful for the calm was the venerable Archbishop of Cashel, Thomas William Croke, who superintended the Catholic faithful in the ecclesiastical province of Munster. The Archbishop directed his flock from the provincial headquarters in Thurles, which he pointedly referred to as "The Palace," suggesting that not all royal halls of Ireland were reserved solely for England's noblemen who toured at their leisure and hunted at will. If this misappropriation of royal symbols offended nobility's privilege, or in any way conveyed disrespect to peers of the realm, it was intended. The Archbishop of Cashel's love of God, Church, and the Holy See was surpassed only by his passionate hatred of English rule and his commitment to Irish nationalism.

Here was no "mushroom patriot," popping up when conditions permitted to wave the green flag, only to disappear at the least sign of royal displeasure. Croke's devotion to the cause was unwavering, his career distinguished by his numerous, forthright expressions of support. "I only like to be praised for one thing," he declared, "and this is for being a good Irishman." And again: "Every Irishman is born with four mothers: His natural mother, his Church, his college, and his country. Now that my natural mother is dead, the mother I love best of the remaining three is my country." In Croke's hierarchy of loyalties, love of country preceded love of Church. He viewed the Catholic Church as the servant of the people and believed that as the Church served the people, the people built a nation. The Church's mission was to improve and elevate the people so they might one day serve themselves. To this end, Archbishop Croke sent forth missives from The Palace, Thurles, intended to hasten the day when the Queen and her regiments departed Erin's soil, leaving the Irish to assume the duties and responsibilities of independence in an orderly, disciplined, and Christian manner.[24]

Ironically, for one so highly placed in the Church hierarchy, Thomas William Croke was the product of a mixed Irish marriage. His father's family came to Ireland with the Norman invasion of the thirteenth century. They were Catholics who, after the initial battles with rival Irish chieftains, more or less settled down and lived among them. Croke's mother, Isabelle Plummer, was a Protestant, the daughter of Brudnell Plummer of Mount Plummer, County Limerick, and Frances Fitzgerald, second daughter of Thomas, sixteenth Knight of Glin, Glin Castle, County Limerick. These families were Protestant colonizers, many of whom came with the hated Cromwell and never left. They imposed their minority religion, language, and system of land ownership upon the majority and, rather than mix, remained aloof. When Isabelle Plummer announced her intention to marry William Croke, a Catholic boy "in trade," she was promptly disinherited. Eight children later, William died suddenly, leaving Isabelle alone and without support. When Isabelle's Protestant brother, the Reverend Richard Plummer, Rector of Killury, refused to help, her Catholic brother-in-law, Reverend James Croke, gave the family a home in his parish at Charleville. Thus young Thomas William knew nothing of his Protestant grandparents beyond their rigid sectarianism and disdain for all that he represented, while his Catholic uncle provided succor to his dead brother's widow and shelter to eight fatherless children.

A bright boy, blessed with a quick mind but no resources, Thomas William turned to the Catholic Church for his education. At age sixteen, he won a scholarship to the Irish College in Paris and left home for good.[25] The college was on the Rue des Irlandais, close to the Sorbonne, in the heart of Paris's student district, where, in the early 1840s, French Catholics demonstrated for free education and democratic reforms. Croke would write of this period, "I imbibed the love of liberty from my earliest years, and have ever been, in heart and act, a rebel against every species of tyranny." Thomas William received his Minor Orders at the Irish College in 1843, and after two years teaching in Belgium, went to the Irish College in Rome to study for the doctorate. At the end of the first year, he competed with twenty-nine students in eight hours of oral examination and won both the gold and silver medals, a feat that led the *Cork Examiner* to brag that, few, if any, had ever "borne away these two medals in any one year." Legend has it that the pious Croke melted down both and sent the proceeds home to help feed the starving in the first years of the Great Famine. In 1847 he returned to Ireland to teach rhetoric at Carlow College, and there saw the devastation for himself. Writing to his friend Tobias Kirby in Rome, he reported, "this part of the world is a frightful place."[26]

In his six-year absence the political situation in Ireland had become more radical. Daniel O'Connell,[27] Ireland's great "liberator," who had won emancipation for the Catholic Church in 1829, died in May 1847, clearing the way for a radical new group of revolutionaries, the Young Irelanders, to seize control of the Nationalist movement.[28] Before his death, O'Connell had been at odds with the Young Irelanders, whose extreme secularism led them to include Protestants within the movement. Once O'Connell was gone, there was nothing to stop the Young Irelanders from pushing their radical, violent agenda for achieving independence from England.

The Young Irelanders quickly captured the Irish imagination when they began to publish a newspaper called the *Nation*, edited by an Ulster Catholic named Gavan Duffy. Its principal writer, Thomas Davis, of Cork, penned a series of essays under a pseudonym, The Celt, exploring questions of Irish nationality and the Irish soul. Davis's essays sent the Young Irelanders back to the great heroes of Irish legend, in particular the mighty Fionn Mc-Cuill, a combination of John Wayne, Pecos Bill, and Prince Charming, the mightiest hunter, bravest warrior, most manly of men. The heroic capers of Fionn and his giant of a son, Ossian, formed the heart of the great Fenian (the word is derived from the name Fionn) legends of Irish folklore. Long before William Butler Yeats would lead a Gaelic literary revival at the end of the nineteenth century, the Fenians conflated Irish history and mythology for political purposes into an ethnocentric form of nationalism tinged with a positive dose of racial pride to counteract negative British stereotypes of the Irish people.[29]

Davis's essays spread like wildfire, appearing across the country in every "repeal" reading room, so named because Nationalists who frequented these rooms favored repeal of the infamous 1801 Act of Union, which bound Ireland to England. Much to the chagrin of British authorities, the *Nation* became Ireland's most widely read newspaper, spurred in the late 1840s by outrage at English policies during the Great Famine.

In 1848, the Young Irelanders mounted an ill-conceived insurrection, which the English quickly quelled, giving them a pretext to deport yet more of Ireland's brave young men across the seas to

England, Canada, America, and beyond. As they sailed away, however, the men of Young Ireland took with them the legends of Fionn McCuill, their passion for freedom, and their hatred of the English. Fionn was their hero, so in his honor, they called themselves Fenians. Since that time Fenianism has become synonymous with radical Irish Republicanism, especially after the formation of the Irish Republican Brotherhood (IRB) in 1858.[30]

Thomas Croke's involvement with Young Ireland was brief yet significant. After Gavan Duffy's arrest in 1848, Croke and another priest named John Barry visited him in Newgate Prison and offered to keep the *Nation* afloat by serving as editor and writer. Duffy declined this generous but foolhardy offer, which undoubtedly kept young Thomas from prison and saved his career as future archbishop. As it was, Croke slipped away quietly and accepted a teaching position at his alma mater, the Irish College in Paris, where he joined a growing colony of Irish exiles. He might have stayed in Paris and enjoyed French wine, stimulating conversation, and a sedentary life had not the Great Famine occurred. In August 1849, his brother, Father William, who served as curate to their uncle in Charleville, died suddenly of a famine-induced fever, and soon Croke returned to Ireland to take his place. As he wrote Kirby, "You will be surprised to hear that I am back in Ireland once more and on the mission."[31] For the next thirty years, Croke devoted himself to the "mission" of preparing his people for sovereignty.

The mission to elevate his people led Thomas William Croke to support movements both inside and outside the Church. He helped organize the Tenant Rights' Societies and served as the first president of St. Colman College in Fermoy. He embraced the Church's devotional revolution, which fostered piety among the people and promoted reforms within the clergy. Before 1850, most priests acted as "little popes" within their parishes. They wore lay clothing, ignored instructions from their bishops, often overcharged their parishioners for baptisms, weddings, and funerals, and basically did as they pleased. Thomas Croke was in the first generation of Irish priests, for example, who had to wear the collar. Many churches were sadly run down, and most sacraments were performed at the priest's house or, for a fee, in private homes. This lack of discipline led to a long list of grievances that Church leaders were determined to correct.

In addition to cleaning its own clerical house, the Church launched a major campaign to wipe out the last vestiges of pagan practices among the peasants, who, for centuries, cherished their pagan Celt traditions— "naturalism, sympathetic magic, attachment to ancestral ground, communal involvement, gaiety and abandon."[32] One strategy used to eliminate paganism was to impose stricter discipline and reemphasize romanized rituals, such as Sodalities, Confraternities, and Stations of the Cross, which had not attracted the Irish before the Famine. To erase vestiges of pagan goddess worship, the Church fostered more traditional, male-oriented rituals directed from Rome, administered by a growing army of priests whose ranks swelled as the Church absorbed substantial numbers of displaced tenant farmers and laborers, resulting in a dramatic increase in the ratio of priests and nuns to parishioners. Cardinal Paul Cullen, Ireland's first Cardinal, threw his weight behind the war on paganism and introduced jubilees, triduums, pilgrimages, shrines, processions, and retreats designed to replace seasonal pagan agricultural pageants, holy wells, charms, effigies, and wakes. By 1875, when Thomas Croke became the Archbishop of Cashel, the Church had beaten back many older forms of paganism.[33] But despite the Church's disapproval of "keening" (wailing at wakes) or visiting holy wells, many secretly practiced the old ways at crossroads, beside the hearth, and at fairy forts or "raths."[34]

As the Church broadened its devotional revolution to include social and cultural institutions, the men of Young Ireland returned home from across the seas, determined to foment a revolution of their own. Their dream was to build a Nationalist movement that was both Irish and secular—a movement that celebrated native Irish culture and revered, rather than feared, its old traditions and beliefs. At stake in this contest between religious and secular forces was the character of the Irish state, whether it would be free of England, free of Rome, or free of the fairies. The competition between the two sides left a fundamental, nearly fatal, fissure within the Nationalist movement that the English were only too happy to exploit. Caught in the middle of this political maelstrom were the peasants, who had good reason to suspect that neither the Church, the Fenians, nor their English landlords cared a whit for them and used them only to further their narrow ideological and economic aims.

The struggle for control of the Nationalist movement, and hence the right to define the character of the future Irish state, revolved around winning the trust of the peasantry, yet both the Church and the Fenians were slow to grasp this political reality. In 1858, James Stephens welded various factions into a truly national Fenian organization called the Irish Republican Brotherhood (IRB). Stephens had joined Young Ireland and become an aide-de-camp to the group's leader William Smith O'Brien but was forced to flee to Paris in 1848 and again in 1865 after failed uprisings. He often made fundraising tours to the United States on behalf of the IRB.

At first the Fenians ignored the land question because it inevitably necessitated getting involved in parliamentary politics.

But when the Fenians' middle-class, Church-sponsored rival, the National Association, did not include tenants' rights as one of its major goals, the Fenians took up the cause of the Irish peasant.[35] In this circuitous fashion Fenianism, and consequentially Irish Republicanism, assumed the mantle of land reform in the 1850s and 1860s. When Cardinal Cullen exhorted priests to stay away from tenants' rights campaigns, many ignored his instructions, especially in the late 1860s, when priests supported an amnesty movement for imprisoned Fenians. Pope Pius IX's condemnation of the Irish Republican Brotherhood in 1865 boomeranged and made Fenianism even more popular among rank-and-file citizens and priests by the end of the decade.[36]

During their years in exile, expatriate Fenian groups in America, Australia, South Africa, and Great Britain linked up and supported the IRB. They swore secret oaths and pledged their lives to win independence for Ireland, secured, if need be, by violent revolution. Those in America honed their fighting skills in the Civil War, after which thousands returned to Ireland intending to join the struggle, for which they were provided generous amounts of Irish American aid. Endowed with support and armed with experience, these Yankee Fenians strolled about with a cocky swagger. Having the United States as a ready refuge, they took more chances at "cocking a snook" at the police and priests of authoritarian, post-Famine Ireland.[37]

Fenians attempted a full-scale insurrection in early 1867, which failed before it got started thanks to English spies within the movement. Key leaders including Michael Davitt and Charles Kickham went to prison, but the rebellion prompted the English to do something about the Irish problem. In 1868, William Gladstone's Liberal Party won control of Parliament, pledging to "pacify" Ireland.[38] Gladstone's strategy was to divide and conquer—throw the troublemakers in jail and keep the others happy with partial repeal of the hated Act of Union. For starters, Gladstone disestablished the Irish Church, Ireland's version of the Church of England, in 1869, which meant that the poorest were no longer obliged to pay tithes to the Irish Protestant Church to which only the very wealthiest belonged. As an added gesture of generosity, the government transferred a number of properties to the Catholic Church, which the more cynical regarded as a gentle inducement, if not an outright bribe offered to the clergy, to disavow the Fenians.[39]

Ecclesiastical reform was followed by the Land Act of 1870, intended to help tenants to buy land. As with many Liberal reforms, unintended consequences followed, and much of the available land was bought up by local businessmen, establishing a new, and often harsher, class of landowners. Franchise reform came next, and produced yet more unintended consequences. In 1874 the secret ballot was used for the first time, the result of which was that Isaac Butt's Home Rule Party won sixty seats in Parliament. The following year a Protestant landlord from County Wicklow named Charles Stewart Parnell was elected to the House of Commons. For two years he sat silent and unnoticed, then burst onto the scene in a blaze of glory. At this particular moment, Butt was leading the Home Government Association, which had revived Daniel O'Connell's idea of home-rule federalism, and using the strategy of "reasoning sweetly" with the English. Parnell quickly tired of sweet reasoning and set upon a determined course to forge a solid Irish bloc in Parliament, strong enough to obstruct Parliament at every turn if Irish concessions were not granted. This aggressive approach caught the fancy of many frustrated Nationalists, and in 1877 Parnell replaced Butt as president of the Home Rule Confederation of Great Britain. Even the Clan na

Gael, the Fenian brotherhood in the United States, restated its opposition to Butt's policy of working peacefully with Parliament and backed Parnell. Ultimately the Catholic Church fell in line, making the charismatic Protestant aristocrat from County Wicklow the undisputed prince of Irish nationalism.[40]

In short order, Parnell succeeded where O'Connell and Butt had failed. He made the Irish Party a savage, fighting force in Parliament. He dramatically changed land tenure in Ireland "with less of social disturbance, and with fewer regrettable incidents" than any other country where land reforms were attempted. And he successfully encouraged the Liberal Party under Gladstone to adopt Home Rule.[41] Yet Parnell's erratically brilliant leadership bequeathed both division and discord in the National movement at home and abroad. In 1880, the *Spectator* described Parnell's public persona:

> Keen, capable, in one sense scrupulous, in another the reverse of scrupulous, with more hatred for the English government of Ireland than love for the Irish themselves, possessed of no small power for terse taunts and no small jealousy of rivalry, with a good deal of the lawyer's pleasures in technicalities and the lawyer's satisfaction in so handing them as to make them serve larger purposes. . . . Incorruptible, sitting apart, jealous, solitary, with great intensive of purpose and very narrow sympathies, his mind reminds us of some of those who were most potent in the making of the great French revolutions, and in Ireland there is undoubtedly enough combustible element for a small, if not a great revolution.[42]

Often silent and always enigmatic, Parnell initiated few ideas of his own, yet his effortless, easy way of making them his own dazzled friend and foe alike. Despite his liabilities, Parnell proved to be an effective leader of the Irish Nationalist movement because he was a thorn in the flesh of English authority.[43]

When the newly installed Archbishop of Cashel, the Reverend Thomas William Croke, took up residence at The Palace, Thurles, in 1875, Isaac Butt was still alive and Charles Stewart Parnell, although newly elected to Parliament, was not yet a political force. Crops were good; prices were relatively high. The Fenians were still smarting from the failed insurrection of 1868, and Gladstone's liberal reforms showed signs of promise. The Catholic Church in Ireland was content because the Catholic faithful were becoming more so, and Cardinal Cullen, the great ultramontane leader of the Irish Church, who worked to increase the power of Rome, naturally enjoyed the full support of Pope Pius IX.

Trouble broke out, however, in 1878 when famine struck again. Crops failed, prices fell, and thousands of tenants were unable to pay their rent. Landlords reacted just as they had in 1847: Rather than using the crop failure to cull goodwill, owners seized the opportunity to clear their land with eviction notices. The Queen looked on with imperial indifference. As George III had done during the protracted conflict with the American colonies, she deferred to Parliament, apparently relishing the opportunity to dispatch another one or perhaps two million Irish Catholics to the New World or to the next world—it mattered not. Police lined up, once again, crowbars in hand, to enforce eviction orders, exposing to no one's surprise the true nature of English colonial "liberality."

From The Palace, Thurles, Archbishop Croke detected more subtle signs of English deviltry, especially English attempts to control the Catholic hierarchy in Ireland. Thanks to Cardinal Cullen's cordial relationship with Pius IX, the Irish Church had been relatively free of interference. For thirty years, Cardinal Cullen imposed an authoritative calm on the Irish Church, strong enough to contain growing nationalism among local priests. Through his stubborn devotion to ultramontane Catholicism, he won the unqualified support of Rome in Irish ecclesiastical patronage and in episcopal appointments. Cardinal Cullen was also fortunate to enjoy thirty years of ascendancy in the Church accompanied by unparalleled relative economic prosperity and political calm.

Change in Ireland's relation to Rome was forecast when Pope Pius IX appointed the moderate John MacEvilly as coadjutor with rights of succession to Archbishop John MacHale of the western province of Tuam. MacHale, often called "the Lion of the Fold of Judah," was a bitter critic of British rule, an avid defender of Irish traditions, and, for years, an outspoken supporter of Nationalist groups at home and abroad. The English wanted him out, and pressured Pope Pius to remove the eighty-seven-year-old prelate. Fearful of rallying Nationalist sentiment against the Church, Cardinal Cullen and Pope Pius delayed, hoping God would intervene and whisk the Lion of Judah to paradise, but He too, chose not to interfere.[44] Finally the old Pope bowed to English pressure and appointed MacEvilly to assist, then succeed, Archbishop MacHale.

In early 1878, a new Pope, Leo XIII, signaled his eagerness to please the Queen, and soon he had his chance. Later that year, Cardinal Cullen died, leaving a vacancy in the Dublin see. As was customary, the prelates of Dublin province met to name a successor. They selected, overwhelmingly, Edward McCabe, Cullen's auxiliary bishop since 1877. McCabe was a conscientious but otherwise undistinguished man, whose popularity with the Dublin clergy was largely due to the belief that, because he was trained at Ireland's national seminary at Maynooth, he would be a strong advocate for the Irish Church. Pope Leo's choice was Patrick Francis Moran, a cousin of Cullen's and a man of much sterner stuff than the amiable McCabe. If the Irish Church was to be brought under the heel of England, Moran would be the better man to fill the vacancy in the Dublin see. With the independence of the Irish Church hanging in the balance, prelates anxiously awaited Pope Leo's decision.

In November 1878, the preference of the Dublin clergy was sent to Rome for the Pope's approval. A month passed, and no action was taken. Christmas came and went, and still no word. January passed. Then came another more troubling indication that the new Pope would clip the wings of the Irish Church. In February 1879, Archbishop Croke exerted pressure on Rome to confirm McCabe's appointment when Prince Altieri, president of the Peter's Pence Association in Rome, asked Irish bishops for an extraordinary collection to celebrate the first anniversary of Pope Leo XIII's consecration. Archbishop Croke respectfully declined and other bishops followed suit.[45] The Pope received the message, and six weeks later, affirmed McCabe as the choice of the Dublin see. Though this relieved the anxiety of Irish prelates somewhat, the delay in McCabe's appointment indicated that Rome was placing a halter on the Irish Church, and the halter bore an English imprint.

As Rome dallied and the Irish Church stewed, the countryside faced full-scale starvation. In 1878, crops failed even as American agricultural imports flooded Irish markets, driving prices for remaining goods even lower. An unusually severe winter compounded the misery, making conditions the worst since the Great Famine. Landowners responded, as usual, by issuing eviction notices; the government responded, as usual, by doing nothing. From Belfast, Bishop Dorrian complained, "Government yet keeps aloof and does nothing!!!" From Tuam, John MacEvilly, who apparently had nothing better to do than write dispatches to Rome, described the distress:

The facts are these: a dire famine stares us in the face. The new
year will open with a general distress throughout the country. The
tenant farmers—the real friends of religion, of the priests, & of the
H. See—will be sorely pressed for food. The landlords as a class—
there are very many noble exceptions—have no sympathy with
the people, with the priests, or the Holy See. . . . As a general rule,
the people are oppressed, the rents far too high, and poor tenant
robbed of the fruit of the sweat of his brow, obliged to pay double
rent for the land his own labor reclaimed from utter barren worth-
lessness. . . . The people are very discontented.[46]

The callous contempt of the English left Church leaders no
choice but to assist the needy. The ever able fundraiser Archbishop
Croke plied his network in France and America; his appeals
brought some relief for the starving, although he complained that
ten times more was needed. While the Church collected pittances,
the Fenians sprang into action. Michael Davitt, a one-armed Fenian
who had spent seven years in Dartmoor Prison, headed west to
Archbishop MacHale's Province of Tuam. There he organized the
Land League, involving radical Fenians and moderate "constitution-
alists" to protect people against rack-renting and eviction. In December 1878, Parnell sailed for the United States, and in two
months, visited sixty-two cities, pleading for aid to feed Ireland's
starving. At each stop, Parnell pounded home his political theme.
Weren't they all a bit tired, he roared, of having their Irish brothers
come hat in hand at every bad season? Wasn't it time to be doing
something about the gloating landowners, the negligent government, and the disdainful Queen? Wasn't it time to address the
whole problem of land ownership that created famine in the first
place? Wasn't it time to be doing something about THAT? The
Irish Catholic community in America responded positively and

sent the Protestant Parnell home with the queenly sum of $200,000 to bolster the Land League's treasury.[47]

In April 1879, the League sponsored a successful protest at Irishtown, County Mayo, to stop tenant evictions, which emboldened Davitt to organize a still larger rally in Westport, to which he invited Parnell. Upon learning that the agitator Parnell was headed to Westport, clergy reacted with alarm. Even Archbishop John MacHale, an avowed foe of the British, was frightened of Parnell's ability to inspire violence; worse, he feared the Protestant Parnell could unite the Nationalists *without* the good offices, patient guidance, and holy sacraments of the Church.

Events proved MacHale right. The Westport rally was an immense success. Parnell came, spoke, and forever changed the Nationalist movement in Ireland. To more than eight thousand tenants, he asserted that a "fair rent" was a rent that a tenant could reasonably pay "according to the times." Furthermore, he declared, "You must show the landlords that you intend to hold a firm grip on your homesteads and lands. You must not allow yourselves to be dispossessed as you were dispossessed in 1847. You must not allow your small holding to be turned into large ones."[48] And how could tenants resist being thrown off their land when the full weight of British law supported the owners? By legal means when possible, by extralegal ones when not. Tenants would be deceiving themselves, he warned, if they believed the present members of Parliament would assist them: "They could help you, but they won't." What they won't do, he went on, you must do for yourself. And remember, he said, "God helps him who helps himself."[49] Those assembled roared their approval, and a fierce Irish Parliamentary Party was born.

In 1879, Parnell stepped forward to lead the newly formed Irish National Land League. All hell then broke loose, both at

Westminster and in Ireland. Under Parnell's leadership, the Irish bloc in Parliament became a veritable gang of obstructionists, frustrating in every way possible the normative efforts at political deal-making while the Land Leaguers launched new campaigns against English landlords.

In County Mayo, the League chose to test a new form of protest upon the unfortunate Charles Boycott, a retired army captain who had become manager of the Earl of Erne's estates in County Mayo. Rather than using time-honored methods of rural violence, the estate's tenants simply ignored the captain. In lieu of shooting him out of the saddle as he rode off for the morning hunt, they cut his family off from all services, supplies, and labor. Unable to withstand the pressure of exclusion, the captain returned to England, and a new word entered the Queen's English. Buoyed by the success of Boycott's boycott, others were organized, and thousands of families were spared eviction.

Even as the Land Leaguers scored success after success in assisting the rural peasantry, the Pope moved to condemn them. Under pressure from the Society for the Propagation of the Faith (or *Propaganda Fide*—the Vatican body that, since the Reformation, dealt with foreign problems), Pope Leo XIII determined that the Land Leaguers were a threat to the established authority of the Queen and the Holy See. He issued his Holy Bull that the Irish Church should have nothing to do with Parnell. In disavowing the Land League, the Church ran the risk of alienating itself from the Irish people and placing Fenians at the head of the Nationalist movement. Patrick Dorrian, Bishop of Down and Connor, spoke up for Parnell and the League, and declared the Church had no choice but to support them. The priests and the people must stay united, he argued, for if the people saw the bishops going against them in their misery, "they would despair and religion would suffer."[50] From Tuam, John MacEvilly concurred. To denounce the Land League was a mistake. If the priests stayed out, "godless nobodies" would take charge and meetings would disintegrate into "scenes of disorder." If, however, the priests participated, "they will keep the people attached to them."[51] The Pope's edict forced the Irish Church to make a choice: Who would it be? The Pope, or the people? From The Palace, Thurles, Archbishop Croke hesitated not a second in stating in the most uncertain, albeit respectful, manner where his loyalty lay. As far as he was concerned, the Church's first responsibility was to stand with the people, and if the people chose Parnell, so be it.

Croke's disobedience did not escape notice. In November, he was informed that he had been cited by Propaganda for using language favorable to a certain violent politician, to which he promptly responded that he had never endorsed violence in any form. Furthermore, "Mr. Parnell's *parliamentary policy* is approved by 99% of the Irish priesthood and people." Speculating on the source of complaints against him, Croke defiantly proclaimed: "Englishmen, I know, do not like me—Irish aristocrats, I know, do not like me; and, perhaps one or two anti-Irish ecclesiastics do not like me. But I have the satisfaction of knowing, that I stand higher in the estimation of the Irish race, at home and abroad, than any living Irish ecclesiastic but one. This is probably the head and front of my offending."[52] Rome's misrepresentation of his view provided more evidence that the English were trying to control the Irish Church through Rome.

The Pope's Bull did not deter the Protestant Parnell. When opening Parliament in May 1880, the Queen made no mention of the crop failures in Ireland and the thousands dying in the lanes. Nor did she utter a single syllable of thanks to those who worked feverishly for two seasons to avert death and destruction, the likes of which had not been seen since the Great Famine, while she and her ministers did absolutely nothing. Not a word! Parnell leapt to his feet at the conclusion of her speech, screaming bloody murder. All hell broke loose on the floor of Parliament. When order was restored, Parnell was up again, demanding passage of his Compensation for Disturbances Bill, which in effect asked Parliament to pay the outrageous rents being charged by British landowners so that the starving tenants could stay in their cottages.

In early August, the House of Lords rejected the bill, which meant that thousands faced eviction in November when rents fell due. Upon hearing this not-so-surprising news, Parnell openly confronted the British minister who supervised Ireland, inquiring if the Queen intended to use her regiments to enforce the evictions. Most assuredly so, was his unwavering reply, and with that, Parnell left for Ireland.

While Parnell waited at his estate in Wicklow, Land Leaguers took to the lanes and villages calling for organized resistance to the Queen's agents who would be enforcing eviction orders. John Dillon, organizer of the American Land League, made an impassioned speech on August 15, at a League meeting in Kildare, after which assaults and crimes against property spread throughout the countryside. Irish bishops called an emergency meeting to condemn those "wicked and designing men" who were going about the country "exciting our poor people," and targeted for censure those within the hierarchy who publicly supported the League, most notably "the A. B. [Archbishop] of Cashel," whose letters and speeches were "doing great mischief." In early September, Parliament prorogued for four months, at which time the Irish members of Parliament returned from Westminster to lead the agitation.

On Sunday, September 19, Parnell made his move. Standing before an agitated crowd in Ennis, he asked: When a man takes a farm from another, what do you do? Amid cries of "Shoot him," and with eight priests on the platform, he continued:

> You must show him on the roadside when you meet him, you must show him in the streets of the town, you must show him at the shop corner, you must show him in the fair and in the market-place, and even in the house of worship, by leaving him severely alone, by putting him into a moral Coventry, by isolating him from his kind as if he was a leper of old—you must show him your detestation of the crime he has committed, and you may depend upon it there will be no man so full of avarice, so lost to shame, as to dare the public opinion of all right-thinking men and to transgress your unwritten code of laws.[53]

The Land League's policy of tendering a fair rent and boycotting those who instituted eviction actions proved highly effective. Many landowners backed off, but in late September, someone "cocked a snook" at Lord Mountmorres in Galway and shot him dead. The British government in Ireland hesitated a month, then on November 2, 1880, police arrested Parnell and four of his parliamentary colleagues.

Archbishop Croke was on his way to Rome with the bishops of Limerick, Cloyne, and Ross when he heard of Parnell's arrest and was thus on hand to dissuade the Pope from doing what British agents were pressing him to do, which was to issue a public statement condemning the League. When he returned home in November, Croke met with both Parnell and Dillon, after which he reported that they had "no object in view except the amelioration of the country, first by procuring for it radical change in the land laws," and, added the unreformed Young Irelander, "repeal of the union, or its equivalent 'home rule'."[54]

Alarmed by Croke's open support of Parnell and Dillon, Tobias Kirby, his friend at the Irish College in Rome, wrote back, urging moderation. This provoked a stinging response from The Palace, Thurles.

> We have tried calmness and what is called *moderation* "ad nauseam" in our dealings with the government, only to be laughed at by them and despised; I predict, now for the first time, that should the day ever come . . . when faith will grow cold in Ireland, and when the masses of the people will fall away from the clergy, it will be . . . because of the pusillanimity . . . and lack of pluck, on the part of more of them. . . . we must go with the people.[55]

What the Archbishop of Cashel realized, and what perhaps Rome did not, was that by late 1880, Parnell had, with the Land League, created a Nationalist movement. Bad harvests, a severe winter, low prices, and the Queen's indifference allowed him to crystallize Nationalist yearnings. The boys of Young Ireland were now the shadowy men of the Irish Republican Brotherhood; they were back in Ireland, armed and oath-bound to excise the country from the British fold. At this crucial juncture in Irish history, Archbishop Croke exercised all the powers of his office and his considerable personal influence to reserve a place for the Catholic Church in the Nationalist movement.

Charles Stewart Parnell and the Gentleman from Mullinahone

By sheer strength of will, Charles Stewart Parnell, the Protestant landowner from County Wicklow, forged the Irish Parliamentary

Party into a solid voting bloc. Aided by changes in the parliamentary system and dissention between Liberals and Conservatives, he was able to frustrate any opponent who stood in the way of Home Rule for Ireland. Although Parnell was a great leader, he was difficult to follow, for one never knew where he might go. He could be fiery, brilliant, and inspiring at one moment, and dark, critical, and morose the next. He could fire up a crowd with his conviction, then change his mind the next day. The sole constant in his life seemed to be his abiding loathing of all things English. Hatred of the English was his firm foundation, his guiding star that none obscured, except perhaps his love for a married woman named Kate O'Shea. Despite his notorious untrustworthiness, the Irish people had chosen Parnell as their political savior, and for their sake, Archbishop Croke asked God's blessings. With his benediction, the priests of Munster marched forward, without fear of censure, to join their brothers, fathers, sisters, and uncles in Land League demonstrations, boycotts, and protests. Many were the sons of tenant farmers themselves, drafted into the priesthood during the post-Famine feast of religious devotionals. When young priests stood toe-to-toe against the Queen's regiments outside a tenant's cottage, the balance of power shifted, the level of violence fell. In these confrontations between crowbar and cross, the people witnessed Church emissaries acting in their interest, giving them reason to trust institutional power. To this end, Archbishop Croke blessed Charles Stewart Parnell and the Land League and saluted the priests of Munster, whose fidelity kept the people within the pale of Church authority.

Parnell's every excess created more opportunity for the Archbishop of Cashel to publicize the Church's loyalty to the people. In early 1881 Croke returned to Ireland from Rome to find the country in an uproar over Parnell's arrest. Supporters organized the Parnell Defense Fund, to which Archbishop Croke promptly and generously subscribed, an act that provoked a stern warning from Rome. Rather than relent, Croke used the occasion to broadcast English injustice to the world. He reminded Rome that the Irish were "the worst fed, the worst clad, and the worst housed people in the world," and the only people periodically forced "to beg for bread" in Europe, America, and Australia. Although these people remained devoted to the Holy See, they chose Charles Stewart Parnell as their leader, and the Church must support their decision. Boldly, Croke personally vouched for Parnell's integrity:

> It is a fact that, though Mr. Parnell is, unfortunately for himself, a Protestant, he is, nevertheless, a man of high honor and unimpeachable moral character. He has repeatedly denied the charge that he contemplates armed insurrection in this Country. He is neither a Fenian nor a Freemason; and his sole aim I believe to be to save his native land, and to emancipate an enslaved people by the means afforded him under the British Constitution.[56]

Croke predicted that the Irish people would triumph over their oppressors by peaceful means, then issued a stern warning of his own directly to the Pope. Ireland would one day become an independent Catholic nation, he asserted, provided Rome did not interfere with her internal political affairs. Any action to the contrary, he warned, would be "attended with the most ruinous results."[57]

The warning was timely, for at that very moment, British emissaries were in Rome urging the Pope to disavow Parnell's Land League. In return, the British government pledged to look favorably on Pope Leo's petition to establish diplomatic relations with the Vatican, and eventually locate a papal nuncio in England, a move that would place Vatican administrative offices in England. The effect of this would have been disastrous for the Irish Church, because affairs of the Irish Church would go to England rather than directly to Rome. But worse, a papal nuncio in England would formally recognize Ireland's union with Great Britain. Though Irish bishops disagreed about Parnell—some, like Croke, steadfastly supported him, and others, like Dublin's Archbishop McCabe, were terrified at the mention of his name—all twenty-four agreed, without hesitation, to a man, even McCabe, that Leo's plans to establish a papal office in England would be a complete, total, and irreversible disaster for the Irish Catholic Church. Better the Protestant Parnell, Michael Davitt, and the whole pack of violent, wild-eyed, fairy-ridden Fenians than subordination to English Catholics.

Despite Croke's recommendation that he not interfere, Pope Leo denounced the Land League in a letter of January 4, 1881, to Archbishop McCabe. Undeterred by the Pope's disapproval, Croke announced his support for the Land League in a letter in which he commended the Ladies Land League for organizing a St. Patrick's Day "monster rally" in Dublin. The timid McCabe denounced the rally, declaring it a "monstrous" thing that ladies should take to the streets, while Croke publicly praised the character of the "good Irish ladies," then went on to express his personal disgust against the "monstrous imputations cast upon them by the Archbishop of Dublin." As if this attack upon a fellow bishop were not enough, Croke hurled a missile toward Rome, declaring: "It is a satisfaction, however, to feel that his grace's political likings and dislikings, though possibly of some consequence elsewhere, carry with them very little weight or significance except with a select few, in Ireland." Upon learning of

Croke's outburst, the Vatican demanded a retraction. Rather than give Rome an excuse to intervene in the business of the Irish Church, Croke issued a formal apology.[58]

In April 1881, Parliament passed the Land Act, intended to break down the rigid system of land ownership in Ireland with famous "three Fs" guarantees of free sale, fair rent, and fixity of tenure. With much fanfare, Prime Minister Gladstone announced passage of the bill, declaring that Parliament had taken a huge step toward the "pacification" of Ireland. The "three Fs," he said, were certain to restore peace in the Irish countryside and ensure political harmony at home.

Parnell thought not and was determined to add a "fourth F" to the list of Land Act guarantees— "Failure." He had no cause to believe that Gladstone's liberalism would do anything but cause more harm. In the meantime, 100,000 Irish tenants faced imminent eviction and starvation, many thousands fell in arrears after two years of crop failure, and, worse, evictions skyrocketed when landlords tried to evict tenants before the Land Act guarantees took effect.

The Land Leaguers were not about to stand by and allow evictions to take place. The government, naturally, knew this, and ordered the Queen's regiments to watch for the first who dared speak out. They did not have long to wait. On May 2, British authorities used the newly passed Coercion Act to arrest Michael Davitt for using "violent and inflammatory language" to protest the wave of evictions that preceded passage of the Land Act. The effect of Gladstone's pincer-like reforms left tenants feeling that they had no recourse under the law. Davitt's arrest was the final insult.

At this moment of crisis, Archbishop Croke calmly embarked on his annual visitation of the province, preaching forbearance, charity, and Catholic Nationalism. *Stay with the people,* he charged his priests. *Boycott! Protest! Organize!* he urged. *Fly the green banners of*

Ireland from the top of every barn, pole, and haystack, but, he warned, *stay within the bounds of law. Show the world the injustice heaped upon the heads of the Irish peasant, but let them show their feelings. Let them vent their despair, their disillusionment, and frustration, but let them also exhibit discipline in their demonstrations of protest.*

And the people did precisely this in dramatic fashion at the town of Clonaulty. As the archbishop approached the town:

> The people came pouring out of every house on the way, and joined from the crossroads. As his carriage passed, they fell on their knees to receive the blessing. On entering their parish we were met by people of Holy Cross accompanied by two bands, and an immense display of green banners. . . . The horse was taken from the carriage, notwithstanding the Abp's opposition, and he was drawn by the people a distance of more than a mile, to the place of meeting. . . . The procession which followed was over a mile in length.[59]

The archbishop was deeply touched that the people were heeding his message.

News of Archbishop Croke's "triumphal progress" through the province reached Rome. Rather than rejoicing at the people's devotion and peaceful demonstration, Propaganda felt even more threatened by the Archbishop of Cashel, heightening their "keen disregard" for him. Despite their disapproval, Croke stood firm in his support for the people, the priests of Munster, and Charles Stewart Parnell, not knowing he was defending a man enmeshed in a secret liaison with a married woman, the wife of a Parnell supporter named Captain William Henry O'Shea. Parnell had met Kate O'Shea in July 1880, and by October, they were lovers.

Through the summer of 1881, Parnell remained quiet, waiting to see how lay the land politically. Moderates, like Croke, urged

him to allow the Land Act to take effect, while radical Nationalists, particularly the Americans, pressed for an open declaration in
favor of Home Rule. Finally in October, Parnell made his position
known. On Sunday, October 9, he stood before the people of
Wexford and openly attacked the "hollowness" of the Land Act.
Referring to Gladstone personally, he declared that,

> . . . the masquerading Knight-errant, this pretending champion of
> the rights of every other nation except those of the Irish nation,
> should be obliged to throw off the mask today, and stand revealed
> as the man who, by his own utterances, is prepared to carry fire
> and sword into your homesteads, unless you humbly abase your-
> selves before him and before the landlords of the country.

On October 13, Parnell was arrested in Dublin under the Coercion Act, charged with attempting to incite violence. From
Sligo, a priest excitedly captured the feeling of anxiety that
gripped the nation when news of Parnell's arrest was made public.
In a letter to Rome, he wrote, "Pray earnestly for us. We are passing thru' perilous times."[60]

Parnell's lieutenants organized protest meetings throughout
the country, and were immediately arrested and sent off en masse
to join their leader in Kilmainham Gaol. Days later, League officials, acting upon Parnell's instructions, issued the famous "no
rent" manifesto, urging tenants to pay no rent at all as long as
their leaders sat in jail. In Ireland, Church leaders uniformly denounced the "wicked Manifesto," although some, like Croke, also
denounced the arrests. Croke wrote to Kirby that he felt "struck
down" by Parnell's action, but he added, "'Twas well I kept with
the people, and that they trusted me."[61] With that retort, Croke

took to his bed with a severe attack of sciatica. In Dublin, Archbishop McCabe denounced Parnell, the manifesto, and those irresponsible tenants who were robbing landlords of their rightful due. To publicly demonstrate whose side he favored, Pope Leo pressed ahead with plans to promote McCabe to Cardinal. The Vatican's drift toward Britannia accelerated when the Queen's special emissary, George Errington, was dispatched to discuss locating the papal nuncio in England.

The situation in Ireland through the winter of 1881–1882 was this: The harvest was bad; the peasants were starving; one hundred thousand tenants faced eviction; Parnell and the Land Leaguers were in Kilmainham Gaol; the Pope was planning to move administrative offices of the Irish Catholic Church to England; and timid Archbishop McCabe was summoned to Rome to receive his red Cardinal's cap. In this season of seething discontent, as popes, politicians, and prelates stormed, Kate O'Shea quietly gave birth to a son whose father was not her husband.

For this reason and perhaps others, when spring came to Ireland, Parnell had had enough of Kilmainham Prison and signaled that he was ready to play according to English rules. In April 1882, he was furloughed from prison to attend his nephew's funeral in France; at that time, he negotiated a deal with Gladstone, jointly announced soon after as the "Kilmainham Compact." In this agreement, Gladstone pledged to extend protection to leaseholders, reduce rents, and drop coercion charges. In return, Parnell promised to behave himself, meaning he would stop the agitation and "cooperate cordially for the future with the liberal party in forwarding liberal principles and measures of general reform."[62]

On May 2, as Parnell and his colleagues walked out of Kilmainham Prison, W. E. Forster, as Britain's chief secretary for Ireland, resigned in protest, fully expecting, as everyone did, that Parnell would return to his old ways. But, amazingly, he did not. Rather, he shifted course again.

Just four days after Parnell's release, Forster's replacement, Lord Frederick Cavendish, and his under-secretary, T. H. Burke, were stabbed to death while walking in Dublin's Phoenix Park. Two days later, on May 8, 1882, a pale, chastened Parnell expressed shock at the murders and offered to resign in a sign of good faith rather than implicate the Irish Parliamentary Party. Gladstone refused to accept his resignation. As a further sign that he was now willing to cooperate, in July 1882, Parnell dissolved the Ladies Land League, over the strenuous protests of his sister Anna and Michael Davitt.[63] Then in October, Parnell launched the Irish National League to replace the old Land League, and for the next three years, quietly went about organizing a national political party to promote Home Rule.

Parnell's newfound collegiality was encouraged, no doubt, by the need to maintain security on the domestic front. The bachelor Parnell now cautiously cohabited with Kate O'Shea, whose lawfully wedded husband, Captain William O'Shea, had recently become a Member of Parliament. Parnell's eagerness to cooperate was also driven by pecuniary embarrassment, for by early 1883, he was broke. The seven-month sojourn in jail, the traveling, organizing, and hefty legal expenses left Ireland's leader penniless and his estate mortgaged. He turned to his friends to save the Wicklow property, and they organized the Parnell Testimonial Fund to raise money to clear his debts. Among the first to step forward with a generous contribution was the Archbishop of Cashel, followed by other bishops and local priests from his province. With the band playing and green banners flying, Archbishop Croke presented the princely sum of £50 to representatives of the Parnell Testimonial Fund on St. Patrick's Day, 1883. This public demonstration of support led detractors of Croke to assume that the donation was intended to energize the Home Rule movement as much as to assist the cash-strapped Parnell.

Opponents could also correctly assume that Croke used the occasion to defy the Vatican. Just weeks before, Cardinal Simeoni, Britain's chief enforcer at Propaganda, declared that any public endorsements in favor of the Irish National League would be looked on gravely. The presentation of £50 to the Parnell Testimonial Fund on St. Patrick's Day was Croke's response. Lest anyone be unclear as to its meaning, the donation affirmed that neither he nor the priests of Munster would be silenced by the Pope. They would not be cowed into forsaking the people or permit the English to neutralize Nationalists within the Catholic hierarchy.

Within Propaganda, whispers of disobedience, defiance, and insubordination followed Croke's name. His public act of support for Parnell, in clear violation of instructions from Rome, demanded action. England's agent at the Vatican, George Errington, threatened to end negotiations immediately if Croke was not stopped. To reinforce this threat, the Tory leader, Lord Robert Salisbury, taunted the Pope's authority, remarking that it appeared to him as if "Dr. Croke was master in Ireland, and that the pope with all his good will was powerless."[64] The pressure leading up to this now visible fissure within the Irish Catholic hierarchy was too much for Cardinal McCabe. In February, he suffered a near fatal heart attack, and as a result, was effectively sidelined. Given these circumstances, the Vatican had no choice but to respond.

On April 19, the Archbishop of Cashel was officially summoned to appear before His Holiness, Pope Leo XIII, and on April 23, he departed for Rome. What happened at the session is unclear, but undoubtedly Croke used the occasion to educate the

Pope on the situation in Ireland, and to express in the clearest of terms his opinion that His Holiness could best strengthen his people's faith and devotion to the Holy See by staying out of Ireland's business. For his part, it appeared that the Pope informed Archbishop Croke that he intended to disregard his advice, and would shortly issue a statement publicly condemning Parnell's Testimonial Fund—a step that every Irish cleric from Croke to McCabe warned against. Suspecting this, Croke delayed his return to Ireland, intentionally wishing to be out of the country when the bomb fell. And fall it did.

On May 11, 1883, Propaganda issued the infamous "Roman Circular" condemning the Parnell Testimonial Fund. While stating that it was not "forbidden" to contribute money to the fund, the Apostolic mandate "absolutely" condemned any collection designed "to inflame popular passions" and lead men into rebellion. In carefully crafted language, the Vatican expressed concern for the people, stating that these collections were designed by wicked men to arouse passions, incite disobedience, and, in the name of patriotism, pressure people to contribute. The order concluded:

> In these circumstances, it must be evident to your Lordship, that the collection called the *"Parnell Testimonial Fund"* cannot be approved by this Sacred Congregation; and consequently it cannot be tolerated that any ecclesiastic, much less a Bishop, should take any part whatever in recommending or promoting it.[65]

By design, Archbishop Croke was in Paris when the announcement was made. When asked to comment, he coolly replied that he saw nothing in the Circular that applied to the Irish National League, and that he was personally as unshaken in his political beliefs as he had ever been. This said, he stated that "the voice of the Vatican would always be heard" by him, and its commands strictly carried out. Croke realized that he need neither say, nor do, more; Rome had done the work for him. Nothing he could have ever hoped, said, or done would prove more effective in uniting the Irish Catholic Church behind the Nationalists. Irish patriots at home and abroad viewed the Circular as undeniable proof that the Pope was implicated in the "deadly intrigues of England";[66] in response Irish patriots everywhere voiced their displeasure by their wallets. Within a month, the Parnell Testimonial Fund had gathered £20,000.

From The Palace, Thurles, "our faithful, devoted prelate" measured his victory humbly by resuming his annual visitation of the province. He would be threatened no more by the Pope, and eventually the Catholic hierarchy in Ireland—aided by the death of Cardinal McCabe in 1885—would unite solidly behind the Nationalists. For the moment, crops improved, tenant evictions subsided, land reforms took effect, and Parnell busied himself with Home Rule, which Gladstone made his last and dying cause. But calm did not prevail.

One reason that peace proved elusive was that the Gladstone government was unable to deliver a Home Rule Bill. By the mid-1880s Gladstone became convinced that Home Rule was the best policy for Ireland, but it never sat well with his own Liberal Party, which viewed it as a betrayal of the Act of Union of 1801, if not of the Empire itself. Gladstone's government fell briefly, replaced by the first conservative ministry of Robert Cecil, Lord Robert Salisbury (1885–1886), but in early 1886, Gladstone returned to power and introduced a wide-ranging Home Rule Bill, which died because ninety-three Liberals voted against it.[67] Even Parnell, who made the greatest speech of his life, could not convince British Liberals to grant Ireland a measure of self-determination. In frustration, Nationalists took matters into their own hands and in late 1886, launched the Plan of Campaign, proposed by William O'Brien, M.P. Under this scheme, landlords who refused to negotiate "reasonable abatements" of rent were obliged to accept rent payments reduced by agreement among the tenants themselves. Should a landlord refuse this payment, tenants were advised to put their rent money in what amounted to an escrow fund until an agreement could be reached. If the owner evicted his tenants for nonpayment, then homeless families could draw on this fund for maintenance.[68] The British government under the second Salisbury ministry (1886–1892) retaliated by outlawing the Plan of Campaign with the Criminal Law Amendment Act in July 1887, ruthlessly administered by the prime minister's nephew, Chief Secretary for Ireland Arthur "Bloody" Balfour. But to no avail. By the autumn and winter of 1886–1887, tenants had refused to pay rents on eighty-four estates in Ireland. As many as sixty landlords finally capitulated to a 25 percent abatement of rents.

The notable exception to the relative success of this campaign proved to be one Arthur Hugh Smith-Barry. Acting on a scheme concocted by Balfour, Smith-Barry became the agent of a secret syndicate composed of wealthy landlords who bought out estates under attack from the Plan of Campaign in order to weaken the effect of the boycott. When the plot was exposed, Smith-Barry became the object of Irish outrage. Nationalists were even more angered when Smith-Barry attempted to thwart the Plan of Campaign on his own estates in Tipperary by creating a new town, called "New Tipperary." Primarily with the support of Archbishop Croke, William O'Brien, and John Dillon, organizers in South Tipperary such as John Mandeville set up the Tenants' Defence League to assist tenants on Smith-Barry lands around Tipperary town and Mitchelstown, but Smith-Barry's wealth allowed him to hold out.

The chaotic state in Tipperary dragged on from the late 1880s until 1895: In the 1887 "Mitchelstown Massacre," RIC (the Queen's Royal Irish Constabulary) police killed two tenants and wounded twenty others after Dillon and O'Brien were jailed for speeches supporting the tenants; John Mandeville was tortured in the Clonmel Gaol and later died of his wounds.[69] Again the Vatican was less than supportive. The Pope sent a mild rebuke to his Archbishop in Cashel, after which Smith-Barry sought Croke's support in obtaining his rent. It came as no surprise that Croke offered him no real help, because the Archbishop had once called Smith-Barry "an aggressive busy-body and virulent partisan," who had "flung down the gage to [his] tenants, never dreaming that they would have dared to take it up." Even though he had once spoken of "exterminating landlords," Croke used his influence to negotiate a settlement with Smith-Barry, thus keeping alive the Plan of Campaign without causing such disruption in other dioceses in the county.[70]

Parnell had been blindsided by O'Brien and Dillon, so he strongly objected to their Plan of Campaign, principally because the idea was not his own. Approaching forty, Parnell drew closer to the aging Gladstone, now in his mid-seventies, and exercised little leadership in either the popular Plan of Campaign or the Tenants' Fund.[71]

Parnell, however, continued to enjoy enormous prestige as the undisputed leader of the Irish Nationalist movement. Because of Parnell's great personal stature, when Captain William O'Shea filed for divorce in December 1889, naming Parnell as corespondent, the Nationalist cause was dealt a devastating blow by association. Parnell's affair with Kate O'Shea had been kept quiet for eight years, largely because the couple was able to secure the cooperation of the cuckolded Captain O'Shea. The captain wanted Parnell's help in winning the Galway seat in Parliament, which provoked poet William Butler Yeats to call O'Shea the "husband who had sold his wife" for a seat in Parliament.

With Parnell's help, he won the seat in February 1886 and was a Member of Parliament when Prime Minister Gladstone called for the second reading of the first Home Rule Bill. Miffed by Parnell's affair with his wife, O'Shea abruptly walked out and resigned his seat. His defection helped defeat the measure that would have allowed Ireland to separate peacefully from Great Britain. As history would have it, this opportunity did not come again until 1894 when the second Home Rule Bill was finally defeated. In the first instance, the peaceful settlement of Ireland's future was jeopardized when personal passions became intertwined in public politics.[72]

Despite this betrayal, Captain O'Shea demanded still more. He insisted that Parnell use his influence with Gladstone to obtain a lucrative government appointment, and refused to grant a divorce until he secured his share of Kate's inheritance. This she would have gladly given up had she been able, but unfortunately, the inheritance was contingent upon the health of Kate's wealthy aunt, Mrs. Benjamin Wood. Irish history might have taken a different course had the aged Aunt Minnie graciously died a timely death, but she lingered and the inheritance coveted by the debt-ridden captain was delayed.[73] When Aunt Minnie finally gave up the ghost, the will was contested, causing still more delay. In frustration, Captain O'Shea filed suit against his wife, in effect, publicly accusing Parnell of adultery.

On first hearing of the suit, Archbishop Croke supported Parnell, but in early November 1890, when the divorce court rendered its decision in favor of Captain O'Shea, Croke let it be known privately that he hoped Parnell would retire quietly. Instead, Parnell veered violently back to his old firebrand, rabble-rousing ways. On November 25, 1890, just days after being unanimously re-elected as chairman of the Irish Parliamentary Party, Parnell issued his famous "Manifesto to the People of Ireland," in which he attacked Gladstone directly, claiming that the "integrity and independence" of the Irish Parliamentary Party had been "sapped and destroyed by wire-pullers of the English Liberal Party."[74] Under "severe pressures" from both Gladstone and Pope Leo XIII, Croke responded to this damning proclamation by telegraphing M.P. Justin McCarthy a statement "intended for publication in the London papers":

> Sorry for Parnell: but in God's name, let him retire quietly, and with good grace from the leadership. If he does so, the Irish Party will be kept together, our honourable alliance with Gladstonian Liberals maintained, success at general election assured, Home Rule certain. But if he does not retire, alliance will be dissolved; elections lost; Irish Party seriously damaged, if not wholly broken up; Home Rule indefinitely postponed; coercion perpetuated; evicted tenants hopelessly crushed; and though last not least, public conscience outraged.

When Parnell refused, Ireland's "saviour" became its "Lucifer" in the Archbishop's eyes. Sadly, Croke wrote to his friend Dr. Tobias Kirby, Rector of the Irish College in Rome, "Parnell will never again, and can never again, be the leader of the Irish Party. . . . Kindly convey from me to the Holy Father . . . that I will use whatever influence I possess in driving the wicked and deceitful man from public life and position in Ireland."[75]

In January 1891 in a desperate effort to retain control of the movement, Parnell methodically divided the Fenian/Church alliance with such skill that within two months of the divorce court decision, Croke wrote Kirby lamenting that there were now "two camps in Ireland arrayed against each other"—the Parnellites and the anti-Parnellites. This division reflected the fundamental fracture between religious and secular Nationalists that existed from the beginning. By supporting Parnell, Archbishop Croke drew the two sides together, but once his support was withdrawn, the old enmity reappeared between those who believed Ireland should be free and Catholic and those who believed the Church should keep the hell out of the state's business. Archbishop Thomas William Croke took a step that profoundly embarrassed and pained him. In March 1891 he issued a confidential circular to the clergy of Cashel and Emly denouncing Parnell for having "sinned against the Christian code" and urging them to prepare for a convention in Thurles to consider the matter. In June, he and other Irish bishops issued a statement declaring Parnell should not be considered as a future leader of the Irish nation.[76] Stung by their rejection, Parnell went on a rampage of political self-destruction in which he willfully and maliciously shattered the Nationalist movement. With unrelenting fury, he toured the country, conjuring up old hatreds that would divide, paralyze, and foment factionalism. To Croke, he seemed driven by madness.

Disavowing Parnell also unleashed the violent, regressive Fenians who had no love for the Catholic Church. Acknowledging the rise of these wilder types, Croke complained, "The lower stratum of society in Ireland is almost entirely for Parnell. Cornerboys, blackguards of every hue, discontented labourers, lazy and drunken artisans, aspiring politicians, Fenians, and in a word all irreligious and anti-clerical scoundrels in the country are at his back." This view was seconded by Bishop Nulty of Meath, who warned his churches that "Parnellism, like Paganism, impedes, obstructs and cripples the efficiency and blights the fruitfulness . . . of the Gospel . . . without which our people cannot be saved."[77] Archbishop Croke feared that the influence of "cornerboys, blackguards and drunken artisans" would supplant the influence of priests in modern Ireland.

With despair, Croke watched as Parnell continued his political rampage. As the weeks passed, his attacks became more desperate, abusive, and distinctly more anticlerical. In May 1891, Croke wrote to Michael Davitt complaining that the "maniac is rushing through the country every week, setting Irishmen at each other's throats, belauding himself, and flinging filth and abuse on all who dare to differ from him."

After years of support for this man, Archbishop Croke was sickened by the destruction of the Nationalist coalition. "I am sick of the whole thing," he declared; "I can never again have the same opinion of our people that I have hitherto had." When he could stand it no longer, Croke left the country in August. He was in Belgium when news reached him that Parnell had died of rheumatic fever on October 6. When he returned to Ireland later that month, he announced, from The Palace, Thurles, "I am done with Irish politics." [78]

With the Irish Parliamentary Party in shambles, Home Rule dead, and Irish politicians at each others' throats, the Unionists could hardly believe their good fortune. The dumbfounded Conservative leader, Lord Salisbury, was at a loss to explain why the Irish bishops had intentionally destroyed the Irish Parliamentary Party. "Nothing in modern history has been shown to equal the influence of Archbishops Croke and Walsh in the recent history of Ireland," he observed. "They have turned the whole of the organization that seemed to embarrass and baffle the British government—they have turned it clear away from the man in whose hands it was, with as much ease as a man turns a boat by leaning on the rudder."[79]

For the most part, Archbishop Croke withdrew from the limelight, but not from politics. He was sixty-eight years old, and not in

the best of health, which the Parnell debacle certainly did nothing
to improve. Over the next few years, he avoided public incidents,
but rather than cede the whole Nationalist movement to the Fenians, he worked furiously behind the scenes to reconcile what became known euphemistically among his group of political allies as
"the split" after Parnell's death. In 1892 Croke and other Catholic
Nationalists organized the Irish National Federation, INF, a
Church-sponsored political party designed to counter the Parnellites' Irish National League and, if possible, save Home Rule.[80]

Two years later, in the Christmas season of 1894, the INF was
beginning to emerge as the dominant force in local politics, especially in the town of Clonmel, where INF candidate Nicholas
Kickham Shee, the "gentleman from Mullinahone," was winning
praise from both camps. He was a good Catholic and loyal INF
man, but more importantly, Kickham Shee was the cousin of Tipperary's lauded poet-patriot, Charles J. Kickham, whose name
shone brightly in the constellation of the county's saints. This was
particularly true from a political point of view in 1894 because, as
an older leader of the IRB, Charles Kickham, before his death in
1882, had never succumbed to Parnell's charm even when the
venerable Croke had. In his life and writings, Charles Kickham
romantically portrayed the spirit of Tipperary's fighting Fenians,
tempered by the ideals of the gentrified tenant farmers, who were
hard-working, tea-drinking, God-fearing, and eager for membership in Ireland's emerging middle class. In Nicholas Kickham
Shee, the INF leaders enlisted a man, appropriated a myth, and
turned both into a serviceable post-Parnell representation signified by the gentleman of Mullinahone. Clonmel's *Nationalist* predicted that Nicholas Kickham Shee's lifelong devotion and
"historic name" would heal the bitterness that so gravely endangered the Nationalist movement.

Nationalists of all stripes stepped forward to support Kickham Shee's candidacy as Tipperary's representative to the INF national council in Dublin. Speaking to INF hard-liners who opposed a lay candidate, the Reverend W. Meagher of St. Mary's Church asserted that Kickham Shee was "a vigorous and healthy Nationalist . . . a Tipperary man of Tipperary men." He urged all within the INF to rally—"Forward for Shee, union, discipline, and victory! Away with disunion, dissension, and deceit!" For his part, Clonmel's former Mayor Edward Cantwell, a known Parnellite, stepped forward to support Shee as did business and professional men. Editors at the *Nationalist* bent over backwards to promote unity: "We shall not add one word which could in any way irritate any of our friends who differed with us in this matter." The victory of Nicholas Kickham Shee, the gentleman from Mullinahone, in January 1895, offered a tiny glimmer, ever so faint, that the Church and the Fenian Nationalists could dwell peacefully together in the homes of Tipperary.

One of those Parnellites who joined with Mayor Cantwell in supporting Nicholas Kickham Shee was Michael Quirke, a local manure dealer who owned property with a laborer's cottage on it in the townland of Ballyvadlea, a mile north of Cloneen and some ten miles "out the mountain" (as local people called the region on the far side of the mountain Slievenamon) from Clonmel. A laborer named Patrick Boland lived in the cottage, shared with his daughter and son-in-law, Bridget and Michael Cleary, both of whom were slowly raising themselves above the common poverty of their rural neighbors through her egg sales and talents as a seamstress and his trade as a cooper. Generally the inhabitants of the cottage were peaceful and well-behaved, but during this particular Christmas season, there were angry, accusing words.

Michael Cleary was disturbed that his spirited, good-looking wife persisted in visiting one of the ancient fairy forts near their home. There was no reason, Cleary insisted, for his wife to visit the old rath. By going too often near the fairy fort, she was surely tempting the fairies to carry her off and he'd abide no changeling under his roof.

Bridget listened to her husband's ranting, then did as she pleased. An unusually independent woman for the time, she was a skilled tradeswoman, ran a thriving egg business, earned her own money, and was bold enough to look a man straight in the eye. The conflict between the two relatively well-off, progressive occupants of the Ballyvadlea cottage indicated that no matter how hard the authorities pushed the peasants to abandon their old beliefs, the fairies were never far off. In the forced march from the Famine to modernity, some had fallen by the way. But not Bridget and Michael. They appeared ready to take advantage of new, modern Ireland of 1895. They were the kind of Irish peasant couple that clerics and politicians were counting on to break with the pagan subculture of violence and move with confidence into the twentieth century.

So passed the Christmas of 1894 in Clonmel. Parnellite and anti-Parnellite politicians raged and railed, but briefly joined hands to support Nicholas Kickham Shee. Merchants plied their wares, offered their bargains. Shoppers browsed and bought in orderly fashion, then hurried home to their firesides. Reports of holiday disturbances were down from previous years, even in the "welkin ring" of "darkest Clonmel." Most significantly, on the eve of Christmas Day, country people silently streamed into town, proceeded in orderly fashion to the cathedral, and knelt at the altar as the choir sang "Adeste Fideles." For these many blessings, small but great, the weary Archbishop of Cashel gave thanks, not knowing that an extraordinary incident in Ballyvadlea was about to disrupt the delicate holiday peace.

2

Gone with the Fairies

'Twas a Strange Story

The momentary show of unity for Nicholas Kickham Shee in 1894–1895 gave hope that the Nationalist movement in County Tipperary might yet bind its wounds and reunite. For his part, the Archbishop of Cashel, Thomas William Croke, withdrew from the public stage after the Parnell debacle and worked to disassociate the Church and the Nationalist movement from Parnell's adultery, claiming that his was a moral stance designed to prevent the "demoralization of the people." For this atypically apolitical stance, Archbishop Croke drew sharp criticism.

After the Catholic bishops broke with Parnell in 1891, His Grace was condemned for saying nothing against Parnell's outrageous and excessive statements against the Church. On the other hand, he refused to rein in ardent supporters of the Irish National

Federation (INF) who vilified Parnell as a moral leper and publicly castigated Parnellites as jackasses and licksplittles. Croke's uncharacteristic silence prompted Frank Hugh O'Donnell, the Member of Parliament from Dungarvan, to accuse him of allowing Ireland to become the laughing stock of the world due to the INF's rhetorical excesses. "Civilized Europe hold[s] its nose over the stench of Irish oratory," O'Donnell charged.[1]

Unwilling or unable to respond to such criticisms, the Archbishop pressed ahead in the early 1890s with his agenda for social, cultural, and political advancement, preferring to battle drunkenness, ignorance, and paganism rather than openly confront Parnellite partisans. In particular, he turned to the Gaelic Athletic Association (GAA), even though his support of this organization had always been ambivalent.

Formed in 1884 by the Fenian and former secretary of the Slievenamon Land League Michael Cusack, the GAA organized competitions for such indigenous Irish sports as football, hurling, and camogie, an ancient form of field hockey. The GAA's "neglect of women" provided young priests with a safe athletic outlet, and the GAA generally kept laymen out of the pubs on Sunday afternoons after Mass. Beneath this seemingly innocent format, the Church feared that the GAA served as a front for the radical Fenian Irish Republican Brotherhood (IRB). Even Croke worried that the IRB, working through the GAA, would overshadow the moderate, Church-controlled Irish National Federation.[2] Though the Archbishop condemned the drinking and radical Fenianism, he recognized the GAA's importance as a social and cultural institution that fostered athleticism, team spirit, and patriotism among Ireland's young men. In truth, the line between politics and the GAA became more and more blurred as both Parnellite and anti-Parnellite Nationalists endeavored to politicize the individual sporting clubs in order to reunite the movement.[3]

On the political front, the Archbishop welcomed the Liberal William Gladstone's return to power in 1892 and supported his second Home Rule Bill and a stronger Land Bill, yet refused to accept the Chief Secretary for Ireland John Morley's plan to help evicted tenants. Although Morley's 1892 bill encouraged tenants to band together, Croke believed that the measure was insufficient because "landlordism though somewhat subdued, is today almost as greedy and mischief-making amongst us as ever." Privately, he continued to nurture the INF, hoping to build it into a responsive institution that would protect the people, defend their interests, and quell rural violence, yet even on the issue dearest to his heart, that of tenants' rights, Croke was conspicuously subdued in 1894 when Morley's Evicted Tenants Bill was defeated.[4]

Croke watched sadly as the now aged and infirm Gladstone in his fourth and final term as Prime Minister stubbornly insisted on proposing a Home Rule Bill, knowing many in his Liberal Party would revolt. When the bill ignominiously failed in the summer of 1894, Archibald Philip Primrose, Lord Rosebery, replaced Gladstone and predictably allowed Home Rule to languish because his foreign policy interests predominated. Conservative backbenchers were barely able to contain their glee that Queen Victoria's empire had successfully survived Gladstone's latest attempt at "dismemberment," and shortly made Prime Minister Rosebery their target, relishing his indifference to Irish nationalism, and awaiting their opportunity to topple his beleaguered Cabinet on any minor pretext.

Clonmel's Unionists looked forward to the Liberal government's demise. Landlords cheered as demoralized Liberals wailed about disunity within the Nationalist ranks; the landlords relished the howls of treachery that filled the air from Dartmoor to Dublin. Sensing that victory was within reach, Unionists disputed "with some acrimony among themselves as to the precise manner in which the happy dispatch should be performed, but they are decently agreed that the painful operation ought not to, and, indeed, cannot be much longer deferred." The leisured, foxhunting class of South Tipperary sensed that their opportunity to topple the Liberals was at hand, but only after the government's fall could the Anglo-Irish nobility "sit down to enjoy their heritage."[5]

Although signs were favorable, a Unionist victory was not absolutely assured. The Irish Parliamentary Party showed faint but worrisome indications of reuniting, particularly in troublesome County Tipperary, where Nicholas Kickham Shee's election signaled the possibility of a new era of unity. Moreover, sentiment was strong in Ireland and America that the Irish people had suffered enough at the hands of their imperial masters. Even in England a sizable minority wanted to disentangle from the Irish. Many resented the havoc wreaked upon the vaunted British parliamentary system by Parnell's renegade Irish Parliamentary Party and supported Gladstone's view that England would be better off without its obstreperous Irish colony. Others simply regarded the entire Irish problem as an interminable bother. To ensure victory, sharp-eyed Unionists stood by, watching for any incident that might discredit either the Nationalists or the Irish people.

An opportunity to attack the Irish Party arose early in 1895 over charges that Charles Parnell while still alive had embezzled £10,000 from the Paris Fund. Parnell's alleged misuse of the Paris account holding the Evicted Tenants' Fund was an issue that Archbishop Croke thought he had resolved in 1892. Unfortunately, the whole affair was dredged up again in early 1895, when the acerbic INF leader Tim Healy used Parnell's alleged misuse of the Fund to attack the Parnellite leader, William Redmond.[6]

The English press relished these internecine squabbles. On March 9, 1895, *Punch,* the satirical London periodical, published a feature entitled "Irish Astronomy," in which Sir Robert Ball was asked if Irish astronomy was not something akin to Irish politics. Sir Robert observed that both were "unusually nebulous, and characterized by the revolution of suns round their satellites, and the prevalence of eccentric comets and shooting stars." In fact, Ball continued, one might write thus of Irish politics:

> *The spaycious firmament on hoigh,*
> *And All the green Hibernian skoy,*
> *And wrangling hivens a foighting frame,*
> *The reign of chaos do proclaim.*
> *What though the "stars" do shoine—and squall,*
> *And on each other's orbits fall!*
> *What though no order, stable, sound,*
> *Amidst those jarring sphayres be found?*
> *Onraison there doth loud rejoice,*
> *At hearing echoed her own voice;*
> *For iver shouting as they shoine,*
> *Our hiven's a Donnybrook divoine.*

The inference was clear. If the Irish could not keep peace in their own political orbs, how could they think of governing themselves? The English relished making sport of Irish politics, which they so ably disrupted, yet at the same time delighted in their own equally debilitating internecine squabbles between Tories and Liberals.

While Unionists in England did their best to foment dissension within the Irish Party, Unionists in Ireland worked hard to maintain peace in the countryside in order to prove that they were more fit administrators of the unruly Irish. One administrative organ responsible for maintaining good order in each district was the Board of Guardians, a body charged with poor relief and peace in the countryside. Over time the Board of Guardians exercised considerable power over the rural population by dispensing just enough public aid to keep the peasants soothed but unsatisfied.[7] The Guardians' tight-fisted management of local funds mimicked parsimonious London's policy toward its indentured republics. On February 2, 1895, *Punch* captured the spirit of London's largesse in a cartoon: A baggy-eyed, pot-bellied street vendor, with cleaver in hand, is carving up a slab of meat. Surrounding the pushcart is a pack of mangy animals eagerly awaiting their share. Three dogs representing the Scotch, Irish, and the laboring classes hover on the curb while a cat representing Wales peers into the cart, looking for hidden stores of food. The Irish dog, by the way, resembles Carrick's ferocious Wheaten terrier.

One of the most tantalizing offerings that the Guardians dangled before the Irish peasant was the coveted laborer's cottage, built to provide housing for rural agricultural laborers, many of whom were former tenants made homeless in the deluge of post-Famine evictions. Local landowners were encouraged, sometimes coerced, to donate small parcels of land upon which the Guardians provided funds for building a small, but suitable cottage, which was leased to the laborer. The cottage program, implemented by the Land Act of 1881, was successful in providing much-needed housing for rural laborers, yet there were never enough cottages built to satisfy the demand.

As a result, rural peasants were pitted against one another in fierce competition for the Guardian cottages. In January 1895, the Thurles Board of Guardians served notice that several of these gravel-sided, slate-roofed residences would be made available. In response to the Guardians' notice, over 122 petitions were received. When the Board convened to consider which of these would receive cottages, a "great crowd" appeared.[8]

Groundbreaking ceremonies for these new cottages were highly publicized events. In June 1888, the Cashel Guardians gathered to celebrate construction of a new cottage, on a beautiful plot near Cloneen in the Drangan district. The cottage had two windows in the front that looked out upon "splendid views across rolling landscape to our most notable local feature, Slievenamon." The cottage plot included a half acre, enough land for a large garden and a few domestic animals. Leaders of the Cashel Board of Guardians attending the groundbreaking included the chairman, Cornelius O'Ryan, and his wife. The Ballyvadlea cottage, completed three months later, was one of 150 built by the Cashel Guardians. A laborer named Patrick Boland and his wife, Bridget, received the lease to this particular cottage and moved in later that year. Their daughter, Bridget, and her husband, Michael Cleary, soon joined the Bolands.[9]

By offering cottages and other forms of aid, the Guardian Boards effectively muzzled complainers and grumblers in the countryside. Nonetheless, readers of Clonmel's Unionist newspaper, the *Clonmel Chronicle*, followed the news closely for reports of fresh outrages, such as a hayrack burned at Marlhill and cattle found dead in County Clare. In County Cork, landowners followed the trial of John Twiss, charged with the murder of an emergency caretaker, James Donovan, hired to manage a farm taken from an evicted tenant. In the closing statement reported in the press, Twiss pleaded for his life, claiming he was a Kerry man and no Kerry man ever found justice in Cork. The jury was unimpressed, and sentenced the unfortunate Twiss to be hanged.[10]

From London came news of the Tories' latest attempt to dilute tenant benefits granted in the Land Act of 1881. After fifteen years, landowners were chafing under the "fair rent" provision that allowed the court to consider the value of tenants' improvements in determining the rent. Owners complained that a high valuation led to lower rents. Liberal M.P. John Morley offered a bill intended to clarify, but not eliminate, the "value of occupation" provision to the Land Bill; Unionists wanted it out.[11]

Unionist readers also took time to amuse themselves with newspaper stories of Irish folly and misfortune recorded in cases brought before the magistrates. One poor soul singled out by the conservative Unionist *Clonmel Chronicle* was Michael Hickey, a laborer who resided on Kickham Street in Clonmel. Hickey was brought before the Resident Magistrate (R.M.), Colonel Richard Evanson, at Clonmel's Court of Petty Sessions, and charged with neglect of his five children, aged one to ten years. Testimony opened as Constable McCormack described the condition of the third youngest child, who was found naked, emaciated, and exposed to drafts because there was no glass in the window of the family's filthy lodgings. Police stated further that the bed was in such a dirty state, no one would touch it. The prosecutor asked if there was a fire for heating and cooking or any food in the house. McCormack replied that there was no fire and just two loaves of bread got from charity, and some milk borrowed from a neighbor. The father was employed by a Mr. Carrothers but earned just fourteen shillings a week. Out of the fourteen shillings, he paid two shillings, nine pence a week in rent.

Colonel Evanson seemed particularly interested in the baby and asked who cared for the child. He was told that an "old woman" named Hannigan watched the baby, as the mother of the children was dead. Hickey had paid Hannigan three shillings a week for three months, but had paid her nothing recently. In spite of not being paid for some time, Hannigan was good enough to look after the children and, sometimes, when there was not enough money, she even pawned some of her own clothes to get food for them.

The trouble started at Christmas when Hannigan spent ten days in the hospital. After being released, she went to look after the children and found them in a very neglected state. In fact, there was no sign that anyone had been caring for them. The infant was within an inch of the fireplace and no one was in the house but the baby. Colonel Evanson asked how the infant survived while Hannigan was in the hospital? Hannigan stated she did not know.

Carrothers, speaking in behalf of his employee, explained that Hickey lived in the country at the time his wife died, leaving him to care for four children and a baby. For a time, people helped out but Hickey soon was obliged to go to town and find work. Carrothers argued that Hickey was a sober, hard-working man who was doing his best under the circumstances. At this inference, the Queen's Resident Magistrate took offense and would not allow Carrothers to proceed with any defense that might besmirch the English administration. Colonel Evanson insisted that this was a most disgraceful case and the defendant and counsel were only making it worse by blaming circumstances. Someone was responsible for the neglect, but it was certainly not members of the English colonial government.

Continuing his warning to Hickey and his ilk, Evanson asserted that any person who would leave an animal in a house by itself without fire or food would be considered guilty of cruelty.

So much greater the guilt when a child was similarly abandoned. If the defendant was obliged to be away at work, he might have asked someone "to do him the kindness of looking after the children." Instead, Hickey had done nothing. Colonel Evanson assured the defendant that the magistrates were fair-minded men, and based on the defendant's reputation for sobriety and industry, they decided to deal leniently with him. The magistrates also expressed the hope that Hickey's case would serve as an example to others in a similarly poverty-stricken position, a cautionary tale for parties guilty of "lamentable ignorance." The sentence: One month imprisonment at hard labor in the Clonmel Gaol.

Carrothers asked if Hickey could pay a fine, and thus be relieved of imprisonment and separation from his children. Evanson responded that the magistrates considered but rejected this option. Too much leniency would dilute the court's object lesson, children be damned. Because Hickey attempted to shift responsibility for his own neglect of his children, a month's hard labor was fair punishment. After judgment was pronounced, police removed Hickey from the courtroom, the five children went to the county workhouse to receive their daily portion of boiled potatoes, and English colonial justice was served once more.[12]

On the lighter side, the conservative readers of the *Clonmel Chronicle* amused themselves with the droll tale of two country bumpkins who assumed airs of civility above their class standing. It seems that Miss Honora O'Brien, a fine, upstanding country girl left standing at the altar, sued the prospective groom, Michael Flynn, County Waterford, for breach of promise. The facts showed that Flynn promised to marry Miss O'Brien for a substantial sum, then reneged on the deal. In his opening statement, Solicitor Molloy warned that the gallery need not expect anything salacious, as the parties were respectable sorts of the farming class, a class that "rarely indulged in romance or in writing love letters" and managed their relations through formal contracts and arrangements.

So said, Molloy stated the facts for the plaintiff. Honora O'Brien was a member of a large, industrious, and respectable family, residing at Brownsford, County Kilkenny, where her father had lived his entire lifetime. Mr. Flynn, a widower, owned a large farm and dairy. While at the races one day, Flynn met Miss O'Brien's brother-in-law, Mr. Cullinane, and together, the two men made "arrangements" for the match. After meeting Miss O'Brien, Flynn approved and the marriage was set for September 27, two weeks hence. To seal the deal, Cullinane paid Flynn £100, after which Honora O'Brien published the banns in her local parish.

Plans for the wedding proceeded, until suddenly, on September 23, just four days before the blessed event, Honora received a telegram from Mr. Flynn calling off the ceremony. The reason? Doctors had discovered cancer of the heart, and advised he could not marry Miss Honora with two large tumors protruding from the organ of love—an observation that drew peals of laughter from the gallery. This story was not to be believed, Solicitor Molloy bellowed. No fools here! Money was at the bottom of it. Flynn had taken the family's money, then left Miss Honora in disgrace. In demanding damages of £500 for the affront to Honora's honor, Molloy disclosed that Miss O'Brien had announced her engagement before the whole congregation of her church, and her honor was irretrievably damaged when news of her rejection was talked of "in every hole and corner in the county." This was a gross wrong, Molloy argued, for which the jury must act in order to teach the defendant that he could not indulge in such behavior with impunity.

For his part, Flynn claimed he never met Cullinane at the races. Rather, he was walking down the street one day, when Cullinane tapped him on the shoulder with his cane and said he wanted to see him about some cattle. The two retired to a hotel to bargain, and it was then that Cullinane proposed the match, but offered £300, mentioning that he, Cullinane, felt this was a good price since he got only £250 for his wife.

At this point in the testimony, His Lordship asked Flynn about the £300. What did he think of being offered £300 to marry Miss O'Brien?

> *Flynn*: I said that was very good, and that will do.
> *His Lordship*: Did you look at the girl at all?
> *Flynn*: I don't know, my lord, whether I did or not; I suppose I did.
> *His Lordship*: But when you said that was very good did you mean the girl or the £300, or, the girl and the £300?
> *Flynn*: Oh, the girl and the £300.

When Cullinane returned, however, he brought only £100. Flynn protested that £300 had been agreed to, whereupon Cullinane promised to bring the remaining £200 the next day. Satisfied with this, Flynn went off to buy a wedding ring for the bride.

> *His Lordship*: Did you pay for the ring?
> *Flynn*: I suppose I did.
> *His Lordship*: What do you mean by "suppose"? Were you muddled?
> *Flynn*: I was about three quarters.
> *His Lordship*: Perhaps you could not see the hole through the ring (*renewed laughter*)?
> *Flynn*: No, I was not that drunk, your lordship.

However, the next day when Cullinane returned with the balance, Flynn claimed he had forgotten all about the agreement. Only when reminded that he had the deposit receipt for the £100 in his pocket, did the whole episode come back to him, "as a dream." When Cullinane went to Father McCarthy to see about the marriage certificate, Flynn's recollection of the marriage was restored.

His Lordship: The dream had passed off.
Flynn: Yes.

And so it went, much to the delight of the assembled crowd. In the end, the court held that Miss O'Brien was entitled to only that amount dispersed by the family, and amidst shrieks of laughter, the case was closed.[13]

Other news of the region included the notice of a suicide near Kilcash, north of Clonmel, on the southern slope of Slievenamon. The story reported that John Dempsey, an egg dealer from Ballypatrick, thirty-eight, complained the previous week of the "state of his head, which, he said was very hot, and his being unable to sleep at night." After taking breakfast on the morning of March 11, Dempsey proceeded to an outhouse and a few minutes later, returned holding a handkerchief to his throat.[14] Upon seeing the blood pouring from the wound, the man's wife sent one of their five children to fetch a neighbor. A priest and doctor arrived shortly. The doctor bandaged the wound and did all in his power to save the man, while the priest administered last rites.

Sergeant O'Connor arrived in time to question the mortally wounded man, asking why he had done this to himself. Dempsey replied, "I do not know; my head was troubled very much." Witnesses stated that the deceased had some losses lately in the purchase and exportation of eggs, in which he dealt extensively, and that it "preyed on his mind." The *Nationalist* also carried a brief notice of Dempsey's "shocking suicide," noting suicides were a rare occurrence in the district. Rumors of his death were initially discounted since Dempsey was well known in the town due to his business of buying and selling eggs. But the rumors proved true for once, leading the paper to speculate that Dempsey suffered from "severe agony" caused by "mental depression."[15] That something more than money matters might have caused him to take his life never surfaced publicly.

Dempsey's suicide was reported on March 16. The next issue of the *Clonmel Chronicle*, on March 20, carried news of another unusual, apparently unrelated incident headlined "Gone with the Fairies." The story went as follows:

> A good deal of excitement has been caused in the district about Drangan and Cloneen by the "mysterious disappearance" of a labourer's wife, who lived with her husband, a farm labourer, in that part of the country. An old woman who had been nursing the sick woman was sitting up with her as usual one night last week, and, as she puts it, the invalid was "drawn" away. A search has been made everywhere, and the police have been communicated with, but up to this afternoon no trace of the missing woman has been discovered. The country-people entertain the opinion that she has "gone with the fairies!"

The police launched an extensive search, but found no sign of the missing woman.[16]

The rumor that a young woman had "gone with the fairies" was a matter of amusement to Unionists and alarm to Nationalists, first, because the story created great excitement among the country people and second, because the Drangan district bordered Mullinahone, the home of the late Charles J. Kickham, Tipperary's poet/patriot, and of INF representative Nicholas Kickham

Shee. The area was well known to hunters because of the vaunted fox cover found on the south slopes of the Slievearmagh hills, particularly near Rathkenny and Kylnagranagh. To Unionists eager for fresh evidence of Irish ignorance, here was a story with the potential of reaching a far larger audience than tales of poor Michael Hickey and the jilted and dishonored Honora O'Brien. To Nationalists, this strange story was a potential disaster.

Scanlon's Field

In the mid-1880s, when the men of the Clonmel Rowing Club entered the pantheon of Clonmel's immortal heroes and the first Home Rule Bill went down to defeat, Michael Cleary, a young man from Killenaule, trudged to Clonmel looking for work. At the time Cleary was in his mid-twenties and unmarried, but entertained thoughts of changing this situation. In appearance, he was somewhat lean at 5'10" and 154 pounds. He had blue eyes, brown hair receding slightly, and a fresh, ruddy complexion. Cleary was a cooper by trade, and, had the times been better, he would have found work in Clonmel's once-bustling barrel industry; but when he arrived, steady work was difficult to obtain. Faced with a tight labor market in Clonmel, Michael Cleary reversed his tracks and traipsed back to the countryside, but rather than return to Killenaule, he settled in the townland of Ballyvadlea, a mile north of Cloneen village.

Initially Michael Cleary found lodging in a crude hut on the property of Michael Quirke, a Parnellite manure dealer from Clonmel. The hut later became a work shed, where Michael stored barrel staves and coopering tools.[17] When there was work, he took jobs in Clonmel, and in the slack seasons, supplemented his income with odd jobs around Fethard and Cloneen. Cleary's

hut was not far from the Kennedy family, whose four sons—
Patrick, Michael, James, and William—were unskilled agricultural
laborers seasonally employed by local farmers. The Kennedy
boys lived with their parents, Richard and Mary Kennedy, in a
traditional, thatched-roof cottage just east of the "low road" that
connected Cloneen with Drangan to the north. Across the low
road, Mary Kennedy's brother, Patrick Boland, lived beside the
stream with his wife, Bridget, and their daughter, also named Bridget, the youngest of their four children. The whereabouts or
deaths of her three brothers cannot be accounted for in existing
records.

The Kennedys and Bolands both had many relatives in the
area, but among them all, young Bridget Boland was the best and
brightest of the lot. She was an intelligent young woman, a top
student at the convent school in Drangan, where classmates remembered her as lively and active. Among her peers, Bridget was
highly social and a favorite with the boys. She was something of
an Irish vixen, described locally as a "handsome well-favoured
young woman of medium height, fresh complexion, with very
dark wavy hair, beautiful [blue] eyes, and pleasing expression."
Her temperament matched her looks—striking, energetic, high-
spirited. Upon her leaving school, probably in the ninth grade,
the Bolands saw to it that Bridget learned a trade. She served an
apprenticeship as a dressmaker, some say in Clonmel, where she
may have met the cooper Cleary. Later, she returned to Ballyvadlea where, it was reported she worked for a time as a housekeeper for a family in Cloneen.[18]

On August 6, 1887, Michael Cleary and Bridget Boland were
married at the Catholic church in Drangan. Michael was twenty-
seven. Bridget was twenty and still working as a domestic, according to the marriage registry.[19] A cousin, Bridget Kennedy,

served as her bridesmaid. The best man at the wedding was not Bridget's cousin, Patrick Kennedy, who was closest in age to the groom, but another relative named John Dunne, who, at forty-seven, was considerably older. Dunne had the reputation of being a "fairy-ridden" character, a reputation exaggerated by his poor eyesight and visible limp. He lived in a cottage outside Cloneen at the base of Kylnagranagh hill with his wife, Catherine, who was an aunt of the Kennedy children.[20]

In the fall of 1888, Patrick and Bridget Boland moved into a newly built Guardians' cottage a half-mile west of the low road, on a hillside overlooking the Anner River valley and the mountain Slievenamon. It was a solid structure with gray stone walls topped with a gray slate roof. The eighteen-foot-wide central room accommodated the cooking and eating area. A ladder gave access to a loft, about eight feet wide, which provided additional storage. There was no indoor plumbing or electricity, but the cottage boasted a recessed fireplace featuring a built-in iron grill for cooking. Adjoining the main room were two tiny bedrooms—really one room separated by a thin wooden partition—both of which opened out into the kitchen/living area. The cottage was large enough to accommodate two couples, and before year's end, Bridget and Michael moved in with the Bolands, and Bridget apparently stopped working as a housekeeper. The newlyweds occupied the back bedroom whose window looked out toward the two stone henhouses set against the hillside. The cottage was set on a half-acre plot where Michael kept his workshop and Bridget, her garden and chicken coops.[21]

For the most part, all those who knew the Clearys, including their local priest, reported that they were happy together, a "united couple." Michael enjoyed his stout, but did not drink heavily. Despite the fact that both he and Bridget had strong personalities, they were not known to argue excessively, something that would have been apparent to the many friends and relatives who routinely visited the cottage. Rather, the two shared the dream of improving their lives and worked hard to do so. As a result, "they were in comfortable circumstances for persons in their station in life." Bridget owned a Singer sewing machine, a significant investment for the time, with which she earned income as a seamstress—a considerable step up from her earlier job as a domestic, which in the 1880s was the main occupation of women in Clonmel.[22]

In addition to sewing, Bridget raised hens and sold eggs in the district, and like her dressmaking enterprise, the egg business also thrived. Bridget and Michael built a first, and later a second, stone henhouse behind their home and had expanded their cottage-enterprise still further by adding a pigsty, which was complete except for the thatched roof for which three stacks of "squtched" (dry) corn had been gathered. For his part, Michael made a good living as a cooper. When work was available, he made barrels and wooden products for Clonmel's two largest manufacturing establishments, the Brewery and the Condensed Milk Factory. He also made butter churns and paddles for the two commercial creameries in Fethard.[23]

Though life appeared to be going well for the young couple, strains began to develop in the relationship. Despite her obvious charm and ability, Bridget Cleary had the reputation of being "a bit queer." Although she and her husband were partners in the couple's entrepreneurial ventures, Bridget exhibited a strong independent streak, which some resented, claiming that she displayed a "certain superiority over the people with whom she came into contact."[24] But the cooper's wife was also something of an enigma because, after almost eight years of marriage, she remained childless, and, what's more, seemed to relish the resulting freedom.

Unburdened by children, Bridget came and went as she pleased, traveling the neighborhood with her eggs and finished goods. Because of her trade skills, she earned her own money, which gave her a small degree of economic independence.

That Bridget showed more spunk than some thought acceptable can be seen in an incident with a priest. Local legend has it Father Michael M'Grath, the parish priest of Drangan, rode by the Cleary cottage and saw Bridget out in the yard straining boiled potatoes. Her dog Badger attacked the priest's horse. M'Grath asked her to call off the dog, and when she refused, he kicked at the dog in order to pass on his way. Whereupon Bridget threw a pot of hot water from the potatoes at both the horse and priest. At which, Father M'Grath cursed her, predicting she would die a violent death by fire for her impertinence.[25] Although the tale may have been conveniently recalled later and embellished to make the priest something of a prophet in his own parish, it rang true to those who knew Bridget because she was not easily cowed by authority.

Moreover, she seemed to harbor an interest in the occult fairy faith of ancient Ireland—an interest she apparently shared with her mother. Another trait that made Bridget a bit "weird" was that she had the disturbing habit of looking men straight in the eye, which was said to be a characteristic of pagan women.

Bridget's growing economic independence, her unflinching defiance of male authority—whether her husband's or the priest's—and her willingness to take risks undoubtedly caused strains in her relationship with her husband. It was Bridget's increasing fascination with the fairy faith, however, especially after her mother's death in February 1894, that set the cooper and his wife at odds.

In the last year of her life, Bridget made frequent trips across the low road to visit two ancient fairy forts, or raths, located in

Jim Scanlon's field on Kylnagranagh hill. The terrain was open, rolling fields, interspersed with furze brush, some recently planted to provide fox cover for the red-coated, horn-blowing hunters. From afar, these particular fairy forts would appear to the untrained observer to be an ordinary grove of trees growing on the hill. But upon closer inspection, one would see that the trees grew around an ancient moat, three to four feet deep in some places, that formed a circle, or ring, around an open, grassy clearing in the center. The larger of the two forts lay on the south slope facing Slievenamon and was over three acres in size, while the smaller was on the gentler, northern slope. It was this smaller, more remote fort that Bridget favored. Because both forts were some distance from the low road, the question of why the spirited young Bridget Cleary bothered to trek up the hill to this remote spot was the matter of speculation around the neighborhood.

The superstitious might say that she went to the forts in hopes of seeing her dead mother among the fairy host. On the other hand, the cynical might say that she went to the remote fort to meet a lover, perhaps Jack Dempsey, the suicidal eggman from Ballypatrick, or a red-coated fox hunter—at least one of whom remembered seeing her quite often and noting her distinctive good looks.[26] Her husband was rightfully jealous, for his wife was a fine-looking woman. But Michael Cleary, like many, also entertained superstitions that these earthen, moated forts were dwelling places of "the people." He, like everyone in the district, knew that if this handsome, overly curious young woman continued her visits to the fort in Scanlon's field, sooner or later there would be trouble.

Anyone who breathed the clear Tipperary air knew stories about the fairies, or "the people." A child's earliest memories included tales of the fairies, circulated from mouth to mouth, whispered at the crossroads, or rehearsed by the fireside. Even in the nineteenth century, the influence of these nonmortal beings remained strong, especially among the rural peasantry who were more likely to encounter the fairies than were their city cousins. The Irish countryside itself seemed to affirm the existence of these beings. To the superstitious, the heather blooming in the cracks of a rocky promontory became a passageway for beings passing to and from the sea. The local mountain, Slievenamon, took the shape of a vessel bound across the western ocean toward mythical Tír na nÓg, the land of eternal youth. An ancient yew tree, believed to be a conduit to the spirit world, watched over Christian graves beside the church. Fairy music could be heard in the hillsides on still, dark evenings. To many in the countryside, the existence of the fairies was surer than mere belief. As a Sligo man said, "Nothing is more certain than that there are fairies."[27]

Even in pious, Christian homes, children were taught proper regard for the fairies. A Catholic priest from the west of Ireland described what he learned from his parents:

> As children we were always afraid of fairies, and were taught to say "God bless *them!* God bless *them!*" whenever we heard them mentioned. . . . In our family we always made it a point to have clean water in the house at night for the fairies. . . . If anything like dirty water was thrown out the doors after dark it was necessary to say *"bugga, bugga salach!"* as a warning to the fairies not to get their clothes wet.[28]

Untasted food was left on the table at night for the fairies. If food spilled from the table, it was not right to take it back, for the fairies wanted it. The luckiest thing to do was to pick up the fallen food, eat just a speck, then leave the rest. Children were warned to stay clear of isolated thornbushes, such as Fanny's Bush,

Sally's Bush, or another in County Sligo near Boyle, because ghosts frequented these spots.

In spite of the fact that beliefs about the fairies originated in Ireland's pagan past, the old teachings coexisted with Christian thought even late into the nineteenth century. Regarding the origin of the fairies, the Catholic priest explained this complex integration of pagan belief and Christian doctrine:

> The fairies of any one race are the people of the preceding race—the Fomors for the Fir Bolgs, the Fir Bolgs for the Dananns, and the Dananns for us. The old races died. Where did they go? They became spirits—and fairies. Second-sight gave our race power to see the inner world. When Christianity came to Ireland the people had no *definite* heaven. Before, their ideas about the other world were vague. But the older ideas of a spirit world remained side by side with the Christian ones, and being preserved in a subconscious way gave rise to the fairy world.[29]

Whether they were good like the Dananns or bad like the Fir Bolgs, mythical beings from the pagan past lived side by side with Christian saints—both were real and both were honored.

Witnesses told of the existence of the fairy tribes. One woman who claimed to have actually seen these invisible beings was quite specific about the physical differences among each race. Gnomes were earth-spirits, perhaps two and one-half feet tall, with distinctly round heads and thick bodies, and appeared to be continually sorrowful. Leprechauns were also small, but were fun-loving and full of mischief. The Little People resembled gnomes and leprechauns, but were very handsome. The Good People directed the magnetic currents of the earth, while the godlike Tuatha De

Danann were the largest of all. The woman conceded there could be other invisible races, but these were the races she had seen.[30]

Among the regal Tuatha De Danann, there were two classes: the shining beings, who reflected light from without; and those beings whose light came from within. The shining beings comprised a lower order and were more frequently seen, while the opalescent beings held positions as great chiefs, princes, or princesses. But whatever their relative rank, all were dazzling beings of great stature. A seer who claimed to have seen them related the following:

> The first of these I saw I remember very clearly, and the manner of its appearance: there was at first a dazzle of light, and then I saw that this came from the heart of a tall figure with a body apparently shaped out of half-transparent or opalescent air, and throughout the body ran a radiant, electrical fire, to which the heart seemed the centre. Around the head of this being and through its waving luminous hair, which was blown all about the body like living strands of gold, there appeared flaming wing-like auras. From the being itself light seemed to stream outwards in every direction: and the effect left on me after the vision was one of extraordinary lightness, joyousness, or ecstasy.[31]

There appears to have been no fixity of gender among the Dananns. Sometimes they took masculine or feminine forms; sometimes neither. Likewise, none appeared to be the leader, nor was there a discernible hierarchy among them; instead, their organization was something like a buzzing hive of bees.

Fairy spirits lived in the Otherworld, which, unlike the Christian spirit world, was believed to be on the earth rather than on some remote, celestial sphere. Many believed that the Otherworld was also populated with spirits of the dead. A woman known as the Dromintee seeress stated:

> These *good people* were the spirits of our dead friends, but I could not recognize them. I have often seen them that way while in my bed. Many women are among them. I once touched a boy of theirs, and he was just like feathers in my hand; there was no substance in him, and I knew he wasn't a living being. I don't know where they live; I've heard they live in the *Carrige* (rocks). Many a time I've heard of their *taking* people or leading them astray. They can't live far away when they come to me in such a rush. They are as big as we are. I think these fairy people are all through this country and in the mountains.[32]

The proximity of the Otherworld to the mortal sphere, coupled with the belief in supernatural intervention in everyday life, created the opportunity for frequent encounters between fairies and mortals.

In fact, the boundary between worlds was so close that mortals could be taken away to live with the fairies in the Otherworld. A civil engineer from County Armagh explained: "When I was a youngster near Armagh, I was kept good by being told that the fairies could take bad boys away. . . . The old people in County Armagh seriously believe that the fairies are the spirits of the dead; and they say that if you have many friends deceased you have many friendly fairies, or if you have many enemies deceased you have many fairies looking out to do you harm." In addition to being spirits of the dead, some among the fairy troop were believed to be mortals taken by the fairies. As John O'Hare said of Cuchulainn's Mountain, site of the famous Cattle Raid of Cooley, "The *good people* in the mountain are the people who have died and been *taken*."[33]

Because the mortal and nonmortal worlds were so close, the chance of encountering the fairies was always a possibility, and in some of these encounters, abductions followed. A man from County Donegal related one incident when he, along with a group of children, encountered the fairies while gathering berries. The children came within a few hundred feet of some "gentle folk" who were dancing. "When they saw us," he stated,

> a little woman dressed all in red came running out from them towards us, and she struck my cousin across the face with what seemed to be a green rush. We ran for home as hard as we could, and when my cousin reached the house she fell dead. Father saddled a horse and went for Father Ryan. When Father Ryan arrived, he put a stole about his neck and began praying over my cousin and reading psalms and striking her with the stole; and in that way brought her back. He said if she had not caught hold of my brother, she would have been *taken* for ever.

Another man recounted that the "gentle folk" in olden times took children and drew the life out of their bodies. Once a spirit was taken, death followed immediately, or, if a fairy spirit was left in the mortal's body, death was delayed, sometimes for years.[34]

The abstraction of the human spirit from the body produced a radical change in the victim's personality. Sometimes this person began speaking in foreign tongues or experienced paroxysms and contortions of the body. Facial expressions and mannerisms were so altered that the possessed individual became unrecognizable. This was particularly true of children who were said to take on the speech habits and even the body type of the inhabiting fairy. One striking example of this is provided by a changeling from Brittany who was no taller than a normal ten-year-old child, but thickset like a thirty-year-old man. His own mother declared that he was not the child she bore.[35]

Another story from Fermanagh told of a careless mother who left her son's cradle unattended. While she was gone, the fairies took him off and left in his place a wizened old creature who smoked a pipe. Imagine the poor mother's surprise when her child popped his head from the cradle and shouted, "Gimme a light for me pipe!" as clear as could be. The old fairy was eventually driven off by the threat of fire, but the woman's son was never seen again. In order to avoid these unwanted exchanges, the mothers of southern Ireland placed bits of iron over the cradles to keep the fairies from taking their babies, since it was known they avoided iron as surely as they feared fire.

Stories of abductions led ethnographer W. Y. Evans-Wentz to observe in 1911 that the prevalence of changelings was a striking feature of the fairy faith. This belief may have been a holdover from a time when the aboriginal pre-Celtic peoples were held in subjection by the Celts. As the more aggressive Celts advanced, these aboriginal tribes were forced to retreat underground, but occasionally kidnapped the children of their conquerors. A few escaped and returned to tell their kinsmen highly romantic tales about living underground in the fairy-world. Another version of this theory states that the Druids, either by their own choice or as a result of being driven back by Christianity, dwelt in secret chambered mounds, or in dense forests. Druids occasionally stole young people for recruits, who were sometimes returned after many years, but only under an inviolable vow of secrecy.[36]

The changeling belief also derived from past eras when people were required to offer human sacrifices to their gods.[37] In these instances, groups gathered up the weak and sickly among them and offered these rather than the healthy. Further, the notion that the spirit could be abstracted from the body led to a similar belief that sickness was the result of the fairies taking off the mortal soul to the Otherworld; hence the connection between changelings and dying spirits.

An Irish poet of the early nineteenth century, Edward Walsh, tells of a fairy nurse who lulls a mortal child to sleep before taking it off to the Otherworld. The poet interweaves the various beliefs about the changeling:

> *Sweet babe! a golden cradle holds thee,*
> *And soft the snow-white fleece enfolds thee;*
> *In airy bower I'll watch thy sleeping,*
> *Where branchy trees to the breeze are sweeping.*
> *Shuhenn, sho, lulo! lo!*
> *When mothers languish broken-hearted,*
> *When young wives are from husbands parted,*
> *Ah! little think the keeners lonely,*
> *They weep some time-worn fairy only.*
> *Shuheen sho, lulo, lo*
> *Within our magic halls of brightness,*
> *Trips many a foot of snowy whiteness;*
> *Stolen maidens, queens of fairy—*
> *And kings and chiefs a sluagh-shee airy.*
> *Shuheen sho, lulo lo!*
> *Rest thee, babe! I love thee dearly,*
> *And as thy mortal mother nearly;*
> *Ours is the swiftest steed and proudest,*
> *That moves where the trap of the host is loudest.*
> *Shuheen sho, lulo lo!*
> *Rest thee, babe! for soon thy slumbers*

Shall flee at the magic's koelshie's [fairy music] numbers;
In airy bower I'll watch thee sleeping,
Where branchy trees to the breeze are sweeping.
Shuheen sho, lulo, lo![38]

When the child's soul was taken away by "the swiftest steed and proudest"; the body left behind soon withered and died. Wives, especially those who were young and comely, were taken from their husbands to become queens to fairy kings. The captive spirit might return, at some future date, but most did not.

The Irish thought of these fairy takings as transfers of spirits that went through portals connecting mortal and nonmortal worlds. Beings of both types could pass back and forth through these passageways. Generally this was not a bad thing, but intercourse between worlds could be tricky. Mortals could profit from the fairies if they understood their ways. One could catch a leprechaun and stare at it continually until it was forced to reveal the location of its treasure, which was easier said than done, according to a man from Mullingar who claimed knowledge of mischievous leprechauns. He heard a report that a leprechaun was captured by the police, but the man from Mullingar had his doubts: "Now that couldn't be at all . . . for everybody knows the leprechaun is a spirit and can't be caught by any blessed policeman, though it is likely one might get his gold if they got him cornered so he had no chance to run away. But the minute you wink or take your eyes off the little devil, sure enough he is gone." A woman from Roscommon said that as a girl she went gathering wild berries and saw a leprechaun in a hole under a stone. He was no larger than a doll and had the most perfectly formed mouth and eyes, but no bag of gold. When she returned home with her story, others chided her for not capturing the creature when she had so good a chance.[39]

Ned the weaver learned that aid from the fairies could be a mixed blessing. Every night before Ned went to bed, he set out yarn on the loom, and each morning found finished woven cloth. But the fairies left the yarn and loom so tangled that it took him hours to set it right. Yet with all the trouble, Ned was no worse off, because the fairies left him household necessities, and any cloth he sold brought triple the price bargained.[40]

A few clever individuals were able to use the supernatural powers of the fairies to their advantage, as was the case with Jamie Freel of Donegal,[41] a responsible young man who worked tirelessly to support his widowed mother. Each Saturday night, he gave her his entire week's earnings, thanking her graciously for the halfpence of tobacco she gave him in return. Mortal neighbors thought him the best son ever. Jamie lived very near an old ruined castle, which was said to be the abode of the "wee folk." Every Halloween its ancient windows were lit, and passers-by saw little figures flitting to and fro and heard the music of pipes and fiddles and great merriment within. Jamie watched from a distance for many years, and finally the night before Halloween one year he announced to his mother that he was away to the castle to seek his fortune. His mother feared he would be killed, leaving her with no means of support, but Jamie replied, "Never fear, mother; nae harm 'ill happen me, but I maun gae." And so he did.

As he approached the castle, Jamie heard music and revelry within and desired to enter, whereupon numbers of the people greeted him warmly. "Welcome, Jamie Freel! Welcome, welcome, Jamie!" cried the company, and the word "Welcome" was caught up and repeated by every voice in the castle. Jamie entered and was enjoying himself in every respect, when one of his hosts announced, "We're going to ride to Dublin tonight to steal a young lady. Will you come, too, Jamie Freel?" "Ay, that I will!" Jamie answered, and off they went on a troop of fine horses, flying high over the countryside all the way to Dublin. They dismounted at a fine house on St. Stephen's Green, where, through a window, Jamie saw a beautiful young woman lying on a pillow in a splendid bed. Then he saw her lifted up and carried away. A stick left in her place on the bed assumed her exact form.

The lady was placed before one rider and carried a short while, then given to another and so forth on the return journey. As the troop approached Jamie's village, the leader asked if Jamie might not want to carry her a short way. Jamie agreed, and when the horses reached his mother's door, he dropped down and, holding fast to the young woman, carried her to the safety of his own cottage. The fairies howled when they discovered Jamie's deception. "Jamie Freel! Jamie Freel! Is this the way you treat us?" they cried. Jamie held fast as the "little folk" tried to retrieve their captive by turning the lady into all sorts of strange shapes—one moment a barking black dog, then a glowing bar of hot iron, then a sack of wool. Still, Jamie held her tight until finally the fairies departed but not before placing a curse on the girl, which left her deaf and dumb. Nevertheless, Jamie and his mother took the poor girl into their home, treated her kindly, and Jamie worked harder than ever to support them all.

The following Halloween, Jamie announced that he would return to the castle. "Are you mad?" his mother cried, "sure they'll kill you this time for what you done on them last year." Jamie made light of her fears and returned as before. Upon approaching the castle he overheard the fairies discussing the trick that Jamie Freel had played upon them the year before. Continuing to listen,

Jamie learned that the curse could be removed if the young woman drank from the glass that one of the fairies was holding. Jamie rushed in, snatched the glass, and returned in an instant to his own house where he gave the girl the last drops to drink. Instantly she regained her speech and hearing. In gratitude for his kindness, she persuaded Jamie to take her back to Dublin and convince her family to accept Jamie as her husband. Soon they were married and all lived happily ever after in the fine house on St. Stephen's Green. This extraordinary turn of fortune was due to Jamie Freel's ability to outfox the fairies.

"She took like a trembling"

On Wednesday, March 6, 1895, Bridget Cleary went about her usual round of duties, tending to her domestic chores around the cottage, then gathering and preparing eggs for her afternoon delivery. Michael warned her against going to the fairy fort as he had done often over the past year since her mother died. She had no business up there, and besides, it was dangerous to be flirting with the fairies.

But Bridget persisted in her trips to the raths and trouble ensued. Michael was adamant; he did not want her going there anymore. Later it was reported that he even threatened to burn her, but she went just the same.[42]

Michael had good reason to fear his wife's fascination with the fairies. The story was told that when he was a boy his own mother went off with the fairies and no one knew where she had gone or if she would ever return. On the third day she came home as suddenly as she had disappeared. And his mother-in-law was also known to be a "wise woman" who took a keen interest in fairylore. Now his wife was following these two in harboring this strange fascination with the Otherworld. His wife was third in a line of women closest to Michael. If one were superstitious about numbers, as we suspect Michael Cleary was, this was cause for concern. Three women, and to boot all named Bridget, and all three seeking something from the other side. Three threes make nine and in Irish mythology, to move beyond nine, or the "ninth wave," is to move into the realm beyond mortal existence. Despite Michael's threats, on the afternoon of March 6, Bridget set out along the low road toward Cloneen with her basket of eggs to call on her usual customers. On her return, she stopped at John Dunne's cottage, which was located at the base of Kylnagranagh hill. He was not at home so she waited for over two hours outside the cottage—or so she said. Rather than wait, she probably climbed the hill and spent the two hours there instead. While she was at the fort, something happened. Did she meet someone? A friend, perhaps, or a lover, perhaps the eggman Jack Dempsey from nearby Ballypatrick, who would soon kill himself, or perhaps she rendezvoused with one of "the people"?

Later that afternoon, Bridget returned home and complained of feeling unwell. Bridget's cousin, Johanna Burke, said that she "took like a tremblin" coming from Kylnagranagh hill. Another witness said she was "left" at Skehan's gate on the low road, a place where the fairies passed on their journeys to and from the hill. When she finally returned home, Bridget exhibited a number of symptoms of fairy-induced illness. She was chilled through to the bone; she ached everywhere and felt miserable. Rather than go about her usual tasks, she sat by the fire, but was so cold that "it would not warm her." Moreover, she was extremely irritable and seemed neither to recognize familiar faces nor to recall events she should have remembered.

The next day, Thursday, March 7, she took to her bed with fever, headache, and congestion. The illness continued, but on Saturday, she went outdoors briefly to supervise a laborer who had come to plough the garden. Afterwards she went back inside, complaining of severe chills. She took to her bed and seemed not herself.[43]

In fairy lore, the sudden onset of Bridget's illness resembles the first sign of a "fairy disease," known as a "fairy stroke," one of several fairy-induced illnesses. This was a very serious disease, known to the Irish as *millteoireacht*, meaning injury, or destruction. If a person had a seizure, this would be viewed as a fairy stroke, especially if the person had not suffered such an attack previously. Osteomyelitis—an infectious inflammatory disease of bone often of bacterial origin marked by local death and separation of tissue—was said to be caused by fairy stroke and was accompanied by a high fever that became chronic and left the patient incapacitated.[44] The "trembling" described by Johanna Burke fit the symptoms of fairy stroke. The signs were more troubling, since Bridget was known to enjoy fine health and a strong constitution. A neighbor recalled that he had known Bridget all her life but had never seen nor heard of her being sick, that as long as he had known her, she was "always healthy and strong." The Protestant caretaker William Simpson, who lived a stone's throw from the Cleary cottage, seconded this opinion, stating that he had never known Bridget to be "delicate in mind or body."[45]

The onset of a fairy-induced ailment was worrisome in itself, but the other fear was that fairy stroke could also be a sign of fairy abduction. One sign of abduction was that if the individual stricken with fairy stroke was also possessed by fairy spirits, then changes in temperament and physical appearance would be immediately apparent. This notion is illustrated in the story of a poor woman who went out one day to fetch boiled bread and milk for her baby and returned to find him greatly changed. When she asked her older son what had happened, he told her the child was playing by the fire when suddenly he heard a rush of wind—a sign of what was called a "fairy blast"—and a great number of fowls flew down the chimney. When he heard the child cry, he ran into the kitchen and found his baby brother "miserable-looking and dirty." The boy's face was like an old man's, and his body, legs, and arms were thin and hairy, but he still resembled the child his mother had left that morning. The child never stopped screaming "mammy, mammy," demanding this and that, and the woman never slept for all his complaining until she was worn to the bone. Surely she would have died, but the neighbors knew the child was not her own, so they came to the cottage one day to intervene. One stout woman came up to the bed, grabbed the imp, and wrapped him in a quilt. Before he could defend himself, she dragged him down the lane with the whole village at her heels.[46]

Changes in temperament and physical appearance were signs of abduction, and Bridget Cleary exhibited both. Immediately after her return from Scanlon's field on March 6, she seemed to be not herself. She crouched by the fire; she was listless and irritable and showed little interest in her usual enjoyments. More alarming was the change in her physical appearance. Michael perceived that she was fully two inches taller than her former self. This sudden alteration of one's bodily structure was possible because the being in possession of the abducted mortal's body was not composed of mortal flesh and blood and so could change its shape at will. Hence the word "changeling." Freed from the constraints of a mortal body, a fairy could take any shape. It could become as huge as a giant or as small as the tiniest baby. It could be a bird, or a cow, or a neighbor down the lane. It could disguise itself so cleverly that only the most discerning could detect the deception.

The ephemeral nature of the fairy body was told in the story of Pat Gill of County Kildare, who, while driving a wagon to market, approached a crossroads and was startled by a woman dressed in long white robes standing vaguely beside the road. She advanced toward him and walked awhile beside the cart. As she did, Pat looked down and saw the stones of the road behind showing through her body. Pat said nothing, and they went on together awhile until they reached the crossroads. Another cart approached, and to Pat's horror, the woman stepped into its path and was struck. Fearing she might be injured, Pat cried out, "By your leave, ma'am!" and stopped his cart. Instead, he saw the woman looking at him intently, her hand shading her eyes. Poor Pat was terrified, and made off, never turning his gaze back until a bend in the road cut off his view.[47]

Michael Cleary also noticed that his wife, in addition to being two inches taller, seemed more "refined" than before her illness. The two alterations were not unrelated. The increase in physical size could be taken as a sign that the spirit in possession of Bridget's body was one of the Tuatha De Dannan, the godlike race closely associated with the mountain Slievenamon and with women. These beings were known to be the largest in stature of all the fairy races, and also the most regal, cultivated, and refined. The Tuatha De Dannan ranked highest in the hierarchy of fairy folk, so if they wished to take away a mortal spirit, they took the finest to be had.

Moreover, fairies, and especially the Tuatha De Dannan, did not arbitrarily abduct mortals. There was usually a purpose for the abduction. Perhaps a fairy mother lost her own child and wished a mortal baby to take its place. Or perhaps a fairy prince sought a bride when none among his own kind pleased him.

One story told of a young woman wooed by a handsome fairy man. In the month of November, when the fairies were said to be active, the prettiest girl in all of the county went to draw water, and as she went, slipped and fell. She quickly recovered but saw that she was in a strange place. Some distance away, she saw a huge bonfire and a crowd gathered round. She drew near, and as she did, they watched her silently. She felt uncomfortable and thought of leaving until a handsome young man with long yellow hair and wearing a red sash embroidered with a gold band approached her and asked her to dance. "It's a foolish thing of you, sir, to ask me to dance," she said. "There is no music." The young man waved his hand and suddenly the sweetest music she had ever heard played all around her. The young man took her hand, and they danced and danced till the moon went down and the stars disappeared. She seemed like one floating on air and forgot everything in the world except the dancing, the music, and the young man with the yellow hair.

At last the dancing ceased, and the handsome young man invited the lovely girl to join the people at supper. She saw an opening in the ground and a flight of steps, and the young man, who now appeared to be the king, led her below, followed by the whole company of people. At the end of the stairs they entered a large hall, all bright and filled with objects of silver and gold, and the table covered with food. The prince handed her a golden goblet of wine and bade her drink. The people pressed the girl to eat, which she was about to do, when a man passed close by and whispered, "Eat no food and drink no wine, or you will never reach your home again."

Fearing she would never see her family again, the girl refused to eat or drink, causing a great uproar. A fierce, dark man stood up and shouted, "Whoever comes to us must drink with us." Then he seized her arm and pressed the wine to her lips. Just as she was about to yield, a red-haired man stepped forward and led her out.

"You are safe for this time," he said. "Take this herb and hold it in your hand until you reach home and no one can harm you." He then gave her a branch of a plant called *Athair lus,* or ground ivy. She took it and ran until she reached her home, then went inside and barred the door. The fairies never troubled her again, but it was a long time before the sound of the fairy music left her ears, a long, long time till the memory of that November night and her fairy lover faded.[48]

The young woman escaped abduction only because she refused to eat the fairies' food and never returned to their fort. Bridget, on the other hand, according to those close to her, willingly went to the fairy fort in Scanlon's field in spite of the warnings, and in doing so, put herself in jeopardy. On March 6, Bridget had gone out selling eggs, as was her custom. We presume that near the end of her route, she stopped at John Dunne's cottage but found no one home. She said later that she waited for two hours for someone to return, but more likely she went to the fort, in defiance of her husband's orders.

While at the fort, Bridget had a "fit of trembling," which in fairy terms meant that her own spirit was taken through the fort's portal into the Otherworld. In exchange, a fairy spirit took possession of her body, which was then "left" on the low road near Skehan's gate, opposite Scanlon's field and the forts, where fairies were known to pass by. According to family members, the changeling looked very much like the cooper's wife, acted something like her, yet was suspiciously strange. It occupied her place by the fire, wore her clothes, but was not the wife of Michael Cleary.

For his part, Michael immediately suspected what he had long feared—that his wife had been abducted and the creature by the fire was a changeling. His suspicions were supported by her father, Patrick Boland, Bridget's aunt, Mary Kennedy, and her cousin Johanna Burke. Two of her cousins, the Kennedy boys, drifted in and formed their concurring opinions as well. John Dunne came by the cottage and, being something of an authority on fairies, confirmed what the others feared, that the strange but familiar creature huddled up by the fire was not their Bridget, but a changeling.

A number of rational explanations could account both for the sudden change in Bridget's physical health and comportment, and for the family's reaction to her altered state. The simplest explanation was that Bridget suffered from a bad case of influenza or bronchitis. Bridget's mother had died the previous year of influenza, so perhaps when Bridget fell ill, the family panicked in fear that the disease would claim the younger Bridget as well. Or perhaps they feared that she suffered an even more serious disease like tuberculosis. Even though tuberculosis was quite common in late-nineteenth-century Ireland, stricken families tried to hide its existence because there was a social stigma attached to it, much like cancer decades later. Some current local residents of Cloneen think that Bridget did, indeed, die of tuberculosis and the family simply covered up the illness by saying the fairies took her.[49]

The second theory involved the operatic themes of love, hate, passion, and vengeance. Many have speculated that Bridget's excursions to the fort had nothing at all to do with the fairies. Instead, the lovely young Bridget met a lover on the hill. Michael, the theory goes, knew of the liaison and became so enraged that he concocted the changeling story to have his revenge.

Rumors persisted that Bridget's paramour was a traveling egg dealer—a plausible supposition given the fact that Bridget raised hens and sold eggs in the district. The addition of a second henhouse at the Cleary cottage indicated that the business flourished, and one could speculate that the second henhouse was built to accommodate the increased demand for eggs generated by access to lucrative markets in the larger towns. And there was the recent mysterious suicide of Jack Dempsey, egg dealer.

Rumors of an extramarital affair appealed to those then and now who assumed that Bridget's independence, coupled with her husband's frequent absences from home, gave her both the motivation and the opportunity to seek a lover. This theory still prevails in the oral culture among many contemporary residents in the Cloneen area. It was raised early in the legal proceedings then dismissed, but the theory has gained strength over the last hundred or so years.

In the 1960s, British writer Hubert Butler took up the eggman thesis, asserting that Bridget's infidelity triggered Michael's jealousy and "unlocked the door to fairyland." Butler noted that although hints of Bridget's affair with an eggman emerged in official proceedings, neither police nor defense counsel followed up on the rumor, so no one was ever named. His disappearance from the trial prompted Butler to comment that "he and his cart might well have been swallowed up into the fairy mound." Thus the causes of the Cleary tragedy, according to Butler, remained a mystery because the eggman failed to receive his due. Instead, speculations about the fairies persisted and became a foil upon which these "oblique and tender-hearted people" cast their guilt and jealousy.[50]

In her recent book on the Bridget Cleary incident, Angela Bourke both agrees and disagrees with Butler. Like Butler, she accepts the notion that the participants used the fairies as a foil for their actions. In her view, the "fairy-narrative" was used as an exercise of patriarchal power by Michael Cleary to justify domestic violence and abuse, and by John Dunne to bolster his failing stock of "symbolic capital in an oral culture [which] had become next to worthless as literacy became general." On the other hand, Bourke also suggests that Bridget was romantically involved with William Simpson, the "emergencyman" (caretaker) who lived near the Cleary cottage, rather than the mysterious, unnamed eggman suggested by Butler. Bourke reminds the reader that both Bridget and Simpson were in their twenties, clever, ambitious, and sexually attractive.[51]

Evidence of Dunne's dwindling "symbolic" influence in a literate Ballyvadlea is suspect since most of the participants were barely literate. In any case, oral folk traditions and their associated superstitions are not eliminated from people's minds and memories by literacy, according to the modern literature on the subject. Over time such lowest-common-denominator societal myths are less likely to be acted upon, but they remain an important part of any nation's cultural heritage and are passed on from generation to generation even when rural people move to an urban setting or migrate to different countries. Ireland's Gaelic-speaking storytellers were remarkably successful in passing their oral traditions to later generations of English-speaking Irish, before and after the English (*Sasanaigh*) domination.[52]

The possibility that Bridget Cleary and William Simpson were lovers seems unlikely. The evidence indicates that Simpson was a supercilious Protestant social climber and a hated symbol of English eviction policy as an "emergencyman," that is, a caretaker living on the property of evicted tenants. Also the two families were neighbors, and they, along with the entire little Ballyvadlea community, would have known of the affair.[53] Lastly, Simpson's presence at the Cleary cottage on one crucial evening during Bridget's illness has never been satisfactorily explained, nor has his initial lying about what went on there. He claimed to be a friendly neighbor (something the Clearys and Kennedys never admitted, probably because of his "emergency" status) concerned about her health. If true, why did he not go to the authorities to protect her from being harmed by a pagan cure he professed not to believe in?

If Bridget Cleary had a lover, the more likely candidate was Jack Dempsey, the egg dealer from Ballypatrick, who slit his own throat a few days after March 6 and the alleged rendezvous on Kylnagranagh hill. Newspapers reported that Dempsey suffered from "suicidal mania" and "mental depression which developed into temporary insanity," the cause of which was vaguely attributed to recent losses in his egg business. This explanation appeared weak given the fact that suicides were rare among Catholics, who believed that those who died by their own hand would be damned in hell.[54] The unusual coincidence between Jack Dempsey's agonizing suicide and Bridget Cleary's strange illness makes him a likely candidate for the unnamed lover.

In addition to the theories about physical disease, infertility, jealousy, and adultery, a third theory asserts that Bridget Cleary was abducted by the fairies, and was, indeed, a changeling, or at least believed that she was. Though rationalists like Hubert Butler would brand this theory nonsense, the product of "oblique and tender-hearted" peasants, ethnographers at the time, and continuing down to the present, do not discount this changeling explanation as part of the belief structure of those involved, accounting for why family members, friends, and neighbors acted as they did.[55] Furthermore, this is the only explanation that privileges the family's obvious advantage of intimate proximity. Those relatives and friends, who knew her all her life, who watched her grow, who sat with her around the fire at night, these intimates *believed* she was taken—first, *taken with* the fairies, then subsequently, *taken by* them. They saw her every day, they watched as she peered from the window, they knew her ways. Based upon their observations, they believed she went to the hill to seek out the fairies and was abducted by them.

According to the stories the Bolands and the Kennedys had heard from childhood, the circumstances for Bridget's abduction were right. Bridget was a bright young woman, locally praised for her good looks and great energy; moreover, she was assertive, feisty, and curious about things that most in the community felt were best left alone. It was known to everyone in Ballyvadlea that she went often to Kylnagranagh hill when she had no good reason to do so. She was, in a sense, they felt, flirting with the fairies and it was just a matter of time until something happened. Whether she sought solitude in a troubled world or was lured by the mysticism of the fairy faith, whether she climbed the hill to meet a lover, connive for riches, or contact her mother, Bridget went to the fairy fort in Scanlon's field more often than she ought to have done. Her wanderings there raised eyebrows, stirred whispers, and worried, if not angered, her husband.

As the days passed following her return from the fairy mound, the creature who bore the semblance of Bridget weakened, grew more unpleasant, and languished by the fire. Rather than bouncing back, as their Bridget would have done, the creature showed no signs of recovery, not even much sign that it wanted to be well. This uncharacteristic lethargy frightened the family more, for it seemed as though the very spirit of their Bridget had gone out of her. Though her body tarried, they knew this too would die. Though it wore her clothing, sat at the table, even laid in her bed, this was not the same woman they knew. Their Bridget was gone and a withered old fairy inhabiting her body sat by their fire. And why shouldn't the family believe Bridget was a witch when tales of changelings had been told around the countryside for centuries? The stories of fairy abductions and changelings were as much a part of their belief system as tales of Fionn Mc-Cuill, Ossian, and the starving black babies in Africa. When Bridget turned up sick after visiting her favorite fairy fort on Scanlon's field and being "left" at Skehan's gate, the family could logically have chosen, on the basis of their collective common knowledge and centuries-old collective wisdom, to believe she was a changeling. Of all the possible explanations available to them, in the end, they believed that Bridget was gone with the fairies.

3

Peasants, Peelers, and Priests

In the Drangan Churchyard

On Saturday, March 16, 1895, the eve of St. Patrick's Day, and ten days after Bridget Cleary was stricken at the fairy fort on Kylnagranagh hill, at just past one o'clock in the afternoon, three men approached the Catholic church in Drangan. Michael Cleary and John Dunne had arrived on foot from Ballyvadlea, two miles south. The third, Michael Kennedy, having spent the night in Drangan after the wake of Michael Cleary's father in Killenaule, was already in town when rumors spread that his cousin, Bridget, was missing. Although he had no direct knowledge of what had happened, he may well have guessed, given the appearance of the two men before him: Michael Cleary looked steely-eyed while John Dunne urged his comrade to seek the priest. Sensing that something serious had happened, Kennedy joined the two men headed to the church, or chapel, as it was called.

At the churchyard gate, the men paused and a discussion ensued. Cleary appeared uncharacteristically haggard; his clothes were rumpled and soiled. A grease stain darkened his tan trousers. Dunne did most of the talking, while Michael Kennedy stood to one side, listening intently, occasionally glancing over his shoulder toward the police garrison across the road. Finally Dunne entered the churchyard alone.

Inside the church, Father Cornelius Fleming Ryan, the newly appointed curate of the Drangan-Cloneen parish, and Father Michael M'Grath, the fifty-six-year-old parish priest, were preparing for the St. Patrick's Day Sunday Mass.[1] Father Ryan lived in a trim, sand-walled cabin on the low road, two miles south of Drangan, down the hill from the Cleary cottage. Father Ryan's duties as curate took him to the townlands between Drangan and Cloneen, where he ministered to the tenants and laborers working the fields around Cloneen, much of it owned by Thomas Lindsay, a wealthy landlord from Cork. Father Ryan at age thirty-seven was a dutiful priest eager to ingratiate himself with his parishioners, who affectionately called him Father Con. He was also eager to please his superiors in Thurles, so in January 1895, he signed on as vice-chair of the Cloneen Branch of the Irish National Federation (INF).[2]

Father Ryan was inside when John Dunne burst into the church, announcing that Michael Cleary was standing outside the gate and was "in a bad way." Father M'Grath instructed Dunne to show Cleary into the chapel, where Father Ryan found him kneeling at the altar in a very "nervous and excited state." Anxious to avoid a disturbance, Father Ryan promptly escorted him out to the vestry, where Cleary began "tearing his hair and behaving like a mad man" saying he wanted confession, and calling upon the name of God, over and over, asking if he could ever be forgiven. Father Ryan later stated that he did not hear his confession because he did not consider Cleary to be in a "proper state of mind." Cleary's behavior was so "strong," that Father Ryan began to feel afraid, so he coaxed him out into the chapel yard. Only outside the church would he listen to what Cleary had to say, perhaps because he already knew what he was about to hear.[3]

In the churchyard, Father M'Grath joined the discussion in progress. Michael Cleary was not making himself understood, so John Dunne approached. He heard Cleary crying. Ryan put his hand up to silence Cleary, then turned to Dunne to find out what was going on, saying, "It is to this man [Dunne] I want to be talking." At this point Dunne blurted out the shocking news that Cleary had burned his wife. Cleary quickly interjected that he was not alone, that "more of them had burned his wife." Dunne retorted that he was not one of those who did the burning, and moreover that he disapproved. Dunne claimed that upon being told of the burning by Michael Cleary earlier that morning, he told him that it was a "droll story [and] that if I had a wife that anyone could not burn her in spite of me." To this remark, Michael replied: "I burned her now and I'm satisfied to suffer it." Dunne told the priests that Cleary and the others wished to give themselves up so they could "give her [Bridget] a Christian burial."

If Dunne was to be believed, both priests were told in the churchyard of the burning, yet neither disclosed this specific information to authorities, and curiously, Father M'Grath's name never surfaced in the newspapers at the time as having been party to such important information. Later when cross-examined as a witness in the case, Father Ryan never satisfactorily answered why he had not disclosed to the police Bridget's death by fire when he heard that dramatic news on Saturday afternoon.[4]

The exchange between priest and peasant in the Drangan churchyard epitomized the Church's troubled relationship with the rural peasantry, many of whom still harbored pagan beliefs. Because the Church officially condemned all pagan practice, the mention of a burning effectively sealed the doors of the Drangan chapel against Michael Cleary and other country people who practiced fairycraft, or what the newspapers initially insisted on calling "witchcraft." In order to keep consecrated ground free of its taint, Father Ryan, or any other priest in the province of Archbishop Croke, knew enough to escort the offender out the door with dispatch. Significantly, it was only after Michael Cleary was safely outdoors that Father Ryan admitted hearing anything about witchcraft. Yet, Father Ryan had been involved in the incident, and if he was not thinking of witchcraft as he claimed, he was the only person in County Tipperary who was not.

Though he feigned innocence, Father Ryan was not naive; he lived among the country people and knew their beliefs. Everyone in the district knew what was happening at the Cleary cottage. For nine days, Bridget lay ill with a mysterious ailment. For nine days, friends and neighbors streamed in and out. For nine days, Michael Cleary stormed over the countryside in search of help, and on at least three occasions, he sought Father Ryan's assistance. Father Ryan visited the Clearys' cottage on Wednesday, March 13, and again, just the day before, on Friday, March 15. On both occasions he met with Bridget and administered Church sacraments. In doing so, he participated in the ritual and probably did so knowingly.

Priests traditionally served as spiritual counselors in matters related to the fairies and were occasionally called upon to exorcise evil spirits, especially when changelings were involved.[5] It was believed (a belief the Catholic Church promoted) that the power of the priest was superior to that of the fairies and that the sign of the cross or the touch of the priest's stole would put the fairies to flight. The presence of the priest was considered the safest, most reliable antidote against mischief-making from the Otherworld. Even if a priest was not available, anyone could make the sign of the cross, pray, or clasp the missal, rosary, or crucifix to ward off the fairies. Not that a priest was infallible. He could sometimes be confused, even deceived, but often his power prevailed.

The alternating vulnerability and power of the Irish priest are illustrated in the story of one priest who encountered the fairies. One foggy night, on a lonesome road, the man lost his way when returning home after making a sick call to a peasant's cottage. As he was crossing an open field, he was hit with a bout of confusion and could not recall the direction he should go. He peered through the fog, but found no familiar landmark and wandered twice around the field. On the third round, he resolved to cross the fence and go straight on, but the dikes were thick with briars, and furze bushes crowned the tops of the steep clay mounds. As he stood there perplexed, he heard the rustle of wings, then heard a voice:

"You will suffer much if you do not find your way. Give us a favourable answer to the question, and you shall be on the road in a few minutes."

The good priest was somewhat startled, but replied straightaway:

"Who are you, and what's your question?"

The voice replied: "We are the Clann Sighe [the fairy folk], and wish you to declare that at the last day our lot may not be with Satan. Say that the Savior died for us as well as for you."

The priest said, "I will give you a favourable answer, if you can make me a hopeful one. Do you adore and love the Son of God?"

To this the priest received no answer; rather he heard weak but shrill cries and the rushing of wings. Then the gloom departed and a faint light shone where he stood, and he saw the path and an opening in the bushes on the fence. He crossed into the next field and shortly was seated before his fire, at his little table covered with books.[6]

Church sacraments administered by a priest were believed to be the most potent charm for warding off the fairies. In fact, the Church promoted this belief to induce the peasantry to partake regularly of the sacraments. Parents of newborn infants, for example, were warned to christen their babies soon after birth, lest they be taken. One young mother's husband was away, so she delayed the christening until his return. Without the protection of the sacrament, the child was taken. When the neighbors learned of it, they came and said to the woman, "Now, ma'am, you see what it is to leave a child without being christened." If she had done her duty, no fairy, no spirit, no "divel" would have had power over her baby. Christen the child, they said to her. So the mother went to the baby and whispered, "Come, Alanna, let me dress you, and we'll go and be christened." Of course the fairy spirit inside the child wanted nothing to do with any priest, so in an instant such roaring and screeching came out of his throat as would frighten the Danes. The mother did not have the heart to have the child christened, so the neighbors took the child away, and cast the devil out, and brought her baby back to her. Needless to say the woman was ashamed of herself on Sunday when Father James preached against the wickedness of neglecting to baptize young babies.[7]

Prior to the ecclesiastical reforms that followed the devotional revolution in the post-Famine period, parishioners routinely paid priests to administer sacraments and provide other spiritual services such as exorcisms. In the instance of exorcism, to receive money in exchange for casting out fairy spirits placed priests in an awkward position because, by accepting payment, they benefited monetarily from the very pagan practices that the Church officially proscribed.[8] Even after the practice of sacraments-for-pay was discouraged, priests led their parishioners to believe that the power of their priesthood was the most effective deterrent against fairies. Late in the century, priests continued to perform exorcisms when called upon, even though they knew that by doing so, they became participants in a fairy-related ritual. Because of this complicity, priests routinely denied any knowledge that fairycraft might be involved in any sacrament or prayer.

Even when civil authority had jurisdiction in a case, the priest was always consulted in matters involving fairycraft. One Irish folk tale tells of a young wife who took sick and died soon after. She was not long gone before her husband took another wife and shortly had two more children. As it turned out, the first wife was captured by the fairies and remained alive in the Otherworld. In the course of time, she became unhappy with her lot and wished to return to her mortal family. The woman managed to make contact with a farmer and persuaded him to write a letter to her husband, advising him that she was alive and wished to be rescued from the fairies. Upon receiving this communication, the husband was at a loss to know what to do. On one hand, he wanted his first wife back with him; on the other, he had a new wife and children to consider. In desperation, the husband turned to the priest for help. The priest determined that the husband should not attempt to rescue the first wife and should instead leave her with the fairies, "though it be a hard thing." Better, he decreed, that she eat the fairy bread than he break God's law by having two wives. The husband accepted the priest's pronouncement and informed his first wife that he would not attempt the rescue.

Upon hearing the news, it was said that she went with the fairies and remained with them ever after.[9]

In light of the importance of the priests' role in matters related to fairycraft and witchcraft, Father Ryan's assertion that he had not thought of witchcraft until told by Dunne in the Drangan churchyard was doubtful, if not downright mendacious. Even if he had no direct knowledge of the family's fears, he should have known that the family might conclude that Bridget was a changeling, and more, that they might take the appropriate action. That Ryan feigned ignorance is all the more likely given that he was a neighbor of the Clearys. In fact, he lived directly between the Cleary cottage in Ballyvadlea and the fairy forts on Kylnagranagh hill. Many in the district, whose population numbered some 300 souls, knew of Bridget's unusual affinity for the forts and her sudden, unexplained illness. As curate of the parish, Father Ryan knew that the illness might signify possession, in which case, he also knew that the family would turn to him for help in casting out the spirit. When John Dunne suddenly burst into the Drangan chapel that Saturday morning, Father Ryan had good reason to suspect something had gone dreadfully wrong and wanted to protect himself, the Church, and the Nationalist movement.

It is also probable that Michael Cleary did not go the Drangan church merely to seek confession. Rather, he went to ask for Father Ryan's help in retrieving his wife from the Otherworld. According to oral tradition, priests could do that. If Bridget's spirit had been taken by the fairies, there was yet time to save her, provided the priest exercised his power in her behalf. In all probability, this was the real reason why Michael Cleary and John Dunne went to the Drangan church on Saturday, March 16—not to confess but to ask Father Ryan to offer prayers and perform sacraments to wrest Bridget from the power of the fairies. Although

Bridget Cleary was missing, there was still time to get her back, provided everyone cooperated.

But rather than cooperate, Father Ryan realized that he was in danger of being implicated, so to hide his complicity, he turned his back on the peasants and referred the matter to the police. After a short consultation with Father M'Grath, Ryan went across the road to the police barracks and returned with an officer. But, rather than tell the police about the alleged burning, Father Ryan reported only that Cleary's wife was missing and that he (Ryan) "suspected . . . foul play." When Michael Cleary realized that Father Ryan had reported the matter to police, he turned cold and would say nothing more than that his wife had run off during the night and was missing. For his part, the officer detected hostility between Cleary, who undoubtedly felt angry and betrayed, and Father Ryan, so he asked Father M'Grath, rather than Ryan, to accompany Cleary home, saying that "it would be better for him [Ryan] if he would not see himself [Cleary] at all." This was agreed upon, and the three men from Ballyvadlea turned and started their walk back home. But Father M'Grath did not accompany Cleary as the officer had asked, for he, like Ryan, wanted nothing to do with the matter. Instead, a constable followed the men home.[10] Like both the priests, the police had heard the rumors concerning the strange events at the Cleary cottage. They heard the stories of fairies, forts, and changelings from childhood, and knew of Bridget's interest in the fairyfaith. They too suspected that more lurked behind the seemingly innocent report that the cooper's wife was missing.

Constable Patrick Egan was the investigating officer who followed the men to Ballyvadlea. He and his ubiquitous fellow officers were the foot soldiers of the Queen's Royal Irish Constabulary (RIC). Constables were known in Ireland as the "peelers," named for Sir Robert Peel, the Irish Secretary who introduced a professional police force into Ireland in 1813. In England, they became known as "bobbies," taken from Peel's first name. After fifty years of cracking Irish heads, in 1867 the constabulary system evolved into the RIC and became the model for Britain's internal security throughout its colonial empire. The RIC was a paramilitary, domestic police force, which included a secret police division. Peelers were housed in army-style barracks in villages as small as Cloneen and were charged with enforcing orders, evictions, and seizures issued by landlords through their surrogates in the Anglo-Irish administration. It was the peelers, backed by the Queen's regiments, who were obliged to quell any violence that erupted in the wake of these orders.[11]

There was, of course, no love lost between peelers and peasants. As the enforcers of English justice, the peelers were everywhere—in the city, at the railway station, in the village, on the high road, the byway, and mountain path—singly or in pairs, and were willing at the drop of a cap to arrest anyone for the least perceived offense. According to local jail records, the RIC routinely arrested local people on such charges as breach of promise, drunkenness, cattle maiming, malicious damage to trees, desertion of family, attempted suicide, disobedience of workhouse rules, leaving employment without fulfilling the proper time, illegal fishing, rabbit killing, carnal knowledge, illegal assembly, unlicensed dogs, obscene or threatening language, begging, bearing false witness, and allowing a horse to wander on a public road.[12]

Moreover, the constable knew everything—who ran the illegal poteen stills, who was behind in the rent, who passed through town, and why, and who might gather in the night. He was a keen observer of the mundane, a wary inspector of the unusual. A traveler described the constable's extraordinary powers of observation this way:

> [The constable] knows articles of American manufacture at a glance, and needs only to see your satchel to tell whether it came from America or was made in England. Talk with him, and he will chat cordially about the weather, the crops, the state of the markets, but all the time he is trying to make out who you are and what is your business. His eyes ramble from your hat to your shoes, and by the time the conversation is ended, he has prepared for the "sergeant" a report of your personal appearance and apparel. "Hat, English; coat, London-made; trousers, doubtful; shoes, American; party evidently an Irish Yankee, who might as well be looked after."[13]

The constable made it his business to know everything because his life often depended upon it.

Typically the Irish constable was the son of a peasant, familiar with the ways of the local community. He tended to be brighter than average but was a social leper in his own community—an insider made forever an outcast because he was too bright to spend his life mowing the landlord's hay, too complacent to leave, and too willing to betray his countrymen. If he needed good ears, sharp eyes, and quick reflexes, the constable also needed a thick skull. Occasionally policemen died in violent eviction brawls. As one Cork man said: "We niver intinded fur to kill him at all, but his shkull was too thin entirely for a consthable, an' brok wid the batin' he was afther gettin."[14] If there were extraordinary rumors circulating around the countryside, Acting Sergeant Egan knew of them. In fact there were indications that the police went to the Cleary cottage two days before to investigate reports that a woman was being mistreated. When Egan learned on Saturday that the cooper's wife was missing, he probably had a fair idea of why Michael Cleary was left standing in the Drangan churchyard and why Father Ryan beat a hasty retreat back into the church.

Egan spotted the trio of Cleary, Dunne, and Kennedy a short distance from town. He followed, making sure to keep his distance. The three men headed west along the main road to Fethard, then turned south through the open fields of the Slieveardagh hills. The road ascended the flank of the Kylnagranagh hill to its crest, then began its descent toward the Anner river valley below. A mile past the top was the townland of Tullowcossaum where Father Ryan resided. Past his gate, the open fields narrowed between the hills, traversed by a stream that flowed on Ryan's side of the road. Thick brush grew along the stream, and between the road and the stream was an area of bog. At the narrowest point between the hills, a bridge, known as the Ballyvadlea bridge, crossed the stream. To the east of the road, on the Kylnagranagh side, was the Kennedy cottage. There, Egan overtook the three men and asked Cleary about the disappearance of his wife.[15] Cleary told him nothing more than what he had already said—that his wife had run off the night before and had not been seen since. When Egan questioned Cleary about the "extraordinary rumor" of foul play, Cleary refused to say more and departed for his own cottage.

Shortly after, four more police officers arrived and a search for Bridget began, but rather than join the others, Egan followed Michael Cleary back to his cottage, arriving there around four in the afternoon. Egan made a cursory search of the house and questioned Michael a second time regarding the disappearance of his wife. Cleary reiterated what he had said before. Bridget left the house about midnight on Friday night. He was asleep at the time and did not see her go. When he last saw her, she was in bed with him. Michael seemed willing, even eager to talk, until Egan pressed him for details. Who else was in the house? Cleary revealed that Bridget's cousin, Johanna Burke, was in the house with Bridget's father, Patrick Boland, who was asleep in the next room. Did he have any idea of where his wife might have gone? No, none. Was there any discord between him and his wife? No. How did he account for his disheveled appearance? Cleary replied he had not slept for the last seven or eight nights. Why hadn't he slept? His wife had been very ill, and he had been up tending her. Why had he gone to bed fully dressed? He was too tired to change. What was the nature of the dark grease stains on his pants? With this, Cleary ended the interview, insisting he knew nothing more, whereupon he went to the bedroom and shut the door. At the magisterial inquiry, Cleary denied any knowledge of this conversation, saying that he "disremembered it all."[16]

Having gleaned all he could, Egan left the cottage and proceeded back toward the Kennedy cottage, where he found Patrick Boland. In contrast to Cleary's calculated coolness, Pat Boland appeared genuinely distraught. He was crying aloud, muttering to himself as if trying to make sense of things. When Egan questioned him, Boland increased his wailing and, after some seconds, sobbed repeatedly, "My daughter will come back home. My daughter will come back home." He would say nothing more, yet his sudden silence aroused Egan's suspicions.

Like priests, police tended to shy away from crimes that involved fairycraft, perhaps because many believed the stories themselves but could not admit it for fear of ridicule. Also the police feared stirring up animosity in the countryside, so when extraordinary cases arose, police and other officials took pains to find plausible explanations for these crimes. This was especially true in cases that involved suspicious burnings. In January 1895, there was a death by burning in Carrick-on-Suir, when Margaret Dwyer, fourteen, caught fire when a tin of paraffin oil spilled from the mantle, igniting her dress. She was visiting a friend at the time, and when she went up in flames, the father of the house quickly conveyed her outside, where he attempted unsuccessfully to extinguish the burning dress. The police were summoned immediately, and determined the death was accidental. Head Constable Hughes concluded that the parties acted responsibly and filed no charges in the matter.[17]

Another burning was deemed suspicious, however. Police investigated the death, in Thurles, of a four-year-old girl, who, her mother claimed, had wandered too near the fire. A neighbor reported that she heard the mother screaming, whereupon she rushed to the cottage and found the child already dead in her mother's arms. When questioned about the matter, the mother held to her story that the burning was accidental. Police asked her to swear to the truth of it by kissing the Bible. This she refused to do, stating flatly that she was telling the truth and she would kiss no Bible to swear an oath. The police, who by then were clearly anxious to close the case, threatened the mother with imprisonment if she did not kiss the Bible and swear an oath. "Send me to jail, then," she insisted, "for I'll not be kissing the Bible to swear an oath." The frustrated constable then took the testimony of the neighbor, who was willing to kiss the Bible, as proof the burning was accidental. No charges were filed, but the scent of fairycraft hung heavy over the grieving mother.[18]

Suspecting that Bridget Cleary's disappearance involved something of this sort, Egan retraced his steps to the Cleary cottage that same evening, arriving around ten. Finding no one at home, he had no trouble letting himself in by a bedroom window. Immediately upon entering, Egan found evidence of a burning. Lying on the floor beside the bed was a pile of soiled clothing, and poking through this, he discovered a woman's nightdress "partly burned." In the main room he noticed that the fireplace was recently swept clean, and in the corner he found a glass vial containing what appeared to be a brackish liquid. Egan remained in the house until around eleven, hoping to question Cleary and Boland further, but neither returned.

Sometime in the early morning hours of St. Patrick's Day, Acting Sergeant Egan returned to the Drangan barracks to file his report. Having found the burned night dress and the glass vial, Egan now had sufficient evidence to allege that foul play was involved in the disappearance of Bridget Cleary. Sometime on Sunday, March 17, District Inspector Alfred Wansbrough of the Carrick-on-Suir office was informed of the allegations. It now appeared that the story of the missing woman involved a serious crime, yet neither Egan nor Wansbrough could have dreamed that the case of the missing copper's wife was about to become an international incident.

The Whiteboys and
the Faithful Priests of Cashel

The following day was Sunday, March 17—St. Patrick's Day in Ireland and anywhere else around the world where an Irishmen might be. This particular St. Paddy's Day dawned fair and mild across Ireland. Newspapers reported that farming operations were in full swing, the "genial" spring weather of the last fortnight in marked contrast to the "arctic severity" of the weather since Christmas. Conditions were favorable for the sowing of all kinds of crops, which enabled farmers "to smile once more" and enjoy a bit of the St. Patrick's Day festivities.[19]

Several celebrations were planned around County Tipperary that year. In Cashel, the Very Reverend Dean Kinane delivered an impressive sermon on the life of St. Patrick and discussed several incidents in connection with his labors in converting the Irish people. Citizens there celebrated in a "very religious and becoming manner, all testifying in marked degree by their general sobriety and peaceful demeanor, to our great love and respect for our National Apostle." In Tipperary town, the regimental brass band, performing in conjunction with the fife-and-drum corps, led a column of four hundred soldiers to morning Mass. Every soldier and officer wore the green "triple leaf" on his breast. The procession was followed by an enormous crowd that filed peacefully into the church, where the organist played the anthem of the day "in a way that was very much appreciated."[20]

In Clonmel, a "glorious festival" was held at St. Mary's Church to celebrate the dedication of a grand new organ. Presiding at this "august" affair was the Bishop of Waterford and Lismore, the Most Reverend Bishop Sheehan, who delivered an "eloquent and appropriate sermon" honoring Ireland's national apostle. Bishop Sheehan imagined that the great St. Patrick was at that moment looking down from his throne in heaven and wished to address the Irish people, scattered far and wide the world over, and say to them, in the words of St. Paul, "Your Faith is spoken of throughout the whole world." Bishop Sheehan called upon those Irishmen cast across the Atlantic, and those who slept beneath the Southern Cross, to join in a "feast" of celebration of the faith of the Irish race, wherein all would be reminded of "their responsibilities" to the apostle and their homeland.[21]

Irish people everywhere did just that. Boston's *Daily Globe* re-

ported on March 18, 1895, that St. Patrick's Day was an "uncommon observance," which featured a grand parade in which
2,500 members of the Ancient Order of Hibernians "stepped
lightly to airs which thrill the souls of every true son of the little green isle." Walls of cheering people lined the streets, illuminated with torches, waving banners of red, white, and green—
the Irish-American tricolor. At the annual festival of St. Cecilia's
Church of Back Bay, a crowd of five thousand heard the Honorable Thomas J. Gargan deliver a rousing address on "Famous
Irishmen," the first of whom was Sir Edmund Burke—"a name
dear to all Irishmen and to all men who believe in a true rational
liberty." Burke labored all his life, with "tongue and pen," to repeal draconian English penal laws that, according to the French
philosopher Montesquieu, "could only have been made by the
devil, and were fit only to be registered in hell." But the greatest
Irishman of the nineteenth century was Daniel O'Connell, "the
liberator" who led the fight for Catholic emancipation, initiated
land reform, and tried to repeal the infamous 1801 Act of
Union.

Other luminaries cited by Gargan included members of the
failed Young Irelanders movement of 1848, many of whom fled to
the United States, including Thomas Francis-Meagher, William
Smith O'Brien, commander of the Irish Brigade in the American
Civil War, John Mitchell, Gavan Duffy, Thomas D'Arcy McGee,
and Tom Moore. The last mentioned in Gargan's list of Irish
patriots was Charles Stewart Parnell. Of him it was said:

> *To his own self not always just,*
> *Bound in the bonds which all men share,*
> *Confess his failings, as we must,*
> *The lion's mark was always there.*[22]

It was hoped that St. Patrick's Day celebrations would draw Irish Nationalists together and repair Parnell's "lion's mark" upon the movement.

In honor of the occasion, the *Globe* printed letters from leading Irish churchmen and political leaders, including Cardinal Michael Logue of Armagh; Michael Davitt, the "father of the Land League"; William O'Brien, M. P.; and Archbishop Thomas William Croke, "the lion-hearted prelate of Thurles," whose St. Patrick's Day greeting was uncharacteristically short and restrained. He expressed gratitude to his countrymen in the United States for their "practical sympathy" toward their less favored countrymen in Ireland but made no other comment. His restrained tone indicated that, after years of standing front and center in the battle to get the Church on the side of the people, Croke was withdrawing from the limelight, "putting up the shutters" of The Palace, Thurles, preferring instead to work behind the scenes for the Nationalist cause.[23]

On St. Patrick's Day, 1895, Archbishop Croke surfaced momentarily to launch a major fundraising drive in behalf of the Irish Parliamentary Party, to which he offered his own practical sympathy in the form of a handsome donation. The *Nationalist* announced in advance that this word, "nay this hint," from so distinguished an ecclesiastic, admired and respected by the Irish people the world over, was sufficient to ensure the "triumphant success of any project blessed by his patronage."[24] The Templemore and Clonmore districts announced similar fundraising drives. In the Moyne district, INF supporters placed posters on the chapel gate to advertise a collection a week hence. In Killea, a special St. Patrick's Day collection was underway, led by "that genuine Irish *Soggarth*," or faithful priest, Rev. M. J. Cleary, C.C., president of the INF's Killea Branch, who stood at the chapel gate on St. Patrick's Day morning to solicit donations as the faithful passed into the church. Other "enthusiastic" members assisted, "keenly alive" to the pressing necessity of supporting the Irish M.P.s who had done so much to throttle the landlordism that desolated the hillsides of Tipperary.[25] 'Twas better far that these enthusiastic members hang posters on the church gate rather than be hanged by the English for shooting a landlord, his agent, or emergency caretaker in the dead of night.

South Tipperary had a long tradition of rural violence and savagery that began with Oliver Cromwell's invasion in the 1640s and continued for over a century as the English invaders massacred the people, expropriated land, and imprisoned priests in their war upon the Catholic majority. By 1800, Irish tenants were living on small, fifteen-to-twenty-acre plots, which relegated them to at most a subsistence level of life. Such tenant farmers were overwhelmingly outnumbered by an even larger, poorer class of agricultural laborers whom historians have divided into descending categories of abject poverty and misery: smallholders, cottiers, and laborers. Together, by 1841, these three groups represented three-fourths of the adult male population.[26] Some of these peasants lived on no more than a patch of land, with a crude mud hut and a hardscrabble potato garden. Abject Irish poverty before the Great Famine remains almost indescribable.

Even the loquacious Alexis de Tocqueville, who toured Ireland in the summer of 1835, found himself at a loss for words to depict conditions on the Galway coast: "a collection of misery such as I did not imagine existed in this world. It is a frightening thing, I assure you, to see a whole population reduced to fasting like Trappists, and not being sure by fasting of surviving to the next harvest, which is still not expected for another ten days." He had even more difficulty trying to assess the violence resulting from

legal, cultural, and political tyranny wrought by Protestant domination. A few years later, a Gaelic-speaking laborer described the
plight of his class in these words: ". . . cold naked, without a coat
or clothing, working in hardships, and anguish under the heel of
enemies, without receiving half the reward their health and
strength deserve, with nothing to eat but shriveled potatoes and a
drop of sour skimmed milk."[27]

Even English landlords abhorred the squalor they created by
their own land policies, but blamed Irish shiftlessness, ignorance,
and drunkenness for the wretchedness, culminating in late-nineteenth-century "Victorian racism." Such cultural and physical
stereotyping was not unique to England, since most "civilized" na-
tion-states considered themselves racially superior to their indentured colonists. However, the English exceeded the norm,
especially with regards to the Irish, seen in Theodor Mommsen's
caricature of Celtic character in his *History of Rome* and cartoons in
London's *Punch*, which equated the Irish with what the British educated classes considered the lowest of the African tribes—the
Hottentots. To the English, the stereotypical "Paddy" was no better than a wild pig, living by the rule "Root, hog, or die!"[28]

As the English learned to rationalize their racism, conditions in
Ireland became worse. The English system of land ownership encouraged subdivision, forcing both tenants and laborers to eke a
living from smaller and smaller parcels. This partitioning became
so complicated that many landlords, even those living in Ireland,
had no idea how many inhabitants occupied their holdings. One
750-acre farm in County Cork was leased to a tenant for a term of
"three lives," then was subsequently sublet to two others, and so
on, until finally, in 1845, the landlord learned that over three hundred inhabitants occupied his land, most living in mud-walled
huts at or below subsistence levels.[29]

More agrarian revolts arose from Ireland's muddy huts between 1750 and 1840 than from anywhere else in Europe. Groups known variously in different locales as Whitefeet, Threshers, Terry Alts, Rickites, Carders, the Defenders, the Molly Maguires, and more commonly as the Whiteboys or Ribbonmen appeared in the last half of the eighteenth century. These were quasi-military, secret societies whose members wore masks and white shirts when conducting their savage midnight raids. To protect against English spies, Whiteboys subjected initiates to elaborate, often pagan-influenced, induction rites and used secret codes and passwords to identify fellow members. These loosely organized, poorly equipped, ragtag gangs were forefathers of later generations of terrorist groups, including the modern Irish Republican Army (IRA).[30]

In the 1770s, the district surrounding Clonmel and Fethard was a fertile field for Whiteboy activity. One gang, the Caravats, surfaced in 1805 at the execution by hanging in Clonmel of one Nicholas Hanley, known for wearing extravagant cravats. One of Hanley's enemies, Patrick Connors, yelled a pun comparing Hanley's necktie to the hangman's rope. Not to be upstaged before his death, Hanley made a sarcastic remark about Connors' waistcoat, and thus the names, Caravats (in Celtic, Carabhaití) and Shanavests (Sean-Bheisteanna, or Ribbonmen) came to differentiate two Whiteboy factions. The middle-class Shanavest farmers generally opposed the erratic violence of the landless and more desperate Caravats, preferring to combine controlled vigilantism with Irish nationalism, while the lower-class Caravats remained committed to local terrorism.[31]

Whiteboys targeted landlords who raised rents, evicted tenants, or enclosed communal land. They leveled ditches and stone walls built by landowners to enclose their holdings, opposed conacre (exploitative seasonal potato-patch) rents, and refused to pay obligatory tithes to the Protestant Church of Ireland. Both gangs routinely raided and robbed the homes of farmers of medium to large holdings, attacked dairy farmers, commandeered horses, and collected contributions for their cause. In reprisal against unjust land laws, Whiteboys occasionally murdered landowners' wives, beat their children, and abducted their daughters. Their murders and attempted murders occurred more often than could be officially recorded in the first decade of the nineteenth century. Magistrates who tried to survey all the damage and deaths from turn-of-the-nineteenth-century Whiteboyism had only rough data on which to base their generalities. One concluded in frustration: "Murders and floggings are so frequent and notorious they need not be mentioned. . . . I omit a list of murders, abductions, mail robberies, and horse stealing." On the other side of the ledger were Protestant landowners and English government officials whose remorseless suppression of Whiteboys caused Edmund Burke as early as the 1760s to condemn them as "monsters of humanity."[32]

Whiteboy violence proved difficult to eradicate because it was rooted in the injustices of the English land system, and reinforced by Celtic mythology and pagan ritual. To a surprising degree, early Whiteboyism did not distinguish between Catholic and Protestant victims. Although Whiteboy violence was condemned by Catholic bishops, the movement was generally viewed by Protestant landowners as a papist plot and, indeed, a number of priests were suspected and a few tried as Whiteboys. Occasionally Whiteboy groups took action against local priests who charged too much for administering sacraments or performing weddings and funerals—sometimes successfully forcing the priests from their parishes.

Rural unrest peaked in 1815 following the disastrous fall in agricultural prices and the corresponding rise in rents that accompanied the end of the Napoleonic wars. Whiteboy terrorism provided the English with a convenient excuse to condemn the Irish and justify its imperial presence. In the 1830s Robert Peel reflected England's view that Ireland's perennial agrarian agitation proved that the Irish had a "natural predilection for outrage and a lawless life which I believe nothing can control." Sir George Cornewall Lewis, who published an astute study of agrarian unrest in 1836, was closer to the truth when he described the Whiteboy secret societies as "a vast trades union for the protection of the Irish peasantry." For the Whiteboys themselves, the use of terror allowed otherwise disenfranchised citizens a method for protesting grievances, but more, the Whiteboys provided tenants and laborers with a sense of solidarity and a safe haven from the intrusions of authority. "I was a very experienced Ribbonman [in the 1820s] and delighted in that business," a government informer later nostalgically recalled. "It was the pleasantest [pastime] that could be found, for there was more real friendship in it than in any other society in the world; I was in it when a boy, and like it in my heart still."[33]

The solidarity and brotherhood fostered by the Whiteboys made the groups difficult to eradicate, especially in and around Clonmel. That this subculture of communal violence flourished despite condemnation by both the Catholic and Protestant churches reflected how little popular, Celtic pagan culture had been displaced by Christianity at the beginning of the nineteenth century. In the 1840s the random, undisciplined violence of the Whiteboys diminished, yielding to the more disciplined forms of agitation supported by Nationalist groups, many of whom won converts by employing symbols from Celtic mythology and pagan rituals.[34]

During the Land War of the 1880s, political organizations had grown strong enough to contain much of the rural violence. The

Land League organized political units and effective rent boy-cotting campaigns. After Parnell, the INF did the same, but even late in the century, the potential for random violence remained whenever evictions occurred.

An example of how violence was rerouted into support for the Nationalist cause was illustrated by the story of Edmond Feehan of Mullinahone, published the week before St. Patrick's Day, 1895. It seems that Feehan's uncle, Michael Feehan, left him land under tenancy that was four years in arrears. The younger Feehan paid up two years of back rent, plus all taxes and fees, leaving just two years' payment in arrears. After accepting Feehan's payment for half the amount due, the landowner, Mr. T. Butler, canceled the lease and took back his land. Nationalists screamed outrage, declaring such a travesty would never occur in a "Nationalist country" free of English rule. Furthermore, they charged that Ed-mond Feehan's complaint was just one of many "bitter experi-ences" suffered by farmers in the Gornahoe and Ballingarry districts. Thus it was a matter of duty and self-protection to put INF branches in "perfect working order immediately." Echoing Parnell's famous line, the writer reminded readers, "God helps those who help themselves."[35]

Because of the movement's success, Archbishop Croke quietly continued to build the INF into an effective, Church-supported political organization that would fight for the people's interests yet create a positive alternative to rural violence, backwardness, and paganism. To celebrate these aims, the priests of Cashel and Emly announced a grand celebration to honor the lion-hearted prelate of Munster, who, for twenty-five years, had stoutly de-fended the Church and Nationalists while leading his people away from ignorance and superstition. Plans for the event began in January, when a meeting of bishops at Maynooth passed resolutions in praise of his Grace in anticipation of his Silver Jubilee. To show the earnestness of their appeal, the priests of Cashel and Emly pledged the princely sum of £1,000 to honor the great Metropolitan of Munster in the largest public celebration ever staged in the county. The date chosen was July 18, 1895, the silver anniversary of Croke's ordination as bishop.[36]

The Irish Party in Nenagh held the first of many meetings in preparation for the celebration and sang the praises of this enormously popular prelate:

> It would, indeed, be impossible to overestimate the services of the noble Archbishop to Faith and Fatherland. He has been a conspicuous figure in Irish National life since the inception of the Home Rule movement, but long before the day of Butt or Parnell he felt the thrill of patriotic fervor and had strived to serve his country by every mean in his power in times when she had few friends. His career has realised the high ideal of the patriotic Irish priest and pastor. His patriotism is not of yesterday, his National convictions are not the fashionable faith of the day. The men of '52 received from him the same generous support, the same inspiring encouragement, the same wise counsel as the men of '82 and '92. For twenty years he has now been first among the foremost in the advocacy of National rights.

He was the patriot who was never found wanting, the leader who never failed, and his union of priest and people was the "surest guarantee of victory" at the ballot box.[37] The town of Clonmel prepared its own celebration, assuring the Thurles committee that "utmost justice would be done by the people as well as by the priesthood to honour the approaching historic occasion."[38]

Yet even as the festivities were announced, a dark cloud appeared that would dim the brightness of the Silver Jubilee. In an odd conjunction of events, a short notice reporting the disappearance of Bridget Cleary, entitled "The Cloneen Horror," followed the article on the Archbishop's celebration. Meanwhile at the RIC's district headquarters in Carrick-on-Suir, District Inspector Alfred Joseph Wansbrough began his investigation. He had in his hands an intriguing report from Acting Sergeant Egan regarding the extraordinary disappearance of the cooper's wife causing such a stir throughout the Drangan district. These were the sorts of rumors that the police followed closely, especially in the region surrounding the Slieveardagh hills, the Anner river valley, and Slievenamon, which some called Ireland's most beautiful and infamous mountain. This was a region famous for agrarian unrest and political uprisings, with a long and honored tradition of rural violence, where pitchfork-bearing peasants and peelers lived in uneasy proximity, always ready for the next spasm of violence to erupt.

Any untoward action taken by police could redound badly on the English administration, yet this particular case might well prove embarrassing to the Irish, particularly the Church and its hero, Archbishop Croke. Talk of fairies and witch burnings on the eve of Croke's Jubilee might prove politically useful to the English. Given the delicate nature of the situation, thirty-eight-year-old District Inspector Wansbrough proceeded cautiously to Ballyvadlea, possibly hoping that his management of the case might attract favorable notice in Dublin and revitalize his lackluster, unlucky career.

Wansbrough had entered the RIC as a cadet in 1881 and had the misfortune of being stationed in Mitchelstown during the "massacre" of 1887, when the RIC killed two and wounded twenty tenants. A subsequent government investigation found fault with the "discipline and morale" of the officers involved in the Plan of Campaign incident.[39] Wansbrough certainly did not want to be involved in quelling agrarian violence again, but he did want to take advantage of the Cleary investigation to enhance his own career. He hoped that the Cleary case, if handled properly, would tarnish the Archbishop's Silver Jubilee and make his celebration a Unionist jubilee as well.

This prospect made the evidence compiled by Acting Sergeant Egan all the more valuable. The discovery of the burned nightdress and the vial filled with brackish liquid provided substantial evidence of foul play, and, given the rumors concerning the involvement of fairies and changelings, Wansbrough surmised that the incident involved an Irish form of witch burning. He realized that any information he could unearth to prove the Irish people still practiced sorcery and entertained evil superstitions would be welcome news in Dublin and London.

"Strange Occurrence at Ballyvadlea"

On Monday, March 18, 1895, constables from the Drangan subdistrict of the RIC continued their search for the missing cooper's wife. To no one's surprise, nothing turned up. Two days was long enough for a drunken husband to sober up, or an aggrieved wife to calm herself, yet there was no sign of Bridget Cleary in the surrounding villages. Two days of searching ditches, fields, and abandoned cottages proved futile. Meanwhile, investigators went to Ballyvadlea to question witnesses about the events leading up to the disappearance. They found the family singularly uncooperative. Michael Cleary stuck to his story that Bridget ran off suddenly on Friday night while he was sleeping and insisted that he knew nothing more about the matter. Patrick Boland, Bridget's father, seconded Cleary. When they tried to stop her, she forced her way out and ran off into the night. Boland was almost inco-

herent. He muttered, babbled, often bursting into tears, repeating
over and over the refrain Egan heard on Saturday that she was
gone but would come back soon.

The Kennedy men were also less than forthcoming, if not
downright hostile. The older boys, Patrick and James, kept to
themselves and said nothing. The third brother, Michael, who
met Cleary and John Dunne in Drangan, was the most vocal, but
rather than shedding light on the situation, he only wanted to
distance himself from the affair. William, the youngest, was as
silent and uncooperative as his older brothers. Their mother,
Mary Kennedy, however, talked a steady stream. She was a tiny,
frail-looking woman, stooped over from years of bending over
turf fires and potato patches, yet she commanded her corps of
grown sons with authority. What would the peelers be wanting
with them, she scolded, and why not ask Michael Cleary about
his wife, and never mind what the neighbors said because Bridget
would be coming back soon.

With Patrick, James, and William stonewalling, Michael saying
he was not involved in any of it, and Mary Kennedy raving and
muttering, there was just one family member who might prove
helpful to the investigation: Johanna Kennedy Burke, who lived
in the neighboring hamlet of Rathkenny, a mile or so west of the
Clearys. When Bridget became ill, Johanna was living at least part
time with her mother and brothers at the Kennedy cottage. She
was the oldest of the Kennedy clan, about thirty-five, and the
only one of the Kennedy children who was married. In 1884 Johanna had married Michael Burke, a laborer, and their first child,
Katie, was born less than a year later, followed by six more.[40] Her
youngest child was barely two months old. Johanna brought
Katie and the infant to her mother's house, presumably leaving

her other four or five children (one may have died) with her husband in Rathkenny.

Unlike Bridget, who enjoyed her independence, Johanna was the family drudge, cooking and cleaning and fetching for everyone. A simple, hardworking woman, she was bright enough to know what was going on, yet vulnerable enough to be bullied. She was close to Bridget, although perhaps somewhat jealous of her freedom, good looks, and comfortable living quarters. Of all the Kennedys, Johanna would be the most likely one to talk because, unlike the others who were unmarried and childless, she was more vulnerable with so many small children at home. As yet, she was as silent as the others, insisting like the rest that Bridget had gone off Friday night.[41]

Another potential witness for the prosecution was the Protestant caretaker, William Simpson, an "intelligent and obliging man," according to reporters, whom he courted during the investigation. Simpson lived with his wife, Mary or "Minnie," and their two daughters on a farm barely a quarter mile from the Clearys.[42] Since Simpson was only twenty-four in 1895 with a wife who was ten years older and a daughter already five, theirs may have been a marriage forced by an unwanted pregnancy. Simpson was an "emergency" caretaker brought in by the district's largest landlord, Thomas Lindsay of Cork, to manage property taken from an evicted tenant. Local newspapers often reported stories about caretakers being shot in the kneecaps, or more often, stoned by rural terrorists like the Whiteboys. A few, during agrarian outrages of the Land War in the early 1880s, were killed. As recently as June 13, 1894, the wife of caretaker Edward Walsh on Mr. Lambert's estate in New Ross found her husband, "his head being blown completely away from the chin." Symbolically, the murder weapon by his side belonged to the absentee landowner, signifying that the gun's owner should be blamed rather than the perpetrators.[43]

These "emergencymen" were universally despised because of their affiliation with the landlords, yet Simpson maintained that he had a good relationship with the Clearys, possibly because he shared an interest in fairycraft (or in Bridget Cleary herself). To outsiders, he liked to portray himself as an authority on the country people and their beliefs, implying that he and his wife took no stock in peasant superstitions. This denial may have been used to cover up their involvement in the fairy trial.

When first questioned by police, Simpson initially repeated the story that the family concocted. Yes, he had seen the Kennedy boys, John Dunne, and others going in and out of the Cleary cottage, but he and his wife had nothing to do with any of it, because neither of them believed stories about the fairies. They were, after all, respectable people. He admitted visiting the Clearys on Thursday evening, but only because he had heard Bridget was ill. Yes, he knew Bridget ran off on Friday night, but only because Michael Cleary told him so. If he and his wife were observers or participants in whatever took place at the Clearys, he volunteered no information.

William Simpson went to Fethard to meet with investigators on March 18 but did not tell all he knew, apparently to conceal his wife's, as well as his own, participation in the fairy trial. Not until his April 1 deposition did he begin to reveal more details about the events of Thursday evening before Bridget's disappearance. In this deposition, Simpson stated he went to the house of Patrick Boland just after nine on the evening of March 14 to visit Bridget Cleary, who had been taken ill. Nearing the cottage, he met Johanna Burke and "inquired from her how was Bridget." Burke responded that "they were giving her at this time herbs they got from Ganey over at the Mountain and that no person would be let in for some time." Upon arriving at the house, which was a "new labourer's cottage," they found the window shutters closed and the door bolted. From the front room, Simpson heard a man shout at the top of his voice, "Take that you bitch, you old faggot or we will kill you."[44]

Soon after, the door opened, and Burke and Simpson were admitted to the cottage, where he witnessed a ritual trial underway. The Kennedy boys were holding Bridget on the bed, while Michael threw herbs mixed in some kind of a liquid at her. The type of liquid used may have shocked the official taking down the information, who recorded that Michael Cleary called for the "uran" and it was brought in by Mary Kennedy in a saucepan whereupon Michael threw the liquid on his wife. While Michael forced the urine into her mouth, he fed her herbs and asked her "in the name of the Father, Son and Holy Ghost, if she were Bridget Boland or what." When this failed, John Dunne suggested they take her to the fire and force her to swallow the herbs. The Kennedys picked Bridget up off the bed, dragged her into the kitchen, and laid her on the fireplace grate. At some point, they seemed satisfied that she was herself, so the men carried her back to bed. This was the end of it, according to Simpson.

When asked how long he had known Bridget Cleary, Simpson responded that he had known her about four years. He claimed he knew nothing about her present whereabouts and finished his statement with his comment that he was disgusted with the fairy trial he had witnessed. As far as he knew, Bridget Cleary left home on the next night and "has not since been found."[45] While offering no clues as to Bridget's fate, Simpson's statement, nonetheless, explained the burned nightdress and gave the police evidence to support a criminal indictment.

With Simpson's deposition in hand, Wansbrough went after a witness key to his case—a witness who could tell investigators what happened on Friday, March 15, the night of the disappearance. The following day, Tuesday, March 19, Johanna Burke, resident of Rathkenny, was summoned to appear at the Petty Sessions' District of Fethard. Though she had less status, and therefore less credibility, than the caretaker Simpson, Burke could tell police what happened to Bridget and where she might be found. But Burke was reluctant to admit anything that might implicate her mother and brothers. In order to get the information he needed, District Inspector Wansbrough was prepared to coerce the witness.

After Burke received her summons to appear in Fethard, Michael Cleary was worried about what she would tell the prosecutors. Before departing, Cleary paid her a visit. "Don't let the peelers dive into you, Han," he warned, and, since he was saying nothing, if she kept quiet, "they would have no one to swear" to the contrary. Knowing Simpson had been deposed the day before, Cleary told her not to go "until you see Simpson, and follow his information." Thereupon, Cleary and Patrick Kennedy escorted Johanna to Simpson's house, as Cleary said, "to see what he says about me." Simpson met them at the door, and after talking to the two men, he called Burke into the parlor where he told her to follow his line. Burke was to vindicate Cleary by saying that "Michael Cleary took no hand in the proceedings." Most importantly, Simpson told her not to reveal that his wife had participated in the fairy ritual.[46] Rather, Simpson directed her to lie and tell the police that only her three brothers held Bridget on the fire. They all agreed to stick with the story that Bridget ran off Friday night, but, unlike Simpson, who answered truthfully that he knew nothing about what happened on Friday night, Johanna

Burke knew the truth. On March 19, however, she told Justice of the Peace W. Walker Tennant in Fethard the story that Michael and Simpson had instructed her to tell:

> [A]fter some time [Bridget] dressed and sat at the fire after some time she went to bed. I went out for some sticks and when I was returning I met her in the door way going out against me with her night dress. I endevoured to hold her and failed. Since that time I have not seen her. Her husband followed her for some time and returned but did not see her. She is missing since they made Search for her.[47]

Not until her second deposition on March 24 and 25 did Johanna Burke begin to reveal what she really knew. Now she said that she met the Simpsons outside the Cleary cottage on the previous Thursday and found the door locked. The three of them went to the window to investigate and heard a voice saying, "Take that, you witch," or perhaps "Take that, you bitch." The three stood listening, and after some time, the door opened. Inside the house, Burke saw Michael Cleary and her brothers Patrick, William, and James Kennedy, along with John Dunne.

Burke described the scene in the bedroom much as Simpson had. Michael was next to the bed, holding a saucepan and forcing liquid into Bridget's mouth. At that point, someone called for more urine, which Burke believed was supplied by her mother, Mary Kennedy. Cleary poured fresh urine over his wife then carried her to the fire, demanding to know in the name of the Father, Son, and Holy Ghost, if she was the wife of Michael Cleary. When Bridget answered in the affirmative, the men put her back in bed. The women then dressed her in a clean chemise and set the old one of striped flannel out to air. In the process of changing clothes, Burke noticed a slight mark on Bridget's neck, but indicated to inspectors that her ordeal in the fireplace had done no serious harm. Johanna stayed through the night, then left at dawn the next morning, apparently with the Simpsons.

The following day, Wednesday, March 20, District Inspector Wansbrough swore out a statement before the Justice of the Peace in the Petty Sessions District of Fethard seeking arrest warrants for members of the Cleary/Kennedy family who took part in the Thursday ordeal, including Michael Cleary, Patrick Boland, Mary Kennedy, Johanna Burke, and the Kennedy brothers—Patrick, James, Michael, and William. Also arrested was John Dunne, who had close ties to the family. Burke was arrested, whereas William Simpson was not, because Wansbrough knew that she would not testify against her mother and brothers unless forced.[48]

District Inspector Wansbrough also arrested two who were outside the family nexus. One was William Ahearn, a sixteen-year-old neighbor of the Kennedys who did nothing more than stand in the corner and hold a candle while the men did their work. Ahearn was one of several neighbors who visited the Cleary cottage on that Thursday night, and throughout the week for that matter, indicating that the strange business going on at the Clearys since Bridget took sick was widely reported throughout the neighborhood. Of this larger group who were aware of the fairy trial underway, only Ahearn was charged; his candle holding amounting to participation in the crime, according to Wansbrough.

The only accused who was not in the cottage at any time was Denis Ganey, the so-called fairy doctor from Kylatlea, across the Anner valley at the base of Slievenamon. Ganey neither participated in the events on Thursday night nor even knew of them. The only reference in the testimony collected thus far implicating Ganey was Simpson's statement that Burke told him the herbs used in the ritual cure came from Ganey, who lived "across the mountain," or "out the mountain," in an area steeped in Irish folklore and superstition. By drawing Ganey into the case, District Inspector Wansbrough used what amounted to uncorroborated hearsay evidence to reach "across the mountain" and indict the fairies, ancient superstitions, and all those who held to them. By bringing Ganey into the courtroom, Wansbrough placed the legal proceeding figuratively at the base of Slievenamon and made Irish folk culture an unindicted co-conspirator in the crime.

With arrest warrants in hand, Wansbrough directed constables of the RIC to remand those charged to the County Gaol in Fethard, which was promptly done. The prisoners offered no resistance. After the arrests, District Inspector Wansbrough suspended the search for a missing person and, instead, ordered constables in the Mullinahone, Drangan, and Cloneen districts to comb the nearby fields and probe the ditch banks for human remains. By now Wansbrough knew full well that the case involved more than ill-treatment and that it was not likely Bridget Cleary would be found alive.

As Wansbrough was making the arrests and reorganizing the search, the first reports of the "strange occurrence at Ballyvadlea" appeared in both of Clonmel's two biweekly newspapers on March 20, 1895. The *Nationalist* reported that the "mysterious disappearance of a young woman" was the "topic of all lips in the neighborhood of Drangan and Cloneen." The conservative *Clonmel Chronicle* decried the "avidity" with which these wild stories were consumed. In the days and weeks to come, the tale of the missing cooper's wife would become the biggest story in County Tipperary since the death of Charles Stewart Parnell.

The March 20 *Nationalist* gave readers two versions of the story. The first reported that a young woman named Cleary, the wife of a cooper, living in a laborer's cottage at Ballyvadlea, took sick a few days prior, suddenly disappeared, and had not been heard of since. Those attending the young woman had called in a medical doctor to look after the patient. Fearing his medicine was ineffective, they apparently discarded his prescriptions and instead "treated her to some fairy quackery." This information was followed by even more startling news:

> Her friends who were present assert that she had been taken away on a white horse before their eyes, and that she told them when leaving, that on Sunday night they would meet her on Kylnagranagh hill, where they could, if they had the courage, rescue her. Accordingly, they assembled at the appointed time and place to fight the fairies, but, needless to say, no white horse appeared.[49]

Talk around the neighborhood confirmed that Michael Cleary, Patrick Boland, and some of the Kennedy brothers had gone to the fort on Kylnagranagh hill every night following the disappearance. In the language of the day, the police learned: "She is gone on a white horse out the mountain," meaning that she had gone off with the fairies.[50]

The second account in the same issue of the *Nationalist* added other details: A woman fell sick and believed she was "going," meaning she was taken by the fairies and would shortly die. A priest was called to administer last rites; thereafter, the woman advised her husband that she would be taken the following night. As predicted, the following night she disappeared even though her husband and father were in attendance nearby. In the aftermath of her disappearance, the police organized several search parties, but as yet nothing more had been seen of her.

In its reporting, the *Clonmel Chronicle* was dismissive of anything as irrational as fairies:

Of course, at the evening firesides wild stories of ghosts, fairies, and "good people" are, under the circumstances, devoured with an avidity that only a mysterious occurrence of this kind can produce. Possibly the appearance of the woman in the flesh, by-and-bye, may rob the case of all the romance. For this reason, I purposely avoid giving names at present.

The *Chronicle* dismissed stories about the "good people," favoring the notion that Bridget would eventually turn up.[51]

In an attempt to affirm or dismiss the reports of fairies, a reporter from the *Nenagh News* toured the Cleary cottage the week after the disappearance, hoping to find something among the Clearys' personal effects that would give some indication of what had happened. He was taken there by William Simpson on midday Thursday, March 21, 1895. The sun was shining brightly, "flitting with delightful fickleness from hill-pitch to hill-pitch." As described by the reporter, the front door opened into the kitchen, which served as the main living area. To the left was a fireplace, inset into the wall. Opposite the fireplace were two doors leading to the bedrooms—one occupied by the Clearys and the other by Bridget's father, Patrick Boland. There was a loft over the bedrooms reached by a ladder in the kitchen. While the kitchen floor was "earthen," the bedrooms had wooden floors. The furniture was small and "naturally rustic," consisting of three chairs, a table, a small cupboard, and a dresser holding blue "common ware" dishes and a prayer book. There was a clock on the wall, still ticking. In the corner were two crosscut saws used in Michael's coopering work. The fireplace was small, the grate being just six by twelve inches. The ashes from a recent fire still lay beneath it. Michael's dog, Badger, and Bridget's cat, Dotie, wandered about the room, seemingly anxious to know where the master and mistress had gone. In the corner lay a mineral-water bottle stained with a thick, yellowish liquid, the medicine presumably prescribed by the district's medical officer, Dr. William Crean. The label bore the instructions "Four teaspoonfuls to be taken in a little water four times a day."[52]

The bedroom where the Clearys slept was about eight feet in width, and had a small window with a view of the hillside behind the cottage. A thin wooden partition separated the two bedrooms. The Clearys' room was almost wholly occupied by the bed but also contained a wooden trunk, Bridget's sewing machine, and a box covered with colored calico. Around the bed on the walls were pictures of a sacred nature; a religious medal hung on the wall; a crucifix lay on the sewing machine. On one wall, hanging on a nail, was a woman's straw hat, black, trimmed with red and navy blue ribbon. The room was a mess. It appeared that Bridget's clothing had been hastily strewn around on the night of the disappearance. However, amidst this "soiled heap" was a new blue handkerchief, which neighbor Simpson disclosed was a present Bridget gave to her husband a few days before she became ill.

On that Thursday, March 21, as William Simpson conducted the Nenagh reporter through the now vacant Cleary cottage, police stepped up their efforts to find the body. The search yielded nothing that day, so reinforcements were called in from neighboring districts. On the afternoon of Friday, March 22, Sergeant Patrick Rogers of Mullinahone, along with Constables Somers, Phillips, O'Connor, and O'Callaghan, searched along an old dike on the west side of the low road, midway between Father Ryan's home at Tullowcossaun and the Kennedy cottage located a quarter mile south.

A little past two in the afternoon, as Rogers was moving north through tangled underbrush along the stream just south of Father

Ryan's, he came to a bend of an overgrown embankment, about thirteen feet wide and four feet high, enclosed on one side by thornbushes and a high fence and on the other by a mass of furze bushes. The dike was well concealed from the surrounding country, allowing a person to work there a long time without being seen. The spot stood only 1,300 yards away, across the fields, from the Cleary cottage. Amid the tangled underbrush, Sergeant Rogers noticed some white thorn brambles strewn on a patch of freshly disturbed soil.[53]

Rogers began probing the loose ground with a stick, which entered the soil without resistance. He climbed higher onto the dike to position himself directly over the patch of loose dirt and thrust the probe in again, upon which he encountered a solid object just inches below the surface that "appeared to be the head of a body." He brushed aside a thin layer of clay soil, exposing the edge of a cloth bag. Rogers called for Constables Somers, O'Connor, and O'Callaghan to assist, ordering one to fetch a shovel.

When the officer arrived with the shovel, Rogers continued digging, revealing first shoulders and then a torso. The cloth bag, he discovered, was pulled over the head like a hood, covering the face and hair of the victim. The torso was wrapped in a white bed sheet. As the constables cleared the earth away, the hole immediately filled with water, requiring that they drain off the excess as they proceeded. The original hole was no more than eighteen inches deep overall and just three feet long, which was not long enough to lay the body flat. In order to fit in this narrow grave, the body was tipped over on its side, the bagged head pointing in a northwesterly direction. The body was almost upright, in a sitting position, the feet drawn up against the buttocks. The legs were splayed apart nine inches at the knees, the arms crossed over the breast.

Having uncovered the body, the constables carefully lifted it out of the hole, moving it some fifteen feet away to await examination by the coroner and the local doctors. Even when removed, the body remained curled up. Rogers took off the bed sheet draped around the torso. The sight was startling. The entire back and lower abdomen were horribly burned, roasted clear to the bone with the vital organs clearly visible. In contrast, the chest, shoulders, and neck, as well as the legs and feet, appeared unscathed. The severity of the burns in the midsection had contracted the muscles and tendons, bending the body into a permanent tuck, like a collapsed letter S. It was a woman's body, a young woman's body. Limp breasts hugged against scorched thighs, a pair of black stockings below the knees, a bit of a blackened chemise burned into the lower torso. Upon removing the cloth bag from the head, constables found the woman's face and hair in nearly perfect condition, though the features were "much distorted."[54]

There was no doubt that it was the body of Bridget Cleary, and even less doubt that she had met a terrible fate, yet Rogers denied any knowledge of the circumstances surrounding her fate. Rogers stated, "I came on the body while searching diligently for it though I did not know at that time that the woman had been murdered at all." He made this claim even though he knew the police had arrested eleven people in connection with the case the day before. Rogers, like everyone else involved in the case, wished to distance himself completely from the taint of fairycraft.

Sergeant Rogers placed a police guard over the burial site and sent one of the constables off to report the discovery to his superiors, instructing those who remained to secure the site pending the arrival of Coroner James Shee. In the meantime, Rogers searched the area for clues. He observed that someone had been careful to remove any sign of disturbance around the grave but found no footprints. Lacking physical evidence from the site itself, constables focused on the bed sheet wrapped about the torso. Police then returned to the nearby Cleary cottage, where they found a sheet in the front room that appeared to be of the same material as that which covered the burnt body. They found no second, matching sheet in the house. Following this significant discovery, the constables retired for the night.

In Clonmel, editors of the *Nationalist* were at work on a feature story for their weekend edition, a long notice of the "further extraordinary developments" in what was now being called, "The Cloneen 'Fairy' Mystery." The article contained new sensational evidence that emerged from the interrogation of the witnesses and the numerous arrests that followed. Readers learned that several suspects were in custody and had been remanded to the jail in Clonmel. Perhaps most sensational, however, was the news that Denis Ganey, the fairy doctor from Kylatlea, was one of those being held.

Word of Sergeant Rogers's discovery was telegraphed to Clonmel's *Nationalist* sometime late Thursday afternoon or early Friday morning, in time to make the weekend edition of March 23. Below the article detailing the "Extraordinary Developments" at Ballyvadlea was the headline: "STOP PRESS—THE BODY FOUND." Beneath this a short notice reported that a telegram from the police in Cloneen had just been received: "Body of Catherine Cleary found in Drangan sub-district." The police sent off the telegram in such haste that they neglected to confirm the victim's name was Bridget rather than Catherine as reported.

4

The Fairy Cures

From the Land of the Banshee

The extraordinary rumors surrounding the disappearance of Bridget Cleary ignited a burst of public interest that undoubtedly warmed the heart of District Inspector Alfred Joseph Wansbrough. Beginning with the inconspicuous notice on March 20 of a mysterious disappearance in "The Land of the Banshee and Fairy," newspapers eager to reap profits from the story seized any scrap of new information regarding the alleged witch burning at Ballyvadlea. On Saturday, March 23, 1895, Clonmel's *Nationalist* published the first depositions of Johanna Burke and William Simpson, which confirmed that the crime involved fairycraft. The arrests of eight family members, two neighbors, and Denis Ganey, the popular fairy doctor from Kylatlea, suggested that the network of practitioners was more widespread than first imagined. The discovery of the body on Friday, March 22, followed by the grisly details from the coroner's report, catapulted the story across the Irish Sea to England, where eager British publicists were only too pleased to report the latest example of Celtic savagery, or what Alfred Lord Tennyson called the "blind hysterics of the Celt."[1]

On Saturday, March 23, several local officials converged to verify the accuracy of the extraordinary rumors emanating from the tiny townland of Ballyvadlea. At just past 2:00 P.M. James J. Shee, District Coroner, convened an inquest in a shed adjacent to Father Ryan's cottage in Tullowossaum, a quarter mile from where the body was discovered. Attending the inquest were several high officials, including Clonmel's Resident Magistrate, Colonel Richard Charles Evanson; Mr. A. E. S. Heard, RIC Divisional Commissioner, Kilkenny; Mr. Wilson, Clonmel, County Inspector; District Inspector Wansbrough, Carrick-on-Suir; District Inspector Huddy, Killenaule; Dr. William Crean, Fethard; Dr. William Kickham Heffernan, Killenaule; and, Dr. C. Moloney, Mullinahone. These officials were joined by six constables of the RIC. Coroner Shee called a jury of local residents to examine the body, hear evidence, and determine the cause of death. The jurors included T. Ryan, foreman, assisted by John Anglim, M. O'Brien, Joseph Maher, the Michael Slatterys, father and son, Ed Brien, Philip Slattery, William Stokes, Francis Bradshaw, Patrick White, Thomas Cahill, and a layman named Thomas Croke. At the request of the jurors, Drs. Heffernan and Crean were instructed to perform a postmortem examination of the body while other evidence was heard.[2]

Coroner Shee opened the inquiry with the standard disclaimer issued by everyone who commented on the case—he was horrified, he had no prior knowledge of the case, and he knew nothing whatsoever about fairy superstitions. Although it was probably true that he was horrified and had no prior knowledge of this particular case, his disclaimer regarding his knowledge of fairy superstitions is suspect, given that Coroner Shee signed the death certificates for most of the burning victims in the county. Shee claimed that he knew only what he read in the newspapers, and just that morning, he learned that the police had discovered the body. For good measure, Shee followed his obligatory protestation of ignorance with some self-righteous editorializing. If the charges proved true, this was certainly one of the most "frightful" things to have occurred in the county for years. "Even among the Hottentots," he opined, one would not expect to hear of such an occurrence. Nevertheless, Coroner Shee recommended that the panel do nothing more than fulfill two requirements prescribed by law—identify the victim and certify the cause of death. Although the law gave jurors the right to call more witnesses, Shee advised the panel to let the matter alone. The jury could go further into the matter if they wished, but, in his opinion, "it was better not [to]," because "we leave the rest to Colonel Evanson."[3]

Thus advised, jury members followed Coroner Shee into the shed for the viewing. There they saw the body lying on the ground, still wrapped in the sheet matching the one found by Acting Sergeant Egan in the Clearys' bedroom. Coroner Shee pulled back this covering. The jurors saw a body, curled in a "most ghastly appearance." Yet, strangely, while the lower torso was charred, burned through to the bone, the woman's face was unblemished. There was no mistaking that this was Bridget Boland Cleary, the cooper's wife whom some of the jurors had known all her life.

Having formally viewed the body, the jury filed back to the priest's cottage to discharge their duty. The first witness, Constable Samuel Somers of Cloneen, identified the woman as Bridget

Cleary: "I have this day viewed the body of Bridget Cleary, now lying dead at Ballyvadlea, in the County. She was married to Michael
Cleary, Cooper, and they resided in this townland. She was about
twenty-six years of age. I knew her about three years." The coroner
asked Constable Somers if Bridget had been healthy. "She was, Sir,
I saw her last about a month or five weeks ago." Shee then asked if
Mrs. Cleary had been reported missing. Somers responded:

> It was reported at Cloneen, on the 16th. inst., that she was miss-
> ing, that she had escaped from her father's house. We had been
> searching for her up to yesterday. I was out with another consta-
> ble yesterday, and I saw Sergeant Rodgers [Rogers] and acting
> Sergeant Dowling, who were searching, too. About three o'clock I
> observed them standing on an angle of a field. We faced for them
> at once. I saw two constables digging in a dike, and after a short
> time they exhumed the body of the deceased, Bridget Cleary. It
> had the appearance of being some days dead and there were
> burned charred marks on it.[4]

At that point, the jury foreman asked Constable Somers how he
identified the woman as Bridget Cleary. "By her features," he responded. "They were not injured. Her features were perfect."

Dismissing Constable Somers, the Coroner called District Inspector Wansbrough to testify. Could he give evidence of when
the death occurred? Though Constable Somers stated the body
appeared to have been dead for some days, Wansbrough offered
no more information and said only that he had no evidence "at
present." Shee next called Dr. Crean. Having established that Dr.
Crean knew the deceased and had last seen her on the morning of
Wednesday, March 13, Shee attempted to determine the state of
Bridget's health before her death:

Shee: On your arrival at her residence on that day how did you find her?

Dr. Crean: I found her suffering. It was simply from nervous excitement and slight bronchitis, she was in bed, I could see nothing in the case likely to cause death and I did not anticipate any danger.

Shee: Did you prescribe for her?

Dr. Crean: I did, and gave the medicine to her husband the same morning.

Crean then repeated his previous assertion that he detected nothing unusual; he had no anxiety whatever about the case. He did not see the deceased afterward, until seeing her dead at Ballyvadlea that day.

After Crean's testimony Coroner Shee requested the examining physicians to present their report to the jurors. It read:

We found the right hip and thigh and lower portion of the abdomen charred and burned; with the internal organs protruding through the burned apertures; the right hand was also burned, the fingers charred and contracted; we also found the same condition on the left side of the deceased's body, but not so severe; the left hand was also burned, and the fingers charred; the muscles of the lower end of the spine were charred and burned, and the bones exposed; there was a gold earring in the left ear; on the inner side of the lips at the right side of the mouth, and the tongue at that side was slightly lacerated; on opening the neck we found the tissues slightly discolored.[5]

Coroner Shee asked if the last detail could have resulted from choking and Heffernan replied, "Yes, or holding." The doctors' report noted that there were "no great marks of violence," including any damage to her brain. Her "lungs were slightly congested, and the left lung hung adherant to the chest wall; the spleen was reptured [*sic*]; we removed the stomach, and found it healthy in appearance." The doctors certified that the cause of death was "shock due to burns," and speculated the woman must have died very soon after these were inflicted, or more probably, "while they were being inflicted."

Coroner Shee questioned the physicians about circumstances surrounding the death. Was the death accidental? Certainly not. Were there signs of violence before the burning? After all, there were marks about the face and mouth, bruises on the neck of the deceased. Could these have resulted from choking? The doctors could not say for certain because these contusions might have come from holding Bridget down, rather than mistreatment with intent to kill. Was there any head trauma or injury to the brain? Both doctors reaffirmed that trauma to the body inflicted before the burning, including the head and brain, was not serious and left only small bruises and abrasions. Were there any signs of poisoning? Apparently not. Doctors had removed the stomach, found it healthy-looking, and therefore decided not to examine its contents for "corrosive" poison. Neither could they indicate whether the victim had been drugged. The stomach was not examined for drugs. Were there any flammable materials found on the body? They made no determination on this. Were there flammable materials on the bits of clothing adhering to the body? No, they could not determine this either.

The jury had no additional questions regarding the condition of the deceased at the time of her death, nor did they wish to call other witnesses. With that, Coroner Shee closed the inquiry, and forthwith the jury returned their verdict:

We find that the deceased, Bridget Cleary, late of Ballyvadlea, was found dead on the lands of Tullacussane [sic], on Friday, 22nd March, 1895, and we further find that death was caused by extensive burns, how, or by whom caused we have no evidence to show.[6]

The jurors had done their duty and that was the end of it, so far as they were concerned.

Also in attendance at the coroner's inquest was a reporter from Clonmel's *Nationalist*, who telegraphed a complete account of the proceedings, along with a transcript of the coroner's report, to James Long, editor-in-chief. This information appeared in a hastily printed second edition of the *Nationalist*, dated Saturday, March 23, placed between "full authentic details" of witnesses' depositions and reports of INF subscription drives. The now-official story that a woman was roasted like a hare created such a demand for extra copies that local presses could scarcely keep up. The extraordinary demand for newspapers was caused in part by lurid details of the burning, but also because the incident was one of the few to break through the official silence veiling pagan beliefs and practice. Even before the burning, news that a changeling had appeared in Ballyvadlea caused great excitement in the Cloneen-Drangan district. Eleven defendants, including the fairy doctor from Kylatlea, sat in the Clonmel Gaol awaiting arraignment at the magisterial inquiry. And significantly, the story broke just as Tipperary's faithful began preparations for the revered and beloved Archbishop Croke's Silver Jubilee.

Interest in the story ran so high that the first printing of the *Nationalist* for March 23 sold out immediately. Editors ordered a special 600-copy second edition, which contained fresh details of the coroner's inquest; it sold out as well. All around the region people hungry for details besieged news agents for extra copies, many of which were sent on to friends and relatives abroad. Ireland once again made international headlines, but like those reporting the death of the disgraced Parnell four years earlier, respectable Irish, whether Catholic or Protestant, did not relish the notoriety; Nationalists, in particular, feared the unsavory publicity would jeopardize future Home Rule initiatives.

Initially local editors reveled in the story's popularity as merchants, eager to capitalize on the unprecedented interest generated by the tale, lined up for advertising space. But as the news spread beyond County Tipperary's borders, Irish Nationalists began to worry about the negative political fallout that the story would have abroad. An early report in the London *Times*, March 26, 1895, suggested what was to follow. The *Times* announced news of a "shocking occurrence, recalling the barbarities practiced in the Middle Ages upon prisoners charged with witchcraft." The article carefully pinpointed the location of this shocking incident in the misspelled village of "Baltyvadhen" situated on the slopes of the misspelled Slievenaman, in County Tipperary. Though Ballyvadlea actually lay across the Anner river valley, some five miles distant, writers in England initially placed the incident directly on the mountain's slope, a perhaps unconscious historical reference to the infamous uprisings that took place on Slievenamon.[7]

The London *Times* article noted, also incorrectly, that two men and a woman had been charged in the death of Bridget Cleary, wife of a cooper, who died after being forced to drink "noxious potions" prepared for her by a "herbalist," after which she was seized and roasted on a fire on the supposition that she was a witch. These "savage orgies" were performed in the house of the woman's father, while her husband stood by and aided in "working the spell." The article went on to report that the body was found buried in a ditch; the cause of death was burning. A full magisterial inquiry was to follow the coroner's inquest, and all defendants, including the "medicine man," were remanded without bail. The specific negative references to the herbalist, his pernicious potions, the working of the spell, and finally the "medicine man" were, of course, explicitly aimed at Denis Ganey. Of all the eleven prisoners remanded to jail, Ganey was the only one not directly involved in the incident, but he was the only one named in the *Times* article. He was specifically hounded out by District Inspector Wansbrough.

In contrast, Irish papers described Ganey as a popular local healer of some renown to whom even medical doctors turned for remedies. Ganey used a variety of herbal cures and bone-setting techniques that he learned from his father, and it was said that he never used the same technique twice.[8] Nonetheless, the arrest of Ganey allowed the British press to trumpet the case as an Irish witch burning, which was sure to embarrass Irish Nationalists at home and abroad. Although not publicly heralded at the time, Wansbrough's ordering of Ganey's arrest constituted a conscious and arrogant attempt to insult traditional Irish folk culture and embarrass a respectable member of the folk community.[9]

On March 27, the *Times* of London explicitly referred to the case as a witch burning. It stated that Colonel Richard Charles Evanson, age fifty-seven and a native of Cork County, convened a special magisterial inquiry court to hear charges against ten persons "charged with having murdered, by burning to death, a woman named Cleary." Further, the victim's husband gave her herbs, forced her onto the fire, and told others "that it was not his wife he was burning, but a witch, and that she would disappear up the chimney." By the end of the magisterial inquiry in April, official court documents all had mislabeled the incident the "Tipperary Witchcraft Case," and headlines in England used the terms witch burning, witchcraft, and witchery interchangeably with fairies and Irish folklore, even though, by the turn of the century most ethnologists agreed, witch-cult, sorcery, and demonology had "never found a home in Ireland as it did elsewhere."[10]

Once editors of Irish newspapers realized how easily the Unionists and the English press could misuse the Cleary story to misrepresent their country, they pulled back from its most sensational aspects. The headline in the *Irish Times*, for example, omitted mention of fairies and witchcraft, referring to the story as "The Extraordinary Case in Tipperary." The subheads that followed stressed order, propriety, and outrage—"Prisoners before the Magistrates; Charge of Murder; Evidence as to How Mrs. Cleary was Burned; and, Popular Demonstrations against the Prisoners." The article acknowledged that the "extraordinary circumstances surrounding the death of the unfortunate young woman Cleary at Cloneen" had excited the "most profound public sensations, and the publication of the details has heightened the popular feeling," which was decidedly unfavorable to the accused.[11]

To forestall further damage to the Nationalist cause and the reputation of Catholic Ireland, most Irish papers minimized the story by reporting it as an unusual murder case, perpetrated by ignorant peasants in a wild and remote corner of the country. The British press exposed the Irish shift in reporting. On Saturday, March 30, the *Times* of London attacked the story that ran in Ireland's *Freeman's Journal*, the official organ of the Irish Parliamentary Party and Dublin's Nationalist voice. The *Times* account stated that though the "witch burning case in the county Tipperary" excited "great interest," some Irish journals, such as the *Freeman*, minimized the case. Contradicting the *Freeman's* evasive account, the *Times* wrote that the case did not take place in a "mountain district, far from any town," as the *Freeman* had indicated; rather the village was only four miles from Fethard, "a town of great repute in the olden times, and ten miles from Clonmel." Nor were the participants "of the lowest class," as the *Freeman* had reported. Rather, Michael Cleary was a cooper who learned his trade in Clonmel, and his wife was a dressmaker, who apprenticed in Clonmel and spent much time there. (Local stories about Bridget's apprenticeship support the statement by the *Times*.) Further, the couple lived comfortably in a well-furnished laborer's cottage erected by the Board of Guardians. "Michael Roland [sic]," father of the deceased, lived with them in "comfortable circumstances for persons in their station in life." The *Times* located the site of the burning as being in the south of the county, near Slievenamon, the site of so many Irish demonstrations against the English.

When Irish attempts to minimize the story failed, *Nationalist* editors shifted the blame to rural Ireland and its peasantry. In Ulster and Dublin, responsibility shifted to Munster, which then passed it on to Tipperary, where most of the opprobrium fell upon Clonmel. "The Tipperary Horror" thus devolved in newspaper headlines into the "South Tipperary Horror," to the "Clonmel Horror," to the "Cloneen Horror," ending finally in the "Ballyvadlea Horror."[12] In the process urban newspaper editors created an artificial division between townspeople, portrayed as too sophisticated for fairy tales, and ignorant country people, who clung to the old ways and caused such an awful stir for their foolishness. In fact, the rural and urban poor shared similar oral beliefs about Irish folklore. The *Nenagh News* smarted from the taint of association and charged that Bridget Cleary died because:

A few foolish men and women clung to the phantoms and bogies of Irish folk lore. They respected the forts which are so common in this country, believing them to be sacred to the fairies, and they fancied that Slievenamon, in the stillness of the night, or when the storm howled through the hills, looked down on mystical revels. They carried the belief to its extreme—its heartless, savage, and appalling extreme—and a life was sacrificed to a spirit which the world thought dead.[13]

Irish newspapers clearly implied that the peasantry's naïve credulity could not be tolerated by a society that was striving to claim respectability as modern, civilized, and worthy of Home Rule. Telling fairy tales was one thing; practicing pagan cures was another. Or as the *Cork Examiner* put it: "When interest [in Celtic imaginativeness] passes from the literary and academic domain . . . not even the most ardent folklorist amongst us . . . could . . . defend it, strong as is their attachment to the fascinating fairyland of our country." Acknowledging that it was also "patriotic to stimulate interest in our beautiful folk lore," this newspaper concluded: "But when the fairies actually play pranks with people, when the bustle of their merry hurling matches is actually heard in the middle of the night, and when all the creatures of the imagination become practical agents in daily life, it is time to pause. Out of such diseased spirit grew the tragedy of which Bridget Cleary was the victim."[14]

On March 27 the *Cork Examiner* railed against the "revolting crime" at Ballyvadlea, which "takes us back to the darkest ages of human superstition and barbarism." Even speaking of this tragic affair "knocked [ten centuries] off the record of progress and civilization." Such a crime would "disgrace the most degraded tribe of African savages." Acknowledging the political damage that might ensue from the incident, the *Examiner* lamented that just when Ireland was being "favorably compared with Europe for enlightenment and humanity" the Ballyvadlea case "brings us face to face with a condition of mental and moral depravity" and was "humiliating to our national self-esteem." The story concluded by calling for "merciless justice [to] be meted out to those who may be found to have participated in [this] hideous crime" and by implication, those responsible for bringing disgrace upon the nation.[15]

Just as Cork wanted nothing of the matter, neither did the good folk of Clonmel wish to bear the opprobrium of association with the murderous and deluded Cleary, Kennedy, and Boland clans. The *Nationalist,* in particular, was anxious that the newspaper appear as a thoroughly modern, up-to-date journalistic enterprise and credited itself for complete and timely reporting of the incident. It was totally at a loss to understand why other papers headlined the case as "the Clonmel horror," especially in view of the well-known fact that the occurrence took place in a remote country district, a dozen miles away, and that no one residing in Clonmel was implicated. Naming the Unionists as the source of this slander, the article concluded, "The Cork Herald might as truthfully have dubbed it, 'the Cork horror.'"[16]

The recriminations of town, county, and country became so heated that local officials in Clonmel intervened to quash publication of any information related to the case. In a move calculated to cool tempers, Colonel Evanson imposed a ban upon the local newspapers, ordering them to refrain from printing anything about the incident. Surprisingly, even James Long, the spirited editor of the *Nationalist,* agreed. In his public acquiescence to Colonel Evanson's edict, Long declared that, while the paper and its advertisers benefited from the unprecedented public demand for information, he was eager to be relieved of the "burthen of the Ballyvadlea case." Acknowledging the sensitivity of the situation, Long pledged to do his part to defuse popular passion and the "countless opportunities for sensationalists and gossips" that so inspired the British press. Further he promised to sustain the "judicious judicial attitude" set by Evanson and assist the Crown by publishing only "sworn evidence." This limitation would not prevent embarrassment, however, since District Inspector Wansbrough, as we shall see, perfervidly saw to it that the sworn evidence contained as many references to the fairies, superstitions, and pagan rites as possible.

Long's willingness to accede to the magistrates' demand was notable given his own history of resistance to the Crown's judicial directives. A native of County Kerry, Long was an ardent defender of tenants' rights and an outspoken foe of so-called land grabbers who snatched up farms from the evicted poor. In July 1890, a case arose in neighboring Thurles in which Edward Ryan, a cattle dealer, obtained from Colonel Fitzgibbon Trant of Dovea a grass farm recently taken from evicted tenants. In defense of the tenants, Long published articles in the *Nationalist*, including one on June 25, 1891, which declared:

> That whilst the brave men of gallant Tipperary and elsewhere are bravely struggling against landlord tyranny and injustice, we cannot but emphatically condemn the unpardonable audacity of the sneaking grass grabber, Edward Ryan (brogue), Thurles, who worms himself into the parish of Inch by cunningly grabbing a boycotted grass farm which forms a portion of a property on which there are several evicted farms, the tenants of which have not yet been reinstated by the Dovea evictor.[17]

Edward Ryan, the newly crowned "Dovea evictor," filed suit, charging that Long threatened, intimidated, and aroused public passion against him. A special court in Clonmel, headed by the same Colonel Evanson, agreed. Under provisions of the Crimes

Act, the court ordered Long to cease and desist his attack on Ryan and sentenced him to three months' imprisonment.

Long's conviction threatened to provoke reprisals. Attempting to prevent any public disorder, Colonel Evanson offered to set aside the sentence if Long pledged to refrain from printing inflammatory material for a year. James Long refused the deal. He thanked the magistrates for their personal courtesy but declared he could not guarantee better behavior since he believed he had broken no "just" law and had merely been "a humble worker . . . in the cause of my country." Because he himself could not be silent, Long would not ask anyone to post a surety bond for him as required by this "exceptional Act." Having rejected clemency, Long was removed under escort to the Clonmel Gaol, followed by a large number of friends who gave him a hearty cheer as he disappeared within its barred portals.

In 1895, Long, although still publishing "land grabber" stories,[18] was now more compliant, and, rather than defend the principle of freedom of the press, he joined the effort to quash the talk of witchery at Ballyvadlea. Likewise, no doctor, priest, or constable wanted any part in the affair. No church, political party, or city official wanted "phantoms and bogies" appearing on their doorsteps. Though everyone knew the tales, no one admitted knowing anything about fairycraft, let alone witchcraft. The official denunciations, including that of the feisty James Long, betrayed the reality that the beliefs, which the world wished dead, were very much alive among the country people, in spite of efforts by the Church, Nationalists, and public officials to relegate them eternally to the Otherworld of dead spirits and traditions.

Back at Cloneen, an eerie drama began unfolding that attested to the strength of the old beliefs among the peasantry. Late in the afternoon of March 23, as the coroner's inquest adjourned, Evanson and other government officials departed for their respective homes, and the reporter from the *Nationalist* rushed off to telegraph the findings back to Clonmel; District Inspector Wansbrough stayed behind to await Coroner Shee's report. When this was written and delivered, Shee released the body to police. Impatient to leave, Wansbrough placed two constables in charge and departed for Carrick-on-Suir to prepare for the formal magisterial inquest, scheduled to open on Monday morning in Clonmel.

Wansbrough's departure left the two constables of Her Majesty's Royal Irish Constabulary in a peculiar predicament. Under normal conditions police would remand the body to the family for burial. In this case, no family members came to claim the body, which was still curled in the bedsheet. Since the immediate members of the Cleary/Kennedy/Boland families were all in the Clonmel Gaol, the police called for clergy. Not a priest in the district, however, would come near the body. Catholic priests were strictly charged against performing sacraments where fairycraft was suspected and the souls of those who died by its practice were refused the comfort of church burial. Father Ryan and his superior, Father M'Grath, were nowhere to be found, having washed their hands of the matter in the Drangan churchyard.

In a macabre denouement, described variously in different newspapers, the "relieving officer" had no choice but to rummage up a rude coffin because no neighbors or relatives would undertake this important task, which the "Irish peasantry regard . . . not only as an expression of respect . . . but as invested with a certain degree of sanctity." Two constables along with three young fellows from the village waited for darkness to fall, and under its cover, quietly removed the body to the Catholic cemetery at Cloneen. In a less than subtle criticism of the local clergy, a contemporary observer wrote that "in such cases as this . . . the Royal

Irish Constabulatory act[ed] like Christians . . . stand[ing] between us and barbarism."[19]

There, beside a rough stone wall, the five men acted out a centuries-old ritual that dramatized the ancient accommodation between the Catholic Church and paganism. The men carried the coffin to a spot outside the churchyard wall so as not to taint the consecrated ground inside. Two of the lads jumped the low stone wall and dug a hole next to the unmarked grave of Bridget's mother. With Bridget's coffin resting outside the wall on unconsecrated ground, the men bowed their heads while one read portions of the burial service by the light of a small lamp. When the service concluded, the men, still standing outside the wall, lowered the coffin into the grave, being careful that the coffin not be allowed to touch consecrated soil on the grave's surface. This procedure allowed the men to bury the "martyred woman" beside her mother without defiling sacred ground.[20] The fact that Bridget was placed beside her mother and that both lie in unmarked graves beside the wall might suggest that the Church considered Bridget's mother a practitioner of the fairyfaith and also denied her a Christian burial. One wonders how many such unsanctified burials took place in Ireland in the last decade of the nineteenth century, indicating that the Church suspected pagan practices, which it insisted no longer existed, had been involved in the deaths of the deceased.

In this simple ritual, the country people honored Bridget Cleary's life and preserved a place for her within their own community. They would not bury her outside the wall in unconsecrated ground, apart from her family and deprived of all hope of salvation, for to do so would be punitive and an affront to the old ways. Nor would they dishonor the Church and defile sacred ground. The lads of the burial contingent simply did what the

Irish had done for centuries—they improvised, and in their own way, honored both systems. Though no headstone was erected, the men placed two upturned stones to mark the site. Local people know where Bridget Cleary was lain and came secretly to pay their respects. She remains there by the wall, near an oak tree, next to her mother, as she should be.

The following day, on March 24, Father Ryan mounted his pulpit in the Cloneen church and delivered a thunderous harangue against the murder of Bridget Cleary and denounced in the strongest possible terms the cruel events that led to her death. Ignoring his involvement in the ritual and his less than forthright reporting to the police, the curate called upon anyone who knew anything of the affair to communicate with the authorities. No mention was made of the Church's boycott of her secret burial the night before or the fairycraft practiced by her immediate family. Two days later the *Nationalist* reported that the priest's remarks reflected the "spontaneous popular indignation" in Clonmel, where his sermon was well received. Father Ryan's public remarks no doubt mollified his superiors in Thurles, but so far as the Nationalists were concerned, the damage was already done: The Unionists were using the Cleary incident to discredit any more land reform and Home Rule for Ireland. In particular, conservative newspapers were asking "how this revelation from the heart of Tipperary will affect Mr. Morley's [the Liberal Chief Secretary for Ireland] opinion of Ireland as fit for Home Rule. . . . We put the question especially to Mr. Morley. . . . Is he still, after the revelations made by the Tipperary horror, inclined to give over Ireland and all her civilization and all her hopes for the future to a peasant-elected Irish Parliament."[21]

Thus, the Cleary murder provided Ireland and the world with a reminder of the country's tenacious paganism and "heathen lore" among the Old Irishry. It was this reemergence of the old ways that transformed the case into a sensational story. More mundane tales of domestic violence were legion and failed to excite similar local, national, and international interest. There were many women who were injured, or who died at the hands of their husbands, but few made international headlines, and none became as well known as the cooper's wife of Ballyvadlea. Local newspapers, however, reported examples of spousal abuse in almost every issue, leading to the impression that mistreatment of wives, and sometimes of husbands, was rampant in the late nineteenth century only in Ireland when, unfortunately, it could also be found in the United States, England, and Europe.

In Ireland, as in other nations, authorities often turned a blind eye because police and priests became inured to repeated calls for help, especially from poor women. By the time authorities intervened, it was often too late. Or if officials did take action, it was often to promote their own careers. The pattern of nonintervention was all too familiar: Reports by wives of abuse were ignored, unsympathetic priests and police refused to intervene, and verbal and physical threats by husbands were considered normal behavior. If the wife was killed, rather than face hanging for a capital offense, the husband was often declared temporarily insane and committed to an asylum or incarcerated for a lesser offense. In all these cases, however, the perpetrator was clearly charged with wife abuse—not with practicing pagan cures.

One particularly gruesome attempted murder of a wife was reported on March 9, 1895, outside of Cappoquin near Waterford, just a week before Bridget disappeared. This case did not receive much attention because the circumstances were considered understandable: The husband was drunk and the wife was annoying him. A recruiting sergeant stationed at the Waterford Artillery

named Corcoran was charged with attacking his wife with a razor. She had come to visit and found him "imbib[ing] pretty
freely for some time back." After they transacted some business at
the local post office, they were walking along Lismore Road when
Corcoran attacked her with a razor cutting her throat from ear to
ear, as well as her wrist and hand, leaving a portion of the razor
imbedded in her head. A cooper named David Browne of Cappoquin came along and saw the woman bleeding profusely on the
roadside at Salterbridge. Browne called the police and a doctor,
who managed to save her life. They found Sergeant Corcoran
nearby with their ten-month-old baby in his arms "besmeared
with blood" but uninjured and "apparently unconcerned" about
his wife. After she recovered, Corcoran was allowed to visit her.
The import of the story was that "the poor creature vented her
feelings most kindly and forgivingly toward him"[22] and so Corcoran was not severely punished.

The Cleary case differed markedly from these run-of-the-mill
instances of domestic violence. It featured elements of fairycraft,
and Michael's "previous character" was said to be exemplary;[23] and
careers, even elections, could be won or lost once the story made
international headlines. The political ramifications of the story, its
sensational aspects, and widespread coverage explain why Father
Ryan thundered from the pulpit and the District Inspector became personally involved in the police investigation. Obviously
this was not a case involving just another dead Irishwoman.

Beyond the Ninth Wave

District Inspector Wansbrough, determined to expose Irish sorcery and superstitions for his own personal and political gain,
made public the details of Bridget's ritual exorcism that had been

carried out over several days. The results of his investigation, the depositions of Crown witnesses, and statements made by defendants provide a cogent narrative of the events leading up to Bridget's murder.

The first indication of trouble between Michael Cleary and his wife occurred sometime around Christmas. Michael was increasingly fearful that his wife would be taken by the fairies if she continued her trips to Kylnagranagh hill. To prevent her going there, Michael purportedly threatened for the first time to burn his wife, but in spite of the unusually cold weather and her husband's harsh words, she continued to go to the fort anyway.

The second incident of trouble between them occurred six weeks later on a day particularly fraught with symbolic meanings from pagan and Christian belief systems: February 1, the feast of St. Brigit. The feast celebrates the life of St. Brigit of Kildare, who defied her father, abandoned her Druid faith, and converted to Christianity before founding the nunnery at Kildare that bears her name. But there are also resonances from the pre-Christian era, when February 1 was the first day of spring and honored Brigit, the goddess of fertility and of healing. Bridget Cleary was childless; perhaps she went to the fairy fort to seek the goddess's help in conceiving a child. February 1, 1895, was also the first anniversary of the death of Bridget Cleary's mother, Bridget Keating Boland, who may have practiced fairycraft. As her mother's only daughter, Bridget may have seen herself as the only one responsible for carrying on folk traditions within the family. If so, little wonder that Bridget defied her husband's wishes and kept going to the fort.[24]

When the weather began to warm in the early days of March, Bridget was out again, selling eggs and making, we believe, furtive trips to the fort. On Wednesday, March 6, she made her final trek up Kylnagranagh hill, knowing from the stories that the fairies were especially active on Wednesdays, which made that a particularly favorable day to encounter the fairies and thus more dangerous to be there.[25] What happened that afternoon is uncertain, but it is known that when Bridget returned home, she was changed. She was cold, she was ill, she was distant. She seemed out of sorts, she looked unlike herself, and she behaved strangely. Of all her trips to Kylnagranagh, this one had grave consequences. Most disturbing, she could not remember how she got from the fort above Scanlon's field to Skehan's gate on the low road.[26]

The sudden onset of illness alerted Michael Cleary to the possibility that his wife had been taken by the fairies. All his life he had been confronted by the family story that his mother had gone off with the fairies for a few days, and now he had come to believe within the last three months that on two prior occasions, the fairies may have tried to abduct his wife but had failed. Now with this third and final episode, it appeared that his wife's spirit had, indeed, been taken. If so, her spirit had been transported to the Otherworld, leaving a clever old fairy "hag" or "witch" in her body for him to cope with. He had warned her time and again to stay away from the fort, but she was a headstrong woman. Likewise, Michael Cleary was a possessive husband, who, despite his wife's stubborn belligerence, fought instinctively for what he believed was rightfully his. To his way of thinking, Bridget belonged to him, and he would rather be damned in hell than allow any other mortal or nonmortal man to possess her.

But even though Cleary believed his wife was taken, folk stories taught that wives abducted by the fairies could be rescued. The taking of a mortal spirit was so serious that "the people" allowed a probationary period of roughly nine days during which the mortal could return, provided that the family exercised all due effort, *and the abducted spirit wished to return.* The family had a nine-day window of opportunity to reverse the effects of abduction, but even if they moved heaven and hell within the prescribed time, the spirit would not return if it chose not to.

Beliefs regarding the spiritual power of the number three and its compound number nine were universal in Celtic and pre-Celtic spiritual systems. The Tuatha de Dannan divided themselves into three classes, *tuathach, dé,* and *dàn,* roughly translated to mean chiefs, artisans, and laborers. In modern times, the Irish Republican Brotherhood replicated this tripartite pattern by organizing units into groups of nine. One of the oldest deities incorporated into the Celtic tradition was Cailleach, or the Old One, variously named the Gray or Blue Hage, the Gyre Carlin, Black Annis, and the Hage of Beare. The Old One possessed vast and ancient knowledge and was said to control the weather and the formation of mountains. Symbols of her power were the "nine loosed tresses" on her head which linked her with the ninefold sisterhood of the cauldron. These nine were guardians of the great cauldron of birth and rebirth and controlled the deadly ninefold cure. It was said that a married woman without children should eat a bite of cake containing special ingredients every night for nine nights before bed. If she told anyone what she was doing, or if anyone saw her, the charm would not work. All the children conceived in this way would be girls.[27]

One of the oldest tales in Irish mythology tells of the time when the ninefold curse was cast upon the men of Ulster by the goddess Macha, who had been forced to run a race against the king's horses while she was pregnant. Though she outran his fastest ponies, the ordeal sent Macha into labor, whereupon she cried out that any man who heard her screams would suffer the pains of birth for five days and four nights. The men of King

Ulaid were thus cursed and their descendants for nine generations thereafter. The so-called curse of Macha—nine half days for nine generations—became known as the noinend, or "novena," of the Ulstermen. It was because of this curse that Fionn MacCuill, or Cuchulainn, later came to defend the Ulstermen, since he was not of Ulster and was, therefore, not affected by the curse of Macha.[28]

The number nine also delineated the boundary between the known and the unknown. Things known fell within the numbers one through nine, but everything beyond nine fell within the realm of the unknown. To sail "beyond the ninth wave" was to voyage beyond the known world into another realm physically and spiritually removed from the revealed, physical world of mortality. A day measured space as well as time, so to move beyond the ninth day signified a movement into another spatial realm. If a changeling was not driven off in nine days, the mortal spirit would pass beyond the ninth wave into the Otherworld, and once there, would likely never return.[29]

According to Mary Kennedy's account, Bridget was taken on Wednesday, March 6, and so, on Thursday, March 7, the nine-day countdown started. On Thursday, day one, a fever appeared and Bridget took to her bed. On day two, Friday, the fever rose and congestion developed. During days three and four, Bridget's headaches grew worse. The family watched her physical symptoms for clues as to the type of malady she suffered and its appropriate cure. Mary Kennedy also reported that Bridget cried out, "If I had my mother, I would not be this way," seeming to allude to her own mother's reputation as a fairy healer. It was said that fairy healers obtained their powers from the fairies themselves, often following their own abductions, during which they learned the ways of the "good people" before being sent back to the mortal world. Not only was Bridget's own mother thought to be a healer, so was Michael's.

Lady Augusta Wilde, the celebrated collector of Irish folklore and mother of playwright Oscar Wilde, recorded a story that described the early stages of a fairy-induced ailment. A certain family feared that one among them had been stricken by a fairy disease, so they called in a fairy doctor to determine the cause of the illness. The doctor took three rods of witch hazel, each three inches long and each marked to indicate maladies of the three most common types of fairy illnesses—those inflicted by a stroke or "fit of trembling," by the wind or "blast," or by casting the evil eye upon the victim. With the three rods before him, the doctor faced the sun and prayed, then placed each of the three rods into the fire. When the rods were burned black, the doctor drew a circle on the floor with the end of one stick, then placed a bowl of pure water within the circle. With more prayers and incantations, he then placed the three burned sticks in the bowl of water and watched to see which one sank first. The doctor then ground up the appropriate rod into a fine powder and placed it in a bottle filled with pure water from the bowl. He uttered more prayers and incantations, then sent the potion home with instructions that it be drunk before midnight, in silence, and alone. The bottle was never to touch the ground and the person carrying it must speak not a word nor look around until he reached home. Finally, the remaining two sticks were buried in the earth in a place known only to the doctor.[30]

In the early days of Bridget's illness, the family undoubtedly utilized their own stock of medicines, cures, and homemade remedies to heal the stricken woman. Friends and neighbors began to stream in and out of the cottage to check on Bridget's condition and offer their own advice. But when nothing appeared to relieve the outward symptoms of the illness, Michael Cleary began thinking of others who might help to rid Bridget of her mysterious illness.

On Saturday, March 9, the third day of the fairy trial, Michael sent his father-in-law, Patrick Boland, off to Fethard to begin what would become a frustrating campaign to get medical attention from the doctor employed by the Cashel Guardians, Dr. William Crean. Under provisions of the Medical Charities Act of 1851, it was Dr. Crean's responsibility to attend to any sick person in his district either at the dispensary in Fethard, or if the patient was too ill to travel, at the patient's home. Applicants seeking medical services could obtain a black ticket for the dispensary, or a red ticket for a house call, either from the dispensary or from any duly elected guardian in the district. Patrick Boland probably obtained a red ticket from Edmond Cummins, a Guardian living in Brook Hill, then presented it at the dispensary in Fethard, requesting that Dr. Crean attend to his daughter. Upon learning that the doctor was unavailable, Boland "noticed" the doctor, meaning he left a notice by posting a red dispensary ticket requesting that the doctor come immediately.[31]

While Patrick Boland journeyed to Fethard in search of a doctor, a laborer hired by the Clearys came to the cottage to plow the garden in preparation for the spring planting. Apparently on this occasion, Bridget felt well enough to go outdoors, even though the weather was cold and wet, to direct the work. But later that afternoon, she was inside and feeling even worse. She complained of a terrible ache in her head, and retreated to her place by the fire, but could not be warmed.

Saturday evening and all day Sunday, the family waited for the arrival of Dr. Crean, still hoping that he could provide modern medicine to supplement their herbal remedies. As they waited, they continued to watch for signs of a fairy-induced ailment. Throughout the day on Monday, March 11, the family waited for the doctor, their concern mounting as the hours passed, and still

Dr. Crean did not arrive. By early afternoon Michael Cleary was clearly frustrated and set off to Fethard himself to file another dispensary ticket requesting the doctor's immediate attention. According to a petition filed from prison ten years later, Cleary stated: "Petitionar went a 2 o'clock the next day [Monday] and had to return without him leaving Word to have him follow if he could be found as quick as possible."[32]

On Tuesday, March 12, day six of the ordeal, there was still no sign of the doctor.

On the seventh day, Wednesday, March 13, Michael Cleary took matters into his own hands. At five A.M. Cleary was out the door and on his way to Fethard to lodge an official complaint against Dr. Crean. To do this, he walked four miles to the home of Guardian Cummins just outside of Fethard. Instead of a dispensary ticket, however, Michael obtained from Cummins a written order demanding immediate attention be paid to the tickets filed first by Patrick Boland on Saturday, and again by Cleary on Monday. Cummins, embarrassed and also angered by Dr. Crean's malfeasance, promised Cleary that "you will have a Doctor in 2 hours at your house." If Dr. Crean could not or would not fulfill the order, Cummins pledged to telegraph Clonmel and request a doctor "even if it cost £20."[33] With Cummins's assurance and "Wrighting" order in hand, Cleary proceeded directly to Dr. Crean's home to serve the order, but the doctor was not at home even though Cleary arrived a little after seven A.M.

While Michael was away from home filing his complaint on Wednesday morning, Dr. Crean finally made his belated house call in Ballyvadlea. The doctor examined Bridget Cleary and determined that she suffered from "nervous excitement and slight bronchitis," neither of which was life-threatening. He admitted that the patient appeared anxious and uncomfortable, but stated that he had no "anxiety" whatsoever about her condition. He determined that the illness could be adequately treated with medication and without the need for further visitations from him.[34] Dr. Crean left instructions that Bridget was to take the medication over the next several days, then left, with no explanation why it took him four days to respond to the family's repeated calls for immediate assistance. Dr. Crean later told the court that he attended Bridget for eight or nine years prior to her illness and that she was "perfectly healthy bodied" and well-nourished, although she appeared to be an awfully nervous and irritable sort of woman, who was likely to suffer from chronic dyspepsia.[35]

Dr. Crean's tardy response and his seeming nonchalance toward her illness did little to comfort the family. While Cleary was frantically searching for the doctor early Wednesday morning, Pat Boland brought news to the Kennedy cottage that Bridget's condition was deteriorating. He told his sister, Mary Kennedy, that Bridget was "very bad . . . with a fairie in her head." So Mary went to the cottage to see for herself. According to Mary Kennedy, she entered Bridget's room and "asked her what way was she." Bridget replied that she was "very bad," that she had a pain in her head and in her temples, adding that she feared her husband was "making a fairy of me now and in Everyway." When her aunt replied, "Don't mind him," Bridget insisted the matter was serious, and that this was not the first incident. "Oh, he thought to burn me about three months ago," she replied to her aunt.

Bridget continued to insist that her husband was trying to make a fairy of her, but each time she made this charge to her aunt, Mary Kennedy, would reply: "Don't mind him. It will be nothing with the help of God bye and bye." Kennedy made this reply each time Bridget made the same charge to others who visited her.[36] Either her aunt did not think Michael would not go to extreme lengths, or she too believed that Bridget was a changeling and was only humoring the fairy within her stricken niece. As it turned out, Mary Kennedy was not the only family member or neighbor harboring fairy beliefs. In her illiterate, incoherent way, she simply reported on them more honestly than others called as witnesses by Wansbrough. That Wednesday morning Mary tried to reassure her niece, and the talk turned to laundry. Bridget indicated that she had "a little to wash," but her aunt begged off, claiming that she was "not able"; instead, she went to fetch Johanna Burke. "I will go up for Hanney and she will wash," Mary Kennedy told her niece.[37]

Having been fetched by her mother, Johanna Burke probably arrived at the Cleary cottage just as Dr. Crean was leaving. She did not report having spoken to him about why he had delayed making a house call for so long, but Bridget Cleary apparently did. According to Burke, Bridget confronted Dr. Crean directly, asking "why he had not come when he was sent for."[38] No doubt Dr. Crean was not accustomed to receiving an affront of this type, especially when delivered by a peasant woman. His irritation with the couple increased when he returned home and learned that Michael Cleary had signed a formal complaint against him with the Guardians. Michael was still waiting at Dr. Crean's home when the doctor returned. Ten years later Michael described his encounter with the medical officer for the Fethard Dispensary District as he remembered it:

> [W]hen [Crean] came back his wife was with him and he was drunk
> he shouted at me that he attend my wife for he [knew] Petitionar
> [Cleary] was very vext to him for the way he was traited with regard
> to his wife. he told petitionar that his wife was very weak and ner-
> vous he proscribed medson and ordered wine which Petitionar

brought home with him and he told Petitionar to tell Edmond
Cummins that was afther attending his wife and also to return the
Wrighting that he got from him Petitionar did as he was desired re-
turned the Writing to Edmond Cummins and went home.[39]

But before returning home, we believe that Michael Cleary had
other errands to do.

It was still relatively early in the morning when Michael left
Dr. Crean's home, perhaps around ten A.M. This allowed Michael
enough time to search out an unnamed woman in Fethard, a fairy
doctor, who provided him with a remedy for fairy-induced illness.
The cure was meant to be taken after other, more benign measures failed. It was called the "Seven Sisters Kill or Cure," and its
name bespoke its mission—it would either cure or kill. It was already the seventh day: Only two more days and the fairies would
have Bridget forever.

In light of Dr. Crean's behavior, it is little wonder that Michael
Cleary turned to a fairy doctor for help. For good reason, the
fairy doctor was still held in a position of esteem among the country and urban poor. The practitioners of these ancient arts healed
ordinary physical illnesses but also afflictions of the spirit that
moderns would refer to as "mental disease." The "old Irishry" relied upon the fairy doctors, and medical doctors resented the
competition, as did civil and church authorities, who viewed the
ancient healing arts as an impediment to the wonders of modern
science and the unchallenged supremacy of Church sacraments.

The fairy doctor prepared salves, balms, and tinctures for treat-
ing common physical maladies such as strains, bruises, fevers, and
even set broken bones. One such affliction was the "fairy dart," a
painful inflammation of the joints, usually in the hands and feet.
To remove the dart, healers used an ointment made from herbs

and unsalted butter that acted both as counter-irritants and pain relievers. In addition, the fairy doctor boiled up a bitter brew made from the bark of the sally rod. Often the ointment and potion were administered with an elaborate ritual of prayers and incantations intended to draw the offending dart out of the victim's body. If successful, the dart was kept as a trophy and proudly exhibited to visitors.[40]

This healing knowledge passed from generation to generation, and often it was said that the earliest healers were ancestors who acquired the restorative arts directly from the fairies or were changelings themselves living among the mortals. This was the case with the famous healer named Morough O'Lee, who lived in the Connemara region, north of Galway. It was said that Morough fell asleep in a fairy fort, and when he awoke, he found himself in Tír na nÓg, the Land of Eternal Youth. Rather than return, Morough elected to stay among the fairies, and remained there a year studying their medical arts. When at last he set out to return home, he was given a book that contained the cures for all diseases, but was told not to open the book, nor attempt to use the knowledge for seven years. After finding his way back from Tír na nÓg, Morough did as the good people instructed and kept the book closed, nor did he attempt to practice the healing arts. After three years had passed, however, a severe epidemic spread through the country and his friends implored Morough to open the book. This he did reluctantly, but because he had not waited the full seven years, he found that he was unable to work all the cures.[41]

In another instance, a man called Ighne from Donegal went off to the mountains one winter day in search of his pony. High and low he climbed, all around the mountain, but nowhere was the pony to be found. At last, the poor man grew so tired that he sat beside a stream and fell asleep. Around midnight, he half awoke and heard people talking in great excitement.

"What are we to do with him?" someone asked.

"Let's kill him!" others responded.

Then one spoke up and declared with authority that none of the fairy host would harm the man, since he and all his people for generations had been good to the fairies. "Nobody of our tribe will be allowed to strike a single blow on his hide," the leader announced.

"Then what should be done to one who comes here among us on the hill at a time when mortals should be at home?" they asked.

"Let us give him a very powerful cure and there will not be a doctor in the country equal to him at curing people," the leader suggested.

Thinking this a good plan, the fairies gathered around Ighne and taught him all about curing diseases. From that very night until the day he died, Ighne spent all his time curing people, even when regular doctors had failed. He was kept so busy fulfilling his new healing duties that he had no time to wander about the fairy fort, especially at times when mortals ought not to be loitering there. Thus all were satisfied—the fairies had their privacy while mortals benefited from Ighne's skill.[42]

Having obtained the Seven Sisters Cure, Michael Cleary left Fethard, but we surmise that, rather than returning home along the usual route via Cloneen, he took the somewhat longer route through Drangan. His purpose was to call at the church and ask for a priest to come to the cottage to help in casting out the changeling spirit. This he planned to do in conjunction with the Seven Sisters Cure. The fairy doctor's potion represented a powerful remedy against spirits, as did the presence of a priest.

Michael reasoned that if he could marshal both forces against the fairy, both would be the stronger. And if Dr. Crean's medicine was thrown in, so much the better. Father Ryan stated that he received the call at about one in the afternoon. He did not say specifically who sent the message, but it was most likely Michael Cleary, returning from Fethard.

Unlike Dr. Crean, Father Ryan responded in a relatively timely manner, arriving by horse at the Cleary cottage about 3:30 P.M., ahead of Michael who had one other errand to attend to. When the priest arrived, Bridget Cleary was there with Johanna Burke, who apparently was still washing clothes or simply visiting with her cousin. Father Ryan was shown into the bedroom where he spoke with Bridget for over twenty minutes, in a conversation he described as "coherent and intelligent," even though she also appeared to be in a very nervous state and possibly hysterical. Although he, like Dr. Crean, did not consider her seriously ill, he thought that her behavior might indicate the onset of "brain fever," a commonly used term to refer to various forms of encephalitis, inflammation of the brain lining. Based upon this determination, Father Ryan decided to administer the last rites of the Church. In doing so, he unthinkingly prepared her for her death from something other than brain fever.

In Father Ryan's defense, it was not unusual, given the high mortality rates in Ireland, for a priest to confer the sacrament of Extreme Unction to a person who was not dangerously ill. In this case, however, the Clearys were close neighbors and Father Ryan undoubtedly heard rumors that Bridget had been taken by the fairies. Furthermore, he should have known the kinds of remedies that would be used to remove the changeling. Whether he realized it or not, Father Ryan administered last rites in the final trimester of the ordeal, shortly before Michael would begin to use deadly force against the changeling. Father Ryan consigned Bridget's soul to heaven, but Michael Cleary would put her through hell.

The implication of Father Ryan's action was not lost on Michael Cleary. Around four P.M., Ryan was just leaving the cottage when Michael returned via Drangan from his eleven-hour journey to Fethard. Michael stated that he returned home to learn that his wife was "afther being prepaired for death by a Priest." The two men conversed. According to Michael, Father Ryan told him that he had prepared his wife for death, that she was very weak. He also asked if Dr. Crean was drunk when he examined Bridget, and Cleary told him that he was. Ryan asked to see the medicine prescribed by the doctor, and upon looking at it, told Cleary that he did not approve of the medicine because "the doctor was never sober."[43] Father Ryan later gave contradictory testimony, stating that he instructed Michael to see that Bridget took the doctor's medicine.

After Father Ryan's departure, Michael Cleary and Johanna Burke were alone in the cottage with Bridget. Shortly John Dunne arrived. Likely he had also been summoned to the cottage by Michael, which explains why Ryan arrived in Ballyvadlea before him. The purpose of his visit was to help Michael administer the Seven Sisters Kill or Cure. This ordeal was witnessed by Johanna Burke, and it is owing to a much later deposition of hers that detailed knowledge of the ordeal exists. Information about the Wednesday ritual never surfaced at the magisterial inquiry; rather this part of the story emerged nearly two months later, when Burke unexpectedly amended her second March deposition in a sworn statement made before the chief magistrate, Colonel Evanson. Burke voluntarily disclosed what really happened on the afternoon following Dr. Crean's visit in an obvious attempt to diminish the culpability of her mother and brothers. Thus, this May 21 document is not above suspicion, but is detailed enough to be at least partly credible.

In this belated deposition, which was also never made public at the trial later in July, Burke recounted that after the visit of Dr. Crean, Michael Cleary sent for Mary Kennedy, asking her to come to the cottage to wash up some bedclothes. This was an indication that the men, perhaps with Mary Kennedy's help, were already administering various herbal cures. These were untidy affairs that left bed clothing and bed coverings soiled. Mary was unable to go herself, so sent Johanna Burke in her place. When she entered the cottage, Michael Cleary and John Dunne were in the bedroom with Bridget. Burke stayed in the kitchen, from where she could see Cleary and Dunne feeding Bridget some herbs on a spoon. Bridget "at first took the herbs off a spoon and asked if they would cure her. She took the herbs freely then." But after a while she would not swallow any more herbs, complaining they were "too bitter."[44]

The men threatened her with physical harm, but Bridget refused to take more of the herbal medicine. Fearing the men would soon apply force to their threats, Burke offered to put the herbs in some milk so as to make them more palatable, whereupon Dunne contemptuously ordered her out, telling her, "Go sit down like a good girl and go about your business [of laundering]; you know nothing about this work." As if quickly regretting his harsh dismissal, he attempted to soothe her, explaining that the herbs represented the Seven Sisters Kill or Cure for changelings. Burke left the room and the men continued to discuss the situation, speculating about why Bridget resisted taking the cure and what could be done about it. At one point in this May deposition, Burke said that she heard Dunne refer to the herbs, saying, "But I am afraid she's left too long . . . they had a right to be given to her on the fifth day."

The two men concluded that Bridget would have to be forced to take the herbs, especially in view of the fact that it was already the seventh day. They then began to force the liquid down Bridget's throat—Dunne holding her by the neck while Cleary pushed the spoon into her mouth. Twice she took the potion, then on the crucial third and final administration, she refused. The men conferred again and decided that she refused to swallow the third dose of the potion because the spirit refused to be driven off. Since it appeared that the herbs alone were ineffective, the two men decided to proceed to the next stage of the ritual or fairy trial.

The story of Rickard the Rake suggested the nature of the ordeal in store for the fairy spirit in possession of Bridget's body. Rickard was a bagpiper who spent far too much time in dance houses and places of ill repute, and it was not long before the fairies had hold of him and no potion could force them to let him loose. So the family called in a fairyman who had knowledge of these things. He came to the house, along with a fairywoman from the next townland, and the two of them stood before the changeling and staged a discussion of their enthusiastically sadistic plans for exorcism. The two of them were fairly shouting to be sure the spirit heard:

She: What do you advise we do with the "anointed" *sheeoge* [fairy]?
He: We'll begin easy. We'll take his neck and crop and hold his head under the water in the turnhold till we'll drive the divel out of him.
She: That'ud be a great deal too easy a punishment for the thief. We'll heat the shovel red-hot, put it under his currabingo [haunches], and land him out in the dung-lough [dungheap].

He : Ah, and I'll put the tongs in the fire till the claws are as hot as the divel, and won't I hould his nasty crass nose between them till he'll know the difference between fiery faces [hardworkers] and a latchycock [ne'er-do-well].

She: . . . I'll go and bring my liquor, drawn from the leaves of the *lussmore* [foxglove, an herb that contains the heart drug digitalis], and if he was a sheeoge forty times, it will put the inside of him into such a state that he'd give the world if he could die.

He: Very well, let's begin. I'll bring my red-hot tongs from the kitchen fire, and you your little bottle of lussmore water. Don't any of yez go in, neighbors, till we have them ingredients ready.

And when the fairy heard what was in store, he departed out the door in a flash, and Rickard the Rake recovered, though he stayed far from the fairy tents thereafter.[45]

As indicated in Rickard the Rake's ordeal, fire applied in conjunction with herbs was the final and most efficacious cure for possession. This often fatal remedy was carried out only in the final days of the fairy trial. Fire was commonly used as a cure, more often than authorities wished to admit. If a child was weak and sickly, he or she was placed on a shovel before the fire, for if an alien spirit possessed the child, it would fly up the chimney and disappear at the first touch by the flames. All too often the poor baby was dreadfully burned and died in great pain. The baby might cry pitifully, but the cries were treated with seeming indifference, for they were not the baby's cries at all, but the shrieks of the possessing fairy. In any case, after the ninth day of possession, the child would be forever lost to the desperate parent. So they had nothing to lose by placing their baby over the flames.[46]

When Bridget refused the third and final course of the Seven Sisters potion, Michael Cleary and John Dunne felt obliged to use fire to drive away the changeling. Burke stated that initially she was "hunted" out of the bedroom by the two men, and the door was shut behind her. In a few minutes Dunne emerged from the room and went to the fireplace. On the open fire, he heated an iron poker until it glowed. Dunne then took the reddened poker and returned to the bedroom. Burke followed him in. Michael Cleary was standing over Bridget with a spoonful of the Seven Sisters potion, which Bridget again refused to swallow. Cleary ordered Dunne to go back to the kitchen and fetch a different spoon. With the reddened poker still in his hand, Dunne did as Cleary asked, returning shortly. At this juncture, the men noticed that Johanna Burke was standing in the corner of the bedroom, and they again ordered her out, demanding that she leave them be and go about her business. From outside the room, Burke heard struggling, then heard Cleary say to his wife, "Is it down? Is it down?" She made some noise as if moaning, then Burke heard Dunne threatening, "Swallow it or I'll put the poker down your throat."

Bridget's refusal to ingest the potion, even when threatened with a red-hot poker, confirmed Michael's suspicions that the Sevens Sisters Cure was ineffective in driving off the changeling or, worse, that the changeling had been driven off for a time, but Bridget's spirit had not returned to her body. Cures were designed to drive away the alien spirit, but even the best of them could do nothing to draw back the mortal spirit if that spirit chose not to return. If the Seven Sisters Cure did work, Michael Cleary faced the sobering, humiliating possibility that Bridget preferred to stay in the Otherworld. This thought made him even more determined to get his wife back.

While Cleary and Dunne retired to the kitchen for a well-earned pint of stout, Johanna Burke was allowed back in the bedroom, where she found Bridget lying in bed, badly frightened.

Finishing his pint, Dunne left for home. Shortly thereafter, Burke finished laundering the bedclothes; then she left as well, returning to her mother's cottage on the low road. Mary Kennedy came later and prepared chicken soup, which Bridget had requested and consumed.

Ganey Across the Mountain

On Thursday, March 14, the eighth day of the trial, the weather was clear and fair in the region around Slievenamon, making it a good day for traveling. Michael Cleary was out for the second day in a row, up early preparing for a journey that would take him across the Anner River valley to the northern flank of the mountain and the village of Kylatlea, home of Denis Ganey, the most renowned fairy doctor in the district. For generations the Ganey family had practiced fairy doctoring in the area around Slievenamon. Two days and one night remained before Bridget's fate would be resolved, one way or the other. Michael Cleary was determined to use all remedies.

Before embarking on the journey to Kylatlea, Michael called for Mary Kennedy to look after Bridget, who showed no improvement from the day before. Cleary told Mary that he would be gone most of the day. Shortly after he departed, Mary walked up to the Cleary cottage, where she spent the day cooking and cleaning.

Michael's journey to Kylatlea led him south along the low road to Cloneen, and from there, east along the main road to Mullinahone, south again across the Anner River and up the gradual ascent along the northern flank of Slievenamon to Gurtnapisha, or Peafield, the spot where the fabled fairy women of Peafield were believed to weave their linen cloth. Denis Ganey lived with his wife and family in a traditional thatched-roof cottage along a nar-

row, winding road, not far from the famous battlefield of Car-
rignaclear, where thousands of United Irishmen died in the
aborted uprising of 1798.

Ganey was a tenant farmer who raised cows along the lush,
northern slope of the mountain, but his claim to fame came from
his skills as a fairy doctor. His reputation extended south to Kilcash and Ballypatrick, and north across the Anner river valley
from Fethard to Mullinahone. Anyone who needed a broken bone
set or an inflammation eased went to Ganey before seeing a
proper medical doctor, especially if it was relief they were seeking. Denis Ganey was known for his inventive remedies, designed
expressly for each case individually.

Ganey devised one of his legendary cures for a man who came
to him after suffering paralysis. Everywhere the man had gone
seeking help, but none, including every Guardian medical doctor
in the county, could restore the man to health. In desperation, he
sought out Ganey, who took one look at him and instantly knew
what was wrong. To effect a cure, Ganey built a large vat in a far
corner of the field and into the vat he heaped up piles of straw,
pig slop, cow manure, and every kind of stinking, rotting material
he could find until the vat was filled to the brim. He allowed the
entire concoction to set in the sun several days until properly
ripened, then instructed the man to strip down and climb inside.
He was not just to put in a toe or bathe the afflicted areas. Rather
he was to sink right down into the muck until the vapors curled
his nose hairs. The man naturally protested, but Ganey insisted
that if he wanted to be cured, down into the vat he must go. Now
the man had already suffered enough and realized he had nothing
to fear from the stinking vat, so he did as Ganey instructed.
When the man emerged, his affliction was gone and he was never
more bothered again, so noxious had been the cure.[47]

In addition to setting bones and curing rare afflictions, Denis Ganey was an authority on fairy-induced ailments and fairy abductions. If there was one in the region "out the mountain" with powers to drive off a changeling, it was Denis Ganey. From Cloneen, it was a good eight miles to Kylatlea and back—a day's journey for a man on foot. Late in the afternoon, Michael Cleary returned from his pilgrimage, tired and a bit footsore, but pleased to have in his possession Ganey's "nine-in-one cure," supplied with the fairy doctor's personal assurances that no more powerful cure could be had. Although a fairy doctor did not charge clients for prayers and incantations, he or she could expect remuneration for herbal remedies. Traditionally clients were obliged to pay in silver.

Despite the time and expense involved in obtaining Ganey's potion, Michael Cleary returned home feeling confident the "nine-in-one cure" would prove effective. However, as he approached the cottage, he heard distressing the news that his father had died in Killenaule that day. This report only strengthened his conviction that his wife was possessed, since it was believed that deaths of other mortals sometimes accompanied fairy abductions to distract bereaved relatives. Michael therefore determined not to express any grief. The timing of his father's death was doubly suspicious to Michael since it came on the eighth day of the trial, just as he was about to administer Ganey's cure. If the fairies had taken Michael's wife and were intent on preventing him from recapturing her spirit, what event could have been more effectively planned, more superbly timed, than the death of his father? This coincidence only hardened Cleary's determination to get his wife back, no matter what the cost.

Upon learning of his father's death, Michael Cleary summoned a neighbor woman, Mary Smith, and asked her to fetch John

Dunne. Shortly thereafter, Dunne arrived, at which time Cleary told him that he, Cleary, wanted him there as he "could not depend on the lot that was about him," referring to his in-laws. By this time, news had spread around the townland of Ballyvadlea that Cleary had received a new cure from Ganey that contained "herbs that there is nine cures in." It was more potent and bitter than the Seven Sisters Cure from Fethard, so he needed help keeping Bridget down while administering it. "It'll be very hard to make her take this," Cleary told Dunne, so "you must give me assistance with it." Feeling confident that Ganey's "nine-in-one" cure would work, Cleary reassured Dunne that once they got the potion down her, "she'll be cured then."[48]

Before attempting to administer Ganey's herbs, Cleary and Dunne sat down for a stout. Young William Ahearn came by, and the three of them each drank another pint. They talked awhile longer, then Ahearn expressed a desire to go home and Dunne agreed to accompany him. Cleary protested that Dunne "could not go home as yet that he [Cleary] wanted to give it to her again and that himself [Cleary] wanted another stout."[49] A little after eight P.M., James and Patrick Kennedy arrived, as Cleary and Dunne were finishing their third pint. Thus fortified, Cleary and Dunne went to work with James and Patrick assisting. William Ahearn held the candle as the four other men went into the bedroom where Bridget lay. Before commencing this latest round of the pagan cure, Michael Cleary locked the front door and shuttered the windows.

The deposition of Mary Kennedy further clarifies the events of that Thursday night. After leaving the Clearys, she returned home where she waited for her son, Michael, to arrive with his weekly wages of nine shillings. He, too, knew of the death of the elder Cleary and asked upon his return home when his brothers planned to leave for the wake; she told him they were already with Cleary. Michael Kennedy gathered his things for the trip to Killenaule, then he and his mother walked back to the Clearys to see what plans were being made for attending the funeral and wake of Michael's father. As the Kennedys and Pat Boland discussed the matter, Michael Cleary suddenly asked Boland to attend in his stead, announcing that he would not be going with them because "he did not care a Devil about him [his father], whether he was dead or alive," and because he had "a little bit of business" to do at home. Apparently this announcement surprised everyone. Mary Kennedy asked, "What have you to do, says I to him, Mike?" Michael replied that they would all see "bye and bye."[50]

Sometime between eight and nine o'clock, after the Kennedys and Pat Boland arrived, Johanna Burke, along with her daughter, Katie, started toward the Cleary cottage, bringing with her a supply of new milk, which was a delicacy in Ireland because it was believed to be a powerful purifying agent. As Burke approached, she met the caretaker of the Lindsay property, William Simpson and his wife, Minnie, who were also on their way to the Clearys. They walked a short way together and, arriving at the home, heard shouts from inside. The three of them went to a shuttered window and heard a man shouting repeatedly, "Take it you witch!" They waited about five minutes before the door opened, whereupon they entered the darkened cottage.

Inside, with windows shuttered and fire low, men were crammed into the dark, tiny, six-by-eight bedroom surrounding Bridget, who was lying on the bed. William Ahearn, wedged in the corner, standing straight as a poker, held the candle. John Dunne sat on the bed, holding Bridget roughly by the hair; Patrick Kennedy pinned one shoulder down and James Kennedy the other. William Kennedy sprawled across her feet at the bottom of the bed. Mary Kennedy asked Michael what he was doing by forcing Bridget to drink down "some green things with a little milk." Michael told everyone "wait until you see what I'll put out the door," Mary answered, "What will you put out the door, says I to him, and what's in it [the liquid]," and he replied, "Oh I haven't Bridgey here, says he to me, for this six weeks." Then Michael said to his wife, "Swallow it, you devil."

Having pinned her down, Michael Cleary approached Bridget with the spoon containing the herbs and milk. "Take this, you old bitch," he shouted, repeating the phrase twice again. Bridget struggled; she complained the herbs were too bitter, that she would not swallow them, which only made Michael more determined to see that she did. He ordered his father-in-law to pry her mouth open. Holding the spoon with one hand, the other hand underneath to catch any material that might spill out, Michael inserted the potion into her mouth, then held his hand tightly over her lips to ensure she did not spit it out. In all it took six men to force the liquid into her, suggesting she had a good bit of strength for a woman who had been ill for over a week and who just the day before had received last rites of the Church.

When satisfied that the herbs had gone down, Michael Cleary repeated three times the following:

In the name of the Father, Son and Holy Ghost, are you Bridget, the wife of Michael Cleary?

After each question he demanded an answer. The question was posed three times because it was generally believed that the repetition of threes strengthened the power of the charm.

The invocation of Christian deity, the triune God, was also believed to be a powerful charm against evil spirits. The efficacy of its utterance was recorded by Lady Wilde, who, along with her husband, Sir William Wilde, witnessed the application of a "very ancient and potent charm" used to great effect in a case of suspected fairy stroke. In this ritual, the fairy doctor laid out three rows of salt on a table in three lines, three equal measures in each row. The practitioner encircled the rows of salt with his arms, then leaned over them, repeating the Lord's Prayer three times over each row, or nine times in all. Then he placed the hand of the victim over the rows of salt and repeated the following: "By the power of the Father and of the Son, and of the Holy Spirit, let this disease disappear, and the spell of the evil spirits be broken. I adjure, I command you to leave this man (naming him). In the name of God I pray. In the name of Christ I adjure. In the name of the Spirit of God I command and compel you to go back and leave this man free. Amen. Amen."[51]

It is not known whether Bridget failed to answer the questions in the proper order or resisted answering at all, but at this point Michael threw "a certain liquid" on her face and chest. Newspaper accounts euphemistically identified the liquid in this way so as to avoid saying what it was: urine. It was believed that urine was also a purifying agent like new milk and salt water. Hen's dung was another agent used to cast out fairies, as in the case of a certain woman who died shortly after having given birth to a child. Her husband, who was away at the time, was informed by a fairy that his wife was not dead, but had been taken, and if he acted quickly he might get her back. The man rushed home and prepared to take action. Late that night, as the man sat alone with his wife's body, the wife's spirit body came in through the door, which the husband had intentionally left open, and crept softly to the cradle where her child lay sleeping. As she peered into the cradle, the husband cast a charm made of hen's dung upon her, then held her fast, shouting for the neighbors to assist him. As they struggled, the wife's spirit returned to her mortal body. Shortly she revived and went on to live a long life.[52]

The repetition of each question three times in conjunction with herbs and urine provided the charm a threefold potency. This ritual was then repeated a second time, then a third. If the all-important third repetition was not completed, then the whole process had to begin again. This exhausting ritual continued throughout the evening because either Bridget would not swallow the potion or she would not answer the questions to everyone's satisfaction. Sometimes she would respond once, sometimes even twice, but she either resisted outright or only pretended to comply on the third repetition, thus nullifying her first two responses.

After over three hours of this, just before midnight, "the witching hour," John Dunne called a halt to the proceedings. This was doing no good, he declared. If they wished the changeling out, the threat of fire was the only answer. Dunne ordered the Kennedys to "take her and put her over the fire, and then she'll answer or die." The men obediently lifted Bridget from the bed and placed her on the floor beside the fireplace. Dunne held her by the throat; the Kennedys grasped her feet and shoulders; Cleary followed them with a saucepan of herbs and milk. At this point, according to Burke, Bridget neither cried out, nor appeared to be in pain. Burke, however, noticed that Bridget's demeanor changed when the men carried her to the fireplace. She looked "wild," even "deranged," and before being put over the fire, she cried out, "Are you going to make a herring of me—give me a chance."

This reference to the herring may have been to the Christian fish symbol associated with Christ's sacrifice of himself. Or it could have meant that she feared being cooked like a herring. More probably, she meant the phrase to mean, to make a woman look rough or seem coarse like a fishwife.[53] Bridget took pride in her appearance, particularly the clothes she made for herself, and was well spoken—quite the opposite of a fishwife.

Alternately, Bridget may have used the word "hare" and been misunderstood by Burke. In pagan lore, witches often transformed themselves into hares to get milk from cows. In almost every county in Ireland, a version of the tale of the hare, hunted and wounded by the hunters' dogs, is told. To escape its pursuers, the hare jumps into a cottage beside a bog, and when the hunters enter, they find an old hag smoking a clay pipe called a dudeen by the fire. When examined, the hag bears a wound on the thigh identical to that inflicted upon the hare. Thus arose the popular adage, "I'll make a hare of you," which refers to the belief that hares were occasionally bewitched. To make a "hare out of a person" could also mean to make a fool of him or her. Regardless of what Bridget's question signified exactly, the utterance of either the word "herring" or "hare" meant that she knew what Michael would do to her next.[54]

Bridget was justified in her fear. While the men held her near the fire, Cleary brandished the poker to force her to swallow the herbs. When she refused, the men began to shove her into the fireplace. For a time her father held her above the grate but soon began to lower her on it when asking more questions. Her position was awkward. The fireplace was no more than four feet by four feet and inset into the wall. Inside the firebox was a small grate about a foot square that sat a foot off the ground. In order to fit her into the opening, Bridget had to be literally "shoveled" over the grate in a fetal position, bent over from the waist on her side, her legs partially projected out of the fireplace. Lodged on the grate, she called to Burke, "Oh Han, Han," but at no time did she struggle or try to escape. According the Burke, there was a low fire burning in the fireplace, large enough to heat the iron grill but not hot enough to boil water.

With Bridget propped partially inside the fireplace, the men performed the ritual exorcism one final time, demanding that Bridget ingest the potion and respond to their questions. Michael ordered her to take the potion, and this time, she complied obediently. Then Michael asked the question:

> In the name of the Father, Son and Holy Ghost, are you Bridget, the wife of Michael Cleary?

Bridget responded clearly in the affirmative; yes, she was indeed his wife.

The group seemed pleased because the fire and herbs appeared to be making her compliant. But John Dunne was unconvinced. The hag, that "Old Deceiver," who possessed Bridget was full of tricks, and just before midnight would pretend to cooperate so as to pass into the ninth, and final day, the last day it could be evicted from her body. And so, for good measure, he insisted the ritual be done again. Still holding Bridget over the fire, the entire process was repeated, but in this round, Patrick Boland also asked her:

> In the name of the Father, Son and Holy Ghost, are you Bridget, the daughter of Patrick Boland?

Each time Bridget responded in the affirmative and answered the final question with familiar and plaintive, "I am, dada." This last childlike, sobbing plea seemed to be the voice of the Bridget they knew and loved.

Based on the evidence of this tender interaction between father and daughter, John Dunne declared her cured. The changeling was gone up the chimney, and soon their own Bridget would be making her own sweet way back into her body. Someone began to clap, and the others joined in, clapping and shouting and dancing around the cottage for joy. Johanna Burke and Mary Kennedy hugged her tight, then the men put their Bridgie back in bed. According to Simpson, they were "satisfied that they had their own—that they had Mrs. Cleary and not a witch." For good measure, they continued to feed her herbs and to shake, slap, and swing her while she "screamed horrible" and they shouted: "Away with you. Come back, Bridget Boland, in the name of God." Then they asked her if she knew everyone in the room, and when she said yes, they were all delighted: They had her back. It was then just before the witching hour of midnight. The changeling seemed to have departed with only one day to spare.

Buoyed by their exorcism of the changeling, the Kennedy men prepared to leave for the funeral and wake of Michael's father in Killenaule. Unbeknownst to them, he was actually being buried six miles beyond Killenaule, making it more like a twelve-mile trip. So they did not return to the Clearys until the fateful Friday night, which proved to be the last for the cooper's wife.[55]

Michael hung back because he alone among them was not convinced the changeling was gone. He'd seen nothing go up the chimney, nor heard a sudden gust of wind or a mournful wailing—the usual signs that accompany a fairy's departure. Lacking any visible or audible sign that the fairy had departed, Michael Cleary reasoned that they may have all been deceived. He was still not sure it was his wife lying in their bed. He might still be sharing his cottage with an unearthly stranger. The Old Deceiver could still be among them, his Bridget still gone. So he determined to seek out "Father Con" one more time—just to make sure.

5

The Fairy Trials

Hunting the Witch

The coroner's report concluded that Bridget Cleary died of burning, willfully inflicted with malice aforethought, which was considered murder under British law. District Inspector Alfred Wansbrough had suspected this, but without a body, there were no grounds for charging the prisoners with more than ill-treatment. Once the body was discovered and the coroner's report signed, however, the charge was immediately upgraded to murder in the first degree. If convicted the defendants would hang.

The law ostensibly afforded all prisoners the protections guaranteed under English common law, including the right to hear charges, review evidence, and question witnesses. However in Ireland, conservative, middle-class Protestants dominated the juries, judgeships, and justices of the peace.[1] Consequently, even by

1895, in so-called modern Ireland, since the poor were never tried by their peers and few were represented by counsel, they could not take advantage of most judicial guarantees. The law did require, however, that the accused receive a hearing within three days, so after the coroner's report was signed on Saturday evening, the ten prisoners were transferred from Fethard to Clonmel—the sole woman, Mary Kennedy, being sent to the women's prison in Limerick—to await a formal arraignment at the Clonmel District Petty Sessions Court.[2] Of the eleven initially taken into custody, only Johanna Burke was released, in exchange for her testimony against the others. On Monday, March 25, magistrates of the Petty Sessions prepared to hear charges incident to the death of the cooper's wife.

Early Monday morning, officials announced that the prisoners would be escorted by police from the County Gaol to the Clonmel courthouse at eleven that morning. In anticipation of this public march, crowds gathered at the jail, the courthouse, and along the streets to catch a glimpse of the "simple countrymen" implicated in the "strange occurrence at Ballyvadlea"—the burning of a witch. Some were so outraged, others so curious, that they waited for up to two hours for the accused to appear. Of the many convict marches to pass through the streets of Clonmel, the procession of the ten accused of the "Ballyvadlea horrour" was unprecedented for the nature of the crime and for the large number of suspects and spectators. Even the oldest residents had seen nothing like it. The sight of the prisoners evoked a storm of shouts, hisses, and jeers—a response more often reserved for the blackest murderer or government informer than a group of bewildered country people. Individually none were particularly noteworthy, but the sight of so many passing through the streets, surrounded by police, made the fantastic stories of witches, burning, and fairy changelings seem more real.

Mary Kennedy had arrived from Limerick earlier that morning, and at eleven the march commenced. A large contingent of police with spiked helmets and rifles at the ready surrounded the prisoners, separating them from the noisy crowds that lined the streets. In contrast to the stern efficiency of the escort team, the defendants appeared disheveled and a bit dazed. The men wore loose-fitting wool jackets and caps; some wore overcoats. Mary Kennedy was completely draped in a dark cloak, her face barely visible behind the ruffled brim of her bonnet. To observers she appeared somewhat nondescript and sickly.[3]

Walking slightly apart from the rest was the cooper, Michael Cleary, age thirty-five. A full goatee and a bushy mustache partially offset his prominent forehead, heightened by a receding hairline. By any standard, he appeared respectably dressed, his features comely, but he seemed somewhat older than his years. His hands bore the scars of his years in the coopering trade. Patrick Boland, sixty-six, and the limping John Dunne, fifty-five, were described as representing an "extremely odd-looking type of countrymen."

The Kennedy boys and William Ahearn paraded past in a cluster. The four Kennedy brothers came in various sizes. The eldest, Patrick, thirty-one, was the shortest. At 5'9" he weighed barely 147 pounds. He was somewhat pinched-faced and stooped, with brown hair, blue eyes, and a mustache. He appeared less robust and strong than the typical farm laborer, perhaps because he had suffered a serious work-related injury to his left leg. Next was Michael, twenty-seven, who had the same hair and eye color as Patrick, but was taller and slightly thinner at 5'11" and 156 pounds. Michael looked a bit more urbane than the others. He

wore his thick hair parted down the middle with stylish bangs going off to right and left and a trim mustache and beard. As a
younger man, Michael had served for a time in the British Army.
He was sent to a foreign climate where he contracted what was
called "fallen sickness," which left him prone to strange "fits" and
memory lapses and was probably a form of malaria. As a result of
this exotic malady, the military authorities had sent him home.
James, twenty-two, stood 5'11" and weighed 163 pounds. He was
the darkest of the boys, the only brother with brown eyes to
match his dark brown hair and drooping mustache. The
youngest, William, twenty-one, was also the heaviest, at 5'9" and
175 pounds. He was also the only one of the four who was clean
shaven. Both James and Patrick Kennedy showed early signs of
balding, accounting for their older appearance and compensatory
mustaches, while William and Michael looked younger, with
more hair and fresh complexions.[4] Of the Kennedy brothers only
the two youngest, James and William, could read and write.

William Ahearn, the seventeen-year-old neighbor of the
Kennedys who held the candle during Bridget's ordeal, stood 5'8"
and weighed a mere 126 pounds. Also literate, he appeared to be
the most frightened and confused of the lot. He was a delicate
boy, not yet employed, who had the look of a young poet with
his thick crop of wavy hair, chiseled nose, heart-shaped mouth,
and receding chin.[5]

The most interesting figure in the group, and the only one
known outside the environs of Ballyvadlea, was Denis Ganey.
Ganey was described in contradictory fashion by regional newspapers as anything from an "ordinary-looking countryman" to a
"peculiar-looking old man." The Clonmel Gaol register reported
that he was fifty-eight years old, 5'8", had blue eyes, and weighed
140 pounds. Ganey walked with a slight limp. He wore a long,

graying, somewhat scraggly goatee that split below his neck into two yellowing spikes, which made him look something like an aged billy goat. Ganey was revered as an honored practitioner of the ancient healing arts and could set broken bones as well as any formally trained doctor. The *Irish Times* reported that Ganey had inherited his fairy-doctoring skills from his father and the practice had been in the family for generations. His herbal concoctions purportedly could heal fairy-induced ailments in both humans and beasts, and he had a reputation for honesty.[6] The crowd erupted when this "well-beloved . . . foe of disease and wicked fairies" appeared, and all along the route, hoots and hollers were directed toward him. Because he treated all manner of illnesses in humans and animals with "mysteriously concocted" herbs known only to himself, some believed he too was a changeling. Before the prisoners appeared on the street, it was rumored that Ganey would never walk down the street with the others. They said he had changed his shape and escaped from his jail cell through a keyhole. His appearance in the parade put the lie to the rumor, perhaps to the crowd's disappointment.[7]

All along the route, the crowd shouted insults at the passing prisoners. Never known for reticence, the townspeople of "rare" Clonmel were outwardly outraged by the shame and scorn cast upon the town, county, even the entire country, yet were inwardly fascinated by the story of the woman who was said to be gone with the fairies, and the family who initially and unsuccessfully sought help from doctor and priest, but finally resorted to extreme measures to get her back. Showing no desire to challenge the armed police, people stayed behind the barriers until the prisoners had passed, then moved into the street and followed the entourage to the courthouse; there an even larger crowd greeted the party with jeers, groans, and "all sorts of cries." The courtroom was already packed to overflowing; the hissing continued as the prisoners were led inside and filed silently, heads bowed, into the dock.

In Clonmel's long, proud history of resistance, never had such a large throng amassed for a nonpolitical criminal trial. Significantly, none of the defendants were involved in local politics; none had participated in rural unrest (although Patrick Boland, when in his cups, sometimes boasted of being a "summer soldier" in the Land War of the early 1880s). Nor had any ever been detained for drunkenness, disorderly conduct, or bad behavior. Yet this nondescript, inarticulate, seemingly compliant lot managed to evoke an extraordinary response from the citizens of Clonmel, which prompted the *Cork Examiner* on March 27 to express its concern about "the danger that popular indignation may assume proportions incompatible with the course of justice." The newspaper urged that justice proceed "steadily and becomingly, and that manifestations of popular feeling . . . be resisted." Joining the impassioned, yet curious citizens of Clonmel were correspondents from major Irish and English newspapers.

When the spectators settled in, Colonel Richard Charles Evanson, Clonmel's resident magistrate, gaveled the official magisterial inquiry to order. Seated beside him was Clonmel's Quaker mill owner, Thomas Cambridge Grubb, Justice of the Peace; they were joined in later sessions by a third magistrate, Sir Charles Gough. Solicitors for the defense included Richard J. Crean, a brother of Dr. William Crean, representing Michael Cleary and Denis Ganey, and Dr. John J. Hanrahan, who stood for young William Ahearn. The other prisoners—John Dunne, Patrick Boland, and the five Kennedys—were without counsel.

William Casey, the court clerk, began reading the charges against the accused. Nine were charged with having, on or about

March 14 jointly and severally, and with malice aforethought, feloniously "killed and murdered" Bridget Cleary. The tenth one charged, Denis Ganey, was accused of being an accessory before the fact in the commission of the crime. When Casey finished reading the charges, the magistrates asked each of the prisoners if they understood the Crown's charges against them. They all nodded.

Presenting evidence for the Crown was General District Inspector Alfred J. Wansbrough of the Carrick-on-Suir district, who rose and addressed the magistrates:

> Your worships are aware of the details of taking the depositions of this matter, and I will now bring the prisoners up with the object of taking the depositions of a few witnesses. Since the case was last before you, the body of Mrs. Cleary has been found with all the appearance of brutal treatment upon it. A coroner's inquest was held, and a verdict returned of death by burning. I will now give evidence as to how the burns were inflicted.[8]

This evidence formed the heart of Wansbrough's case. To show how the burns were made (and hoping to indict as many as possible), he would present evidence to prove that all the accused contributed, either directly or indirectly, to the death of Bridget Cleary. This required that he show not that Bridget died of burning itself, which only Michael Cleary was directly responsible for, but rather that she died as a result of the ritual that led to the burning in which all the assembled defendants participated. By taking this approach, Wansbrough cast a wide net over the family and their beliefs and exposed both to public ridicule, in effect putting the fairies on trial along with the ten defendants. In the process, he planned to elicit information about a "fairy trial," conducted by the family, that took place in the Cleary cottage during the final week of Bridget Cleary's life—a trial that culminated in death by burning.

Denis Ganey's herbal potion was the most important piece of evidence for the prosecution. Wansbrough would show that, in the course of the family's fairy trial, the participants forced her to ingest Ganey's herbs, which rendered Bridget "insensible" and unable to defend herself when threatened with fire. Wansbrough would show that had Bridget Cleary been in possession of her senses, she could have defended herself by calling for help, thereby preventing the burning. Using this argument, Wansbrough could charge Ganey, and, in the bargain, broadly indict all those who still believed in and practiced the old pagan traditions. This strategy also allowed Wansbrough to use the magisterial inquiry to put the fairies on trial by asking not only "how," but "why" the burns were inflicted. Why had this happened? Why were so many involved? What was wrong with the people of Catholic Ireland?

To produce evidence to show both "how" and "why" the burns were inflicted, Wansbrough selected two witnesses—Johanna Burke and William Simpson. Burke was valuable in telling "how" and "by whom" the burns were inflicted. As the family's designated scullery maid, she was called in to care for her cousin, and she was present on both Thursday and Friday nights. To produce evidence as to "why" the burns were inflicted, Wansbrough relied on the caretaker, William Simpson, who was present on Thursday night when Ganey's allegedly debilitating potion was administered. Unlike the peasants in the dock, Simpson was not an Irish Catholic tenant farmer or laborer; he was an Episcopalian, he held a position of responsibility as caretaker of a large estate, and he dressed in a somewhat ostentatious way—a kind of dandified imitation of the landed gentry. Because of his foppish clothing, he appeared older than his twenty-four years. Simpson was an outsider in the community, yet Michael Cleary apparently trusted him enough to give him the key to the cottage on the day he was arrested. He told Simpson that he "would be back in a few days," and asked him "to keep an eye on the place and feed hens till he should return and his wife turn up."[9]

William Simpson would make a good witness for the Crown, because he, like Wansbrough, was an opportunist. Here was the chance of a lifetime to promote himself and be noticed—to be respected in a way that caretakers and emergency men seldom were. When the story exploded, Simpson, instead of acting like a friend of the Clearys, talked to reporters, answered questions about the defendants, and led tours through the cottage, pointing out significant points of interest such as the fireplace, Michael's coopering tools, and the pile of ashes beside the hen house. It was Simpson who took upon himself the mantle of authority and disdain regarding native superstitions and primitive beliefs still nurtured among the unlettered peasantry. If Michael had entrusted him with the key to cottage, he made a mistake. Simpson trumpeted himself as the resident expert on changelings, alien spirits, and encounters with the "good people" and was only too willing to enlighten the world with his vast knowledge at the expense of the "old Irishry." All this bravado and self-promotion obscured the degree to which he, and particularly his wife, Minnie, had been involved in the ritual.

Conversely, Johanna Burke, who knew more about the proceedings at the Cleary cottage, was reluctant to talk because her testimony could convict her mother, brothers, and uncle. To get her to say anything, Wansbrough had to coerce her testimony by first arresting her, then offering her immunity from prosecution.

Yet Burke still refused to cooperate fully, even after a prison priest threatened to withhold Church sacraments from her and her family. Even then, Johanna Burke remained a reluctant witness throughout the hearing. Misleadingly, the *Nationalist* asserted that Burke "did not hesitate to give evidence against even her own mother's brothers, and other relatives," in order to counter Unionist claims that the ritualistic killing proved Irish citizens were not ready for self-government.[10] Burke became a pawn in the hands of both Nationalists and Unionists.

For any Irish person to testify on behalf of the Crown in a murder case, especially one involving kin, represented a betrayal of Irish people that took generations for a family to outlive. If a witness accepted blood money in return for testifying, the crime against country and clan was still greater. There was no evidence to indicate that Burke, poor and dependent as she was, took fees from government officials to testify, although she apparently received clothing and housing expenses in addition to some form of police protection for a time after the trial. Only one thing is clear: She was a most reluctant witness whose already destitute life was further ruined by Wansbrough's strong-arm tactics.[11]

After the charges were read, Colonel Evanson directed District Inspector Alfred Wansbrough to call his first witness to the dock—Johanna Burke, resident of Rathkenney and Ballyvadlea. A murmur swept through the courtroom as Johanna, holding a two-month-old child, rose and slowly made her way to the stand, accompanied by her daughter, Katie, clinging to her skirts. When she reached the witness stand and turned to face the defendants, another murmur went up from the crowd. Chief Magistrate Colonel Evanson banged his gavel and ordered silence.[12]

District Inspector Wansbrough opened by asking Burke to recount the events of Thursday, March 14, the night she and her daughter Katie met William and Minnie Simpson outside the Cleary cottage. Burke dutifully told the story of finding the front door locked, hearing voices shouting within, then waiting until the door was unlocked. She recounted the scene in the bedroom where the men forced Bridget to swallow Ganey's "nine-in-one cure," while Cleary repeatedly asked, "Are you Bridget Boland, wife of Michael Cleary, in the name of God?" She answered it once or twice, and then her father asked a similar question. Michael Cleary, she thought, threw a certain liquid on his wife, after which they put the question to Bridget again, and she repeated the words they wanted to hear.

Burke testified that it was John Dunne, rather than any of her brothers, who suggested that they force Bridget into the fireplace. "Hold her over the fire and she will soon answer," were his words. Dunne, Cleary, and Patrick Kennedy then lifted Bridget off the bed and placed her in a kind of sitting position over the kitchen fire, which was barely burning. Even so, when placed on the fire, Bridget's appearance changed, and she became "wild and deranged." Nevertheless, the men repeated the question, and she answered desperately, "I am Bridget Boland, daughter of Pat Boland, in the name of God." Burke testified that Bridget turned toward her and cried softly, "Oh Han, Han," pleading for protection, after which the men put her back in bed. If Wansbrough hoped to show that Bridget was rendered "insensible" after taking Ganey's potion, Johanna Burke gave him little to go on, but she did establish that Bridget was forced to take the potion, and that the threatened application of fire was the primary inducement.

At the hearing the following week, William Simpson's testimony did more to support Wansbrough's case that the belief in fairies and the fairy doctor's potion was crucial to understanding how and why the burns were inflicted. Wansbrough opened his questioning by asking Simpson to recount the events of the evening of Thursday, March 14, when Simpson and Johanna Burke went to visit the Clearys, only to find themselves locked out of the cottage. Wansbrough wanted to know why the door was locked. Since it was rare for doors to be locked in rural Ireland, it would seem to signify that the ritual was already underway.

Simpson stated that he arrived between nine and ten in the evening, somewhat later than the time given in Burke's account. From inside, he heard male voices shouting, "Take it, you old bitch or I will kill you," or "We will kill you."[13] Upon hearing the cries inside, Simpson stood listening for a few minutes at the window. Soon the door was opened. From the bench, Colonel Evanson asked why the door was opened. Was it opened to admit them, or opened for another reason? If the latter, who was it that the men were allowing in or out? Simpson replied that he thought the door was opened to let the fairies out.

Solicitor Richard Crean, representing both Cleary and Ganey, objected that any reference to the fairies could not be admitted as evidence, for to do so would imply that the court regarded the fairies as real. Wansbrough rephrased his question.

Wansbrough: Who opened the door?

Simpson: I can't say. It was opened without any knocking.

Wansbrough: Did you hear anything when it was opened?

Simpson: Yes, I heard loud shouts of "away she goes, away she goes."

Wansbrough: Who said that?

Simpson: I can't say, they were all saying it, the men who were holding her said it.

Wansbrough: And what did they mean, "away she goes"?

Simpson: I understood it to mean that it was the witch they were sending away.

Once inside the cottage, Simpson and his wife, Minnie, were then able to see what was taking place. According to Simpson's memory, the ordeal was more violent than Burke recounted. He believed that Bridget was in pain; she was struggling and appeared exhausted. Wansbrough pressed him for damning details about the forced feeding of the potion, its effects, and the subsequent use of fire. How did Bridget react to this treatment? Did she resist ingesting the potion? Did she protest? Did she appear to be in pain? Simpson responded that Bridget did little to resist taking the herbs except to keep her mouth "closed against it." When the medicine went down her throat, and when the men shook her body and slapped her hands, she screamed horribly.

Wansbrough: Did they say anything when they shook her?
Simpson: Yes, they all said, "Away with you. Come home, Bridget Boland, in the name of God."

Wansbrough asked his witness if other substances besides the herbs were forced into Bridget's mouth. Simpson indicated he was not near enough to Bridget to see, but "another liquid" was called for and thrown on her. According to Burke's May 21 deposition, which was never made public, Cleary asked if anyone had any "piss." Initially Mary Kennedy passed a cup beneath her skirts to supply the urine, after which Michael threw it on Bridget's face and chest in intervals of twenty minutes. When Mary's supply ran low, the cup was passed to Simpson's wife, Minnie, who did her part to keep the ritual supplied with this crucial cleansing agent.[14] Burke disclosed that Minnie Simpson took a cup and put it under her clothes behind her

[Burke's] back and asked her to stand behind her, "in her shade," so to speak. After she urinated in the cup, Michael Cleary told Minnie to throw it on his wife and she did. Then Cleary asked if anyone else could supply more urine. Apparently no one else volunteered.[15] Thanks to Mary Kennedy and Minnie Simpson, enough urine was thrown on Bridget during the course of the evening to soak her chemise. The amount of urine from Minnie Simpson never became known because Wansbrough could not afford to have it known that the wife of his star male witness participated in a pagan ritual.

After the administration of the urine, the ritualistic questioning resumed. First from Michael: "Are you Bridget Boland, wife of Michael Cleary, in the name of the Father, Son and Holy Ghost?" Then Boland, "Are you Bridget Boland, daughter of Patrick Boland, in the name of the Father, Son and Holy Ghost?" Wansbrough asked if Bridget responded to these queries, and Simpson replied that she spoke so low that he was unable to hear exactly what she said. Others also had trouble hearing her response. This prompted Wansbrough to ask who was in the room besides the family and why there was such a large crowd at the cottage that evening. Were others there to "drive out the witch"? Crean objected again, stating Simpson did not say that, but Simpson declared, "I did say witches." Colonel Evanson allowed Simpson to proceed, adding that he seemed to be an intelligent man and the magistrates were eager to learn all they could about the proceeding from him. Simpson's status as a Protestant added weight to the prosecution's evidence and explained why neither Simpson nor his wife was arrested for the parts they played in the ritual.

> *Simpson:* I believe they went to hunt the witches. I saw them at it, but I can't say what motive they had in going there. I saw them doing it when I was there.

Wansbrough: What?

Simpson: Hunting out the witches.

He hastened to add that he and his wife, on the other hand, merely went there to inquire about Bridget Cleary's health. Then Simpson described how and why the "hunting" of witches turned deadly. He gathered that this process was not going well. Bridget answered her husband and father's questions once or twice, then floundered, or refused outright to respond; thereupon the process began again, with more herbs, more threats, and more questioning. Finally, according to Simpson, as the hour grew late, it was John Dunne who suggested the fire.

> *Wansbrough*: Was there anything said after the questions on the bed?
>
> *Simpson*: Yes, I heard some one say, I believe John Dunne, "Make down a good fire and we will burn her, and make her answer."

There was a low fire burning in the kitchen, so Dunne carried her there and set her beside the hearth. William, James, and Pat held her there while Cleary and Boland repeated the former questions.

> *Wansbrough*: Did she answer? Did she appear to be able?
>
> *Simpson*: Yes, but her eyes were wandering around as if she was frightened.

The questions were repeated more than three times. Receiving no answer, they then forced her into the fireplace. John Dunne cradled her head, while James Kennedy and William held her feet. Pat Kennedy grasped her shoulders, and her father kept

Bridget off the grate to prevent her body from touching the hot bars. Then Boland allowed his daughter to fall on the grate, and the men hoisted her in a sideways, sitting position over the fire.

> *Wansbrough*: Did she give any evidence of pain?
> *Simpson*: No.
> *Wansbrough*: Did she scream?
> *Simpson*: No, she had her night dress and, I believe, chemise on; she was held over the fire and on the fire for about ten minutes.
> *Wansbrough*: Did you get a smell of burning?
> *Simpson*: Yes.

Wansbrough then asked Simpson to identify a chemise. Was it the chemise Bridget wore when she was put to the fire? Simpson answered in the affirmative. Wansbrough showed the magistrates a hole burned into the garment approximately four inches across. He asked Simpson what the others were doing.

Simpson admitted that he did nothing to intervene and grew more "excited" as the men did their work. Wansbrough asked if anyone else in the room attempted to stop the ritual. Simpson indicated that no one did. "At all events, they made no signs of disapproval?" Wansbrough asked. "No," Simpson replied. When asked "his excuse for his presence and non-interference," the caretaker lamely responded: "the door was locked, and [I] could not get out."[16]

While on the fire, Bridget apparently answered the questions in a manner that satisfied everyone, especially after she responded to Boland's questions with the familiar and pitiful, "Yes, dada." Everyone appeared very relieved by this response, thinking for the first time that evening that the potion was effective after all. Wansbrough asked what this meant? Why did they appear happy? Because, Simpson replied, they were satisfied that they had their own. That Mrs. Cleary was not a witch.

Following this ordeal, Bridget was put back in bed. Simpson heard Mary Kennedy and Johanna Burke say that they should put some dry nightclothes on her, which was done. After Bridget was in bed, Patrick Boland, James and William Kennedy, and John Dunne went back into the bedroom. Shortly, Michael Cleary followed, carrying a saucepan in his hand. They all asked her to identify those in the room and explain the relationship of each to her. Each Kennedy son in his turn she correctly named as a "first cousin." As Bridget named each person in the room, Simpson observed that they asked each other if they thought "it was she that was in it." Each seemed satisfied that it was Bridget responding and not the witch, and they all appeared delighted.

By this time, the ordeal had been underway for over three hours. Wansbrough asked when this break in the proceedings occurred. Simpson answered that it was around 11:30 P.M. He knew this because some in the room expressed concern that the questioning be concluded by midnight.

Wansbrough asked if the defendants expressed concern that the questioning be concluded before the "witching hour of midnight"?

Simpson: What do you mean?
Wansbrough: That if she was not asked before 12 she would be taken in spite of them. Did anyone say that?
Simpson: Yes; they all said it.

With that, Colonel Evanson adjourned the court for lunch.

When the court session resumed, Wansbrough asked Simpson about the red poker. Had he seen it used on Bridget? He replied,

no, that it had been used the day before, but the fairy trial participants in the Cleary cottage had told him about it. They believed
that they had to touch her on the forehead with it. Indeed, he had
seen a slight mark on Bridget's forehead and small bruises on her
neck. He also believed there were other bruises on her arm. The
participants also told him that there had been two sessions prior to
the Thursday night ritual during which Bridget had been forced to
take herbs. Simpson saw Bridget again briefly the day after the
burning that he had witnessed Thursday night. At that time she
was still in bed and appeared very weak but was taking milk. He
spoke with her, asking if she knew him, and she replied that she
did. That was the last time William Simpson saw Bridget Cleary
alive. This was all he claimed to know about Bridget's "trial."

On Tuesday, April 2, Mrs. Mary "Minnie" Simpson was called
to testify. In order to distract the magistrate's attention from her
complicity, she stressed her respectability and her disdain for anything remotely associated with fairycraft. Unlike her husband, a
self-styled expert on fairy lore, Minnie claimed to know nothing
about such things. Wansbrough, however, could not be so easily
outdone in his determination to obtain more fairy evidence. He
immediately set to work to learn what she could tell the court
about the fairy trial.[17]

Minnie's version of Thursday evening's events followed her
husband's closely. Upon approaching the Cleary house on Thursday evening, she heard voices from within shouting "Take that,
you trap!" Or perhaps the term was "strap," she could not be certain. When the previously locked door was opened, she then
heard the men inside say, "Away she goes, away she goes," as
though they were driving someone out of the house, someone
who was not Mrs. Cleary but who occupied her bed. Wansbrough
asked who this "someone" was supposed to be. Minnie said that

she did not know. "Do you believe it was Mrs. Cleary in the bed?" Wansbrough asked.

Mrs. Simpson: Certainly I did.
Wansbrough: What were they driving out?
Mrs. Simpson: They thought it was a witch; but I did not.

Crean, representing Cleary and Ganey, objected that the witness could not say what the others thought. Colonel Evanson asked Minnie to explain what she meant. She explained that the men were holding Bridget in bed while Michael Cleary dispensed herbs "from Ganey from the mountain," because they believed it was not Mrs. Cleary, but a witch in the bed. Crean objected, asking who had told her about Ganey's herbs. Minnie responded that Mrs. Burke, when the defendants were not present, had told her the herbs came from Ganey. Crean objected again, and the objection was sustained. Wansbrough asked Minnie to proceed.

Minnie stated that once she, her husband, and Johanna Burke were allowed in the cottage, Michael Cleary said to them, "All that's inside must stay inside, and those outside must stay outside." Wansbrough asked if this remark had anything to do with the "charm" business? Minnie quickly retorted, "I don't know; I don't know anything about witchcraft at all." This comment evoked a burst of laughter from the crowd in the courtroom. Mrs. Simpson then stated that Cleary forced the potion into his wife's mouth, each time asking her to identify herself. After each ministration of the herbal compound, Michael called for a "liquid" and threw it at her. Minnie asserted it was Mary Kennedy who provided it. Then John Dunne said, "Bring her to the fire." Wansbrough asked if Bridget said anything while the men carried her to the fire. Minnie said that Bridget asked the men, "Are you going to make a herring out of me?"

Once Bridget was forced onto the fire, Minnie described how both Michael and Patrick Boland questioned her repeatedly for about five minutes. She reported the fire was low, not hot enough to boil a kettle of water. Unlike her husband, who claimed that he smelled something burning, Minnie testified that she smelled nothing. Wansbrough asked if anyone attempted to prevent "this brutal treatment." Mrs. Simpson replied that no one did. Did anyone dissent in any way? No. When Bridget had answered to their satisfaction the same men took her back to the bed.

Once Bridget was back in bed, Minnie stated that she helped Mary Kennedy put dry clothing on her, by which time Bridget was "raving," said Minnie. She corroborated the assertion of her husband that all the questioning had to be completed before twelve o'clock. Wansbrough asked why they seemed concerned that the questions be answered before midnight. "It appeared to me," Mrs. Simpson stated, "that they could not drive away the witch after twelve o'clock." Upon hearing this answer, the courtroom broke out in laughter again.

But it was no laughing matter at the time for Michael Cleary and the others assembled in the cottage. It was near the witching hour of midnight. The four Kennedy brothers, as well as Pat Boland, were all for stopping the ordeal, and were anxious to leave for the wake of Michael Cleary's father in Killenaule. Everyone assumed Michael would be going with them. While the others seemed confident that the witch was gone, Cleary was not so sure. Rather than leave to attend his own father's wake, Cleary announced his intention to stay. Perhaps they were disturbed or even startled by his announcement, but they left without him.

Fragments of testimony from all the witnesses reveal that the ritual continued through the early morning hours of Friday, March 15, after Patrick Boland and the Kennedy brothers left for Killenaule. The tone of the proceedings changed after midnight, however. Rather than violently threatening, the atmosphere was much gentler. They all believed, at least for a time, that Ganey's potion had worked, and that the witch had been hunted out and driven off. Still, there was more work to be done. Having hunted out the witch, Michael had now both to prevent the witch from returning and entice Bridget's spirit to return.

To this end, Michael, and those who remained, maintained a vigil throughout the night. John Dunne and William Ahearn stayed at the cottage until about two A.M. Michael Cleary and William Simpson remained with Johanna and Katie Burke, Mary Kennedy, and Minnie Simpson throughout the entire night, while Bridget stayed awake. To Minnie, Bridget appeared "nervous and not sensible," although aware enough to ask occasionally for something to drink. In further support of Wansbrough's insensibility theory, William Simpson stated that while he was talking to her, she asked him if the police had been there and why the kitchen was filled with smoke (apparently forgetting that she herself had been violently forced into the fireplace just a short time before). In order to mollify and reassure her, Simpson pretended that there had been two RIC police, or "peelers," at the window and she remarked that they were nice men. "I told her the police were there to satisfy her mind," the Protestant caretaker testified, but "the police were not really there at that time." With such a large gathering packed into the cottage for that length of time, and with rumors rampant in the area for over a week, the peelers might plausibly have indeed come around to keep an eye on things. While there was some evidence that the police were alerted to the possibility that a woman was being mistreated, none of the witnesses claimed to have seen or spoken to the police during the fairy trial. While the Simpsons threw their weight behind the insensibility theory, Johanna Burke was initially more interested in attempting to minimize her brothers' role by maintaining that Bridget was not in pain and did not appear to suffer from her ordeal on the simmering fire.

It was not until six on Friday morning that this phase of the fairy trial in the Cleary cottage concluded. Just before daylight, Mary Kennedy, Johanna and Katie Burke, and the Simpsons finally left, having been there over eight hours. Significantly, Michael Cleary left the cottage at the same time, not for his father's wake, but to fetch Father Ryan. The unwitting priest was about to be called upon to take part in a ritual he would later deny knowing anything about.

Mass in the Morning

After an adjournment for the evening, testimony at the magisterial inquiry in Clonmel resumed on Tuesday, March 26, when Johanna Burke took the stand to tell of the events of Friday, March 15—the ninth, and final, day of the fatal fairy trial at Ballyvadlea. In the courtroom were the ten defendants, surrounded by police, members of the press, and city officials. On the previous day, the gallery had been filled to overflowing with curious onlookers, some of whom had spent several hours on the sidewalks outside the courthouse for the chance to hear details of the now infamous witch-burning. When order was established, Magistrates Evanson and Grubb entered the court and directed District Inspector Wansbrough to resume his interrogation, upon which he recalled Mrs. Johanna Burke to the stand.

The courtroom grew still. People shifted in their seats to catch a glimpse of Mrs. Burke as she walked toward the witness box, again with babe in arms, an older child clinging to her skirts. As she approached the box, Burke glanced over at her mother and brothers, then burst into tears, dreading to say what she was about to disclose. The police rushed forward to stop the untoward (and sympathy-generating) outpouring of feeling but could not, so Burke was unceremoniously escorted out of the courtroom until she regained her composure. Already expectant and impatient spectators packed in the courtroom's gallery waited another long half hour for the inquiry to resume.

When Johanna Burke was again escorted to the witness dock, the District Inspector pressed her to explain the events leading up to the burning of Bridget Cleary. As she resumed her testimony from the previous day, the court learned that the Kennedy family began to have doubts that the herbs, incantations, and, ultimately, the fire had drawn out the changeling spirit. For, according to Burke, William and Minnie Simpson, herself, Mary Kennedy, and Michael Cleary, all stayed with Bridget through Thursday night and early Friday morning, shouting, clapping hands, and performing other types of rituals intended to draw Bridget's true spirit back once Ganey's herbs had successfully driven out the changeling. Since Friday was the last day when herbal potions, incantations, and even fire could be used as exorcising agents, Michael Cleary was out at dawn, once again, to call for the priest. He had only eighteen hours left to rescue his Bridget from the fairies.

Wansbrough wondered why Michael Cleary was so anxious to get the priest into the cottage so early in the morning after what must have been an exhausting ordeal the previous night. He was even more curious to know why Father Ryan was called back to the cottage, when just two days before he had administered the last rites. Johanna Burke, as usual, remained noncommittal on this point. Father Ryan was called, she stated flatly, to say Mass.

In his testimony, however, William Simpson had provided more information, stating that as he and his wife left the cottage very early Friday morning, Cleary left with them to fetch the priest. "Why," Wansbrough asked, "did he send for the priest?" Simpson answered that Michael told him he thought there were some evil spirits in the house and he wanted to have Mass said to banish them.

Other evidence shows that Michael Cleary asked Father Ryan to come the day before, on Thursday, as he returned from his journey to Kylatlea. Father Ryan avoided this call, but Friday morning, Cleary insisted that Father Ryan come immediately. Though he claimed to be annoyed by this request, Ryan later testified that he went at once. He went, he said, because he had a breakfast appointment at the home of Bridget Shee, and the Cleary cottage was on the way. Whether he revealed exactly why Michael wanted him to say Mass, the curate certainly had reason to suspect that something more than Catholic religiosity was going on in Ballyvadlea.

It is true, as Burke testified, that on Friday morning, Cleary specifically asked Father Ryan to say Mass at the cottage, a somewhat unusual request, given that he had already administered last rites, but certainly not without precedent. Although house Masses were less common in Ireland after the Great Famine, when the Catholic establishment built more churches and encouraged regular attendance on Sunday, they were still performed, attended by neighbors, passers-by, and family members. The importance of conducting Mass *in* the Cleary cottage was, first, to drive off the intractable spirit residing in the cottage, and, second, to administer the Holy Eucharist to Bridget. If a fairy spirit resided in Bridget's body, it would not abide a holy instrument of such power as the Host possessed. But, if it really was Bridget's own spirit in her body, the wafer would be gladly received. So the ceremony had a dual purpose, as both remedy and diagnosis. Both purposes were of utmost importance to Michael Cleary, and his increasingly frantic desire to accomplish them explains his early-morning, unannounced visit to Father Ryan. Although the request was sudden, inconvenient, and a bit of a bother, Father Ryan came, as did several others in the neighborhood.

At around 8:30 A.M., Father Ryan arrived at the Cleary cottage and prepared to celebrate Mass. Johanna Burke was already there, as she said, "to wash shirts," which might seem strange given the fact that she had been up all night. Clearly, she too was interested in seeing how Bridget would respond when given the Eucharist. In his questioning concerning this impromptu Mass, Wansbrough was still trying to establish that Bridget had been rendered insensible by the administration of Ganey's herbal potion.

> *Wansbrough*: Were you present on Friday morning . . . when Father
>   Ryan, of Drangan, celebrated Mass in the house and gave Holy
>   Communion to Bridget Cleary?
> *Burke*: I was.
> *Wansbrough*: What state was she in then?
> *Burke*: She looked nervous.
> *Wansbrough*: Did she get up at all during Mass?
> *Burke*: No, she was not sensible.

Jumping at this opening, Wansbrough pressed his witness. How did she know Mrs. Cleary was not sensible? What signs did she give of insensibility?

    Burke: I know she did not swallow the Holy Communion. I saw her
      take it out, that is why I say she had not the whole of her senses.

Once again, in probing for evidence of Bridget's insensibility, Wansbrough had stumbled upon more evidence of the fairy trial ritual and the participants' stubborn superstitions, born of their (to Protestant eyes) equally ludicrous pagan and Catholic beliefs. Any Irish Catholic knew that to refuse the wafer was tantamount to blasphemy, a sign of paganism, and a true indication that the Old Deceiver was still present. Johanna Burke had noticed that Bridget pretended to take the wafer then spat it out, and if she had seen it, certainly Michael Cleary had also seen his wife's blasphemy.

This revelation made Wansbrough all the more suspicious of Father's Ryan's role in the ritual. When Father Ryan took the witness stand, the prosecutor asked him to explain his relationship to the Clearys and to describe his visits to the cottage prior to the burning. Ryan stated that the Clearys were members of his church and had been under his "spiritual charge" for a year and a half, since he had become curate, and during that time, he never observed any signs of "mental derangement" in Mrs. Cleary, until he attended her on Wednesday, March 13.

Wansbrough asked Father Ryan to tell the court about that visit, and in particular, why he had seen fit to administer last rites, which seemed peculiar, given that Dr. Crean had examined her earlier that day and determined she was not gravely ill. Father Ryan stated that the first he learned of Bridget's illness was on Wednesday when he was summoned and that he arrived at the cottage around 3:30 P.M.[18] When Father Ryan entered, he found Mrs. Cleary in a "very nervous state," possibly even hysterical, so he concluded that her condition might be "the beginning of mental derangement." Having said that, he contradicted himself by

Parnell Street, Clonmel. Statue commemorating the Croppy Boys of '98 stands to the right in front of the old Town Hall.

The Clonmel Quay. Barges bearing barrels filled with Irish foodstuffs depart for England.

Slievenamon as seen from Mullinahone, home of Charles J. Kickham. *(photo courtesy of Marian Yeates)*

Archbishop Thomas William Croke
(courtesy of the Archdiocese of Emly
and Cashel, Thurles)

The Drangan Church
(photo courtesy of
Marian Yeates)

Contemporary photograph of the Cleary cottage, 1895
(courtesy of the Irish National Archives, Dublin)

The room in which the burning is supposed to have taken place.

The place where the body was discovered. (The cross indicates the exact spot.)

THE SURVIVAL OF WITCHCRAFT IN IRELAND:
SKETCHES ON THE SCENE OF THE TRAGEDY.

Contemporary sketches of the Cleary cottage, burial site, and Sergeant Phillips from the Daily Graphic *(courtesy of the British Newspaper Library, London)*

The fireplace inside the Cleary cottage where Bridget Cleary was burned to death (photo courtesy of Marian Yeates)

Father Cornelius Ryan's cottage in Tullowossaum
(*photo courtesy of Marian Yeates*)

Out-building adjacent to Father Ryan's cottage where the coroner's inquest was held
(*photo courtesy of Marian Yeates*)

The Clonmel Courthouse

District-Inspector Alfred J. Wansbrough

Interior of the Clonmel Gaol
(Reg. No. 1987.433, courtesy of the
County Tipperary Museum, Clonmel)

Prison photo of Michael Cleary, 1895
(courtesy of the Irish National Archive, Dublin)

Prison photo of John Dunne, 1895
(courtesy of the Irish National Archive, Dublin)

Contemporary sketch
of the prisoners' march
from the Clonmel Gaol
to the Court House,
March 25, 1895, from
the Daily Graphic
(courtesy of the British
Newspaper Library,
London)

Contemporary sketch of
witnesses and prisoners from
the Daily Graphic. Top
row (left to right): Father
Ryan, Mary Kennedy,
William Simpson. Bottom
row: Michael Cleary (1),
Michael Kennedy (2),
William Ahearn (3),
Patrick Boland (4), Patrick
Kennedy (5), William
Kennedy (6), James
Kennedy (7),
Denis Ganey (8), and John
Dunne (9)
(courtesy of British Newspaper
Library, London)

Prison photos of Michael Cleary, 1901
(*courtesy of the Irish National Archive, Dublin*)

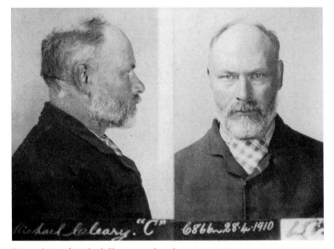

Prison photos of Michael Cleary upon his release in 1910
(*courtesy of the Irish National Archive, Dublin*)

stating in the next breath that they carried on a "coherent and intelligent" conversation for over twenty minutes. Admitting that he found nothing unusual in Bridget's behavior, nothing to "attract special attention," he administered last rites of the Church because he thought "her condition might lead to something dangerous such as brain fever." He added that on the following day, Thursday, March 14, he received a second call to come to the Cleary home, but declined, since he had just seen Bridget and had already administered last rites.

Wansbrough let this statement pass then turned to the Friday Mass and Burke's testimony regarding the desecration of the sacrament. Who had called him and for what purpose? Ryan stated that Michael Cleary had come to his house very early Friday morning and explained that Bridget had "a very bad night," so requested that Ryan come to the cottage to celebrate Mass. Since he was preparing to leave for a breakfast engagement that same morning, Ryan followed Cleary on horseback back to the cottage, arriving there about 8:15. Bridget was lying in bed, and there were already several other people at the cottage. Ryan remembered that Michael Cleary and Patrick Boland were present but "could not say who else may have been there." According to testimony of other witnesses, those present included Johanna Burke, William Nagle of Rathkenny, Thomas Daniel, and Miss Bridget Shee, who was accompanying Father Ryan to breakfast that morning.

Wansbrough: What state was she in?

Ryan: More nervous and more excited than when I saw her on Wednesday.

Wansbrough: Did you have any conversation with Michael Cleary, or any one present, as to the incidents that had happened, or to the state of Mrs. Cleary?

Ryan: No, I did not suspect anything.

Wansbrough: She was quite sensible?

Ryan: Yes, for notwithstanding her wild and excited look, her conversation with me was intelligent and coherent. She was in a sitting posture in bed.

Defense Attorney Crean examined Father Ryan about the communion service and Burke's charge that Bridget spit out the communion wafer. Crean asked who was present in the bedroom at the time.

Ryan: Only Mrs. Cleary, the boy serving Mass, and myself.

Crean: Would it be true if it were stated that Mrs. Cleary took the Holy Communion out of her mouth, and did not swallow it?

Ryan: I would not swear that it was not true, but I don't believe it.

Crean: If Mrs. Burke swore it, it would not be true?

Ryan: I don't believe it. I did not see Mrs. Burke in the room; there were some people outside the room; I noticed that Mrs. Cleary's mouth was dry and parched, and after I administered the Holy Communion I watched her until I thought she had swallowed it, thinking she might want some water to assist her in swallowing, but after awhile I did not consider it necessary.

Solicitor Crean wanted to press the matter further and show that, given the culture of belief around them, his clients had reason to suspect Bridget was a changeling and that the priest believed the same thing, but Magistrate Grubb interrupted. None of the magistrates was comfortable with this line of questioning. Grubb said that Father Ryan had answered properly and no more questions would be allowed. Crean relented. Then Colonel Evanson tried to change the subject. He asked if Bridget said anything to Father Ryan about her treatment. Did she protest? Did she ask for help? Father Ryan stated that she did not protest at any time and said nothing whatever about her treatment.

But Father Ryan was not finished refuting the charge that Bridget spit out the wafer while under his watchful eye. In his own defense, he informed the magistrates that he wished to make a statement: "I wish to add regarding the Holy Communion that if any Catholic saw Bridget Cleary taking the Blessed Sacrament out of her mouth, that Catholic would be strictly bound to tell me at once, so as to save the sacred species from profanation."

After this blame-shifting denial, Wansbrough resumed his questioning, asking if Father Ryan had noticed anything unusual either about the cottage or its occupants. He responded that he had not until he spied the medicine bottle left by Dr. Crean. Ryan asked Cleary if Bridget had taken the medicine, and Cleary responded negatively, saying he had no faith in the doctor's medicine. Contradicting what he purportedly told Michael on Wednesday about Crean's prescriptions being suspect because the doctor was never sober, Father Ryan said he remonstrated, insisting the medicine was good and Bridget should take it, to which Cleary replied, "People may have some remedy of their own that would do more good than doctors' medicine." At this reference to "people," District Inspector Wansbrough pounced on his witness, demanding to know how he, a priest, could have not known that "people" referred to the fairies and that the ritual, in which he participated, involved witchcraft. Father Ryan insisted he had heard nothing of witchcraft, "absolutely nothing." Wansbrough paused, then took direct aim at his witness, asking, "Don't you think that very extraordinary?"

Father Ryan: No, I don't. The Priest is very often the last to hear of
   things like that generally, I should say. I heard a rumor on the
   Saturday after that Mrs. Cleary had disappeared mysteriously. I
   had no suspicion of foul play or witchcraft, and if I had I should
   have at once absolutely refused to say Mass in the house, and
   have given information to the police at once.

Sensing that the magistrates would not tolerate the public hu-
miliation of a priest, Wansbrough dropped the matter and allowed Father Ryan one final statement. Ryan returned to the
matter of the sacrament, saying that he knew of nothing that occurred during the Mass which would "cause an impression on the
mind" that Bridget Cleary could not or did not swallow the Holy
Communion properly. He reasserted that he had kept her under
his observation until he was satisfied she had swallowed it and he
could not understand how anyone could suggest otherwise.

But Johanna Burke had suggested otherwise. She was standing
beside Bridget during the Mass and testified that she saw Bridget
take the wafer into her mouth and act as if she would swallow, but
did not. According to Burke, Bridget held the Host in her mouth,
then later, when she thought no one was looking, turned her head
to the side and spit it out. Burke later found the undissolved remnant stuck to the bedding. This indicated to the superstitious that
the old witch pretended to take the communion wafer, then secretly spit it out so cleverly as to deceive even the priest. Johanna
Burke saw the desecration of the Sacred Host because she was
watching for Bridget's reaction, recognizing that the saying of the
Mass would discern if the changeling was still in possession of
Bridget's body. If Johanna Burke saw this desecration, others saw
it, too. Father Ryan may have seen it as well but could never admit it. His career as a priest would be ruined if it was shown that

he had allowed desecration of the Sacred Host; he had no choice but to insist that Bridget swallowed the wafer properly. More likely, however, he had not paid that much attention and let the peasants make of the ceremony what they would. By looking away at just the right moment, Father Ryan did what Catholic priests had done for centuries, which was to accommodate pagan practice.

Despite Father Ryan's denials, Wansbrough tried to show that the priest either knowingly participated in the fairy trial, or allowed himself to be used by the peasants. On at least three occasions, his conduct was suspect—on Wednesday, when he administered last rites and purportedly told Michael to disregard the doctor's instructions; on Friday morning, when he said Mass at the cottage and administered the diagnostic wafer; and on Saturday, when he was told of the burning but failed to report it to police.

Regarding this third incident, Wansbrough asked why he had failed to report the burning after being told about it by John Dunne. Wansbrough confronted the priest directly: "Will you say how with that foul crime having been revealed to you, why you took no steps whatever to bring any of those criminals to justice, or to inform the police?" Ryan admitted only that he had gathered from the men's conversation that foul play was involved in Bridget's disappearance, not fairycraft. John Dunne had said something suspicious, but Michael Cleary was acting as if he was out of his mind, so Ryan went to the police barracks and told Acting Sergeant Egan to "keep an eye on Cleary." After reporting the men to the police, Ryan said, "I did not see any of them after that or since."

Wansbrough pressed Father Ryan about why he did not tell the police specifically about the burning, which was something very different from reporting a missing person. He reminded Ryan that, as a matter of fact, John Dunne had told him explicitly that "the woman had been burned." Wansbrough asked Ryan to explain his failure to inform the police, observing, "I would like to know your reason for it, because it seems extraordinary." Before Father Ryan could respond, Wansbrough backed off, knowing the magistrates would not allow a priest to be publicly exposed as a perjurer. Rather, the whole matter was politely quashed and the embarrassed priest quietly left the stand.

Whether as willing participant or unwitting dupe, Father Ryan played a role in the fairy trial of Bridget Cleary. On Wednesday, the seventh day of the fairy trial, Father Ryan gave last rites to the ailing Bridget Cleary prior to the Seven Sisters Kill or Cure remedy. On Friday, the ninth day, he administered the Sacred Host, which, to the onlookers, seemed to expose the presence of the changeling but failed to drive it away. As Father Ryan rode off to breakfast that Friday morning, the family was left to draw their own conclusions—the herbal cures were ineffective, the priest was powerless, the Old Deceiver was still among them, and it was the ninth day. In the wake of his failure, the family was left to its own devices.

The Fairy Shilling

In the aftermath of the morning Mass, the fairy trial conducted in the cottage at Ballyvadlea resumed in deadly earnest and with redoubled zeal. With only twelve hours remaining until the witching hour and the irrevocable separation of Bridget's spirit from her body, Michael Cleary called in anyone and everyone who could add certainty to the issue. One was William Simpson, who stopped by, he claimed, simply to visit with Bridget after the ordeal of the previous night. He went inside, chatted with Bridget, and observed that she appeared somewhat weaker but was taking milk. Intending more than neighborly banter, Simpson questioned Bridget in a way designed to discern if she was herself or if the Old Deceiver was again in possession of her body. He asked if she knew him. She said she did. Simpson had his dog with him. Did she know his dog? Her answer was evasive. She initially had trouble identifying Simpson's dog, but later was able to do so. After this informal interrogation, Simpson remembered seeing Michael Cleary and John Dunne out in the yard deep in conversation—a fact that Dunne had conveniently forgotten to mention in his deposition. He did not join them. Simpson left, leaving Bridget alone in the cottage.

Johanna Burke, her daughter Katie, and Mary Kennedy in separate statements revealed to the magistrates some more events of that Friday afternoon. Burke spent part of the afternoon at the cottage after Simpson left, washing shirts and sheets soiled in the messy goings-on of the previous night. Her testimony continued to be guarded, every word calculated to protect her brothers. But the ever persistent Wansbrough harried his witness for more details of the fairy trial, and as he did, other, more disturbing information emerged that showed the family's struggle to determine Bridget's identity. It seemed that the issue of whether or not Bridget was a changeling was decided definitively by, of all things, the curious matter of a fairy shilling.

Based on what can be gathered from Burke's willfully obtuse testimony, it appeared that sometime that Friday afternoon, Bridget asked Johanna Burke to go and buy her some new milk. When Michael learned of this request, it probably set him on edge. It was commonly believed that fairies loved milk and received nourishment from it. For this reason, Irish farmers often let a bit of milk spill from their pails to assuage the fairies. If Bridget was inhabited by a fairy, Michael feared that giving her milk would only encourage the fairy to stay. The fact that Bridget was asking for milk at all was suspicious, especially when Bridget had sent Johanna Burke on a special errand just for the purpose of obtaining new milk.

When Burke returned that afternoon, her daughter, Katie, her mother, and a neighbor, Johanna Meara, were with Bridget, who asked her to drink some of the new milk. According to Mary Kennedy, Bridget later told her: "I sent Han, says she, for milk and he would not give me a drop of it and I never asked [for] any milk, says she, without buying it." Hearing his wife's request for a drink of milk, Michael asked Johanna Burke how she paid for it. Burke replied that Bridget had given her a shilling in payment, which Michael immediately demanded to see. Johanna produced the coin from her pocket and Michael examined it closely, looking for tell-tale signs of its authenticity. Bridget knew full well why he wished to see the shilling, so she asked to see it as well. Michael handed her the shilling then she slipped it under the bedcovers, pretending to rub it on her leg, just as a fairy would do.[19]

This was a fatal mistake, perhaps. Bridget knew full well how Michael would interpret this seemingly innocent act. She knew that he would take it as a sign that she was a fairy masquerading as his wife, and that she possessed the power of enchantment required to endow the shilling with its special properties. She knew that it was the ninth day and he was desperate for any clue to help him discern the identity of the wifelike creature lying in his bed. She knew him well enough to know that if he believed she was a fairy, he was prepared to burn the impostor to get his wife back. And knowing all this, Bridget intentionally slipped the shilling beneath the bedcovers and rubbed the coin on her leg just as a fairy would do.

Why did Bridget deliberately provoke her husband at this particular moment? Was she merely teasing him? Trying to show him that his fears were silly? Maybe she was thinking: He believes I'm a fairy. I'll take the shilling and rub it on my leg and, when I give it back to him, he'll see that it is just an ordinary shilling and he'll come to his senses.

Then again, maybe Bridget wasn't teasing. Perhaps she believed that she was a changeling and she was signaling him that she did indeed have the power to produce a fairy shilling from beneath the bedcovers. Maybe she believed this. And maybe it was true.

Whether Bridget was tempting, teasing, or telling her husband something, the gesture made with the shilling affirmed Michael's conviction that the creature was not his wife. To his mind, she acted just as a fairy would act if it was trying to take away his wife. She warded off the power of the priest, she removed the Sacred Host, and she resisted Ganey's most powerful potion. Now she used a fairy shilling to purchase milk and acknowledged it as such by rubbing the coin on her leg. This last gesture confirmed to Michael that he would be required to carry out the last phase of the ritual if he were to retrieve his missing wife.

The significance of the incident revolved around the belief that the fairies dispensed special coins—usually a shilling—that possessed magical properties. Legends of the fairy shilling arose from the belief that fairies could produce coins at will by rubbing any object on their person and turning it into a coin. Since fairies had no use for coins themselves, they frequently gave out shillings to mortals—sometimes for good ends, sometimes for mischief.

The story of Paddy O'Grady illustrates the promise and peril of the fairy shilling. Paddy was making his way home one fine moonlit night, when he spied a woman standing beside the road with a basket beside her. He greeted her and she greeted him, then she picked up the basket and walked with him, step for step, along the road. Thinking the basket was too heavy for a lady to carry, Paddy asked if he could carry it, and the woman thanked him and handed him the basket. When he took it, he was surprised because it had no weight to it, so he thought it must be empty. They walked on awhile, neither one asking the name of the other.

When they reached a crossroads near Paddy's home, Paddy said he'd be turning off, and she said she'd be going the same way, that she was going to Jimi Jeck's house, who happened to be Paddy's neighbor. They continued on together and when they arrived at Jeck's house, Paddy handed the woman her basket, and she asked him if he drank. Paddy said naturally at a fair or market he was sure to take a pint. So she put her hand in her pocket and handed him a shilling.

"Now," said she, "next time you have a pint, drink to my health!" With that she departed, and he saw her no more.

Next morning, Paddy rose and thought to ask his neighbor, Jimi Jeck, about the woman. "Blast you!" said Jimi, "I saw no woman at all!"

Between then and nightfall, Paddy wanted a bit of tobacco, so went to the shop and gave the clerk the shilling for the tobacco and got some change back for it. On his way home, he put his hand in his pocket to feel his change, and there was the shilling back again.

This shilling was spent and returned to his pocket repeatedly for several years. Whenever Paddy went to the tavern for a pint or bought a bit of tobacco, he paid with the shilling and each time got it back again. After a few years, he feared he was drinking too much because of it, so he went to the priest and told him what happened. The priest put his stole around his neck and made the sign of the cross on the shilling, and it disappeared forever. And that was the tale of Paddy O'Grady's fairy shilling.[20] The virtue of having a fairy shilling was that, even though it was spent, it would reappear and could be spent again. The vice of it was that having such a remarkable coin could lead a mortal into trouble. Fairy intervention of this sort was always a mixed blessing.

Bridget's seemingly playful gesture with the shilling set off a dispute that continued through the late afternoon and on into the night with Michael refusing to allow her to drink the milk, insisting instead that she drink the water from the glass bottle called a "naggin" containing Ganey's herbs. At one point, Mary Kennedy interceded on Bridget's behalf, asking Michael, "What nourishment is a cup of water for the creature?" At that, Cleary took the bottle of milk away and would not give her even ere a "tint" of it. "No matter, Bridgie," said Mary Kennedy, "Hanney will give you a cup bye and bye." It is not clear whether they insisted on the ritual questioning at this time, but at some point Bridget insisted that two neighbors be called to settle their dispute. One of them, Thomas Smyth, a fifty-four-year-old farmer living nearby, had been to the cottage earlier that afternoon.

When his turn came to testify, Smyth said as little as possible and minimized his own involvement in the ritual by pretending to know nothing about fairy lore. Smyth stated that he had been plowing in a field adjoining the Clearys' house and hearing that Bridget was ill, went to visit around two P.M. on Friday afternoon. Bridget was in bed, attended by her husband, Johanna Burke, and John Dunne, who apparently had come inside after talking to Michael. According to Smyth, Bridget was clearly ill; she had a "delicate appearance" and looked "washy." He asked her how she felt, whereupon she made some reply that he later said he did not understand, but others reported that she had told him that her husband was making a fairy of her. He believed, however, that she had recognized him. He claimed to have had further conversation with her. When pressed by Wansbrough to reveal more details of what had happened in the cottage, Smyth said that he had asked Cleary and Burke if Bridget was eating anything. They said she was. Smyth thought they were serving Bridget "a cup of tea, or a cut of bread, or something like that." Wansbrough asked if Ganey's herbs were being forcibly administered on Friday, but Smyth could not answer this. Smyth stated that he was in the cottage just ten minutes that afternoon, then left.

After Smyth's departure, Michael and Bridget continued to quarrel over the fairy shilling on into the evening. In order finally to decide the matter, Bridget suggested that "two honest men" be called to the cottage. According to Johanna Burke, Bridget felt that Michael might be persuaded that she was herself again if others could convince him. Bridget said to Burke, "If I had Tom Smyth and David Hogan they would settle what is between me and Mike." Once again, "Hanney" and her daughter, Katie, became messengers to fetch Smyth and Hogan.

A little after eight P.M. Johanna Burke knocked on Smyth's door and asked him to come back. She told him that Bridget had requested that he help settle an argument with Michael. Along the way, she also called on David Hogan, and they all went back to the Clearys' cottage together, Katie Burke with them. When they arrived around 8:30 P.M., they found Mary Kennedy, Patrick Boland, and an assortment of neighbors, including Thomas Anglim, Johanna Meara, Patrick Leahy, and Tom Lehy.[21] It appeared that a ritual was underway to which Smyth and Hogan were summoned as witnesses.

Thomas Smyth, like the others, was reluctant to reveal details of the fairy trial and tried to couch events in terms that authorities would find acceptable. According to Smyth, Michael Cleary said to his wife, "Here's Tom Smyth and David Hogan, now." When the two entered the bedroom, Cleary was urging his wife to ingest a certain fluid drawn from a small bottle which he held in his hand.

Cleary asked his wife, "Will you take this now, as Tom Smyth and David Hogan are here?" Smyth asked Cleary what was in the bottle and claimed that Cleary told him that it was Holy Water. More than likely, this was untrue. By now, everyone in the neighborhood knew that Cleary was giving his wife herbs from Ganey across the mountain—herbs contained in a small "naggin" bottle. Smyth continued, stating that Cleary asked Bridget to drink the liquid "in the name of the Father, Son, and Holy Ghost, which she did." After Bridget drank the liquid as instructed, Michael asked her to drink milk, which she did. Wansbrough asked Smyth if Cleary told him why he had been called to the cottage. Smyth again was less than truthful and reported that Cleary asked him no questions. He saw no marks on Bridget's body that would indicate harm, but pleased Wansbrough by stating that she "did not appear to be right in her head," yet she answered all questions put to her. He saw nothing suspicious and would have the court believe that Michael did nothing more than bless some milk in the name of God before giving it to his wife to drink.

Wansbrough sensed that Smyth was hiding something so he pressed ahead in search of more details. Upon further questioning, Smyth disclosed that late that night, perhaps around eleven, Johanna Meara, Patrick Leahy, and Tom Lehy left for home, leaving Smyth, Hogan, and Tom Anglim alone in the cottage with Bridget and the family. The three visitors—Smyth, Hogan, and Anglim—retired "down to the fire." Meanwhile, Michael Cleary, Johanna Burke, and Mary Kennedy disappeared into the bedroom where they began to dress Bridget in her finest clothing.

The details of this ritual dressing remain murky, but the outlines emerged through bits of various witnesses' testimony. According to Smyth's account, it was Bridget who first suggested that she be dressed in her finest clothes. He stated that after leaving the bedroom, the men retired to the fire where Michael told them Bridget wanted to get up and get dressed. Shortly she appeared wearing a frock and a shawl. When pressed for a more complete description of the clothing, Smyth added reluctantly that Johanna Burke aired her jacket and corset.

Mary Kennedy, however, claimed that it was Michael who insisted that Bridget get dressed up. She stated that the three of them—Michael, Mary Kennedy, and Johanna Burke—laid out both her petticoats, one red and the other striped, her navy blue flannel dress, a gray corset, navy blue cashmere jacket, black stockings, boots, and her gold earrings. Beneath her fine clothes she wore "an ordinary calico chemise." When asked in her March deposition why she had put on her best clothing at this late hour, Johanna Burke disclosed that Bridget dressed in her finest "to give her courage to go amongst the people."

Burke's reference to "the people" could be interpreted in different ways. Bridget could have been referring to the men assembled by the fire—Smyth, Hogan, and Anglim—who would shortly pass judgment on her true identity. Or perhaps she wanted to dress so she could go out to meet the police, suggesting that the police were at the cottage and that she might try to secure their help.

Smyth disclosed that after Bridget was fully dressed, but before leaving the bedroom, she suddenly said to Michael, "the peelers are at the window and mind me now." Provoked by this remark, Michael picked up the chamber pot and threw urine on Bridget, some of it soiling her cashmere sweater, some landing on the window where the peelers were said to be. Apparently Michael was angered by his wife's demand that he "mind" her wishes (obey her), or he may have feared she might try to call for the police and disrupt the ritual. Wansbrough urged Smyth to explain the incident. Were the peelers actually there, or was she imagining it all? Smyth believed that she only imagined the peelers. Smyth's observation reinforced Wansbrough's argument that Bridget was incapable of defending herself.

The most likely meaning of Burke's statement that Bridget prepared "to go amongst the people" was that she dressed in her finest clothes to go among the fairy folk. In questioning Smyth about this possibility, Wansbrough wondered why Bridget would dress in her finest clothes at that late hour. He specifically asked if she said anything about dressing to meet the fairy folk. Smyth denied hearing anything about the fairies, except what other witnesses had already divulged in court, but he recalled hearing the dispute over the fairy shilling. In the course of questioning, Smyth disclosed that the discussion about the fairy shilling continued *after* Bridget was dressed in her finest attire.

From this information, we can reconstruct what took place in the Cleary cottage an hour or so before midnight of the ninth day of the fairy trial. Johanna Meara and other friends and neighbors had gone home, leaving only the three men—Thomas Smyth, David Hogan, and Tom Anglim—who had been called to judge whether the woman claiming to be Bridget Cleary was herself or a changeling. Shortly after eleven, Bridget emerged from her bedroom dressed in her best clothes, as Burke testified, "to go amongst the people."[22] She sat down with Smyth, Hogan, and Anglim by the fire, prepared for the ordeal that awaited her.

Mary Kennedy indicated that the discussion about milk taking place in the bedroom continued when Bridget went to the kitchen.[23] When Bridget emerged from the bedroom dressed in her best clothes, Smyth asked how she was doing. "Middling," she replied, then complained that Michael "was making a fairy out of me now."

"Don't mind him, Bridgie," Mary retorted, "don't be afraid."

Then Mary asked Michael for some milk, presumably to give Bridget. Michael refused.

"Well I never asked [for] milk without buying it," Bridget declared, again alluding to the fairy shilling dispute.

Perhaps fearing Michael's response, Mary Kennedy told her to "hold her tongue, and not be minding him, that she could drink it bye-and-bye." According to Mary, Bridget said nothing more about the milk.

Wansbrough pressed Smyth for details of what happened next. In his eagerness to prove Bridget's insensibility, Wansbrough asked about Bridget's state of mind. He asked Smyth if Bridget spoke coherently. Smyth evaded the question by responding that Bridget was incoherent because she was talking about fairies, an answer that assumed that anyone talking about fairies was by definition incoherent. Wansbrough asked if there was anything said about *pishogues?*

> *Smyth*: Well there was. She said that she never got a bottle of milk or anything but she paid for it, nor did she get anything from her mother [meaning either a bottle of milk or a shilling]. I heard her ask Johanna Burke—"Did he give you a shilling?" and she said not; Mrs. Cleary repeated the questions, and she again denied it; Mrs. Cleary then said—"Thanks be to God; there is no use in me saying anything now," and I think she also said— "There's no *pishogues* in me," or something like that.
>
> *Wansbrough*: What do you mean by that?
>
> *Smyth*: Something like witchcraft, I understand.

By stating that *pishogues* were akin to witchcraft, Thomas Smyth evaded the question, disclosing much less than he knew. The fairy *pishogue*, common in Irish folklore, is from the Irish *pisreog* meaning a charm or spell, usually an evil charm or spell meant to do harm. If, for instance, one wished to bestow bad luck upon a neighbor, one might throw rotten eggs over the fence into the neighbor's yard. It was believed that the eggs carried the *pishogue*, or evil spell, and as the eggs rotted further, the neighbor's good fortune departed. Like the casting of the evil eye, the *pishogue* was feared in rural Ireland for its power to do material damage, such as cause illness, make a cow go dry, or rot a potato patch. In order to avoid the harmful effects of the charm, one must constantly be alert to the *pishogue* and be prepared to counteract its effects. It would be entirely appropriate for the aggrieved family to call in others to determine the source of the spell and prescribe what, if any, steps should be taken to neutralize the charm.

But Smyth's less-than-forthcoming testimony disclosed that possession was the real concern regarding the *pishogue* and the fairy shilling because both were a sign that an alien spirit possessed Bridget's body. Michael Cleary seized upon the incident with the fairy shilling to demonstrate that there was a *pishogue* in his wife, meaning that she was possessed. Apparently Bridget fought back, insisting that she was herself and not a fairy.[24] Michael charged that Bridget had asked Johanna Burke to buy milk in the village and paid her for the milk with a fairy shilling. As proof he told the three witnesses that she had taken the shilling, hid it beneath the bedcovers, and rubbed it on her leg as a fairy would do. Bridget did not deny the charge, but angrily retorted: "There's no *pishogues* in me, thanks be to God." Bridget then countered his charge with one of her own, insinuating that Michael only accused her of being a fairy because his own mother had once "gone with the fairies," saying: "Your own mother used to go with the fairies, and that is why you think I am going with them." Michael immediately demanded to know if his mother had told her this, and Bridget replied in the affirmative.

As Michael and Bridget exchanged charges, the three men listened silently, each deciding whether or not they sat before Bridget or the changeling. Smyth did reveal that they reviewed details about the alleged "fairy blast" on March 6, when the possession was believed to have occurred. Again, Smyth's testimony indicated that the discussion went back and forth. Bridget denied there were any *pishogue* about her then blurted out: "They left me on the road by myself at Skehan's yard or about Skehan's Gate." Someone else recalled that Bridget returned home that day in a fit of trembling. Sensing that the evidence against her was mounting, Bridget tried to make light of the situation as she had done when Michael accused her of rubbing the shilling on her thigh. Smyth disclosed that after making the statement about Skehan's gate, Bridget pointed to someone in the room and said, "There's Jim Skehan now." Since Jim Skehan was not in the room, Smyth claimed that this was proof that Bridget was "not right in the mind."[25] Smyth's claim was clever. He knew Wansbrough would accept this response since this was the testimony he was trying to elicit in order to try the fairies at the magisterial inquiry. Yet, it was also a way of saying that he, and the others, believed that Bridget was not right in the mind, meaning she was indeed a fairy and not herself. This ended the conversation about fairies and *pishogue*, but apparently the three men had reached a decision.

Before Thomas Smyth was dismissed, Wansbrough asked how long he had stayed at the cottage. Smyth replied that he had stayed until midnight, then left with Hogan and Anglim. Wansbrough asked again if there was any more conversation about witchcraft. Rather than perjure himself, Smyth simply stated that he did not hear anything more. In contrast, Johanna Burke stated that the conservation that evening went on for so long that she forgot all that was said. By this time the presentation of the "evidence" in Wansbrough's fairy trial was deemed conclusive and damning. Perhaps with just a nod or gesture, the three men rendered their verdict. After all the potions, charms, prayers, sacraments, and the application of fire, the changeling still possessed the body of Bridget Cleary. Ironically, Bridget herself was sensible enough to realize what was happening. "Thanks be to God," she said, "there is no use in my saying anything now."

The depositions revealed nothing more about the evening's events. As Smyth, Hogan, and Anglim were preparing to leave, Patrick, James, and William Kennedy returned dog-tired and probably hung over from the wake of Michael's father. They were no doubt surprised to see Bridget sitting by the fire in her finest clothes, but one greeted her saying, "Bridgie, I am glad to see you up." They joined with the other men around the fire, chatting and undoubtedly hearing about the day's events. They talked awhile as Johanna Burke fetched tea. Then Smyth, Hogan, and Anglim departed for home, at which time the Kennedys went "into the old man's bed" and fell asleep.

It was now near midnight of the ninth and final day of Bridget Cleary's fairy trial. Johanna Burke was clearing up the dishes just as midnight came. Michael and Bridget sat together by the fire looking for all the world like close companions—Bridget still dressed in her best clothes. It seemed a cozy, domestic scene. But the time for deception, contradiction, and guessing had now passed. What was done was done. It was now time for her to "Go Amongst the People."

6

"To Go Amongst
the People"

The Witching Hour

As midnight approached on Friday, March 15, Bridget Cleary sat by the fire, surrounded by her family. Her father, Patrick Boland, and husband, Michael, were there, as were her aunt, Mary Kennedy, and her cousins, Johanna Burke, Patrick, James, and William Kennedy, and ten-year-old Katie Burke. The only family member missing from the inner circle was her cousin Michael Kennedy, who stayed the night at his employer's farm outside Drangan. There were nine gathered round the fire as the clock struck midnight, marking the end of the ninth and final day of the trial of the cooper's wife.

Patrick, James, and William Kennedy had arrived back at the cottage just as Tom Smyth, David Hogan, and Tom Anglim were leaving for home.[1] When the last neighbor was gone, Michael Cleary secured the lock on the door and put the key in his pocket. Johanna Burke noticed him do it. The three Kennedy boys sat down by the fire and talked with Bridget, curious to know how she was feeling. She appeared to be more like her old self, and they told her that they were glad she was feeling better. After talking awhile, the Kennedys were apparently satisfied that Bridget was herself once again. They had left for Killenaule the night before believing she was cured, so knew nothing of the Mass earlier that morning, the desecrated communion wafer, or the grave dispute over the fairy shilling. As far as they knew, Ganey's potion, fortified by fire, had driven off the changeling, and they wanted to be sure that Bridget held nothing against them. The three of them seemed satisfied that all was right between them, so they went off to the "old man's room," where they fell into his one tiny bed and were soon fast asleep.

That left just the six by the fire—Bridget and Michael, Patrick Boland and Mary Kennedy, Johanna and young Katie Burke. It was a strange scene in the cottage that night. Bridget had dressed in her finest clothes—now stained with urine—to "Go Amongst the People." Johanna Burke was jumping up to fetch and do whatever anyone wanted. Michael paced about like a nervous cat, watching the clock, listening for any unusual sounds. Pat Boland and his sister, Mary, stared at the fire, fearing what might happen next.

Having received tacit agreement from three of his neighbors, Michael Cleary was even more certain that the creature by the fire wearing his wife's finest clothes was not his wife but a changeling. He was convinced of it. Moreover, he believed that it didn't matter what he did to her because, in the end, she would die anyway. Despite his own best efforts to get help from the doctor, priest, and herbalists, Bridget seemed to grow worse. As he recalled later, she had become so "despondent and emaciated" that he entertained no hope of her recovery.[2] Father Ryan had administered last rites, leading Michael to believe that the priest thought she would die. The folk tales foretold her death. Everyone assembled that night in the cottage believed she would eventually die if the changeling were not expelled. It seemed a foregone conclusion. Yet Michael Cleary also believed that even if his wife, or the creature imitating his wife, should die, he might still have his wife back again. The stories told him so.

Other husbands in Ireland had lost their wives to the fairies; only some had won them back. Michael would likely have heard and believed stories like the one about the shoemaker from Donegal who had a wife who was about to deliver a child when the fairies took her. The shoemaker had gone to fetch a midwife to see to his wife, and as he returned home, a flock of birds swooped down upon him, alerting him to the fact that something was dreadfully wrong at home. He threw a handful of iron nails into the air to ward off the spirit birds, and no sooner had he done so than he heard something fall beneath the horse's feet. He quickly dismounted and saw a woman lying in the road who resembled his wife. Fearful that his wife had been taken by the fairies, the shoemaker returned home where he learned that his wife was dead in their bed. But since he had seen her on the road, he believed that the creature in the bed was a changeling and there was yet time to save his wife. On the chance he was right, he ran to the barn and in a flash returned with a pitchfork and made straight for the creature lying lifeless in the bed. But before he could drive it through her, the creature rose out of bed and departed through the open window in a rush of air. He had no fear about piercing the woman with the pitchfork, for he knew the creature lying in his bed was not his wife. After the changeling was driven out, the wife's spirit returned to her own body and her health was restored. In due time the child was born safely, and the shoemaker and his wife were troubled no more.[3]

Happily the shoemaker recovered his wife and all ended well, but he'd never have had her back had he not thrown iron nails at the birds and raised the pitchfork at the creature lying in his bed. Michael Cleary sought similar traditional remedies when he fetched the Seven Sisters Cure from the woman in Fethard. He asked John Dunne to help him administer the potion and followed Dunne's suggestion that they use fire to drive off the changeling. He called for the priest every day and twice the priest came. He also repeatedly summoned Dr. Crean from the medical dispensary in Fethard. And for surety, he went across to the mountain for Ganey's "nine-in-one cure." And just as he walked up the lane to his cottage with Ganey's cure in his pocket, he heard the news of his own father's death in Killenaule.[4] Emotionally and physically exhausted, he could easily believe that "the people" were playing a deadly game with him, perhaps even taking his father as a means of distracting his attention from exorcising the spirit. After the nine-day ordeal, it was clear that if he wanted his wife back, he would be obliged to fight harder still.

But after all the trouble he'd gone to, what haunted Michael the most was the thought that Bridget did not wish to return, in which case all the charms, priests, and potions in Ireland could not bring her back. He might have heard the tale of young Biddy Purcell, who was as pure and clever a girl as could be found in seven parishes. At just eighteen, Biddy was suddenly "whipped away" by the fairies one day when she and her sister were out gathering rushes in a bog beneath an old castle. A very strange old woman approached, demanding that Biddy give over a portion of the rushes to her, to which Biddy replied that the bog was big enough, there were plenty of rushes and she could go pick her own. The words were no sooner out of her mouth than the old woman erupted in anger, drew forth a large stick, and proceeded to give Biddy a good whipping about the knees. The old woman then left and Biddy and her sister ran home. That night Biddy took sick, screeching and bawling with pain.

The family knew for certain that Biddy was taken, but in all her raving, she insisted that they do nothing to get her back. She said it was no use trying to save her, for she'd seen a whole heap of male fairies riding on horses, and every one had girls following behind them. One of the fairies was waiting for her and would come for her on a certain day, at a certain hour. She implored them to do nothing to save her. Hearing these words from Biddy's mouth herself, the family was uncertain. Should they believe her story and let her be? Was it Biddy herself speaking to them, or only the changeling?

The family sent for a fairy doctor, who provided a test for determining if the spirit was Biddy's or that of a changeling. They were given a bottle of simple green herbs with instructions to boil the herbs and watch for any change in color. In the Celtic cosmology, green signified eternal life and immortality, which was why fairies were commonly seen in green attire. The color green was also associated with abduction. While green was the color of life, gold, like the number nine, signified transition and transformation. This meant that if the herbs stayed green after being boiled, Biddy would recover, but if they turned golden yellow, she was gone, her spirit was transformed, and nothing could be done. The family did as instructed, and when boiled, the herbs turned yellow as gold, meaning the creature was a changeling. The diagnosis was confirmed when Biddy drank the golden herbs and died five minutes later.[5]

Though Biddy passed away, the family found comfort in knowing that they did everything possible to save her in the time allotted, and if she went after all, she went of her own volition. They could think of her riding off with a young, handsome fairy man and living happily ever after in the Otherworld. Who among them would blame her for desiring that existence? With all the trouble and confusion in this world, why would she want to stay? A similar thought that Bridget may have willingly gone off troubled Michael Cleary, and the image of her riding away with some fairy prince disturbed the jealous husband even more. Bridget Cleary was his wife and belonged to him. Only he had the right to possess her, and he'd be damned in hell before he allowed some fairyman to be riding off with his wife.

These thoughts must have obsessed Michael Cleary as he paced back and forth in front of the fireplace just before midnight on the ninth day of the fairy trial. As the six family members gathered around the warmth of the fire, Johanna Burke stood and busied herself by preparing more tea. Michael stared at his wife as she sat by the fire and wondered if the spirit looking out at him was his wife or the Old Deceiver come again to torment him. Impulsively, no longer willing to be tormented by his own dark thoughts, Michael decided to repeat the ritual one last time. Johanna Burke offered both Michael and Bridget a cup of tea, but Michael objected, saying he wanted Bridget first to eat three pieces of bread and jam. He handed her the first bit of bread, repeating three times the question, "Are you Bridget Cleary my wife in the name of God?" Twice she answered yes and ate the bit of bread with jam. On the third round, she refused to answer the questions or eat the bread and jam. That was all the remaining evidence Michael needed. Bridget's refusal to answer the question the third and most important time meant that the changeling was back again, or had never left. There was only one course of action remaining to him.

Johanna Burke's testimony at the hearing reveals in horrifying detail Michael's last, desperate attempt to retrieve his wife's spirit. It was to be Bridget's final ordeal. Upon her refusal to answer his question the third time, Michael jumped up and threw her to the floor so hard that she may have hit her head on the flagstone in front of the fireplace. With his knee to her chest and his hand on her throat, the cooper forced the bread into his wife's mouth, shouting, "If you don't take it, down you will go. Swallow it. Is it down? Is it down?" Wansbrough asked if Burke said anything to him.

> *Burke*: I said, Let her alone, don't you see it is Bridget that is in it?
> *Wansbrough*: What did you mean by that?
> *Burke*: I meant that it was his wife he was mistreating and not the fairy.

At this point Wansbrough paused to ask the question running through everyone's mind: Why had no one tried to stop the attack? Besides Burke, there were two other adults in the room, and three men sleeping not more than ten feet away behind a flimsy partition. Burke claimed that she threatened to go for the peelers if Michael did not desist. To this threat, he retorted, "the peelers are on the road where they are wanted and they are not here tonight," implying that the peelers had been there previously and confirming Bridget's earlier, seemingly delusional observations.[6] Wansbrough asked why the Kennedy brothers did not try to stop the attack. Burke could only offer a feeble defense. She stated that she called out to her brothers, telling them that Michael was choking Bridget and asking why they didn't come out and take him away or something like that. Then she added sadly that one of her brothers, she didn't recall which, called out from the bedroom, "Let him do what he likes with her. Hold your tongue and let us sleep."[7]

Knowing that no one would intervene, Michael continued his attack on his prostrate wife, who now lay helpless on the flagstone before the fireplace. He ripped at her outer jacket, forcing it up over her head and shoulders. Then he took a "red stump" off the fire and held it over her mouth, demanding to know if she was his wife or a fairy. Bridget struggled, but was unable, or unwilling to answer. Holding the lighted stump over his head, his knee still on her chest, Michael demanded once more: Are you a witch? Are you a fairy? Are you the wife of Michael Cleary? Wansbrough asked what happened next. Burke stated that she saw something like a bloody froth come out of Bridget's mouth. She could see blood from the froth run through his fingers as he was forcing the bit of bread into her mouth. Although his hand was still on her throat, Bridget managed to roll to the side and whispered, "Oh Han, Han."

Hearing these words, Michael Cleary jumped up and shouted from the dock: "Excuse me, I cannot listen to this any longer!"[8] Colonel Richard Charles Evanson ordered silence, then instructed Cleary that he would have an opportunity to question the witness later in the proceedings. Johanna Burke was instructed to continue with her testimony. She stated that Michael grabbed the lighting stump off the fire and held it over Bridget's mouth.

> *Wansbrough*: What happened then?
>
> *Burke*: Michael said the words to me, "Begor Han I believe she's dead."
>
> *Wansbrough*: When Cleary knocked her on the floor, did you hear her knock against the flag?

Burke: Yes, Sir, I heard her head knock, but I don't know whether he did it or not.

Seeing Bridget was unresponsive, Michael put the stick back on the fire and asked Burke to turn down the bed clothes as he wanted to carry Bridget back into bed. As Burke turned and left the kitchen, Michael continued to strip off Bridget's clothing. From the bedroom, Burke saw him tear off her cashmere sweater, blouse and skirt, leaving her clad only in her chemise and stockings. She turned back the bedcovers as instructed, and as she returned to the kitchen, Burke was horrified to see Bridget Cleary's chemise on fire.

Wansbrough: When you came back into the kitchen what did you see?

Burke: I saw her eyes then turned up and they were closed after that. I ran and caught the chemise and took a piece of it away with me. I said I would take it to the barracks and Michael Cleary took it from me and threw it on the fire.[9]

Then according to Burke, Michael Cleary grabbed an oil can from the dresser beside the fireplace and threw the entire contents of the can on his wife then set her on fire. To use the words of young Katie Burke, "She lit up like a blaze." Burke screamed and lunged toward him, but Michael pushed her away.[10] The commotion in the kitchen brought Mary Kennedy and Pat Boland to their feet and the three Kennedys into the room. Upon seeing the conflagration, Burke testified that they sobbed "to be let out" rather than intervene. Belatedly, the Kennedys attempted to intercede, yelling at Michael to "leave her alone."

According to Burke's May 21 deposition, both she and her mother tried to put out the fire but Cleary stopped them. Burke said, "My mother ran to Bridget Cleary and he shoved my mother also." Mary Kennedy confirmed that Michael Cleary "gave me a shoulder and knocked me against the side of the table in my side." Having been pushed aside, Johanna pulled her mother into one of the bedrooms from where they watched Bridget burn. Michael warned them not to interfere, threatening, "If you come out any more, says Cleary, I'll roast you down as well as her." Just to make sure the fire would kill her, he doused more oil on the burning body until the can was completely empty. A burst of flames leapt up around the woman, filling the tiny kitchen with black smoke and the acerbic stench of burning clothing, flesh and bone. Had there been any opportunity for the bewildered bystanders to stop the conflagration it vanished when the last drop of oil was hurled into the flame.

Magistrate Grubb asked Burke to describe again how many times Michael Cleary threw oil on his wife.

Burke: Three.

Wansbrough: Did anyone attempt to extinguish the fire? Did anyone throw water on her?

Burke: My brother William fell into a weakness so my mother threw Easter holy water on him.

Wansbrough: Then no one threw water on Bridget?

Burke: No.

Wansbrough: Did any attempt to rescue her?

Burke: They feared burning themselves and were suffocated with smoke and stench.

Wansbrough: Did you say anything to him?

Burke: I said something to him and Michael says to me, "Hold your tongue, Han. It is not Bridget I am burning, you will see her going out the chimney."[11]

At this last revelation, a "deep sensation" ran through the Clonmel courthouse. After all the laughing, the jokes about fairies, changelings and witches, the grim facts describing how the woman died silenced the crowd. But more disturbing than how she died was the realization that even when doused with a can of paraffin oil and set on fire, the woman never screamed out in pain.

As magistrates and spectators pondered this strange and inexplicable occurence, testimony continued. Burke revealed that rather than rush forward to douse the fire, the Kennedys weakly attempted to flee the cottage, but the door was locked, the key tucked securely in Michael Cleary's "breeches pocket."[12] He had intentionally kept the door locked during the ritual, believing that if the changeling was expelled by the herbal charms, incantations, or fire, it might attempt to reenter the cottage via the doorway. One of the brothers fumbled through the pockets of Michael's jacket, but, unable to locate the key, turned to Michael, begging to be let out. He refused, insisting that no one could leave until "he would bring back [or get back] his wife." Again he insisted, "It is not my wife," then declared "I am not going to keep an old witch in place of my wife, so I must get back my wife."[13]

As if to prove his claim that the creature was not his wife, Cleary held up a scapular of the Virgin taken from Bridget's person. Pointing to the amulet, he said, "What wonder is it that she deceived me—she deceived the priest—look at what Father Ryan put on her neck." Only he, among the lot of them, was not fooled by the Old Deceiver. He understood its cunning, its intelligence and determination; he also knew his wife better than they did. Cleary reproached the lot of them for allowing themselves to be deceived and, worse, for not fighting back. "You're a cowardly dirty set," he shouted. "You would rather have her go to the Fort than to have me have her." As the flames died down, the group watched the burning corpse until Patrick Boland muttered, "Anything I can do to bring back my child I will do."[14]

It took fully thirty minutes for the paraffin oil to burn off, during which time none of the Kennedys tried to force the door or overpower Cleary. Even though the smell inside the cottage must have been suffocating, none made a serious effort to leave. William Kennedy claimed that he did attempt to get out several times but was barred by the locked door. But apparently no one tried to climb out a window, which clearly was possible since Acting Sergeant Patrick Egan had no trouble entering the Cleary cottage through a bedroom window during his investigation. Perhaps they did not make a serious effort to leave because they believed Michael Cleary and were still not certain about who, or what, had been burned.

When the flames finally died down, Cleary approached the body and asked the men to "lift her on to the fire and she'll go up the chimney and we will have Bridgey in a few minutes." Her body was lifted onto the grate by her father and Pat Kennedy. As they lifted her, Michael Cleary slid a steel spade under her thighs and wedged her torso into the fireplace. There was no sound of the changeling rushing away. Nothing but smoke went up the chimney. It was an awful silence.

When Johanna Burke concluded her account of the burning, Chief Magistrate Evanson ordered that her entire testimony be read to the prisoners to ensure they understood it and to allow the prisoners and their attorneys to cross-examine the witness. As the court reporter read back the transcript, Johanna Burke stood in the dock and wept openly. Evanson asked if there were any questions, but only Michael Kennedy had anything to say, insisting that he was not there on Friday night. Burke confirmed to the court that his statement was correct. Solicitor Crean, defending

Cleary and Ganey, said that he had not yet had a chance to read all the depositions and asked the court to call a recess. Evanson agreed but allowed Wansbrough first to call his next witness.

District Inspector Wansbrough rose and called Katie Burke to the dock. Again, a murmur went through the crowd in the courtroom, expressing a "thrill of interest" in what the youngest witness might say. Solicitor Crean rose to object, questioning the propriety of bringing a child into the proceedings on the grounds that she probably did not understand the nature of an oath—an untenable position as the Catholic Church maintained that children reached the age of reason at age six. In response to Crean's objection, the court clerk, William Casey, stated that Katie, like her aunt Bridget, attended the convent school in Drangan, where she said her prayers morning and evening, and believed that if she told a lie she would go to hell. With this matter laid to rest, Evanson bid Wansbrough to proceed with the witness.

Katie Burke was a "pretty, intelligent child," not unlike her cousin, Bridget, and, by all accounts, told her story "clearly and without confusion."[15] She began by stating that she lived with her grandmother, Mary Kennedy, at Ballyvadlea, possibly because her grandmother's home lay closer to her school in Drangan. In her account of the burning, she stated that she saw "Mickey" Cleary give Bridget some medicine. Then she saw Mickey knock Bridget to the flagstone threatening to put a lighted stick in her mouth if she did not eat the last bit of food. "Then when she did not eat it," Katie explained, "he caught her and laid her on the fire."

Wansbrough: And then what happened?
Katie: Then he took fire and he got lamp oil and he put it on her.
Wansbrough: What happened next?
Katie: She lit up like a blaze.

The powerful simplicity of this innocent child's testimony was enough for the prosecution. Colonel Evanson once again asked the prisoners if they wished to question the witness. None did. With this, the magisterial inquiry investigating the burning of Bridget Cleary was recessed until Monday, April 1, which allowed Solicitor Richard Crean time to review the depositions and prepare to examine the witnesses in defense of his clients, Michael Cleary and Dennis Ganey.

To the Fort

For at least thirty more minutes after the fatal burning of Bridget Cleary, the corpse lay smoldering in the fireplace—smoke now rising up the chimney gently in a gray, silken plume. The body remained in the same position in which Michael Cleary, Patrick Kennedy, and Patrick Boland had placed it: Rolled on her side, propped upon the grate, her body bent up in two like a jackknife, hips inside the fireplace, the crown of her head and soles of her feet resting on the flagstone apron. Her arms were drawn up against her chest, as if in prayer. Her knees buckled up, locking calf against thigh, a single black stocking dangled uselessly from a foot. The other foot was bare. The buttocks and midsection were horribly burned, charred through to the bone, leaving the internal organs partially exposed. The parts of her body lying outside the fireplace, however—her upper torso, shoulders, neck, and hair—were untouched. Not a feature of her face was blemished, not a hair singed, although there was a soot mark on her forehead.

The stench and smoke should have driven them all out of the tiny cottage, but no one left or even tried to get out. Johanna Burke said she threatened to go for the peelers, and Mary Kennedy claimed that since her son, William, fell in a faint, she was busy dousing him with holy water. But none of the others made a serious effort to break out of the cottage and seek help.[16] Michael Cleary had locked the door, fearing that the Old Deceiver would steal back in through the door once it went up the chimney. Even though the door was locked, they could have escaped through a window, or the three strapping Kennedy brothers could have wrestled Michael to the flagstone and fished the key out of his pocket. Instead they did nothing as the body burned slowly on the fireplace grate while the eight of them passively watched the grisly spectacle.

During this macabre period of quiet, Michael Cleary persisted in repeating the ritual meant to drive the changeling away. "Away with you! Away with you!" he shouted, waving his arms over the smoldering corpse of his wife so as to guide the smoke up the chimney. With each repetition, they all paused to listen for any unusual sound made by the departing spirit—the rushing of wind; a banging window; objects moving about the room mysteriously; movement outside where there might be a procession of fairies coming to escort the Old Deceiver home with them, making a sort of noisy celebration of the fact that she had lasted the nine days and neither the best of the fairy doctoring, nor the power of the priest, could make her go.

This ritual was punctuated by occasional protests to Michael that it was Bridget they were burning, but with each such whimper, Michael retorted that it was not his wife on the grate, but the old witch. The old witch was dead, he declared, but his wife was being held captive at the fort. Although the nine days were past, they could still rescue Bridget if they dared go to the fort and confront the fairies. Michael assured the reluctant Kennedy boys that he was willing to try but he needed their help as well. Pat Boland continued his sobbing, promising to do anything to bring his child back to him.

Michael quickly formulated a plan: Just past midnight on the

coming day, they would all go to the place where Bridget was being held captive, to the fairy fort on Kylnagranagh hill. There they
would wait for the fairies to pass through the portal, and when
they did, Bridget would be riding on a gray horse. If they could
catch hold of her, and hold her tight, they could have her back.
But this could only happen if they had courage, armed themselves
properly, and were themselves willing to risk being taken.

If all went well, events would unfold just as they had done for
a certain farmer from Coolgarrow whose wife had been taken.
She had three small children, the youngest of which she was still
breastfeeding. One Sunday morning, the husband and children
went off to Mass while the wife stayed behind to consult a fairyman about a sick cow she had. The appointment ran late and she
was late for chapel, which displeased her husband and the priest
as well. But she received her due when, late that night, the man
heard his children screaming. When he asked why they were
screaming, they told him their mother was out the door with a
troop of little men and women dressed in white and red and
green. The man ran out and searched everywhere, but heard
nothing from his wife or rumors from neighbors. The poor miserable man was beside himself and was often seen crying over his
neglected, dirty, and motherless children.

About six weeks after his wife's disappearance, the farmer was
going off to work when a midwife in the village began walking
along beside him, step for step, whispering that there was something she needed to tell him. She said that just as she was falling
asleep the previous night, she'd heard a horse's tramp in the yard
and a knock at the door. When she went out to investigate, she
saw a fine-looking dark man, mounted on a black horse, who bade
her go with him. As soon as she put on her cloak, he took her by
the hand, and drew his fingers across her eyes. Then she saw
nothing and felt no ground beneath her feet. She did not know

whether she was going backwards or forwards, nor how long she traveled, till he took her hand and she felt the ground again. He drew his fingers the other way across her eyes, and she looked and saw a castle door. Behind it was a big hall, all painted in fine green colors, with the finest carpets and chairs and tables, and fine ladies and gentlemen walking about. At last they entered a bedroom where a beautiful lady was about to give birth. The midwife realized she was brought there to help with the birth. Before long, a fine baby boy came into the world. Seeing the baby and the lady were safely delivered, the fairyman closed the midwife's eyes and returned her home again. When she opened her eyes, she found herself on an earthen dike.

Now there was no reason for the midwife to be telling the poor farmer this strange tale, except for a part of the story she omitted. When she was coming out of the castle, imagine her surprise when she spied the farmer's wife standing outside. The wife drew near and told her that she had been brought to the Otherworld to give suck to the child of the king and queen of the fairies, but she was miserable without her own children and wished to go home. She then told the midwife that there was to be a large procession of fairies leaving the fort next Friday. All the fairy court was to pass by the cross of Templeshambo on their way to visit the fairies of Old Ross. She could meet her husband then, if he would come to rescue her. She would be riding a horse, she said, and if her husband could catch her by the hand as she rode by and had the courage not to let go his grip, then she'd be safe with him once more.

When he heard the midwife's tale, the farmer was overjoyed, and they both determined they would go to the fort together on the following Friday eve. At the appointed time, they were waiting where the mountain road crosses the road to Ross. It was the dead of night, and only a little moonlight was shining from over Kilachdiarmid. By and by, they heard the faint jingling of bridles and soon a procession of fine horses passed. Among the throng they saw the man's wife riding on the outside so as to be able to rub up against her husband. The two joined in the procession, making like they were part of the fairy crowd going off to Ross. Their hearts were beating hard and fast in their chests for fear they would be discovered before they reached the woman. But as they drew near, the farmer stretched out his arms wide, and just then a great hullabaloo rose up like an earthquake. He immediately found himself surrounded by horrible-looking creatures, roaring at him, and yanking and pulling at his wife. But he made the sign of the cross, and suddenly his arms seemed to be made of iron. In a moment everything was silent as the grave, and there lay the wife, secure in her husband's strong, stout arms.[17]

This folk story was familiar to Michael and his in-laws, and he hoped that like the lucky farmer, he would go to the fort and seize Bridget as she rode by. Michael convinced the others that this was the only way to save Bridget and themselves as well. For if they didn't recover Bridget's spirit from the fairies, they would have a difficult time explaining their actions of the evening to the police.

After the body had cooled sufficiently, the men prepared to remove it from the cottage. Together, Michael Cleary and Pat Kennedy laid out a bedsheet before the fireplace. Then the two men wedged the shovel under Bridget's charred midsection and gingerly hoisted the corpse up off the grate and onto the sheet. As they did so, a terrible moment of clarity seemed to dawn upon Michael. "She is burned now and God knows I did not intend to do it. It's Jack Dunne I may thank for it all," he wailed pathetically, attempting to shift the blame onto the man who had indeed urged Michael several times to "treat" Bridget's malady with fire.[18]

No one in the room would have been horrified at the sight of a dead body. But neither had anyone there seen a corpse like this one, roasted to the bone, doubled over and bent up, so it could almost sit up straight of its own accord. No matter how they wedged and pried the body, it refused to lie down flat as was necessary for a proper Christian burial. The men finally gave up trying to unbend the corpse and instead wrapped her up so no one would have to look at her. They fashioned the sheet into a sort of makeshift hammock, its midsection bulging and the two ends twisted so the men could more easily heft the deadweight. When the body was thus wrapped, Michael told the others that they could not leave until he returned from the burial. To ensure they stayed put, he took the key from his pocket, unlocked the cottage door just long enough to get the body out, then secured the door again, locking them in. Bringing a spade and shovel each, Michael and Patrick Kennedy headed off, carrying the weighty load between them.

The sound of barking dogs that night awakened Tom Smyth. It was lambing season and barking dogs often signaled the birth of a new lamb. Smyth went out to check and noticed lights at the Cleary cottage. When he checked his sheep, he found no new lambs. He would learn later that it was likely the smell of burning flesh that had provoked the dogs' howling.[19]

Michael Cleary and Patrick Kennedy buried Bridget Cleary's body in an earthen dike, near the stream running along the low road. Two hours later they were back at the cottage with the spade and the shovel. As they entered, Michael locked the door behind him so no one would leave until they all agreed upon a story, which he had worked out. Basically the story was that as he, Michael, slept in his bed late Friday night, Johanna Burke came rushing in, saying that Bridget had run off.

William Simpson initially vouched for the concocted story, stating that he believed Cleary's story because he had heard Bridget "raving about leaving house and going home." Simpson also believed Cleary when told that he and the Kennedys had searched everywhere for his wife, but she was nowhere to be found. Simpson never revealed, however, at the magisterial inquiry that Michael had also told him to lie about his, Cleary's, participation in the fairy proceedings on Thursday night and to blame three of the Kennedy brothers instead, or that Simpson himself had told Burke "not to mention anything about his wife Minnie" taking part. For a man who, within days of the arrests, was conducting tours proclaiming that he did not believe in fairies, Simpson tried to have it both ways: to serve as dutiful Crown witness and cover the extent of his own, and his wife's, involvement in the fairy trial. There is also the possibility that Cleary blackmailed Simpson into falsely testifying in his first deposition about Bridget's leave-taking by threatening to reveal Minnie Simpson's role in providing urine for the ritual.[20]

The story was simple enough, but Michael instinctively feared that Burke and Pat Boland would tell all. "Hannah," he said, "it is hard to depend on you. If you were to be kept in Gaol until you would rot, don't divulge." He demanded that she swear an oath. He ranted and raved about going to America; he even threatened to go to the police, or worse, if she didn't swear. Not knowing what he might do, Burke threw herself on her knees and said: "I declare before God and man that until the day I die I will never tell and if she [Bridget] is found I will say that I know nothing about it." Pat Boland followed suit and threw himself on his knees swearing, "Now that my child is burned there is no use in saying anything about it, but God help me in the latter to the end of my days." Michael was not convinced and demanded they swear a second and third time, saying "I dread the two of you." They threw themselves on their knees and swore until he was finally satisfied. Certain the oath was safely done, Michael unlocked the door and allowed the Kennedy clan to leave. It was now about four Saturday morning.[21]

John Dunne testified that on Saturday morning, March 16, as

he was walking up the low road toward the Cleary's cottage, he saw his neighbor Tom Lehy digging in his garden. Upon seeing Dunne approaching, Tom straightened up and shouted:

"Bridget Cleary was left."

"Where is she gone to?" Dunne asked.

"Oh, she is broke away in the middle of the night and there is no knowing where she went."

Dunne took no credit in Lahy's words, so he walked on to learn more for himself. As he turned off the "low road" and made for the Cleary cottage, Dunne encountered Patrick Boland crying in the lane.

"What ails you Paddy?"

"Bridgey that's gone away."

"Where did she go, Paddy?"

"Oh, I don't know."

Approaching the cottage, Dunne found Michael Cleary out in the yard. He asked Cleary the same question.

"Where's she gone?"

"I don't know."

Michael related to Dunne his concocted story, telling him that late in the night he was "stretched out on the bed," when Johanna Burke called for him. And he got up in time to see his wife in the field with two fairymen to the right of the door.

"Why didn't you follow her?"

"It was no use for me, ten men could not hold her," says he.

Dunne may not have known exactly what happened since he had seen Michael last, but he did sense that Michael was not telling all he knew. Like William Simpson, John Dunne was eager to minimize his involvement in Bridget's "trial" and murder, so he told the court that Michael Cleary deceived him with all sorts of "fibs," which he claimed that he did not believe and which he

deemed unfit to repeat in open court. Cleary told him, for example, that Bridget was "always talking about Kylenagranagh," and
Dunne reminded him that "She used to be meeting an egg man on
down at my place on the lower road about a mile and a half."[22]
Dunne's claim that these statements were "fibs" meant to deceive
the court without perjuring himself. He could acknowledge what
he knew yet dismiss the information by characterizing it as untrue. Yet Dunne tried to persuade the court that he used Michael's
so-called fib regarding Bridget's relation with the eggman to lure
Michael into telling him about Bridget's disappearance. In truth,
John Dunne probably knew full well what had happened early
that Saturday morning.

In any case, Dunne suggested that Bridget might be hiding at
the fort on Kylnagranagh hill and asked Michael if he had looked
for her there. Michael said he had not, so Dunne suggested they
go there to search.

"Well come on with me," said Dunne, "there's no place there
that I don't know and if she's there we'll make her out."

So they went up the hill to a site Dunne described as a "waste
place" near the fox cover below the fort. They searched a row of
abandoned huts, then walked through the kitchen garden and
around a cottage, but found nothing. Certain that Bridget was not
there, Dunne confronted Michael, saying, "She's not in Kylenagranagh—there's nothing but open fields now and we could see
her." He demanded to know what really happened.

"Oh don't even speak of it," Michael begged.

Dunne pressed him until Cleary confessed.

"She was buried last night. I burned her."

Dunne made certain that the court knew that he was horrified
by Cleary's admission.

"Oh you Vagabond!" he cried. "Why did you do it?"

"It isn't my wife I had," says he. "She was too fine a woman to be my wife. She was two inches taller than my wife."

John Dunne took full credit for convincing Cleary to go to the authorities then made sure he did so by going to Drangan with him. "You'll have no living on this earth," he said, "until you give yourself up and take your punishment." A few hours later, Dunne and Cleary, accompanied by Michael Kennedy, appeared at the Drangan churchyard seeking an audience with Father Ryan, according to Dunne, to confess so his wife could have a Christian burial.

There is the distinct possibility, however, that Michael Cleary did not go to "Father Con" to confess, but rather to seek another kind of help. Throughout the ordeal, Michael had repeatedly asked the priest to come to his cottage, perhaps as much to drive off the evil spirit inhabiting Bridget as to seek official Church sacraments. Although the priest's power had proved ineffective before his wife's death, they had one last chance to recapture Bridget at the fort. If he hoped to confront the fairies directly, Michael would need the help of God to cut Bridget from the gray horse. We suspect that the men—rather than seeking a Christian burial, as Dunne claimed—went to the Drangan church to ask the priest to go to the fort that evening and help them recapture Bridget. This is something we shall never know for sure.

When the police questioned Cleary and Dunne outside the Drangan churchyard, Michael appeared calm, belying Ryan's description of his disturbed mental state. There was no raving then, no indication of nervous breakdown or weeping or pulling of hair, as the curate had testified. Rather, Michael Cleary seemed intent upon mustering strength for the next episode of the ordeal. On their trip back to Ballyvadlea, Cleary discussed with Dunne his plans to go to the fort to rescue his wife from the fairies. He asked Dunne to go with him, but Dunne claimed that he refused, saying, "I told him I would not do that, that [his plan] was only moonshine." This was a strange response from someone who, by all accounts, was himself a notorious expert on changelings, abductions, and superstitions. Cleary insisted that Bridget would be there, and they could avoid trouble with the priest and the peelers if she was brought back safely. Dunne, clearly trying to distance himself from Cleary, testified later that he did not believe this was possible, and replied:

"You're sure a woman is there after you burned her?"

"It was not she I burned," Michael insisted.

"Well," Dunne replied, "if it be only to look for the one you burned, I'll have nothing more to do with you."

Dunne claimed that Cleary offered "various excuses about burning her," and by then they were back at Ballyvadlea. There the two parted company. Dunne continued on to his cottage, while Michael stopped by the Kennedy cottage, where Sergeant Egan caught up with him and began his questioning. Unsatisfied with what he learned at the Kennedy's, Sergeant Egan followed Michael Cleary back to the cottage and questioned him there. Again, Cleary told him nothing more than the concocted story, which was that his wife ran off in the night and had not been seen since. With that, Cleary went into the bedroom and shut the door, but not before Egan spotted a suspicious-looking nightdress and bedsheet lying on the floor.

Later that night, on St. Patrick's Eve, Egan returned to the Cleary cottage again and found it empty. Cleary, Patrick Boland, and the Kennedys were all gone. If he had inquired as to why they had all gone off, leaving no one behind in case Bridget returned, they most likely would not have told him the truth: that they were at the fort on Kylnagranagh hill waiting for a procession of fairies.

The journey on Saturday night to the fort on top of Kylnagranagh hill was just the first of several over succeeding nights. On
Sunday night about seven or eight o'clock, Michael Cleary paid a
surprise visit to William Simpson to make a startling request. He
asked if he could borrow Simpson's revolver. When Simpson inquired as to why, Cleary explained that "those parties" who had
convinced him that his wife was taken off by the fairies were now
refusing to go to the fort, just above the fox cover, on Kylnagranagh hill. Cleary needed the revolver to "oblige" them to go.

Simpson testified that he had "heard a noise at the fort" the
night before, that is, on Saturday, St. Patrick's Eve. Since that was
a physical impossibility, because of the distance between Simpson's home and the fort, we surmise that he had gone along to the
fort with the others on their first vigil, but the cagey caretaker
made it sound as if he had not been there. Then he patiently explained to the court that the fort was "supposed to be a fairy
ring"—a fairy "inhabitance."

At the magisterial inquiry, Wansbrough asked William Simpson to explain how Cleary expected his dead wife to appear.
Simpson stated that Cleary told him that she would be riding a
gray horse and that he was to cut the ropes tying her to the saddle. He believed that if he could rescue Bridget from the gray
horse, "then she would stay with him if he was able to keep her."
Wansbrough then asked if Simpson had given Cleary the revolver
as requested. Simpson claimed that he had not, but that he saw
Cleary later with a table knife in his pocket while on his way to
the fort for the second vigil.

If Simpson did accompany Michael on the first visit to the fort
on St. Patrick's Eve, he probably was part of a fairly large group:
Michael Cleary, Patrick Boland, all the Kennedys, William Simpson, and perhaps other neighbors and family members, including

Johanna Burke, Mary Kennedy, young Katie, Minnie Simpson, and perhaps even such neighbors as Tom Smyth, Johanna Meara, Patrick Leahy, Tom Lehy, David Hogan, and Thomas Anglim. Most likely, even John Dunne, despite his denial, was there as well. Indeed a large and curious crowd may have turned out to see the fairies, but they were all to be disappointed for no fairy band appeared. After the first night of waiting on the hill in the cold, Michael had difficulty recruiting helpers for the second night's vigil. He went to the fort that night, however, and the third, and would likely have gone every night until the following Friday had not District Inspector Wansbrough arrested him.

Michael Cleary went to the fort to recapture his wife from the fairies, just like a certain man from Currgraigue whose bride was carried away on their wedding night. In this tale, probably known to Cleary, a group was toasting the health of the absent bride and groom, when a man rushed in crying that the bride had been abducted. A great search was launched, but she was not to be found. That night the bride appeared to her distraught husband in a dream, still dressed in her bridal clothes. At first he was alarmed, but she reassured him that she was well, though she had fallen under the power of the fairies.

The bride explained that on the following Friday, which was May Day Eve, the whole fairy court would ride out of the old fort at midnight and she would be in their company. Now, she instructed, "Go there and sprinkle a circle with holy water, and have a black-hafted knife with you. If you have courage to pull me off the horse and draw me into the ring of holy water, all they can do will be useless." Further, she asked him to leave her bits of food each night, and she would come for them, for she dared not eat the wondrous food of the fairies lest she be tempted to stay forever.

The husband did as he was asked. Each evening he left out a bit of food and each morning it was gone. On Friday night of May Day Eve, the groom went to the fort shortly before midnight and formed a circle of holy water just by the entrance. His black-handled knife was at his side. Just as it struck midnight, the dark bushy hedges around the fort were suddenly transformed into a beautiful castle, with a thousand lights flickering from the windows. From out of the gates came a magnificent cavalcade of richly attired ladies and gentlemen riding directly toward him. As the fairies rode by laughing and jesting, he was unable to discern whether they noticed him, yet he watched each face intently, hoping to catch of glimpse of his own dear bride.

At last he caught sight of her, borne upon the back of a milk-white horse. She recognized him well enough but was unable to guide the horse to the holy circle where he stood. Seeing that she might be taken away, the groom leapt from his secure place and, with superhuman courage and spirit, forced his way through the cavalcade toward his bride. Cries of rage and fury arose from every side once the fairies realized his intent, but, before he could be taken himself, he pulled forth his black knife and wielding it high overhead, cut a huge circle in the air creating a protected space that none dared violate. Quickly, he seized his bride and, amid shouts of derision and defiance, rushed back to the safety of the sacred circle. As the end of the procession filed past, the mortal pair held each other tightly, until the bright light of the fairy troop and castle dimmed and once again the rath was restored to its original shape.[23]

Capturing someone was a risky business. Anyone undertaking such a rescue needed information on the date and location of fairy processions, the right instruments, and extraordinary courage. Rescuers must exercise superhuman power to match the magical power of the folk and, even then, be blessed with a bit of luck. Yet all the mortal armies of the world could not bring back a human taken by the fairies who did not wish to return to the earthly realm. This was Michael's particular anxiety—that Bridget didn't want to be rescued by him and return to their home. (It was a situation that William Butler Yeats memorably caught in "The Stolen Child": "Come away, O human child/ To the waters and the wild/ With a faery hand in hand/ For the world's more full of weeping than you can understand.") In order to recruit help, however, Cleary told family and neighbors that they were going to the fort at his wife's request, indicating to them that she wanted to be rescued so that would make their task much easier.

It was not as though Michael Cleary was afraid to go alone, because he was not. He had traveled up and down the district seeking help for his ailing wife in every quarter, and when all else failed, he burned his wife with no fear of retribution from the British authorities. No, the fairies did not intimidate Michael; rather, they angered him because they had taken his wife, and they had no right to do so. Michael Cleary would have gone and fought them all bare-handed if it were left solely to him. Yet, over those nine days, Michael Cleary had come to believe that the forces he faced were bigger than himself. This was no ordinary witch that fought him and tricked and deceived them all. The strength of the spirit, its intelligence and determination, convinced Michael Cleary that his wife was taken by the fairies for some high and worthy purpose. So he needed all the help he could muster. He needed a small army of souls at the fort.

What he did fear was that Bridget would not return. His wife was a strong-willed woman and becoming maddeningly more so as she matured. If she did not want to come back, then there was no way to force her. The ritual of return would only be successful if the mortal rescuer was willing to cross over and be taken himself, and the one taken actively participated in her own rescue. What would happen, he wondered, if they were all at the fort, with the holy water, the priest, and the black-handled knife, and it was just past midnight, and they heard the jingling of bridles, and the countryside became illuminated, and the radiant fairy procession came into view, and their hearts were pounding in their chests, and they saw their Bridget riding upon the gray horse, and they stepped forth bravely into the host. And just as they rushed out to cut her down, she coldly and indifferently turned away. What then?

Nine Prisoners

In the second week of the magisterial inquiry investigating the death of Bridget Cleary, General Sir Charles Gough and Colonel W. A. Riall joined Colonel Evanson on the bench, bringing the inquiry to its full complement of magistrates. On Monday, April 1, District Inspector Wansbrough resumed the questioning by bringing Crown witness William Simpson to the dock, followed by testimony from Minnie Simpson, Father Cornelius J. Ryan, Thomas Smyth, and Sergeant Patrick Rogers. It was Sergeant Rogers who had headed the search team that discovered the body of Bridget Cleary, and to him, Wansbrough, and the other constables involved, Colonel Evanson expressed his high opinion of their prompt action, which led to the discovery of the body in "this very unfrequented spot." The court so noted Colonel Evanson's commendation. Questioning of these witnesses continued through Tuesday, April 2.

Wansbrough entered evidence culled from his own investigation. He testified that he visited the house of Michael Cleary after he heard a report of ill-treatment at the laborer's cottage on March 14.[24] This statement was deliberately vague. Did he hear the report on the 14th, or did he visit the cottage on the 14th? If he visited the house on Thursday, March 14, then Bridget Cleary's references to seeing peelers at the window were not a delusion. Moreover, Wansbrough's statement indicated that the police were aware of the abuse of Bridget Cleary before Father Ryan reported her disappearance two days later. The inspector's statement indicated that the police received information that Bridget was being abused, perhaps in grave danger *before* the killing, but they, like her family, neighbors, and priest did nothing to stop it.

Wansbrough added that he searched the house on March 23, after Bridget's disappearance, at which time he found a spade and shovel on the premises. The spade was comparatively new. The handle was stained with what appeared to be paraffin oil as though it had been carried by some person with an oily hand. He also found traces of black, boggy soil on the spade, similar to that found on the empty oil can that Cleary had used to douse his wife. Then he dramatically sniffed the handle of the spade saying that it smelled of paraffin lamp oil, and pointedly made it clear that "all the windows would admit of a person getting in or out," and that there was a full view of the fireplace from both small bedrooms.[25]

The magistrates asked if the prisoners had any questions for Wansbrough. None did, except Michael Kennedy, who wanted to return to the question of the cottage windows. He asked how a person was to get out through the windows without breaking them? Wansbrough retorted that he was not an expert on witchcraft, but he supposed that one could go out simply by opening the window. The Inspector's sarcasm drew a great roar of laughter from the spectators. Michael Kennedy protested that the windows were covered by screens, but Wansbrough retorted that the screens were flimsy and easily removed. After this exchange, Colonel Evanson unexpectedly announced that the court would recess until Thursday, April 4.

The reason for this unanticipated delay was soon evident. A telegram had been sent on April 2 from the Under Secretary of the State Home Office in London to the Royal Irish Constabulatory at Dublin Castle requesting that one of two Sessional Crown Solicitors be dispatched immediately to take over the prosecution of the inquiry. Authorities in London now thought the inquiry had dragged on too long and felt Wansbrough's interminable probing of the fairy issue was fruitless. Rather than pursue a group of ignorant peasants and an eccentric fairy doctor, London saw an extremely tempting opportunity to pursue bigger game. The telegram, copied to District Inspector Wansbrough in Carrick-on-Suir, stated that the local police needed the assistance of the Crown Solicitor in "perfecting depositions and replying to applications for trial [where difficult] points of law might arise."[26] Pursuant to London's direction, Sessional Crown Solicitor Michael Gleeson was dispatched from Nenagh and arrived in Clonmel on Thursday April 4, just as the magisterial inquiry resumed. Attendance in court fell off noticeably that day because of a counterattraction. According to the *Cork Examiner*, Defense Attorney Crean had to point out to Gleeson that everyone was at the races at Fethard.[27]

When Crown Solicitor Gleeson arrived, he learned that Wansbrough had not summoned Doctors Crean of Fethard and Heffernan of Killenaule to testify as to the cause of death—two witnesses he deemed of utmost importance for reasons he would shortly make clear. Gleeson ordered Wansbrough to telegraph these two doctors, who had conducted the autopsy for the coroner's inquest. To await their arrival, Gleeson applied for a short adjournment to consult with Wansbrough, and for the rest of this race-day inquiry, the magistrates heard desultory and unilluminating statements from Acting Sergeant Patrick Egan and Johanna Burke.

In his statement, Egan confirmed that it was he who had followed Michael Cleary, John Dunne, and Michael Kennedy to Ballyvadlea on Saturday, March 16. He stated that after having talked briefly with Cleary at the Kennedy cottage, he had searched the Cleary cottage and found a "partly burnt nightdress." When the clerk asked Cleary if he wanted to cross-examine the witness, he replied: "I know nothing about what I have said on that occasion." Likewise, Pat Boland said that he was "too troubled" to remember anything about talking to Egan on that day. None of the other prisoners asked any questions.[28]

Colonel Evanson questioned Johanna Burke yet again about how many days Bridget had been forced to take the herbs mixed in new milk. (He was not yet aware that Gleeson would shift prosecution tactics and leave off probing the peasants' practice of fairycraft and the insensibility theory.) Burke indicated that they were administered beginning on Wednesday, March 13. Cleary had told her that he had obtained the herbs from a woman in Fethard, and that was all she knew. The solicitor for William Ahearn, Dr. John J. Hanrahan, cross-examined the witness, asking her if his client had been in the bedroom on Thursday night holding a candle when the men forced Bridget to drink the herbs and new milk. Burke could not remember his being in the bedroom but saw him later in the kitchen, which was lit with a lamp.[29] The magistrates asked more questions, all of which seemed pointless to the newly arrived and impatient Crown Solicitor.

Having heard his fill of this tired and twice-told testimony, Crown Solicitor Gleeson suddenly rose and abruptly asked for an adjournment, announcing that he would have no further questions until the arrival of Drs. Crean and Heffernan. Furthermore he declared that he would call no other witnesses, ask for no additional depositions, and, after the doctors testified the next day, he would ask the magistrates to arraign the prisoners on capital charges.

With this announcement Gleeson signaled that Dublin and London wanted the prosecution to shift its focus. On Thursday, April 4, Gleeson complained to the Under Secretary in Dublin that Wansbrough proposed unnecessary witnesses for that day and that the current magistrates seemed to "resent any suggestion that the Inquiry might be closed today" on the grounds that some vague new evidence might be produced if "fresh depositions" were taken from some of the accused. Gleeson flatly disagreed, stating that while the existing depositions were "lengthy, mixed, and contradictory . . . at this stage it is impossible to have them condensed or remodelled." He promised the Under Secretary that he would promptly conclude the investigation the next day.[30] Gleeson and his superiors in Dublin were eager to get on with their new plan.

Finally on Friday, April 5, the magisterial inquiry officially resumed. Crown Solicitor Gleeson unveiled the government's revised strategy for prosecuting the now celebrated "Tipperary Witchcraft Case." Gleeson called Dr. William Richard Crean to the dock and asked him to report on the cause of Bridget Cleary's death. Newspaper accounts described Crean as "a highly esteemed medical man," who had occupied the chairmanship of the Fethard Town Commission "for the past ten years uninterruptedly," but made no mention of Cleary's complaint to the Board of Guardians.[31] Gleeson, like everyone else in the county, knew that Crean suffered from alcoholism, so he asked only perfunctory questions that required little more than perfunctory answers. Dr. Crean reiterated the findings of the coroner's report that described the nature of the burns and other marks found on the body. He indicated there was no evidence to support the conclusion that Bridget Cleary had died by poisoning.[32] Then, Gleeson asked, if poisoning was not the cause of death, what was? Crean replied that Bridget Cleary died from the effects of burning, adding that the rupture of the spleen would itself have caused death.

Colonel Evanson asked the doctor if the contents of the stomach were examined. Crean replied there was no need, as there were no signs of irritant poison and no abrasions. In seeking to know if Bridget Cleary may have been fatally injured when Michael threw her down on the flagstone hearth, Evanson asked if there was any external mark on the head corresponding to the effusion of blood to the brain? Crean said no.

Gleeson inquired into the general state of Bridget's health prior to the onset of her illness on March 6. Was she a woman of good constitution and physique? Dr. Crean replied that generally she enjoyed good health, but added that she appeared to be "awfully nervous." In the eight or nine years that Dr. Crean attended her, it had been his impression that Bridget was a "nervous, irritable sort of woman." Gleeson asked for Dr. Crean's assessment of the nature of that nervousness. Was it caused by dyspepsia? Following the prosecutor's suggestion, Dr. Crean stated that this might have been the source of her nervousness since dyspepsia could irritate the brain. Yes, Crean concluded, it probably was dyspepsia. He then added that he did not think that Ganey did the woman any harm. Colonel Evanson allowed that that information could not be entered and the witness was excused.[33]

The Crown Solicitor's next witness was Dr. William Kickham Heffernan, of Killenaule, who, in Gleeson's judgment, was the more reliable of the two doctors and the one Gleeson would use

to establish the prosecution's strategy. The prosecution's old tactic, pursued by Wansbrough and supported by the magistrates,
was to show that Ganey's herbs contributed to the death, which
would implicate Ganey, the fairy traditions, and the ignorant,
lawless rural peasantry, but in effect no one else beyond the individual prisoners, all of whom were worthless to the Crown. Gleeson's aim was to lay the ground for a prosecution ploy that would
implicate not some insignificant fairy doctor, but the venerable
Catholic Church itself and the backward, superstitious culture it
fostered in Ireland. He set out along this path by asking if the
herbal potion supplied by Denis Ganey played any role in Bridget's death. Did Ganey's potion contain drugs potent enough to
render Bridget "insensible "? No. Were these drugs strong enough
to prevent Bridget Cleary from crying out while she was being
burned? No. Did the herbal remedy obtained from Denis Ganey
contain narcotics or poison? Although the contents of the stomach were not analyzed, Dr. Heffernan stated that it was his opinion that no poison or narcotic was used.[34]

From the bench, Colonel Evanson asked if even the strongest
narcotic would have prevented Bridget from feeling the effects of
burning. Dr. Heffernan replied that even under the influence of
morphia, the strongest of all narcotic poisons, a person would
scream when put on the fire. But of course, he added, this was "all
theorizing" since he found no evidence to make him believe that
any narcotic was given to Bridget Cleary.

All this led to Gleeson's most significant question: If Ganey's
drugs did not contribute to the death, could something else have
killed her or made her comatose *prior to* the burning? In asking
this, Gleeson suggested an alternative cause of death. Rather than
show that Bridget was rendered insensible by Ganey's potion,
Gleeson wanted to establish that Bridget suffered so severely due

to her ill-treatment on Thursday night, that she actually died of shock prior to being burned in the fireplace on Friday night. This would explain why she did not scream. By establishing the cause of death as shock prior to burning, Gleeson cast a net of guilt around all those who were present either Thursday or Friday night, and not just Michael Cleary. All of the accused were thereby equally guilty, eliminating the need for separate charges. To elicit evidence for this new Crown claim, Gleeson went to work on Dr. Heffernan:

> Gleeson: Supposing this woman in ill-health and suffering from nervous debility, and that persons put her on the fire and burned her, or even scorched her, and that people for a lengthened period—for half an hour, or longer—ill-treated her and threw noxious stuff on her, and otherwise ill-treated her, and stated in her presence that they would put her on the fire and burn her, would such acts be likely to cause death?

Dr. Heffernan, perhaps a bit stunned himself by this verbal barrage, found himself saying "Yes." Following up on the question why she did not scream, shout, and make an uproar, he responded that her senses would have been so blunted by the first shock that she would not feel the shock afterwards.

Evanson reminded the new prosecutor that this legal hypothetical would apply only to those present the second night. So Gleeson restated the question so as to include anyone who was present, either night. Even if Bridget had suffered shock on Thursday night, might she still be incapacitated the following night?

Dr. Heffernan replied, "A woman suffering from irritability of the brain, or nervous excitement, if put on the fire or near the fire, would suffer from increased nervous delinlity [*sic*] or irritability of the brain; and, if she lived long enough, it could eventually materially affect her condition, and might cause her death." Under cross-examination by Dr. John J. Hanrahan, representing young William Ahearn, Dr. Heffernan reiterated that it was possible for shock not to set in for twelve or twenty-four hours. "I have seen very serious symptoms supervene . . . after a very slight burn . . . and people died from shock." Obviously this answer did not help Hanrahan's client.[35]

Finally realizing where Gleeson was heading with this line of questioning and seeking to defend the value of his earlier prosecutorial strategy, Colonel Evanson hastened to comment that he and the other magistrates throughout the proceedings wondered why the woman never cried out. Gleeson's long list of hypotheticals that "might" cause death was broad enough to include any shock suffered either night, but excluded any effects of Ganey's harmless potion. Bridget Cleary died of shock *before* the burning, the magistrates quickly concluded. This change in tactic effectively cleared Denis Ganey, but laid the groundwork for an attack upon the Catholic Church to be deployed later.

The theory behind Crown Solicitor Gleeson's strategy asserted that Bridget Cleary died as a result of delayed shock incurred at the Thursday night ordeal. This tactic assumed that Ganey's herbs had no effect on Bridget's physical condition or her state of mind. Rather, the effect of being repeatedly slapped, gagged by bitter herbs, soiled with urine, deprived of sleep, denied adequate food, and finally placed upon the fire finally weakened her to the point where she was unable to defend herself and subsequently fell into a state of shock. Michael's sudden, violent attack on Friday night sent the already stupefied woman into a final, fatal state of collapse that killed her before she ever reached the fireplace.

Dr. Heffernan stated under oath that death due to shock was medically possible, although unusual, and it was not impossible for the effects of shock to prove fatal over twenty-four hours after being induced.

Although Gleeson's theory strained the limits of medical authority, it promised to reap rich political rewards by placing the blame for Bridget's death at the feet of the Irish Catholic Church. In essence, Gleeson argued that the shock that killed Bridget Cleary was incurred during the Thursday night ritual, which made the ritual itself the lethal agent rather than Ganey's herbs. Furthermore, the Thursday night ritual was but a part of a larger culture that condoned, even fostered, pagan practice and belief in the occult world of the fairies, and this culture of ignorance and superstition was officially condemned yet tacitly supported by the Catholic Church. In effect, Gleeson's theory opened the door to the charge that the Catholic Church officially turned a blind eye to pagan rituals practiced by the peasantry all the while unofficially allowing them to continue.

Solicitor Richard Crean rose and asked that given this new prosecution track, the magistrates dismiss his client, Denis Ganey. Gleeson replied that he had no quarrel with this request. Though he had the disadvantage of not being involved in the case from the commencement and present when all of the witnesses were examined, he found no evidence in the depositions that indicated Ganey should stand trial. With a stroke of the gavel, it was so ordered, and Denis Ganey, the fairy doctor from Kylatlea, was free to go. There were now nine prisoners.

In an attempt to make it eight, Solicitor Hanrahan spoke for his client, William Ahearn. He stated that he did not oppose the witnesses; rather he wished to ask their worships, in all fairness, was there enough evidence to charge this sixteen-year-old boy with any crime when all he did was hold a candle in the corner of the cottage on Thursday night, while Cleary dispensed innocuous herbs from a saucepan? After all, Ahearn went to the Cleary cottage in the first place only because his mother sent him on an errand. Did this justify the charge of willful murder? The magistrates ruled that indeed it did. William Ahearn stayed in the prisoners' dock.

All the accused who were not represented by counsel then had the dubious opportunity to defend themselves. Michael Kennedy began the questioning on his own behalf by calling his employer, Edward Anglim, to the stand. Anglim was duly sworn. He told the court that he was called by the police at the request of Michael Kennedy, but he had no knowledge at all of the case.[36]

From the prisoners' dock, Michael Kennedy asked Mr. Anglim if he remembered that he (Kennedy) had asked for his wages on Thursday, March 14, for the purpose of taking the money to his mother. Anglim replied yes. Did he remember Kennedy asking for money for his mother on other occasions? Again, Anglim answered yes. Michael Kennedy then stated that he had nothing more to ask Mr. Anglim and he thanked him for coming to testify in his behalf.

As Edward Anglim left the stand, Colonel Evanson asked Michael Kennedy what he meant to show with this evidence. Michael Kennedy replied that he meant to show that he went to the Cleary cottage on Thursday evening only after giving his wages of nine shillings to his mother. Because she wanted to go to the Clearys' cottage, he was obliged to go there, otherwise he would not have been there at all on Thursday evening. Kennedy elaborated on his point, stating that he had not gone to the Clearys for the purpose of participating in the ritual, but rather to accompany his mother. Was it fair to charge him with willful murder when all he did was to hand over his nine shillings?

The magistrates were not moved. Michael Kennedy's plea for dismissal was denied. There were still nine prisoners. The magistrates allowed each of them to make statements in their own defense. Michael Cleary spoke next. In a speech that grew increasingly incoherent and paranoid, he pathetically attempted to defend himself, casting aspersions on Johanna Burke and her family:

This is in reference to Johanna Burke. She stated in her evidence that I threw paraffin oil on my wife. I threw no paraffin oil on my wife nor neither was there paraffin oil in the house on that occasion at all, only what herself [Burke] put out of a bottle into the lamp that was lighting at the aforesaid time. She stated also in her evidence that I placed my wife on the fire. I have not placed my wife on the fire nor neither would I have done it. I'd sooner put myself on the fire than put her on the fire but her and her family often made an attempt to injure both me and my wife. We were not "great" at all only for the last twelve months. Both her and her brothers left no stone unturned to injure both me and my wife in our way of living and they never got a chance of doing so until they got a chance of destroying my wife and anyone in the country that would wish to tell the truth could tell that. I worked here in this town of Clonmel four years ago and her father who is dead now and herself alive yet when they could do nothing to me were running away with my character behind my back to my wife. Her father used to say, "Ay, it's seldom he'll come home to her now—he have plenty of women where he is, seldom will [he come-?] to see her." She [Burke] used to go on another occasion previous to that and fall on the road and say I used to put a rope before her to kill her. Her father used to leave no stone unturned to get law of me to know if it was the fact and she could prove it. So this is the wind-up of the whole of it between them. So that is the whole. I have no more to say now, but I have a broken heart.[37]

At the end of his remarks, Cleary was only asked what he meant when he had said he and his wife were not "great" (which had the meaning of not getting along well). In a disjointed, confused reply, he said that Pat Boland was an uncle to the Kennedy boys, and Pat Boland's wife and his wife were not "great," and the boys did not come into his house except when they wanted a smoke.

At the conclusion of Michael Cleary's statement, Patrick Boland tottered to the dock, complained that he was getting a "weakness," and asked to be allowed to sit. The magistrates bade him do so. Boland stated that on Thursday night, Michael Cleary put Bridget on the fire because she refused to take the herbs. Cleary said to him, "Have you any faith? Don't you know it is with an old witch I am sleeping?" Boland asserted she was no witch. "You are sleeping with my daughter," he hotly reminded Cleary. Later that night, Boland went off to Cleary's father's wake and returned Friday morning to find with relief that his daughter was "grand." He had nothing further to say about Friday evening except that Michael tried to force Bridget to eat some bread, and when she would not, he burned her. The prison priest, Father Ryan, not to be confused with the priest from Drangan, told him to tell the truth, and that, he said, was what he was doing. At the end of his statement Boland asked Colonel Evanson to allow him to go home. "I am only a half a mile from it and am willing to come back any time you like. I want to go home because I am losing my sight. The Sergeant can see me every day because I am only half a mile away from him and

could you see your way to be decent towards me," Boland concluded, "I would be very grateful to you." Evanson told him that
his request would be addressed later.

After hearing the statement by Bridget's father, Cleary could
not contain himself. "In a very excited manner" he stood bolt-up-
right in the dock and yelled:

> I would make an objection to that statement. There is not one
> word of truth in it, and, if I am to get justice between them—they
> are all one—any man can say what he likes, but I want justice, and
> if I am not going to get justice here, I will get it in Heaven. Not
> one word of all that is true. They are all one lot, and they are af-
> ter doing their best against me, and the father is the worst after
> doing that on me. I am to get justice—I don't care whether I will
> or not—I will get it in another place. It is their badness and dirt. I
> did not do it, but they did it, and buried her.

Johanna Burke made some remark to Cleary at this point from
where she was sitting in the courtroom. He swung around toward
her and shouted: "You had your say. You need go no further than
Fethard for your character," implying that Burke had a reputation
throughout the district. Turning back to his fellow prisoners in
the dock he growled at them: "I am satisfied whatever way it goes.
I am not cowardly like ye, ye dirty set. It is only her brothers and
first cousins could do such a thing as that." With these words,
Michael Cleary ended his own defense more dramatically than
his attorney. If anything, Solicitor Crean had conducted a more
spirited defense of the herb doctor Denis Ganey, but then, Crean
had grounds for seeking Ganey's dismissal since he was never at
the Ballyvadlea cottage. On the other hand, the Crown had an
eyewitness who saw Michael Cleary throw paraffin oil on his wife

and deliberately set her afire. This would have been a difficult case for any defense attorney to handle.

Mary Kennedy offered a long, rambling, incoherent account of when Bridget went "Amongst the People." All that could be discerned clearly in her statement was that on Wednesday, March 13, Michael called for her to attend to Bridget, who complained of a pain in her head and said Michael was making out that she had "a fairy in her head." Otherwise Mary Kennedy's statement, at least those parts that could be understood, followed witnesses' testimony. When she finished, Cleary shouted out to her: "You did well, Mary," and she replied, "I did so." Then he sarcastically added: "I hope you will do it in heaven as well." "Indeed, I will," said Mary Kennedy, "with the help of God."[38] At the conclusion of this charged exchange, it was half-past six, at which time the inquiry adjourned for the day.

On Saturday, April 6, the magisterial inquiry reconvened for the final time to hear statements from the remaining prisoners. The first was Patrick Kennedy, a smallish, mustached farm laborer thirty-one years of age. Patrick affirmed his mother's testimony, and only added that he returned to the Cleary cottage on Friday night, about 10, and was very tired after the twelve-mile walk from the wake for Michael's father. He went into Patrick Boland's bedroom to sleep, only to be awakened by a commotion in the kitchen. Michael told them he was burning not his wife but a witch who would "go out in the chimney." Cleary then locked them in the cottage, threatened them with a knife, and coerced them into accompanying him to the fort at Kylenagranagh three nights in a row to rescue his "Bridgey."

Patrick Kennedy maintained that he had been forced to help bury Bridget's body when Michael threatened him with a knife, saying: "I'll call your name three times and if you don't answer me

and come to me I'll drive the knife to the handle in through you."
This part of his statement created "considerable sensation" in the
court as he described Michael throwing his wife's body on its side
and pressing her down into the boggy ground with his feet. Obviously upset, Patrick concluded his testimony by saying, "I have
no more to say. I am not steady. . . . I am cracked after it, for to
see my first cousin burned. I am under the care of Dr. Crean for
six years. This is as true as God is above me."[39]

Twenty-two-year-old James Kennedy, the tallest of the brothers, provided the most detail about Michael Cleary's belief that
his wife was a changeling. On Friday night, James claimed he attempted to stop Cleary from harming Bridget by saying, "For the
love of God, don't burn your wife." Michael's reply, according to
James, was this:

> She was not his wife—she was an old deceiver that was sent in
> place of his wife; "she was after deceiving me," says he, "for the last
> seven or eight days, and deceived the priest to-day, too," he says,
> "that she won't deceive anyone any more. As I beggined [sic] it
> with her, I'll finish it with her."[40]

James testified further that when his brother William threatened to break a window to get out of the cottage, Michael Cleary
drew a knife on them all and William "got a weakness at the room
door." After catching his fall and shaking him, Mary Kennedy
threw Easter holy water on him and stretched him out on a bed.

James Kennedy described Cleary as being in a "terrible state"
for several days following the murder, threatening to "do away
with himself" and insisting that Bridget would appear at the fort.
After three nights of vigil at the fort, the Kennedy brothers refused to accompany him again, and instead urged him to give

himself up, for he would surely be arrested "one of these days" for the killing of his wife. Michael continued to protest that "it was not his wife he killed, but a witch sent in her place." James claimed that up until the time of the arrest, he had urged Michael to give himself up and stand trial, but he'd refused and said that none of them should speak about what "he's done until the day we'd die." Following James Kennedy's damning (and refreshingly coherent) statement, the Court adjourned for lunch.

When the session resumed, twenty-seven-year-old Michael Kennedy made a statement that showed he felt himself to be the least involved, and begged the court to consider his physical disability acquired while serving in the British army. He repeated his prior statement that he was in the Cleary cottage only to accompany his mother after delivering his wages to her. And although he saw the others place Bridget on the fire, he turned away and went into Boland's bedroom, because

> when I got a fit which I am subject of getting—fallen sickness. I was sent home from Foreign Climates with this. The fit takes my memory off me for half an hour—more or less—I could not say and I found myself in bed. I commenced to get my senses again. I walked out on the floor [of the kitchen]. I looked around me and I see the crowd within the room. I then turned and I sat down at the table. I could not say any more about what occurred in the house.[41]

Michael Kennedy then reiterated that he and his brothers went to the wake of Cleary's father, but that he had not returned with them to the Cleary cottage on Friday night, staying instead at the Anglim house near Drangan. It was not until Saturday, March 16, that Michael met up with Dunne and Cleary on the road to Drangan and heard that his cousin was missing. After reaching his house, he joined in the search for her body and continued to search until he was arrested, being unaware how Bridget had died and had been buried by Cleary and his own brother Patrick. That's all he knew of it, and "I never heard a word of what was done to Bridget until I was here [in] the dock that's where I am." Michael was unable to sign his name to his deposition.

The youngest of the Kennedy boys, William, twenty-one, was the heaviest and best-looking of the lot, clean-shaven with a full head of hair. He frankly admitted his participation in the events of both nights, but, like his brothers, said he was asleep when the final burning began. When he awoke to the unimaginable sight of his cousin Bridget burning in the fireplace on Friday night, he asked Michael what he thought he was doing. Michael in essence told him to mind his own business. When Cleary threatened to kill them all with a knife if they attempted to leave the cottage, William "got a weakness and I had to be brought back to the [bed] room [of Patrick Boland]," from where he heard Michael forcing his brother Patrick to help bury the body. William also admitted going with Michael Cleary to the fort every night from Saturday through Tuesday.[42]

The last of the accused to testify was William Ahearn, the young candleholder. His statement was short and to the point: "My mother told me to go to see Mrs. Cleary that was sick. I would say that the evidence of William Simpson and Mary Simpson is correct about Thursday night. I know no more about it. I am no relative of those parties whatsoever. That's all."[43]

Having heard the testimony of the Crown witnesses and statements from all the prisoners, the magistrates asked Gleeson if he had any concluding remarks. He summarized the prosecution's position. There were two classes of prisoners, he declared: those present on the night of March 14 and those present both nights.

There could be no question, he admitted, that the parties present on the night of March 15 would be returned on the charge of murder. These were the abettors of the crime, and none made any attempt to prevent the death of Bridget Cleary. Those present on the 14th only, however, would also be charged with murder, for the medical evidence indicated that the cause of death may be attributed to the shock administered to Bridget Cleary on the night before her actual murder. The question of whether those present on the 14th were equally as culpable as the others should be left for a judge to decide.

The magistrates deliberated less than an hour before reaching a decision on the fate of the nine prisoners before them. When they returned with it, Colonel Evanson addressed the packed courtroom. After careful consideration of the evidence, there could be no doubt, he declared, that each of the nine prisoners had taken part in events leading up to the death of Bridget Cleary, although there were different "degrees of culpability" among them. Furthermore, the magistrates held that there was a "distinct question" that the occurrence of Friday night, March 15, was a "legal continuance" of the "great and cruel torture" inflicted upon the deceased on Thursday evening.[44] In other words, the magistrates accepted the Crown Solicitor's thesis that the trauma inflicted upon the deceased on Thursday, March 14, precipitated a state of shock that actually killed the victim sometime before the burning the following night. The magistrates ordered the nine prisoners bound over for trial at the next assizes to be held for County Tipperary, South Riding district, scheduled to open July 4, 1895.

The magistrates' decision allowed the Crown to commit all the remaining nine prisoners for trial, yet allowed each to be charged, and subsequently tried, according to varying degrees of culpability. By accepting Gleeson's contention that the murder itself was a "legal continuance" of the "torture" inflicted on Thursday night, when all the prisoners were present, the Crown's prosecution implicated the greatest number, although did so selectively—the two key omissions being Minnie and William Simpson. Furthermore, the magistrates made no recommendations regarding indictments for each prisoner. This was left to the discretion of Crown Solicitor Gleeson, who was to enter specific charges against each prisoner individually, ranging from murder in the first and second degrees to lesser crimes of manslaughter and aiding and abetting. By accepting Gleeson's legal theory, the magistrates granted the prosecutors maximum latitude and flexibility so English justice could appear both firm and fair.

The ruling also addressed a central mystery in the case, which was why Bridget never attempted to seek help or even to cry out in pain when set ablaze. Both questions troubled the magistrates exceedingly and ultimately had some bearing upon weighing degrees of culpability. For if Bridget never sought help, or even cried out when subjected to the excruciating pain of being burned alive, it would imply either that she was complicit in her own murder or, more frightening, that she was indeed a fairy changeling. Both of these suppositions defied the rational demands of English justice, so both were discarded. By asserting that Bridget died from delayed shock syndrome because of the ordeal of days-long torture, rather than by Ganey's herbs, the magistrates addressed logically, then dismissed summarily, the whole issue of the occult—of fairies, changelings, and magical cures.

When the prisoners emerged from the courthouse doors following the close of the hearing, a large crowd awaited them outside the gates. Inside, the police escort formed rank and prepared for the final march back through the streets to the infamous Clonmel Gaol, where rebels and murderers were held before their final walk to the gallows across the square. With bayonets fixed, the police led the contingent out among the assembled citizens of Clonmel, who joined the procession, loudly expressing to the perpetrators of the "Ballyvadlea Horror" their contempt for these simple country people who had done so much to disgrace their town, county, and the entire country. At the top of Nelson Street, the formation turned left in front of the Hearne Hotel onto Parnell Street, where stood Clonmel's monument to the Croppy Boys, who had fought and died on the flanks of Slievenamon in an attempt to win independence in the failed rising of 1798. From there, the prisoners marched onto Emmet Street, at the top of which stood the towering gates of the Clonmel Gaol—Tipperary's oldest house of incarceration—where disrupters of social order learned English civility by breaking rocks and patriots prepared to meet their God.

For most of the nineteenth century the Grand Jury that sat in Clonmel during the Assizes did not earn a reputation for mercy. Far from it. The town witnessed many hangings at the gallows opposite the jail, most attended by huge crowds. Priests ministered to the condemned while officials prepared to carry out the death sentences. An anonymous eighteenth-century poet portrayed the plight of a young man—perhaps a Whiteboy terrorist or Croppy Boy revolutionary—who languished in the Clonmel Gaol while awaiting his date with the hangman:

> How hard is my fortune,
> And vain my repining!
> The strong rope of fate
> For this young neck is twining!
> At my bed-foot decaying,
> My hurl-bat is lying;

> *Through the boys of the village*
> *My goal-ball is flying;*
> *My horse 'mong the neighbors*
> *Neglected may fallow,*
> *While I pine in my chains*
> *In the jail of Clonmala.*
> *Next Sunday the patron*
> *At home will be keeping,*
> *And the young active hurlers*
> *The field will be sweeping;*
> *With the dance of fair maidens*
> *The evening they'll hallow,*
> *While this heart once so gay*
> *Shall be cold in Clonmala.* [45]

It was said that a certain hangman of Clonmel dropped his victim gently down, so as not to break the neck, leaving the condemned to die a slow, agonizing death by strangulation. So hated was this particular executioner, that when he retired his position, he lived out his days *inside* the Clonmel Gaol as authorities could guarantee his safety nowhere else in County Tipperary. [46]

As the nine prisoners shuffled past these gallows, to the chorus of abuse hurled by their countrymen, and returned to the echoing silence of the gaol, they surely wondered whether their blood would soon mingle with that of Ireland's greatest patriots at the foot of the hanging gallows opposite the Clonmel Gaol.

7

Tales of Slievenamon

The Raths of Kylnagranagh

As the nine prisoners disappeared through the massive prison gates, the townspeople of Clonmel were eager to put aside the tragedy at Ballyvadlea and prepare for Holy Week. On Good Friday, all public offices, banks, and businesses closed. No trains ran in the district. Neither the morning papers nor the midday post were delivered, making the occasion still more fit for contemplation. The spiritually attuned contemplated the extraordinary configuration in the heavens when the stars of the constellations, together with the sun, moon, and planetary bodies on this Good Friday occupied exactly the same positions as were seen on the night that Jesus died on Calvary more than 1800 years before. Some might say that this rare alignment of stars and planets caused disturbances in the Other World, manifested by the tragedy at Ballyvadlea, or perhaps the stars foretold a significant conjunction of events yet to come.

One upcoming event of stellar importance was Archbishop Croke's Silver Jubilee, the largest public celebration ever held in County Tipperary. Throughout the early months of 1895, the faithful priests of Cashel raised over a thousand pounds to launch a series of ceremonies planned to pay homage to the peerless prelate who stood against Pope, Parnell, and English skullduggery to preserve the autonomy of the Irish Catholic Church and save the Nationalist movement. At the first formal meeting of the Jubilee Committee May 1 at St. Patrick's College, Thurles, the priests announced the first of several venues planned for the celebration, on July 18. A subcommittee, appointed to implement details of this "remarkable and interesting event," directed that the money contributed by the clergy would go to remodel The Palace, since Croke himself had "persistently refused to accept money from clergy or laity on the occasion of his Jubilee." All through the country, preparations went forward with a degree of extravagance that embarrassed the prelate personally, although he, more than anyone, recognized that the celebration was more political than religious.[1]

Other groups followed the lead of the priests of Cashel. In mid-May the Thurles Teachers' Association elected a jubilee committee, which bore testimony to the archbishop's good work in behalf of the diocese's teachers. The citizens of Thurles formed a committee, chaired by Maurice Power, who exhibited great enthusiasm when announcing that a testimonial would be written to honor the archbishop. Above the shouts of the crowd, Power roared that there was nothing left for him or anyone to say about "the high position and glorious prestige of our great Archbishop," or the "kindly and affectionate regard in which His Grace is held" by the people of Thurles; nevertheless, a committee was called upon to conjure up something suitable for the jubilee celebration.[2] From Dublin, the Irish Parliamentary Party unanimously passed a formal resolution praying that its members be allowed to associate themselves with this joyful celebration so "warmly commended and endorsed by the Irish race at home and abroad." A meeting to determine the party's contribution to the event would be called wherever a town hall could be secured, to which duly accredited delegates from municipal boards, Guardian Boards, and INF branches would be invited to attend.[3] As other organizations came forward, the strange conjunction of groups, not often seen clustered together, added to the luster of Archbishop Croke's Silver Jubilee.

Even as the Irish prepared to celebrate Croke's Jubilee, the English authorities in Dublin kept close watch on the archbishop's activities. In April 1895, the Crime Branch Special (CBS, aka the Secret Police) wrote up a report that contained information about Croke's association with the Gaelic Athletic Association (GAA).[4] Secret Police reports—like those of the FBI and other such organizations—usually contain all kinds of hearsay and unsubstantiated evidence—in this instance, about Croke and others involved with the GAA clubs, which police believed were connected to secret Fenian societies. Although the Church thought the same thing when the organization was formed back in 1884, Croke now vehemently denied this claim and publicly stated that the GAA "was purely an athletic body and that alone." He even proposed a resolution at the spring General Council Convention at Thurles that the GAA "should steer clear of politics and that no club should assume any party name." English authorities remained unimpressed and concluded that the GAA would continue to give support to the Irish Nationalists.[5] Believing that Croke was linked to the GAA

more than was publicly acknowledged, police kept him under surveillance, especially when he attended GAA athletic matches. On
April 22, the CBS police reported that the archbishop attended a
football game in Nenagh with his secretary, the Very Reverend
Arthur Ryan, Canon of Newchapel. A vignette included in the report illustrated the divisiveness of Irish politics in early 1895. The
officer noted that when Croke and his secretary left the match two
hours later, a few supporters near him attempted to applaud when
he left, but the fans were too involved in the game and most of
those in his immediate vicinity were Parnellites and were "indis-
posed to cheer him."[6]

While the Secret Police kept tabs on Croke, Unionists, also
sensing an imminent and rare confluence of events, watched the
heavens for signs that a new government might arise. Hints came
from London in a speech by Arthur Balfour, former Tory Irish
Secretary. He reassured the earnest advocates of empire that
Conservative and Liberal Unionists were about to unite in "one
Government, drawn together by one great object, and carrying
out the one great work by which they should have earned the
gratitude not only of their time but of posterity." This promised
coalition of Liberal and Conservative Unionists, he proclaimed,
had no intention of ceding one acre of Irish soil, but would fight
to preserve the empire.[7]

On the battle line of empire was the Queen's Resident Magistrate in Clonmel, Colonel Richard Evanson. Having concluded
the lengthy inquiry investigating the "Ballyvadlea Horror," Evanson found himself embroiled in another highly charged incident,
one that had the potential to shatter Clonmel's thin veneer of civility. On April 20, Assistant Sheriff Mitchell set off to serve an
eviction order on the recently widowed Minnie Fahey of Currenstown. Mitchell, along with two bailiffs named Ryan and Shea, ar-

rived at the widow Fahey's cottage and pounded on the door, not knowing that the widow, two sisters, five children, and a friend were barricaded inside. The sheriff pounded on the door again, demanding it be opened, at which time he was told in no uncertain terms where he could go to be finding the key.

The men tried to knock the door down but found it fortified, at which time the sheriff ordered Ryan and Shea to enter through a window, while he waited at a safe distance outside. The two bailiffs did as they were told and went in through the window, where the widow, lying in wait, dowsed them both with a bucket of limewash. Blinded by the lime, Ryan fell to the floor, where he received a furious batting about the head from Mary Davin, the widow's sister, while the other sister, Almyra Davin, held his hands. Meanwhile the widow and a friend, Mrs. Purcell, heaved more limewash over him, just to be sure he'd think twice about entering a poor widow's cottage uninvited. While the female furies were distracted by their labors with Ryan, Shea unlatched the door where Sheriff Mitchell stood ready to serve the order.

By this time a crowd of neighbors had gathered, some of whom offered to remove the widow's furniture, hoping to avoid further confrontation. But Mitchell was in no mood to back down. He was out for the widow's blood as well as her home, and rather than restore calm, he ordered the women out of the cottage. At this point Mary Davin turned her stick on Mitchell, all the while howling, "Remember Mitchelstown!"—evoking memories of the 1887 eviction that resulted in the police killing two and wounding twenty tenants. Sheriff Mitchell grabbed widow Fahey and attempted to drag her out of the house, at which point Mrs. Purcell and the two Misses Davins grabbed her, and a tug-of-war ensued with women screaming, children crying, dogs barking, and the crowd becoming more agitated all the while. At this, the bailiffs wisely retreated, but later that night forty police were dispatched from Clonmel, and, without further discussion, the widow Fahey along with her three sisters-in-arms were unceremoniously turned out of the house and thrown into the Clonmel Gaol.[8]

On Monday, April 28, the so-called Currenstown Four were brought before Colonel Evanson, where charges were read by District Inspector Shoveller. Evanson asked each if they had any questions. None did. Speaking for them was Solicitor Richard J. Crean, also counsel for Michael Cleary. Crean pleaded that the court grant bail, arguing that all were "respectable" women unlikely to flee prosecution, more so because the widow's father-in-law had belatedly agreed to pay the back rent due the landlord, Mr. Perry. Moreover, Mrs. Purcell was ill, and Minnie Fahey had a babe in arms and four children, the eldest being only eight years old, all of whom were now homeless and without parents. Shoveller protested that the wounds inflicted upon bailiffs Ryan and Shea were serious, though not life-threatening, and argued that the crime was clearly premeditated and of an "aggravated nature." To drive home the point, Ryan and Shea were carried into the courtroom on litters, where they testified despite the thick bandages wrapped about their heads.

After weighing both sides Colonel Evanson acknowledged that this was a difficult case. He agreed with defense counsel that the prisoners were unlikely to flee, yet concurred that the offense was serious, and the women intended to inflict bodily harm by preparing the lime wash in advance. Furthermore, it was always an "exceptionally serious" matter when citizens opposed the law. No matter whom the bailiffs were, they represented the law and operated under its authority; and the law must be respected. Evanson stated that, personally, he regretted charging four respectable women with such a serious offense. He would have preferred to arrest both the landlord and the widow's father-in-law who had allowed the matter to get out of hand by not settling their differences sooner and allowing the eviction to proceed. But despite his personal opinion in the matter, Evanson upheld the law. He ordered that the four women be committed for trial and remanded to the Limerick female prison without bail, even though the widow's father-in-law had agreed to pay the back rent.[9]

In another small but newsworthy incident that added to the growing cluster of strangely related events, the Fethard Dispensary Committee heard an unfavorable report from the Local Government Board charging malfeasance on the part of the dispensary's chief medical officer following a routine inspection of his office. Speaking in defense of Fethard's medical officer, committee members Robert O'Shea and P. Anglim requested that the board ignore the report, claiming it was issued in anger following an unpleasant incident between the doctor in question and the board inspector. O'Shea and Anglim explained that on the day of the inspector's visit, the medical officer had not breakfasted until noon and was not in the best of humor. Moreover, the officer had not been very strong of late and the slightest perceived provocation would cause him to be irritable and excited. Nonetheless, the officer's books were found to be in good order and during his ten years as Fethard's chief medical man, not a single case of misconduct had been brought against him. He was a "first-class physician and surgeon, and his medical services, especially amongst the poor, proved him to be skillful, patient and painstaking."[10] The medical officer cited was none other than Dr. William Crean, who was known by everyone in the district to suffer from alcoholism and who had to be repeatedly asked to attend Bridget Cleary when she was believed to be gravely ill. Despite the local committee's plea for leniency, the Cashel Poor Law Guardians voted to fire Dr. Crean and immediately began advertising for his replacement.[11]

On the lighter side, the *Clonmel Chronicle*'s voice of the Tipperary Hounds, Mr. Larky Grigg, offered a thoughtful "Retrospective Glance" upon the just-concluded fox hunting season in "South Tipp." It was a grand season thanks to the efforts of Richard Burke, Master of the Hounds, who had done so much for the sport's popularity in Ireland. To house his hounds, Burke built a new kennel in Clonmel large enough to stable a pack of dogs and twenty horses as well. To repair battered relations with local farmers who resented having their fields and fences torn to shreds by leaping horse and baying hound, Burke collected money from members of the well-heeled Tipperary Hounds and dispensed over £150 per season to affected farmers. He also encouraged a breeding program for young foxes and initiated a reclamation project designed to cultivate gorse cover in key areas such as Kylnagranagh hill. Through Burke's sterling leadership as pack master, South Tipp boasted some of the finest hunting anywhere in the United Kingdom, "the shires" of England included. The Hounds hoped that development of the sport would attract other Protestant bluebloods into the area to occupy the many deserted manor houses in the county and possibly shore up English hegemony in the Irish countryside.[12]

The much praised foxhunting line, from Mullinahone across Kylnagranagh hill to the Anner River valley, traversed a region rich in Irish folklore and history, dominated geographically by Slievenamon. As mountains go, Slievenamon is not particularly imposing. It rises along a gentle incline from the west to its 2,300-foot summit, then drops off precipitously eastward toward Ahenny and the Lingaun River. To the southwest lies Clonmel and the River Suir, which divides south Tipperary from County

Waterford; to the northeast, Callan and Kilkenny; to the west, the fortress towns of Cahir and Cashel. Though not mighty in its aspect, Slievenamon holds sway over the surrounding, hilly countryside just as it dominates the mythology of the area, known anciently as Slewdale, or Sliabh Díle.[13]

The mountain's first inhabitants were said to be a cultivated, pre-Celtic race that migrated northward from Eurasia. These early residents were part of a larger migration to Ireland led by Scota, the daughter of an Egyptian pharaoh. Scota ruled with great wisdom, so her sons called her followers Scoti, in her honor. The people of Scota worshiped the fertility goddesses Eriu, Banba, and Fotla, represented by the Triple Spiral seen on pre-Christian monuments. The goddesses were believed to help bring forth children, ripen crops, and promote smithwork, healing, poetry, and cooking. These endeavors required peace, so to that end, the goddess Eriu required that all who wished to enter Ireland pledge to abide by her law. In her honor, Ireland came to be called the "Isle of Erin." In the mild, fertile region surrounding Slievenamon, the people of Scota introduced the art of cultivating and weaving flax and hemp called O *Shiris*, an art associated with occasions when young women and girls came together to card wool or spin flax. It was said that these women gathered on the mountain at Gurtnapisha, or Peafield, meaning "field of vetches," or "field of peas," which lay directly across the Anner river valley from Cloneen and west of Denis Ganey's home in Kylatlea. In later lore, these weavers became the fairywomen of Peafield, who were said to slip into a peasant's cottage at night to weave their cloth.[14]

This peaceful, matriarchal culture produced a succession of strong female figures who survived in legend as rulers, healers, and seers, and who often became associated with Ireland's rivers, mountains, and streams. One was Bóand, the goddess of the river Boyne and its valley, where the Scoti built Newgrange. In that region, Bóand was called upon to make the rivers flow, ripen the crops, and protect the children. The people of Scota imagined the goddess as a celestial cow who nourished the earth with her milk (indeed, the Irish word for "cow"—"bo"—derives from the goddess's name). The milk of the Sacred Cow was honored for its purity and healing powers (a belief whose persistence is attested to by the attempt to feed Bridget Cleary new milk).

Another of the great Irish goddesses was Brigit, meaning "high" or "exalted." Brigit personified the feminine ideal, and was believed to be a manifestation of the great goddess Danu, mother of all gods and regarded as the mother of memory, and as such was greatly revered by the Druids. In addition, Brigit was the protector of poets, a healer of the sick, and a patron of the domestic arts, including the art of forging iron.[15]

Brigit was also a fertility goddess whose feast day was Imbolc, meaning "ewe-milk," celebrated on February 1, the first day of pagan spring. On this day, it was believed that Brigit emerged from the Otherworld and breathed new life into the dead of winter, thus beginning a new cycle of rebirth and regeneration. Brigit was the great lawgiver who codified the ancient legal code of Ireland known as "Brehon Law"—a code administered by generations of "brehons," learned men and women who committed the law to memory and administered justice. These laws were still in use when the English imposed their legal system upon the Irish people.[16]

In honor of these ancient female goddesses who blessed the land, the people of Scota named the mountain Slievenamon. The origins of the name was explained by John Dunne (1815–1892), a schoolmaster from Poulacapple who became a great collector of folklore in the region of Sliabh Díle. In his exegesis of the name,

Dunne discussed several possible translations, all of which refer to the influence of the early matrilocal culture that dominated the area prior to the arrival of the Celts. These variations include "the mountain of the fair women," or "the mountain of the people of Mann" (the people credited with teaching native women the art of spinning). Of these variations, oral tradition favored the Irish name Sliabh-na-m-ban, meaning simply, "the mountain of the women."[17]

A major figure associated with the mountain was Grainne, whose story represents the integration of the older, matriarchal culture with that of the patriarchal and warlike Celts. The legends of Slievenamon suggest how the "mountain of women of Mann" became the mountain of "Fionn's women." According to legend, Fionn McCuill, Ireland's greatest mythological folk hero, was a bit of a ladies man who cast his attentions upon the maids of Sliabh Díle, leaving each one believing that she was his favorite. The women talked among themselves, and, upon learning that Fionn spoke sweet words to many, they carried on with such implacable acrimony that the entire countryside was threatened with chaos. To restore the peace he had disturbed, gallant Fionn devised a stratagem to soothe the female furies. He organized a race up the mountain, offering himself as the prize to the fair maid who reached the summit first.

But crafty Fionn was not content to take his chances, for among the competitors was one whom he favored. She was Grainne, meaning "grace," the daughter of Cormac Ulfhada, king of Ireland. To her alone, Fionn whispered a strategy to ensure her victory. When race day arrived, the others surged ahead leaving Grainne far behind, but they soon tired and fell by the wayside. Grainne trudged up the mountain, maintaining a steady pace as Fionn had advised, and reached the summit first. In doing so, Grainne won the prize and married the man, but thereafter the summit of the mountain bore Fionn's name, Suí Finn, or Finn's Seat. The ascendancy of Fionn marked the peaceful transition from the ancient culture of the mother goddess Danu and her followers, the Tuatha De Dannan, to the patriarchal culture of the Celts.[18]

The mountain quickly became a repository of Fenian folklore. The story goes that Fionn was an old man when he married young Grainne, and, in due time, her eyes fell upon Fionn's handsome lieutenant, Diarmuid, whose chest bore an enchanted beauty mark. Upon seeing the mark, she was instantly smitten and determined to have the man of her choice. Grainne persuaded Diarmuid to take her away by invoking a clause in the Fenian oath that prohibited a Fenian from causing offense to a woman. Torn between his loyalty to his chief, Fionn, and the requirements of his oath, Diarmuid reluctantly agreed and off they went, with furious Fionn in pursuit. For sixteen years, Fionn followed the beleaguered couple up one side of Ireland and down the other, until at last King Cormac interceded and put a stop to the chase. He gave Fionn another daughter to marry and allowed Diarmuid and Grainne to settle at Rath Grainne, where they produced four sons and a daughter.[19]

Fionn's exploits on Slievenamon enriched the folklore of the area. The story was told that on one occasion Fionn was attacked by a giant, and, rather than retreat, he drew his sword and pursued the giant down the mountain. Fionn delivered an awesome blow which the giant deftly avoided, but the force of the blow cut a gorge in the mountain, thereafter named Buile Chlaimh, meaning "sword-stroke." In another instance, Fionn caught a salmon in the River Suir and was broiling it over the fire when a fairy appeared, snatched away the meal, then disappeared into the hill.

Unwilling to relinquish his dinner, Fionn took up the chase and followed the fairy back to a mysterious palace in the mountain. Just as the fairy was about to slam the palace door shut, Fionn thrust his thumb in the jamb. Smarting with pain, Fionn stuck his throbbing thumb in his mouth, and, to his amazement, discovered he was able to see into the future. Hence the saying "he has the thumb of knowledge." The site of the fairy palace, known as Sidhe Gamhna, the Fairy Palace of the Yearling Deer, can still be seen north of the mountain's highest point. It is said that women live beneath this fairy palace and any mortal who stays out too late at night is in danger of falling under their power.[20]

As Fionn and his band of Celt warriors grew in strength and the wisdom of this world, Grainne and the older matriarchal traditions of Sliabh Díle retreated to the Otherworld. Men ruled the mountain and stories of their martial prowess replaced the older tales of women's weaving, nurturing, and seasonal regulation. In this cultural shift, Grainne's reputation suffered. Before her marriage, she was Grainne— "grace." In later legends, she became "Granu," or "Old Granu" which in Irish is closely related to "grana," meaning "ugly." She had been transformed from an ideal of feminine beauty to the stereotypical loathsome hag of folklore. A site associated with Grainne near Slievenamon was Kylnagranagh hill, meaning the sanctuary or wood of Granu.[21]

After centuries of this new patriarchal dominance, however, the Celts too waned in power, and the tales of Slievenamon record a second cultural shift. After Fionn was slain in battle at Rathbrea in 294 A.D., his son Ossian led his band of Fenian faithful to various hunting spots across the island, including Slievenamon, where they shared great adventures hunting deer and elk upon the mountain. After a time, Ossian was taken away to Tír na nÓg, the "Land of Eternal Youth," ruled by the mythical Queen Mab, but after spending centuries there, the Fenian longed to rejoin his band of warriors. Queen Mab granted Ossian's wish but warned that if he lingered too long in the mortal world, the spell of immortality would be broken and he would assume his mortal form. Ossian was so charmed by his old sporting life that he tarried too long. The spell was broken, and Ossian was immediately changed into an old man, worn by the infirmities of two hundred years.

Legend has it that in the first half of the fifth century, St. Patrick came upon Ossian in a weakened state and took the old giant into his residence on Cashel Rock in hopes of converting the pagan chief to the Christian religion. Ossian greatly disliked the fasting, austerity, and early morning bells of the Christian sect and longed for the melody of the mountain birds and discordant music of the hunt. Patrick humored Ossian by asking him to recount tales of his exploits, many of which took place on Slievenamon, symbolically beginning what would become a centuries-long dialogue between Christianity and the old pagan traditions.[22] The dialogue between Ossian and St. Patrick represents the blending of the Celtic and Christian culture. Rather than destroying Ossian and his stories, St. Patrick sheltered them both and forged a bridge between the two traditions, an accomplishment unique among European nations. No other Catholic apostle peacefully converted an entire country.

Following this cultural alliance between Christian and Celt, the goddesses of the older pre-Celtic culture receded ever further into Slievenamon, yet the folklore of Sliabh Díle told of powerful, though mischievous, female figures such as the wily old Granu, Peafield's weavers, the fairy queens of Sidhe Gamhna. There were some who believed that the legends associated with the Slievenamon, especially those associated with women, lured Bridget Cleary to the large fairy forts on the brow of Kylnagranagh hill and ultimately played a role in her murder. There were rumors that Bridget was ill, even that she was dying of consumption, and so went to Kylnagranagh hill to seek a cure. Her mother, Bridget

Keating Boland, was said to have been a "wise woman," schooled in the ancient healing arts. If one were superstitious, one could readily view her death on February 1, 1894—the ancient holiday of the goddess Brigit and later that of Saint Brigit, also—as a sign of her special status.[23] If Bridget was indeed ill, she might have gone to the fairy fort either to seek her mother's comfort or her cure. If Bridget was in good health, as contemporary accounts indicate, she might have been going to the fort to seek a cure for her apparent infertility. To remain childless so long after marriage in rural Catholic Ireland carried a stigma. Perhaps the pre-Celtic feminine goddesses of fertility could help Bridget if she paid homage to them at their ancient residence. Or perhaps she sought a lover there, either a mortal man or, as some believed, a fairy prince. The tales of Slievenamon contained a treasure trove not just of occult belief but also of cultural and political history.

One contemporary poet who linked Bridget Cleary's illness and subsequent murder to the tales of Slievenamon was Thomas Ryan, the "Drangan Boy." Ryan was born near Drangan in 1849, where he attended a National School. When just eighteen, he joined the Irish Republican Brotherhood, took the Fenian oath, and thereafter wrote poems and patriotic ballads. One, "Moonlight Drill: A Fenian Memory," described the Fenian leader Rory Oge ("But never throbb'd in manly breast an Irish heart more true"), leading his men up Slievenamon one dark night "to join the moonlight drill." Rory Oge was modeled after Charles McCarthy, a native of Clonmel arrested by the British and thrown into an English dungeon. After twelve years of imprisonment, McCarthy returned to a hero's welcome in Ireland and, in 1878, purportedly died in the arms of his friend Charles Stewart Parnell.[24]

On May 11, 1895, a poem by the "Drangan boy" with the intriguing title "Fairy Redivivus—Apologia" appeared in the poetry section of Clonmel's *Nationalist*. In it, Ryan refers to the times when Crom, a pagan god, and Queen Mab, Queen of the Fairies, ruled—days when "pagan baelfires shone/O'er glen and wold and cromlec hoar/Around old Slievenamon." Though by 1895, Crom and Mab no longer ruled, their tales still had a seductive power especially around the fairy forts:

> *The magic rath, enchanted by*
> *Old weird fireside tales,*
> *Sends forth its airy beings to ride*
> *On lonely midnight gales,*
> *Impulsive people hear the croon,*
> *And sighing thro' the trees,*
> *And whisper—"They're the Davine Maith*
>   [good people or fairies],
> *Who're passing on the breeze."*
> *'Tis told again how Aileen pined,*
> *And how her beauty waned,*
> *As she was woo'd to Tir-na-n-oge,*
> *And in its mansion reigned;*
> *But longing soon to see again*
> *The friends of early days,*
> *Her lover cuts the bridle rein—*
> *She 'woke in his embrace.*

The "impulsive people" reciting these tales are the peasants at Ballyvadlea wooed by the romance of the old stories. Bridget, like Aileen, becomes the once beautiful, but now aging, woman who wants to believe that she is being wooed to the land of eternal youth. She is taken away by the fairies and believes her lover will rescue her by cutting the bridle rein. She awakens in his embrace.

Ryan explains that the romance of the old stories is embedded in the landmarks around Slievenamon, and the tales are so ubiquitous, that these "impulsive people" cannot escape the weight of their culture pressing down upon them from every familiar landmark. Thus they are seduced:

> *And rev'lling in those legends of*
> *The dim, far distant years,*
> *When druids sat 'neath oaken boughs*
> *In pride of no compeers,*
> *Alas! that in Tipperary's vales*
> *A group of peasants grew,*
> *Who seem'd to think that* Crom *had come*
> *His empire to renew.*
> *'Tis but too true, yet down the vale*
> *Mark'd by the sand of time,*
> *Past landmarks linger on the way*
> *In every ancient clime;*
> *And where old Slievenamon points out*
> *Those scenes of mystic lore,*
> *No wonder celtic fancy bursts*
> *And stirs the uncultur'd store.*

Then Ryan offers an "apology" for their behavior, a "tragic sequel" to the story. In this explanation he writes that, had the Irish been left to rule themselves, had they been able to teach their legends appropriately and use the stories for instilling patriotism and cultural pride, this tragedy and others like it would not have taken place. The final two stanzas assert:

> *But oh! the tragic sequel that*
> *Has quench'd for all and aye,*

> *Those dying rays of elfin lights,*
> *Which glimmer'd in our sky;*
> *The Saxon bann'd the teacher and*
> *Let him not now recall*
> *The crimson stain clung to his name*
> *In days of Erin's thrall.*
>
> *He dimm'd the light in our fair land*
> *Far as his torture could;*
> *He draped its every window with*
> *A coat of Irish blood;*
> *His fetters dangled overhead,*
> *Our every Irish school,*
> *We conquered and he knows it—*
> *"The exception proves the rule."*

Ryan concluded with the hope that even though the English forcibly imposed their own culture upon the Irish, they failed—"We conquered and he knows it." Although the "impulsive" peasants in Ballyvadlea carried matters too far, becoming deluded believers in fallen tradition rather than proud scholars of it, Ryan defends the Irish people and their love of the old stories. Although he would prefer the people be scholars rather than deluded practitioners of the old ways, Ryan recognized that the prevalence of Irish oral tradition in the countryside prevented the Saxon from ever making Englishmen of the Irish.

"Like Rory of the Hill"

On Thursday, March 21, as District Inspector Alfred Wansbrough began his hunt for the body of Bridget Cleary, the landowning Tipperary Hounds enjoyed a grand run across Kylnagranagh hill. If they noticed any unusual police activity in the area, it concerned them little, as they hunted the "bent-necked" vixen streaking through the finest foxhunting line in the county—it was a ritual wryly described by a character in Oscar Wilde's *A Woman of No Importance* (first produced in early 1895) as "the unspeakable in full pursuit of the uneatable." After losing one fox in the cover at Garryricken, another was found at Ballylennon, and immediately the hounds vanished "like smoke." The chase led in a right-hand half circle through Killaghy up to Kyle, where they managed to trap the fox in the Priesttown sewers. In a desperate effort to save itself, the fox broke for the Drangan cover, but the hounds were quickly tearing at its throat, concluding a sporting run of seventy minutes.

The thirsty hunters paused to refresh themselves at a local pub, then reconvened for a second ride. This time the hunt led the Hounds into the Slieveardagh hills, south of Drangan, toward Kylnagranagh, where the hounds raised a grand "old relic" that was at once "on his legs and away." The chase led down toward the River Anner through Kilbarry, where the fox turned north toward the old castle near the Ballinard wood outside Cloneen. After leaving the wood, the chase continued up Bennett's hill east of Fethard, then careened toward Rathkenny, thence away to Peppardstown, where the fox wheeled again and ran on, as if making for the cover on Kylnagranagh. Having convinced the Hounds and their hounds that this was to be its destination, the old fox suddenly veered and disappeared into the cover at Rathkenny, vanishing into the dense brush as though it were mysteriously able to change its very shape and form. Nonetheless, it was a grand day for Burke's Tipperary Hounds, which had ended with a magnificent run of ninety-five minutes. The dogs ran hard, the foxes were quick, and the hunters challenged by the twisting, twelve-mile line. At day's end the horses were so "done to a turn," it was with considerable difficulty some of them hobbled home, or so reported the voice of the Tipperary Hounds, Larky Grigg.[25]

If the aristocratic Tipperary Hounds failed to notice District Inspector Wansbrough's constables scouring the hills, they were likely unaware that the district was mourning the loss of a leading citizen, Thomas Kickham, the gentle, genial, somewhat eccentric younger brother of Tipperary's poet/patriot, Charles J. Kickham, who himself had died earlier, in 1882. Thomas died early on Monday, March 18, two days after Bridget Cleary had disappeared, just as the St. Patrick's Day's festivities were winding down. His death greatly saddened his many friends, colleagues, and family members.

The conservative, Unionist *Clonmel Chronicle* merely reported that the funeral cortege was "large and respectable." The *Nationalist*, on the other hand, was more effusive in eulogizing the loss of this "sterling Irishman" whose death severed the Nationalists' last link with his late brother, the prominent actor in the "stirring political scenes of '67" and author of the Irish classics *Knocknagow* and *Sally Cavanagh*. Though eclipsed in life by the "noble and brilliant historic figure" of his brother, there was no truer Irishman than Thomas Kickham whose patriotism was of the "most genuine stamp." No consideration ever seduced him from the "right path." He stood by his famous brother in the stormiest of times, took an "active interest" in every movement for Ireland's nationality, and was consistently a "modest but familiar and welcome figure" at Nationalist gatherings all around Slievenamon, at which Thomas and his pony, "Little Wonder," were familiar figures. The *Nationalist* also gratefully acknowledged that Thomas donated some of his brother's manuscripts to the newspaper's archives.[26]

On Tuesday, March 19, Thomas Kickham received full civil and religious honors at a large funeral attended by a great number of prominent people, Nationalist politicians, and a large contingent of priests, including Reverend Cornelius J. Ryan, curate of the Drangan church. After funeral prayers were recited, the clergymen knelt at the grave and offered prayers to speed Kickham's passage to heaven.

Later that afternoon another ritual took place. An unobserved reporter watched as an old man named Morris, a drummer in the famed Drangan band, came to the grave of Thomas Kickham, and, believing himself to be alone, knelt down and wept. After a time, the man reached beneath his coat and drew out a miniature Irish harp wrapped in green. Ever so gently, he laid the offering upon the grave, then rose and departed, still wiping the tears from his face. The token, like the priests' prayers, was meant to aid Master Thomas on his passage to the next world, in this case to the ancient Otherworld—with the harp signifying transition or passage, the green for Ireland.[27]

The first Kickham in Ireland was an Englishman, a farrier sergeant with Cromwell's army. If he had not been minding the horses, he might have been one of the men who stormed the breach during the siege of Clonmel, where the brave Hugh Dubh O'Neill and the men of rare Clonmel were waiting. After the English Civil War, Sergeant Kickham remained behind and settled near Clonmel. He prospered there, and his descendant, James Kickham, lived for a time in Knockkelly Castle, near Fethard, between Bennett's hill and the fox cover at Rathkenny. James Kickham married a Catholic girl, and their descendants were raised Catholic.

Their grandson, Charles Joseph Kickham (1752–1815), was a blacksmith who established himself as a merchant/farmer in the Mullinahone district and raised a large family. His ventures prospered to the extent that he was able to give each of his five sons a good start in life.

James, the eldest, inherited the family business on the Square in Mullinahone, while Charles and Roger studied for the priesthood at Maynooth. Thomas acquired a farm outside Mullinahone, and John (father of Charles J.) established a drapery business on Fethard Street in Mullinahone. Thomas and John married two sisters from Cashel named Mahony. John and his wife, Anne, had a large family. The eldest, Charles Joseph, was born at the Mahony home on May 9, 1828. Charles had two brothers who survived to adulthood, Alexander and Thomas, as well as four sisters, Maria, Bridget, Elizabeth, and Anne.[28]

The unusual intellectual ability that Charles displayed as a boy led his parents to hope that he would pursue a career in medicine, but at the age of thirteen, when a flask of gunpowder exploded in his face, seriously impairing both his hearing and eyesight, their hopes were dashed. The injuries were so severe that even the possibility of joining his father's business seemed remote. Thus crippled, he never achieved his family's traditional hopes for him.

Unable to be either doctor or draper, Charles was left to develop his considerable literary talents and pursue his growing passion for popular movements, the first of which was the temperance crusade launched by Father Theobold Mathew in 1838. When Charles was nearly sixteen and still healing from his accident, Father Mathew came to Mullinahone in March 1843, and in a very infectious, banner-waving, testimony-bearing ceremony, called for converts to step forward and "take the pledge." Young Charles responded without hesitation and became a lifelong apostle of temperance, and from that day to his last, not a drop of alcohol passed his lips.[29]

In 1842, Charles's uncle, James Kickham of the Square, became a distributor for the Young Irelanders' new Nationalist newspaper, the *Nation*, edited by Thomas Davis, who wrote under the pseu-

donym The Celt. Uncle James saw to it that a copy of the newspaper was delivered to his brother's home, where Davis's essays
were read with great interest by young Charles and his mother,
Anne. Writing about the experience many years later, Kickham
reflected that the death of Davis in September 1845 filled him
"with a vague sense of loss," which was shared by the whole family, particularly his mother, who actually shed tears for the man
"whose name she had probably never heard while he lived," a man
known to her simply as The Celt. From these readings, young
Charles forged a romantic yet durable vision of an independent
Catholic Ireland, founded upon principles of civility, land ownership, and security of land tenure.[30]

In addition to reading the *Nation* with her son, Anne Mahony
Kickham filled young Charles with patriotic tales, especially of
the ill-fated Rising of 1798 and the battle of Carraigmoclear on
Slievenamon. The uprising began in the north of Ireland,
spawned by nonsectarian agrarian unrest and hopes that France
would help the Irish as it had helped George Washington's army
during the American Revolution. Local, ragtag military units in
the north, comprised of Catholics and aggrieved Protestants,
joined with rebel bands of the Society of United Irishmen in the
south to resist the English, but the arrest and subsequent execution of most of the leaders of the Society left the group flounder-
ing by the time of the Carraigmoclear defeat.[31]

Although sporadic resistance continued in Leinster, the United
Irishmen needed a solid victory, akin to the American victory at
Saratoga, to convince the French, and themselves, that they could
beat the English. Carraigmoclear was one of their last chances for
a victory, but it was not to be. A few days before the battle, the
English caught some rebels at Ninemilehouse Inn, and though a
messenger went to Carrick-on-Suir for help, the rebellion was ir-

reparably damaged. In the meantime, the English discovered a larger plot was afoot, and in a successful attempt to thwart the uprising, soldiers lit a signal fire, drawing the rebels into a trap. Volunteers were sent out to urge more rebels to the mountain, but few came. Without supplies and with virtually no leadership, the English cavalry, Yeoman regulars, and Hessian troopers from Kilkenny drove the rebels up the mountain as easily as a "cow at the fair in a shepherd's care." With this humiliating defeat, the Irish rebels' land campaign was over, at least for a time. But there was always the sea.[32]

Two years before, in 1796, one of the founders of the Society of United Irishmen, Wolfe Tone, a Dublin Protestant, advocate of Catholic emancipation, and admirer of the French Revolution, had almost single-handedly convinced the French to send ships and troops. The resulting huge invasion force of 14,000 men and forty-three ships was badly organized, however, and on reaching the Irish coast was dispersed by a storm. In August 1798, the French belatedly intervened again at Tone's request by landing a squadron at Killala Bay, County Mayo. In September, in Donegal, along with three thousand of his men, he was captured, wearing the uniform of a French general, which to the English was tantamount to treason. Rather than be hanged by the hated English as a traitor, he cut his own throat, dying a hero to the Irish cause in November 1798. Thus ended one of the bloodiest episodes in Irish history. By the time the English completed their round of hangings and the dead were counted, over 30,000 Irishmen had lost their lives. But the greater tragedy was that the Rising of '98 had deteriorated into an intractable civil war setting Catholic peasants against their Protestant counterparts, destroying a powerful alliance against a common enemy, and commencing the sectarian violence that would roil the island for nearly two more centuries and distract both sides from their true oppressor—the English overlords.[33]

After the uprising was smashed, English vengeance was swift and certain. Hundreds of suspected rebels were summarily hanged, famously memorialized in a line by Don Boucicault, "They are hanging men and women for the wearing of the Green." In Mullinahone, a local leader named Daniel Norton was shot under orders of William Despard, proprietor of Killaghy Castle and Captain of the Yeoman. After the execution Norton's head was impaled on a spike and displayed at St. John's Castle. Ever resourceful, the Fenians auctioned off the infamous spike in 1864 in Chicago to benefit their treasury.[34]

In addition to the lives taken after the Rising, the English made the Irish pay dearly in political terms. In an effort to exercise stricter control over the recalcitrant island, Ireland was forced to accept the odious Act of Union in 1801, which effected the political consolidation of England, Scotland, Wales, and Ireland into a single empire ruled from London. As a result of this paper union with England, the Irish Parliament in Dublin was shut down and the government of Ireland was removed to Westminister, demoting Dublin from the nation's capital to its administrative center and mere colonial outpost. One hundred years later, Nationalists were still trying vainly to recover Ireland's Parliament through passage of the Home Rule Bill. In the 1900s, the undoing of the Act of Union continued under British Prime Minister Tony Blair's New Labour government, with inauguration of an independent Scottish Parliament, a semi-independent Welsh legislature, and diligent and serious peace talks in Ulster.

Although the Rising of '98 was in many respects a political and cultural disaster, it inspired countless poems and ballads like "The Croppy Boy" and President John Fitzgerald Kennedy's favorite,

"Kelly, the Boy from Killane."[35] The haunting subject matter was courage in defeat, praise of martyrs, and righteous polemics against oppression and subjugation. In his famous "Rory of the Hill," the poet/patriot Charles Kickham admits the importance of knowledge, education, and political action but maintains that if Ireland was to be free, the rough-and-ready men of the hills must be prepared to fight. The final stanza reads:

> Oh! knowledge is a wondrous power,
> And stronger than the wind;
> And thrones shall fall, and despots bow
> Before the might of mind:
> The poet and the orator
> The heart of man can sway,
> And would to the kind heavens
> That Wolf Tone were here to-day!
> Yet trust me, friends, dear Ireland's strength,
> Her truest strength, is still
> The rough-and-ready roving boys,
> Like Rory of the Hill.[36]

Kickham foresaw the day when Rory would be back to fight on the mountain, armed with more than learned words.

Such a day came fifty years later. Inspired by the republican revolutions throughout Europe, in 1848 Irish Nationalists staged a massive demonstration on Slievenamon to protest English indifference to the Great Famine. Unlike the motley assortment of men at Carraigmoclear, the 1848 monster rally drew an estimated fifty thousand Young Irelanders and men of the Irish Confederation to the mountain on July 16, 1848. Crowds jammed the roads and clogged the nearby towns of Clonmel and Carrick-on-Suir long before the scheduled meeting time. The roads from counties Cork, Waterford, Wexford, Kilkenny, and Limerick, extending to the banks of the River Anner and the whole length of the "Golden Vale," teemed with club members, largely from surrounding towns, marching behind their respective presidents. Michael Doheny alone led a contingent of six thousand Young Irelanders from central Tipperary.[37]

Though the day was hot and the slope steep, marchers made their way up the mountain, greeted as they climbed by "the widest exclamations of delight and defiance from townspeople of both sexes—who were physically unfit for the arduous task of breasting the lofty mountain." A hush fell over Sui Finn, or Finn's Seat, when keynote speaker Thomas Francis Meagher rose. Standing before the immense gathering that literally blackened the mountainside, Meagher delivered a scathing indictment of the English administration:

> A scourge came from God which ought to have stirred you into greater action. The potato was smitten; but your fields waved with golden grain. It was not for you. To your lips it was forbidden fruit. The ships came and bore it away, and when the price rose it came back, but not for the victims whose lips grew pale, and quivered, and opened no more. . . . The fact is plain, that this land, which is yours by nature, and by God's gift, is not yours by the law of the land. . . . I stand here upon the lofty summit of a country which, if we do not win for ourselves, we must win for those who come after us.

After his fiery remarks, a resounding "Hear! Hear!" echoed across the mountain.[38]

As the fifty thousand dispersed following the rally, no one appeared quite certain how, when, or where the rebellion would be-

gin. Over a week later, on July 25, two leaders of the Irish Confederation, William Smith O'Brien and John Blake Dillon, stumbled
into Mullinahone "in search of a rebellion" and looking to start
something there. Naturally, the appearance of these would-be revolutionaries caused great excitement, especially for twenty-one-
year-old Charles Kickham, who impressed the visitors with his
knowledge of revolutionary arts, gleaned from articles in the *Nation*.
He figured that their presence in town signaled that the revolution
was about to begin, and, knowing that all revolutions needed
plenty of pikes, cut down an ash tree. While O'Brien and Dillon
were conferring, Charles darted off to get the local blacksmith
started on making pike heads, then raced off to ring the chapel bell,
because, as he read in the *Nation*, no "proper revolution could start
without the sounding of the tocsin." If there was to be a revolution,
young Kickham would make sure it was conducted properly.

Despite Kickham's efforts, the rising of 1848 never got off the
ground. O'Brien botched an attempt to seize firearms from the
constabulary in Mullinahone, thanks to interference from two local priests. Having failed in Mullinahone, a small band of Young
Irelanders marched on a mining company in the Slieveardagh
hills, where they were confronted by a military contingent from
nearby Ballingarry. In a scene fit for low comedy, the soldiers
chased the Young Irelanders into widow Cormack's cabbage
patch, where they were forced to surrender their weapons. This
less than glorious surrender did nothing to diminish young Kickham's enthusiasm, though he realized that full-scale rebellion
would await another day. As expected, the English took strong re-
taliatory action. From July through September, soldiers smashed
isolated disturbances; the courts suspended habeas corpus and re-
voked gun licenses. In short order, the massive demonstration va-
porized, leaving its leaders mystified and the people bewildered.[39]

The Church's failure to support the Nationalists in '48 was followed by what some perceived as clerical indifference to the ravages of the Great Famine.[40] As the death and devastation mounted, many religious leaders advocated emigration rather than attacking the English and their predatory land policies. One cleric prominent in the emigration campaign was Father James Maher of County Carlow, whom Kickham adamantly opposed, believing strongly that emigration was a hemorrhage of the country's lifeblood. In response to Father Maher in particular, and the Church in general, Kickham wrote a "Remonstrance," which was an ironic adaptation of a famous eulogy to the faithful priest, Soggarth Aroon by poet John Banim. In Banim's poem, the priest stands by his people, but in Kickham's verse, the people are uncertain if the Church will support them in their fight with the English. The people ask Kickham's Soggarth Aroon:

> *And will you leave us too, Soggarth Aroon,*
> *You who were always true, Soggarth Aroon,*
> *The thought made our cold hearts glow—*
> *You'd be the last to go,*
> *Whether come weal or woe, Soggarth Aroon.*

By invoking the image of Soggarth Aroon, Kickham attempted to taunt the priests of Ireland into fighting with the people for just reforms.[41]

For his own part, Kickham joined with two curates, Fathers O'Shea and Keefe, who organized the Callan Tenant Protection Society in October 1849 to resolve tenant disputes.[42] In addition, Kickham published poems, stories, and ballads to portray the hard lot of the Irish tenant farmer. One poem in particular decried the injustice of crop seizures. Under the law, landlords could not seize crops until after the harvest and only during the daylight hours. To save the crop, farmers began the practice of night harvest, which Kickham captured in a poem that described cutting the ripened corn beneath the "harvest moon." The final stanza reads:

> Then let fools have the ripe sheaf strewn, my boy,
> To scorch in the sultry noon, my boy,
> Oh! our toil is more light
> In the cool dewy night,
> 'Neath the smiles of the harvest moon, my boy.[43]

In the late 1850s, Kickham published his most famous poem, "She Lived Beside the Anner," which appeared in the *Celt*, a weekly newspaper published by Dr. Robert Cane of Kilkenny, a former confidant of Thomas Davis and Charles Gavan Duffy of the *Nation*. In this poem, Kickham told the story of an Irish girl who was forced to emigrate because there was no place for her in Ireland:

> She lived beside the Anner,
> At the foot of Slievenamon,
> A gentle peasant girl,
> With mild eyes like the dawn;
> Her lips were dewy rosebuds;
> Her teeth of pearls rare;
> And a snow-drift 'neath a beechen bough
> Her neck and nut-brown hair.
> How pleasant 'twas to meet her
> On Sunday when the bell
> Was filling with its mellow tones
> Lone wood and grassy dell!

And when at eve young maidens
Strayed the river's banks along,
The widow's brown-haired daughter
Was loveliest of the throng.
O brave, brave Irish girls—
We well may call you brave!—
Sure the least of all your perils
Is the stormy ocean wave,
When you leave your quiet valleys,
And cross the Atlantic's foam,
To hoard your hard-won earning
For the helpless ones at home.
"Write word to my own dear mother—
Say, we'll meet with God above;
And tell my little brothers
I send them all my love;
May the angels ever guard them,
Is their dying sister's prayer"—
And folded in that letter
Was a braid of nut-brown hair.
Ah, cold, and well nigh callous
This weary heart has grown
For thy hapless fate, dear Ireland,
And for sorrows of mine own;
Yet a tear mine eye will moisten
When by Anner's side I stray,
For the lily of the mountain foot
That withered far away.[44]

The poem became an anthem of protest against English-inspired emigration, which Kickham believed was a deliberate, calculated effort to murder a nation through exsanguination. One reason for the poem's popularity was that every town in Ireland had a gentle, mild-eyed "peasant girl" with a similar story, although not every town had a poet who could elevate the maid into the realm of myth.

Had Charles Kickham been content with the life of a moderately well-to-do country gentleman, he would have ended his days quietly in Mullinahone helping tenants, writing poems, and occasionally speaking out against heartless landlords or hypocritical clergy. But fate would not have it so.

In the late 1850s, James Stephens set out to build a truly national, politically active organization by gathering together disparate and scattered remnants of the Young Irelanders, United Irishmen, and various repeal clubs (for repeal of the Act of Union) into one umbrella Fenian society, known as the Irish Republican Brotherhood (IRB). Stephens asked Kickham to join, but he at first declined, apparently uncomfortable with the Brotherhood's insistence on secrecy and unquestioning loyalty to Stephens. In 1860, however, he changed his mind, convinced by the Fenian John O'Mahony, who was visiting Ireland from America, that the IRB was trying to broaden its base and needed men like himself. Convinced, Kickham became a member, pledging to secure, through any means including violence, an independent, republican government for Ireland. By joining the IRB, Kickham risked excommunication from the Church as well as surveillance and possible arrest by the police. Kickham ignored these risks and by 1862 was head of the IRB's Mullinahone branch.[45]

In keeping with his love of public display and commitment to a more open, democratic IRB, Kickham made no attempt to conceal IRB activities in his unit, and in fact made IRB drills occasions for community picnics and celebrations. In July 1863, the Mullinahone unit made a four-mile trek to Carraigmoclear, where they were met by cheering boys and girls from neighboring villages. Music, dancing, and readings of poems by Thomas Davis completed the outing.[46] The first drill/picnic was such a success that a larger event was planned for the following month to include IRB units throughout the region. The site selected for the August 15 gathering was, naturally, Suí Finn on the summit of Slievenamon. James Stephens opposed such a public, culturally charged location, fearing unwanted attention from the police. In keeping with the new open spirit of the IRB, however, he relented eventually, but insisted on remaining in the background. With Stephens and other IRB leaders reluctant to take part actively, it fell to Charles Kickham to make the keynote speech.[47]

Undaunted by the danger of this foolhardy act, Kickham mounted the ancient monument atop Slievenamon to address the crowd of a thousand Fenian faithful. Despite his impaired hearing and poor eyesight, Kickham was in his prime. At forty-five, he was a stout man who wore his hair in long black ringlets to his neck, a black beard partially covering the facial scars from the childhood gunpowder accident. With restrained eloquence, Kickham pleaded his argument familiar to readers of "Rory of the Hill": Words alone were not enough. The Irish, he claimed, had the unlucky knack of indulging in the delusion that when the speech was done, "we have done our duty." They had the reputation for assembling for a grand cause and vowing with "clenched hands up lifted" to fight to the death, only to fly "terror stricken to the emigrant shop or lie down to die patiently of hunger." And so, the Irish were "reviled and scorned, or at least pitied, but never respected, never feared." Irish rhetoric must be ribbed with Irish action, he asserted, if Ireland was ever to assume its rightful place among the free and independent nations of the world. Restating the ideals of the Rising of '98, Kickham invoked the legends of Slievenamon, in his somber advice:

> This highest pinnacle of Slievenamon derives its name from the chieftain of the Fenian heroes of ancient Erin. I am not going to treat you to an Ossianic lecture. I shall merely ask you to join with me in the hope—and labour for its realisation—that on the spot where long ago their prototypes have left their footprints the Fenians of our own day may yet assemble, with their noble chief—the tried and trusted John O'Mahony—in their midst.[48]

Though the speech was reasonably moderate, a magistrate who had climbed the mountain to keep tabs on the demonstration sent a detailed report, with a synopsis of Kickham's speech, to the Crime Branch Special (CBS) of the Queen's Royal Irish Constabulary in Dublin Castle, where it merited the attention of the Lord Lieutenant of Ireland, Lord Carlisle, who briefly considered pressing criminal charges against Kickham. Though this idea was later dropped, Carlisle did send the report on to Prime Minister Palmerston in London. Thus for the first time, a file containing Kickham's name reached the highest level of the British government.[49]

Kickham's role in the 1863 demonstration on Slievenamon precipitated his modest rise into the upper echelons of the IRB leadership. In 1863, Stephens and O'Mahony launched an IRB newspaper, the *Irish People*, and invited Kickham to Dublin to serve as an editor, along with Thomas Clarke Luby and John O'Leary. An extended journey to the United States delayed his acceptance, but when he returned late in 1863, Kickham pulled up stakes in Mullinahone and moved to Dublin. In his articles for the *Irish People*, Kickham developed a reputation as an articulate, passionate propagandist and an outspoken critic of the Church. While other

IRB leaders believed the Church had no role in politics whatsoever, Kickham disagreed. He wanted to see priests and Church leaders actively involved in the political arena, but only if they fully supported the interests of the Irish people. His anti-Church polemics expressed disappointment that the people could not rely upon their priests for support and advocacy in times of adversity and personal need, as proved to be only too true in the Cleary case. One of the few Kickham poems to appear in the *Irish People* was an adaptation of his 1850 poem dedicated to the faithful priest, Soggarth Aroon, in which he questioned the Church's devotion to the people. In the 1863 version, Kickham accused the Catholic Church of wholesale desertion, charging that, because of the Church's unfaithfulness, the people were hunted and slaughtered like animals:

> *On those dark days we now look back,*
> *Soggarth Aroon,*
> *When the bloodhound was on your track,*
> *Soggarth Aroon,*
> *Then we spurned the tyrant's gold,*
> *The past then we never sold,*
> We are still what we were of old,
> *Soggarth Aroon.*

Though Kickham chided the Church for its failure to stand against the English, he never denied its importance. Though Nationalists berated the Church for making accommodations with the English in return for monetary advantages and piecemeal reforms, Kickham maintained that the people needed its ritual, discipline, spiritual guidance, and teachers to defend them against the wealthier, better-educated English. Whereas others in the IRB took the attitude "No priests in politics, ever!," Kickham's view was, "No priests in politics just now."[50] In his principled but un-flinching criticism of the Catholic Church, Kickham spoke for the vast majority of Nationalists, both inside and outside the IRB, who remained faithful Church members—a somewhat ironic po-sition that nevertheless made him a prominent voice within the IRB and on the pages of the *Irish People*.

For twenty-two months, the police tolerated the Fenian publi-cation, but their patience ran thin when rumors reached Ireland that bands of armed Fenians, recently discharged from fighting in the American Civil War, were on their way. On the evening of September 15, 1865, Dublin police raided the headquarters of the *Irish People*, seized the contents of the office, and arrested all staff members on the premises. Their prime target, James Stephens, was out of the office, as was Charles Kickham, and both men es-caped arrest. Initially Kickham was not slated for arrest, but on September 30, fellow editors O'Leary and Luby were brought be-fore a police magistrate. Officers uncovered a document that had been signed by James Stephens that empowered O'Leary, Luby, and Charles Kickham to exercise executive authority over the IRB in the event of the chief's absence. Although Kickham probably never knew about the document, the evidence sealed his fate and a warrant was issued for his arrest. After being on the run for two months, Charles Kickham, along with James Stephens, was ar-rested on November 11, 1865, in their safe house at Sandymount. Both were charged with high treason.[51]

Knocknagow

After their arrests, James Stephens, John O'Leary, Thomas Luby, and Charles Kickham were brought before the Dublin magistrates on Tuesday, November 14 to hear the government's charges. The following day, the inquiry was over, its outcome a foregone conclusion. Based on evidence gathered from the office of the *Irish People*, the four were bound over for trial before a commission, representing not a special court but special session of the regular assize court. Just ten days later, Stephens staged a spectacular escape from the Richmond Jail, and subsequently fled the country. Although Kickham was in the neighboring cell, he was left behind probably because of his physical disabilities.[52]

In January 1866, the special crown commission convened to try the case against Charles Kickham. The chief witness for the defense was Kickham's brother, Thomas, who testified that Kickham was in Mullinahone in March 1864 when Stephens signed the damning document naming Kickham as one of his successors to lead the IRB. Since Kickham had no knowledge of Stephens's act, his solicitor argued that he could not be held responsible. In an attempt to counter this argument, the prosecution produced handwritten documents, purportedly written by Kickham, which were alleged to show his involvement in the IRB leadership. In a moment of high drama, prosecutors tried to trap Thomas into identifying his brother's handwriting, but the heretofore underrated Thomas rose to the occasion and evaded the questions with great skill and resourcefulness. His artful dodging, however, did nothing to change the outcome of the trial.[53]

After a short deliberation, the jury found Kickham guilty as charged. He then made a final, somewhat subdued, but eloquent appeal on his own behalf and that of Ireland to Judge William Keogh before his sentencing on January 6, 1866, saying in part:

> What Irishman looking back on the history of Ireland for the last eighty-four years—its bright gleam of prosperity and glory—its years of treachery and shame—the sufferings of the people and

the famine which desolated the country—could hesitate to say to the enemy, "In God's name give us our country to ourselves, and let us see what we can do with it?". . . I have endeavoured to serve Ireland, and now I am prepared to suffer for Ireland.[54]

Unmoved, Judge Keogh, whose treachery against the Irish people had been attacked again and again in editorials in the *Irish People*, ordered Kickham to serve fourteen years' penal servitude, a term deemed merciful given the fact that Luby and O'Leary received twenty.[55]

Kickham actually served only three years of the sentence. After several lengthy stays in the infirmary, he was released in March 1869 from Pentonville Prison outside London. A feisty, unbowed, and somewhat vain Kickham described his return to Ireland:

I kicked up a row about my own clothes but I was told they were rotten. I insisted on seeing them and picked out a black frock coat and trousers, which the tailor's goose and clothes brush made tolerably presentable. . . . I was ordered to go to Bristol and from that as a deck-passenger to Dublin. Mind that—and I have been in the hospital since 5 January. . . . Yet they would send me across the Channel on deck, without even an outside coat. The officers left us at the first station, and I pitched them to the divil.[56]

After a week's rest in Dublin, Kickham left for Kilkenny, where a large procession accompanied him to the hotel. Later that night, he departed for Mullinahone. In spite of the lateness of the hour, townspeople gathered at the station there, to await the return of "Master Charles." Before his arrest, he was virtually unknown outside of Mullinahone; after his release, he was a national hero.[57]

Although O'Leary and Stephens were much more important leaders of the IRB, they never achieved the same following as Charles Kickham, the gentleman from Mullinahone who was ever the immovable advocate of Nationalism yet retained "the innocent enthusiasm of boyhood" throughout his life. Long before the Gaelic Athletic Association came into existence, Kickham organized nationalist outings for youth groups and helped to mediate land disputes between tenants and landlords. But ultimately, his literary rather than political writings captured the "popular Irish sensibility" and placed him in the pantheon of Irish literary figures.[58]

After his return from prison Charles Kickham had neither the strength nor the inclination to fight the English administration head-on, and turned instead to writing as a means to promote the Irish cause and earn a living. English justice had made him a chastened and impoverished Fenian. Earlier, in December 1865 while awaiting trial, Kickham had assigned his entire portfolio of rental properties, along with the income derived therefrom, to his brother, Alexander, with the understanding that, upon his release, they would be restored. Expecting his brother would be locked away for some time, Alexander used the Mullinahone property as security for a warehousing scheme, which tied up his assets and left him without an income. In short, he was broke. Not surprisingly, he tendered his literary talents for hire, and fortunately there was no shortage of offers. Kickham's first full-length work of fiction, *Sally Cavanagh, or, the Untenanted Graves*, was published in March 1869, and because of the book's success, publishers on both sides of the Atlantic were eager for more prose fiction from Kickham. Badly in need of money, he was happy to write all the prose they could publish.

Buoyed by this encouragement and pressed by impending poverty, Kickham set to writing his most ambitious novel. He

called it *Knocknagow: or, The Homes of Tipperary*.[59] A literary master-
piece it was not; nor was it the expected seething polemic against
the English administration in Ireland. Rather, Kickham painted an
idealized portrait of Irish rural life that dramatized the dilemma of
an inherently good people living under an inherently evil system.
The plot is rambling, implausible, poorly constructed; the dialogue is stylized and difficult to follow. Yet this shaggy, over-
stuffed, sentimental wreck of a novel became Ireland's best-loved
tome, and for generations thereafter, thousands who left county
Tipperary for Boston, Liverpool, or Butte, Montana, carried with
them a copy of *Knocknagow*.

The story takes place in the decades after the Great Famine in
the mythical townland of Knocknagow, owned by an absentee
English landlord, Sir Garrett Butler. The action opens on Christmas Day, at the home of Maurice Kearney, a prosperous tenant.
The Kearneys are playing host to Sir Garrett's nephew, Mr. Henry
Lowe, whom Kickham describes as a young gentleman who
knows "little of Ireland from personal experience, having spent
most of his life in what is sometimes oddly enough called 'the sister country.'"[60] After attending Christmas Mass, Mr. Lowe accom-
panies the men to "the fort" where a wren hunt was underway,
after which the group returns to the cottage for tea. Through the
course of the day, Mr. Lowe is impressed by the respectability, religious piety, and intelligence of his host, and also charmed by the
beauty and refinement of his daughters.

In contrast to Henry Lowe, who seems capable of doing little
more than hunting wrens and sipping tea, the novel's hero, Mat
Donovan, known to everyone as Mat the Thrasher, can do any-
thing and everything twice as well and twice as fast as any man.
Though only a peasant, Mat is drawn as the virtual offspring of
Fionn McCuill—the biggest, bravest, strongest man in all the dis-

trict, yet a man so good and honorable that no mother would begrudge him her daughter. He is a simple, landless rustic on his way to becoming a landowning, God-fearing farmer and father. Unlike the scruffy, illiterate, superstitious Kennedy brothers of Ballyvadlea, Matt is the romantic embodiment of rural Ireland. The evil figures in the novel are Sir Garrett's unscrupulous land agent, Mr. Isaac Pender, and his dastardly son, Beresford. Together they lie, connive, and conspire to terminate the leaseholds, evict the tenants, and destroy Knocknagow.

The threat to tenants like the Kearneys, Mat Donovan, and his neighbor Tom Hogan, is immediate, but Kickham also points out that the plight of the tenant farmers is symptomatic of the threat to the entire Irish nation. The English are not simply evicting tenants, he argues; rather, English policies are calculated to exterminate the Irish. As one Irish landlord returns from the English army minus an arm, and another advises that his land was taken, the commentator observes, "The Irish landlords were encouraged to exterminate the people . . . and when the work was done, many of themselves were exterminated. England cares just as little for them as for the people."[61] Tales of English injustice hang like a shadow over Knocknagow, darkening the landscape and blighting the people.

However unjust the system, Kickham condemns the futility of random violence. In his youth he called for a well-organized armed revolt; now he calls for a higher, more civilized standard of conduct. His prescription for Irish resistance is dramatized one tragic day when "magnificent Tipperary" shows its true colors. That is the day when sheriff and soldiers march on Knocknagow—this time to serve eviction orders upon Mat Donovan and Tom Hogan. Rather than react violently, Mat the Thrasher watches silently as the bailiffs do their work. After the destruction, the sheriff hands Mr. Isaac Pender a twig from the fence and a bit of stubble from the ground, which in turn, Pender offers Mat, as a mocking expression of sympathy for the loss of his "little garden." Only then does Mat lose his composure, but does nothing more than denounce the agent as a "robber and a hypocrite."[62]

Sheriff and soldiers then troop off to Tom Hogan's cottage, led by the bailiff Darby Ruadh, who knocks at Hogan's door.

> The door is open, and Darby Ruadh enters, looking flurried and excited, as if he expected to be knocked down at any moment. . . . Nancy Hogan [Tom's courageous daughter] is looking very pale, but so beautiful that for a moment Darby forgets everything else in his admiration of her. Her mother is sitting upon a stool, quite calm. The house is soon cleared, and mother and daughter walk out quietly. Darby is obliged to have recourse to the cotton pocket-handkerchief, he is so much affected. He thought he would have been obliged to use violence, and is quite moved to find Mrs. Hogan so reasonable and considerate. And now Tom Hogan himself walks into the yard, and *won't* see the police drawn up along the barn—that barn that is as good as Attorney Hanly's and better than Maurice Kearney's—nor the party of soldiers on the road. Nancy covers her golden hair with her cloak and shades her face from their gaze. "God save you, Darby," says Tom Hogan quietly, as he walks towards the door.

When the first blow of the crowbar crashes into the cottage, it is as if it goes right through poor Tom Hogan's heart and he falls senseless to the ground. When the sheriff and soldiers have done their work, half of Knocknagow has been "swept from the face of the earth."[63]

Though the fictional Knocknagow was decimated, Kickham offered those few who remained hope for the future. The Irish people, he argued, could not afford the ill-conceived, unorganized acts of terrorism that plagued the countryside; nor could they afford leaders who engaged endlessly in parliamentary debates that would ultimately do nothing but appease and divide. By participating in either random violence or parliamentary politics, as he had earlier as a Young Irelander and member of the IRB, Kickham maintained that the Irish were playing the English game—a game they would inevitably lose. Rather than dissipate their strength, Kickham advocated a single-minded program of rural, cultural, and economic advancement in preparation for armed rebellion. Only by developing an educated, thinking people could the shadow of the curse be lifted from Slievenamon mountain and all Ireland.

Knocknagow is a romantic portrayal of rural bourgeois values superimposed on one relatively prosperous, but nonetheless indebted Irish tenant family.[64] There was almost no reference to Irish mythology or language in the novel because Kickham did not consider them necessary for achieving Irish independence. He believed, as did one of the characters in his tale "White Humphrey of the Grange," that the "Saxon tongue has taken root in the country, and must ere long be the language of the majority of the people" and insisted that "the language of the stranger, may be as thoroughly Irish as if written in the [Irish] language." The only Irish-music enthusiast in *Knocknagow* is a niece of the absentee English landowner, Sir Garrett Butler. There is only one Fenian agitator, a fiftyish doctor named Kiely who exhibits the "liberality of the aristocracy" and is writing a book about Irish antiquity. Kickham makes only passing references to folklore or belief in fairies. Billy Heffernan is the character most representative of the poor Irish peasantry and its innocent identification with the land, but he is portrayed only as "superstitious," not "fairie-ridden" like the real-life tenant farmers and laborers of Ballyvadlea. There is no spiritual or supernatural dimension to Kickham's politics or his idyllic description of the middle-class virtues embodied by the Kearneys, their friends, and their subtenants. While a few priests are openly hostile to the "damnable [British] government" because of the "suffering of the people" during the Great Famine, their unusually prominent role in Irish politics, which Kickham opposed as a young Fenian, is also ignored in *Knocknagow*.[65]

The discrepancy between this secular, moralistic portrayal of Irish family life in the 1860s and Kickham's radical Fenian views can be explained in part by his financial needs and his devotion to the area around Slievenamon. Roiling beneath the glossy surface of the novel is Kickham's anger over the forced evictions of honest, upright, hardworking tenants and the indignities of the crowbar destruction of their cottages. Kickham's outrage at these cultural atrocities is one enduring hallmark of *Knocknagow*. The other is his simple faith in the Irish people.

Addressed primarily to Irish Catholics in Ireland and the United States, *Knocknagow* appealed to their desire for respectable antecedents to counter discrimination at home and abroad. Despite its multiple editions well into the first half of the twentieth century, *Knocknagow*'s moderate commercial success at the time did not save its author from financial ruin. When friends in Dublin heard of Kickham's financial embarrassment, the *Freeman's Journal* announced in November 1878 that a fund had been organized to help. Within days, money began to arrive from various parts of Ireland, and later from England, America, and Australia. By February 1879, the fund had gathered over £1,200, which was invested in American, rather than British, securities.

Contributors included Charles Stewart Parnell, Isaac Butt, and Gavan Duffy, as well as several bishops and clergymen. One of the first to contribute was the Archbishop of Cashel, Thomas William Croke.[66]

That Kickham had any support from Church leaders was surprising, given his consistent criticism of Church policy toward the Fenian movement. Although the Church withheld sacraments from known Fenians from the early 1860s on, its policy was carried out with varying degrees of enthusiasm, depending upon the politics of individual priests. Kickham did receive sacraments while in prison; after his release, however, the issue became more vexing. In 1870, the Pope explicitly condemned Fenianism by name, and this precluded Kickham from receiving the sacraments.

Despite the state of limbo in which the Church's policy had placed him, Kickham remained a devout Catholic and sought reconciliation with the Church. In December 1877, his hope was bolstered when he read a letter published in the *Freeman's Journal* from Archbishop Croke, urging the release of Fenian prisoners. Croke's appeal gave Kickham cause to hope that he had found a kindred spirit within the Catholic hierarchy, and indeed he had. Like Kickham, Croke never betrayed his nationalist roots, but Croke buried his political beliefs until he had safely established himself as Archbishop of Cashel. By 1878, Croke felt secure enough to let his nationalist colors show.

Sometime in the spring or early summer of 1878, Charles Kickham traveled to The Palace, Thurles, along with T. P. O'Connor, to meet with the archbishop. Without prior notice, the two men knocked at the door of the Palace; they were informed that His Grace was unavailable but could meet with them later in the day. When they returned, Croke himself greeted them at the door and ushered them into his parlor. A copy of *Knock-*

nagow was lying on a table, intentionally set apart from other books as if it had just been put down.

Kickham wasted no time getting to the purpose of his visit: the archbishop's permission to be readmitted to the sacraments. He explained, however, that he could not possibly abandon his immovable conviction that the only effective means of winning their nation's independence was through physical force. Croke listened politely, then offered a defense of the Church's ban on secret societies, questioning the Fenians' insistence on using force rather than the parliamentary process. In reply, Kickham reiterated his oft-stated belief that the British would never agree to peaceful separation with Ireland and that adopting the Church's policy of complicity would only delay the inevitable break with England. Croke begged to disagree, and a tense moment ensued. Kickham asked His Grace point blank whether he was an English priest or an Irish priest. In the face of this aggressive challenge, Croke relented. The archbishop asked Kickham to nominate a confessor, promising to write at once, granting permission for Kickham to be admitted to the sacraments.[67]

Archbishop Croke later recounted his recollection of this interview in a letter to the *Freeman's Journal* accompanying his £10 contribution to the Kickham Fund. He recalled that Kickham came to him on a matter of "vital moment to him" and commented:

> I can safely say that, apart altogether from and independent of his attractions as an Irish poet, scholar and patriot, I take him to be of all men that I have ever met about the gentlest, the most amiable, the most truthful, and the most sorely and searchingly tried, at the same time that I believe our most holy mother the church has few more dutiful sons than he, and no more thoroughly devoted to her interests, or more resolutely and reasonably faithful.[68]

To refer to Charles Kickham, even in his more moderate post-prison political mode, as a dutiful son of the Church was certainly courageous, and defiant, of the Archbishop of Cashel, given the Pope's ban on Fenians.

By the 1880s, Thomas Croke and Charles Kickham were more alike than dissimilar in their vision for Ireland. Both were thoroughly committed to independence, although Croke was more sanguine that the parliamentary approach would prove fruitful, and both were committed to the idea that the Church should play a major role in winning independence for a future nation that should be both Catholic and Irish. Kickham's earlier criticism of the Church had been based on its lack of consistent support for Irish nationalism, but he saw that under Croke's leadership the Catholic devotional revolution was evolving into a social and cultural revolution in support of Irish independence. Although Croke eschewed violence, he agreed with Kickham that the nation must build up a sober, physically strong, disciplined, well-educated citizenry that was prepared to fight for its independence if necessary. Finally, both agreed that paganism was an impediment to progress. The cultural and political revolution they envisioned for Ireland was modern and bourgeois, not rooted in the country's pagan, ignorant, poverty-stricken past.

Despite the Archbishop's public testimonial on behalf of Kickham, other priests were neither as forgiving of him nor as bold in his defense. After Kickham's death at age fifty-four in Dublin on August 22, 1882, IRB leaders organized a massive funeral cortege of Fenians from across Ireland and England, which passed through the streets of Dublin from Blackrock to Kingsbridge Railway Station. Some three dozen carriages followed, carrying nationalist dignitaries of all stripes, including M.P.s John Dillon, R.B. Sullivan, and Tim Healy, and joined by eleven marching bands from Dublin trade unions. At Kingsbridge Station, prayers were recited, then the coffin was put on a train bound for Thurles.[69]

Unfortunately Archbishop Croke was away when the cortege arrived in Thurles. The official story was that he was in England; unofficially, it was said that he was secretly in Rome, lecturing the Pope on the realities of Irish politics. Had Croke been in residence at The Palace, he would have approved the Fenians' wish that the body lie in state in the cathedral, allowing for an orderly outpouring of public feeling for Tipperary's beloved poet/patriot. In Croke's absence, the parish administrator, Father James Cantwell, flatly refused to grant access to the cathedral, which left the funeral detail in confusion. The body stayed overnight in a private home, and on the following day, Monday, August 26, a procession formed to accompany it from Thurles to Mullinahone.[70]

Another awkward event took place at the Mullinahone cemetery when leaders found the gates locked and no priest in sight. After a moment of consultation, they forced the lock and held a short, impromptu graveside service. Because no priest was in attendance, a seminary student stepped forward and led the crowd in a recitation of the *De profundis*. Belatedly, the local curate arrived to close the grave, after which John Daly of Limerick, one of Kickham's faithful IRB followers, offered a short oration.[71] Sometime later, Archbishop Croke learned of Kickham's death and wrote his brother, Alexander, to express his condolences, stating that had he been in Thurles, Charles Joseph Kickham would have been extended "all due honour."[72]

From The Palace, Thurles, and through the pages of *Knocknagow*, Thomas Croke, the archbishop, and Charles Kickham, the poet, forged common links between priest and peasant, Catholicism and Fenianism in behalf of the Nationalist movement sworn to protect the interests of the dispossessed, humiliated Irish peasantry. Thirteen years later, in another strange conjunction of events, ancient forces from deep within the culture clashed with modern ideas for progress and civilization when a cooper's wife was burned as a witch in the shadow of Slievenamon.

8

The Archbishop's Jubilee

Of Sorcery and Superstitions:
The Trial of Michael Cleary

On July 1, 1895, "Jubilee Month" opened with a series of celebrations to honor the "Metropolitan of Munster," the Right Reverend Archbishop of Cashel and Emly, Dr. Thomas William Croke, a man who was widely considered the greatest prelate to serve as archbishop since St. Lawrence O'Toole. Underscoring the Archbishop's immense popularity, committees of every type and kind throughout the county prepared to pay tribute to Tipperary's "illustrious prelate" and "unflinching Irish Nationalist." In Burrisoleigh, crowds were turned away when the Archbishop paid a private visit to the town's church; otherwise the people would have filled the streets with boisterous cheers and bright green banners.[1]

Jubilee well-wishers polished their prose in preparation for Tipperary's grandest event ever. Thomas J. Condon, M.P., rallied support from Clonmel's faithful Catholic Nationalists, declaring that no figure in County Tipperary was as universally loved and admired as Archbishop Croke. Indeed, there was not an Irishman who rendered more "signal services" to Ireland's cause than his Grace of Cashel, especially in the dark days of 1891, when Parnell shattered the Irish Party with his recklessness and indiscretion. It was an absolute fact, Condon declared, that, "next to God, it was [to] his Grace's stand in that terrible juncture that they owed the preservation of the National movement."[2]

Next to God, Croke loved his country best. Throughout his career, he labored to lead his people from political bondage and spiritual darkness. He believed that Ireland's union with England was destroying his country so he helped build the Irish National Federation (INF) into a national political party. He loathed persistent violence in the countryside, so he supported the athletic activities, but not the drinking habits, of the Gaelic Athletic Association (GAA), which channeled civil unrest and cultivated a corps of able-bodied, disciplined, sober young men who might one day be called upon to fight for their country's freedom. Finally, Croke abhorred the persistent ignorance, sorcery, and superstition that kept the people in darkness and exposed them to ridicule. In order to foster progress, he promoted education, art, and the best elements of Irish culture and folklore, believing that if the Irish could be introduced to the right influences, they would turn away from the old folkways and become a truly civilized people.

And so it was fitting that Jubilee Month open with a concert of light opera and musical highlights presented by schoolgirls from the Ursuline Convent in Thurles, attended by His Grace and a delegation of priests and dignitaries. In honor of the occasion, the hall was brightly lit and specially decorated to show respect for the Archbishop, who had encouraged the progress of the school with "more than a father's care." The recital opened with an instrumental piece played by the school's orchestra, followed by a tribute to his Grace, clearly and sweetly delivered by a student, Miss Mary Pekenham. This was followed by some French light opera, which was perhaps intended to pay tribute to Croke's Paris years. The evening closed with a specially commissioned choral composition performed by the convent's Jubilee Chorus. After this touching and entertaining tribute, the Archbishop expressed his appreciation to the nuns, priests, and, above all, to the fine young women of the Ursuline convent who had worked so hard and performed so remarkably well.[3]

As the Ursuline girls departed for summer holiday, darker forces appeared to cloud the glittering opening of Croke's Jubilee. On Wednesday, July 3, Clonmel's citizens learned that Michael Cleary and the other prisoners held in connection with what English officials called the "Tipperary Witchcraft Case" were to be arraigned the next day before Justice William O'Brien at the Clonmel Courthouse. It was expected that Cleary's trial on the capital charge of murdering his wife would be begun "without delay." The timing of the trial could not have been worse for the Jubilee celebrants, the Nationalists, and the Archbishop personally because a protracted witch-burning trial, reported in newspapers around the world, would certainly cast a shadow over Croke's Jubilee, scheduled for July 18 in County Tipperary, and could possibly affect the outcome of the national parliamentary elections to be held the same day in County Tipperary. English authorities in London and Dublin recognized the opportunity made possible by this strange conjunction of events and relished the discomfort they might inflict upon the Nationalists and the Archbishop of Cashel. To capitalize upon this rare opportunity, English authorities devised a cleverly crafty legal theory designed to convict not just the nine prisoners charged with the murder of Bridget Cleary but also the Catholic Church and the superstition-ridden culture it allegedly fostered.[4]

It fell to Justice O'Brien to deploy the British government's plan to implicate the Church in the Cleary trial. Ironically, O'Brien was a Catholic himself, just one of four Catholics, out of a total of eighteen judges, to serve on the Superior Courts in Ireland. O'Brien had risen from a lowly background to his seat on the bench, starting out as a reporter and editor of the *Cork Examiner* before the Liberal Sir Edward Sullivan, the Irish Master of the Rolls and subsequently Lord Chancellor, became his mentor.[5] Even though he was a Liberal Catholic appointment to the bench, O'Brien appeared willing to do Dublin's bidding and effectively brand the Catholic Church as an unindicted co-conspirator by eliciting evidence to show that Catholic prayers and sacraments were used in the witch-burning ritual. Yet, O'Brien was prepared to go just so far in embarrassing the Church.

On the morning of July 4, 1895, the nine defendants awaiting trial for the murder of Bridget Cleary emerged from the gray walls of the Clonmel Gaol, surrounded by a contingent of armed officers. Once they were outside the gates, a large crowd, eager for a glimpse of the now-infamous nine, jeered the prisoners, who "looked something the worse" for their incarceration since the magisterial inquiry. Michael Cleary appeared noticeably thinner, "the peculiar pallor" of his face more pronounced, his beard longer and shaggier than in March. He wore clothing similar to his earlier public appearance: a flannel shirt, corduroy trousers, suspenders, and blue tweed cap, the weather being too warm for his tweed jacket and vest.[6]

The police escort moved out along its usual route down to Parnell Street, past the ever youthful, ever hopeful monument to the

Croppy Boys, heroes of the failed Rising of 1798, outside Clonmel's town hall, then down Nelson Street to the Courthouse, where Her Majesty's Quarter Session Court for South Riding, County Tipperary, was about to convene. Outside the courthouse, another large crowd awaited the prisoners' arrival, but unlike the noisy gatherings outside the courthouse preceding the March magisterial inquiry, this time there was "no demonstration of sympathy or otherwise." The more subdued response expressed the crowd's respect for the heavily armed military escort, sympathy for the prisoners, and the dulling effect of the summer's heat. Inside, the courtroom was packed with the press, members of the specially called Grand Jury, and spectators from "all classes of society," some of whom had waited over two hours for a seat. At exactly 11:30 A.M., spectators were asked to rise as High Sheriff Robert Malcombson and Sub-Sheriff Arnold Power, Esq. accompanied Justices O'Brien and Holmes to the bench. With a bang of the gavel, the clerk called the regular summer session of the South Riding Assize to order. While the court dispensed with preliminary business, the prisoners remained in an underground holding cell.[7]

As was the custom, the Presiding Crown Justice, O'Brien, opened the South Riding Quarter Session by delivering a judicial "state of the county" address to members of the district's Grand Jury. In his quarterly report, he took note of the number and types of crimes committed, reviewed cases to be heard, then made his recommendations as to how the largely Protestant, upper-class members of the Grand Jury could do their part to maintain good order in the district. The report for the Summer Session of 1895 was generally favorable. Justice O'Brien was encouraged by "evidence of great and beneficial change," especially when contrasted to years when lawlessness and violence were the order of the day in County Tipperary. He felt relieved that citizens of the district could now go about their business unmolested and sleep through the night without fear of outrage. Unlike the turbulent days of the Land Wars, today there was a greater sense of security for person, life, and property, so much so, that he felt confident enough to predict that the "evil times have passed away," at least for the present. Qualifying his sanguine report slightly, O'Brien warned that he was, as always, "prepared for the recrudescence of disturbance in Ireland."

Justice O'Brien cited figures from the Royal Irish Constabulary indicating that ordinary crime was down, as were "recorded outrages" in the countryside. However, the judge interjected, the decline of *ordinary* crime did not prevent South Riding from achieving distinction in the category of *extraordinary* crime. Indeed South Riding had succeeded in producing a case of such unimaginable horror that its notoriety had spread "to the end of the civilised world." This case was so unprecedented, so outrageous, and so tantalizing that the judge could not resist instructing the jurors on how the English government could best make use of this rare opportunity. This most bizarre situation, he lamented, arose "out of a superstitious belief in witchcraft," and unpleasant as their duty might be, he warned the jury that they must face the fact that even in modern times, yes, even in "Christian communities," women were burned to death while screaming they were innocent. To help make sense of this horrible event, His Honor had consulted Sir Francis Bacon and William Shakespeare, who led him to conclude that "from the depths of human delusions and folly we are altogether not so far removed as we thought we were."[8]

Having invoked the gods of English philosophy and literature, O'Brien then laid out the administration's legal theory to the largely Protestant Grand Jury. He began by making the distinction between legal witch burnings, such as those conducted in England within the confines of law and under orders of the state, and extralegal burnings like that of Bridget Cleary, which took place outside the bounds of constituted authority. The perpetrators, he declared, acted not under the direction of law, as would have been right and proper, but "under the influence of religion." The reference to "religion" undoubtedly alerted the politically attuned in the courtroom to the direction of O'Brien's argument. He had no need to name the religion to which he referred, or mention the feverish preparations taking place throughout South and North Riding to honor the beloved prelate of Munster. No, indeed, these things went without saying. But those within the sound of his voice understood that the judge was going to try the Catholic Church for murder along with the nine prisoners.

To support this theory, O'Brien asked the jury to pay particular attention to the rituals preceding the murder, especially those that incorporated a "curious and singular mixture of religious incantations and sacred names" used to expel the witch, the consequence of which now confronted the court. Also they were to note that the effect of these incantations was not limited to one man alone, but to an entire group. While Michael Cleary apparently "conceived the idea that his wife was under some preternatural influence," O'Brien, like most other right-thinking people, found it incredible that so many persons—as many as eleven—young and old, men and women, were "incapable of emotions or pity or sympathy with suffering" and failed to intervene on Bridget Cleary's behalf. The jurors must ask themselves: How could so many be bound by darkness? How could so many become laden with superstition? How could so many be rendered incapable of pity? The only possible explanation was that all of the accused shared a common belief in the Catholic religion, which, he implied, had for so long accommodated pagan superstitions in Ireland.[9]

In casting blame upon the collective beliefs of the accused, O'Brien portrayed Bridget Cleary as an innocent victim. This young woman who was "respectful in all her conduct," he declared, was in no way responsible for her death. She did nothing to provoke this "barbaric" treatment and committed neither harm nor offense to others. Indeed, her attempts to save her own life called to mind lines from *Macbeth*:

> Pleading like angels, trumpet tongued,
> Against the deep damnation of *her* taking off.

Justice O'Brien suggested that Bridget Cleary failed to save her life because her family, friends, and neighbors secretly practiced sorcery and harbored superstitions fostered by *that* religion.

His Lordship explained why jurors should regard the crime as a capital offense. If a murder occurred in the course of a sudden quarrel or burst of passion, the offense could be reduced to manslaughter, but such reduced charge was not appropriate in cases in which death resulted from a "delusion raised in the mind" or "where the act was the result of a belief in witchcraft." Though the jury might be tempted to reduce the charge, the judge recommended that they not consider manslaughter because, he declared, it would be "exceedingly dangerous to the lives and happiness of the community if the existence of such a delusion as that in the mind of any person could arrest the quality or nature of a crime that resulted in the taking away of human life." Nevertheless, he advised members of the jury that it was within their prerogative to reduce the charge to manslaughter if they saw fit despite his stated contempt for such a course of action.[10]

By mentioning the possibility that the murder charge could be reduced to manslaughter if accepted by the Grand Jury, O'Brien revealed his own plan for mitigating the damage to his own Church and people. He would satisfy his superiors in Dublin by showing the extent to which Catholic prayers and sacraments were used in the pagan ritual, yet he would attempt to end the trial quickly by obliging Michael Cleary's defense attorney to enter a guilty plea to the lesser charge of manslaughter. If the manslaughter plea was entered, O'Brien hoped the trial might end in days rather than weeks, before, rather than concurrent with, Croke's Jubilee and the national elections.

Following O'Brien's recommendations, the Grand Jury delivered true bills of indictment against Michael Cleary, Patrick Boland, Mary Kennedy, James Kennedy, and Patrick Kennedy. True bills of wounding were issued against John Dunne, Michael Kennedy, William Kennedy, and William Ahearn. Standing ready to press the Crown's case against Michael Cleary and the Catholic Church was a team of prosecutors selected from the Queen's Counsel (Q.C.), led by William Ryan. At his elbow were two assistant prosecutors, Stephen Curtis, Q.C., and C. Molloy, Q.C., advised by Crown Solicitor Michael Gleeson. Dr. John Boursiquot Falconer, assisted by Richard J. Crean, was engaged to defend Michael Cleary.

Prosecutor William Ryan announced the Crown was prepared to proceed with the case against Michael Cleary. Moments later, Cleary was led into the courtroom from the underground cell, his hat gripped tightly in one hand. He walked solemnly to the front bar of the prisoners' dock rail and looked quietly around the courtroom, causing one reporter to observe that he seemed a "matter-of-fact sort of person."[11] When Cleary heard that the charge against him was willful murder, his calm facade was shattered and he looked visibly shaken.

O'Brien: Are you guilty or not?
Cleary: I am not, sir.[12]

Queen's Counsel William Ryan rose and laid out the Crown's case, which began by affirming Bridget Cleary's innocence. There was no evidence, he asserted, to support the claim that Bridget Cleary exhibited supernatural powers. Michael Cleary's fears that his wife had "gone with the fairies" was nonsense bred of ignorance and superstition. Further, the killing was nothing less than "willful murder," and he urged the jury not to accept a lesser charge of manslaughter in order that the case would stand as "an example to others and of putting a stop to anything of this kind occurring in their great country again."[13]

At the conclusion of his statement, Ryan called his first witness, Johanna Burke. Ryan began questioning her. In her July appearance, Burke was much more aggressive in defending her family, and even Michael Cleary, than at the magisterial inquiry, and attempted to place the blame squarely upon John Dunne. To establish Dunne's responsibility, Burke now recalled incriminating new evidence that Bridget had a blister on her hip from the red-hot poker wielded by Dunne; in earlier testimony, she had indicated the poker was used only to threaten Bridget. As Dunne was forcing Bridget to swallow the herbs, Michael stopped and asked for a cork to put in his wife's mouth, "as the spoon would hurt her." It was Dunne who rejected this suggestion, because she might bite the cork rather than ingest the cure.[14] She insisted that it was Dunne who first spoke of getting the "small spoon" to help administer the herbs and brought the hot poker into the bedroom to persuade her to swallow them.[15] Dunne whispered a charm to Michael Cleary, which Burke could not hear. Burke insisted that "Cleary made no fairy of her; that it was all Dunne's fault." She hurled so many charges against Dunne that the judge felt obliged to warn the jury that Burke's sympathy for her family might prejudice her evidence against him.[16]

Undaunted by the judge's warning, Johanna testified that she did not blame Michael for the murder, because he was "very fond" of Bridget and "loved his wife very much." To illustrate her point she stated that as Michael bent down to wrap the body, he said, "She's burned now and God knows I would never do it but for Jack Dunne. It was he told me my wife was a fairy. . . . He [Dunne] did tell Mike Cleary that, because I heard him." Burke insisted that Dunne's whisperings fanned Cleary's fears, aided by a "bellyful of whiskey." Her accusations against Dunne continued until the prosecutor asked Burke to identify Cleary's trousers entered as evidence, stained with oil and the burned flesh of Bridget's body. Upon seeing the trousers, Johanna broke down and wept openly.[17]

To the prosecution's delight, Burke testified that as Michael mixed Ganey's herbs, Dunne ordered him to boil them and he "made the sign of the cross over them and go around the house making *pishogues* and cutting the sign of the cross over the saucepan." Cleary was fond of his wife, Burke maintained, and had the priest attend to her. Burke even related how Michael had put his arm tenderly around his wife's neck on Friday evening, as if to coax her to answer the questions correctly.

The prosecution team pushed Burke to reveal more instances in which Catholic holy names and signs were used in the rituals. The most prominent of these was the chant "In the name of the Father, Son, and Holy Ghost," repeated three times and recited as each dose of herbal potion was administered. Burke and others testified that on numerous occasions throughout the ordeal, Michael Cleary, joined by Patrick Boland, invoked the names of

the holy trinity for the purpose of strengthening the herbal potion by adding to it the weight of divine power. This testimony
showed that, in fact, the names of the Father, Son, and Holy
Ghost were as much a part of the ritual as the pagan cure.

Upon prompting from the Queen's counsel, Burke disclosed
other instances where the name of God was used to aid the
process of exorcism. In damning new evidence, Prosecutor Mal-
loy forced Burke to concede that, just after the burning, Cleary
invoked the name of God to get his wife back, and, that as Bridget still lay smoldering on the fire, Michael declared: "I got you
by the law of God and [now] come back in the name of God,"[18]
then Patrick Boland allegedly told Patrick Kennedy: "Come and
we will do it and maybe we will get her back. God is good." After
Bridget's dead body was removed from the fireplace, Burke's
mother, Mary, screamed out: "In the name of God let ye go on
your knees and say the rosary. It was the devil whispered it into
his ear." Obeying their mother's request, the family prepared to
say the rosary, to be led by the youngest son, William. Michael
Cleary refused to join in the prayer. Burke also recalled that on
Thursday, Michael took a cross from his wife's hands, saying she
had no business with it. Burke later retrieved Bridget's cross and
testified that she held it in her hands as William recited the rosary
after the burning. This was all the prosecution wished to hear
from its witness.[19] It completed its direct examination of Johanna
at seven P.M. and court adjourned until ten the next morning. The
jurors were sequestered in a nearby hotel for the night.

On the morning of July 5, Dr. Falconer, counsel for Michael
Cleary, began his cross-examination of the Crown's star witness.
Falconer rose and tried to defend his client by demonstrating that
Michael Cleary genuinely believed his wife was taken by the
fairies—a tactic that proved futile, when at every turn, His Lord-

ship disallowed any reference to fairies. Falconer insisted that Cleary "fully believed that his wife was a witch" because she had "got a blast," meaning that her illness was fairy-induced. To thwart this line of questioning, the judge blasted him, demanding, "When you asked had she got a 'blast' you must specify what it is because I have heard of 'blasts' of various kinds. . . . I have heard a great many maladies described as 'blasts.'" Falconer attempted to show that Bridget incurred the "blast" when returning from the fort on Kylnagranagh hill. He asked Burke to describe the event, specifically if Bridget had a cold, flu, or bronchitis, or if she "took like a tremble coming up from Kylnagranagh." Before she could answer, the judge interrupted again, asking, "Does Dunne live there?" Burke responded that he did, then elaborated by saying that Bridget had told her "she was coming from Dunne's house when she took like a trembling coming by Kylnagranagh," adding that Dunne lived a "few fields under the fort." When Falconer asked her if the fairies were supposed to live at the fort, O'Brien stopped him dead in his tracks.

> *His Lordship*: I will not allow a question, that question. If you persist in putting illegal questions I must put an end to this line of examination.
>
> *Falconer*: The connection between fairies and Kylnagranagh was brought out in direct examination.
>
> *His Lordship*: I will not allow a question as to where fairies are supposed to be. They may be supposed to be in this courthouse. We are not here acting in a play, but to inquire into matters of fact.[20]
>
> *Falconer*: But you are inquiring into a question of tragedy.

Tragedy or not, there would be no questions about fairies. Yet Falconer persisted. Turning again to the witness, he asked Johanna about the circumstances surrounding the onset of Bridget's illness. She reiterated that Bridget came home ill and could not be warmed by the fire. She recalled that Bridget was unusually cross and argumentative, which led Michael to believe that she was possessed by a fairy spirit. The couple argued openly about the possibility that Bridget had been abducted at the fort. Bridget denied this and retorted that Michael's mother had gone with the fairies for two days. Michael countered with the charge that Bridget's mother also had gone with the fairies. Judge O'Brien objected to this testimony, labeling Falconer's questions "pure extravagance." Falconer protested that he was only trying to determine if the mother, Bridget Boland, "was reputed to be a wise woman about witches and fairies" because, if she had been, then Michael would have had more reason to fear that his own wife was taken in the fairy blast. Justice O'Brien disallowed Falconer's questions. Realizing he could not introduce evidence about supernatural influences, either directly or indirectly, Falconer relented, stating that he would drop the matter of "Boland's wife" going with the fairies. Justice O'Brien concurred, adding, "And I think that for the present you might also drop the fairies."

Nonetheless Falconer made one more attempt, asking Burke if she had ever heard Patrick Boland tell Michael Cleary about the fairies. O'Brien allowed this question, to which Burke meekly answered, "I never did," adding that she believed Pat Boland and his son-in-law were on good terms, though she occasionally "saw some quarrels between them." Falconer did succeed in eliciting from Burke that Michael Cleary had told the caretaker William Simpson that the cottage "was full of fairies" on Thursday night and that several would be going out the door. Also Burke said that Cleary had insisted repeatedly that he never burned his wife, but believed that it was a fairy he put on the fire to get it out the chimney.[21]

The court was more receptive to Falconer's questions about the Friday Mass celebrated at the Cleary cottage, hoping this evidence might show the priest's role in the pagan ritual. Falconer asked Burke if, to her knowledge, Bridget swallowed "the Sacred Particle." Burke replied that she did not know, but that Bridget had told her that Father Ryan put something in her mouth to cure her. To demonstrate, Bridget put her finger in her mouth and, drawing out the communion wafer, said to Burke, "Look here." Burke thought that Bridget had removed what she took to be the "Sacred particle" off the roof of her mouth, then set it on the blanket of the bed. Falconer reminded Burke of her testimony at the magisterial inquiry in which she stated that Bridget had not swallowed the communion wafer. With this equivocal testimony, Burke attempted to avoid this crucial issue, because if she saw Bridget remove the communion wafer, then Father Ryan would have seen this desecration of the sacred host as well.[22]

Falconer pressed the witness to clarify this discrepancy from her earlier testimony. Burke replied that she believed it was the Holy Communion but could not be sure, since prior to the Mass, Bridget had eaten bread for breakfast and could have removed an uneaten remnant on her finger. Burke testified that upon seeing the bit of bread, she asked Bridget if she had swallowed the wafer. Bridget implied that she had received the sacrament properly, yet her response was open to interpretation. According to Burke, Bridget said, "It couldn't be the Holy Communion, Han, for didn't you give me my breakfast." When Falconer asked Burke to state definitely whether or not Bridget swallowed the communion wafer, O'Brien objected, ruling he could not ask Burke for an inference. At this point, Falconer asked if she had heard that Father Ryan had been called to say Mass in order to "banish the evil spirits out of the house." To which Burke firmly replied, "No, and there was nothing of the kind said."[23]

Realizing that his line of questioning was going nowhere, Falconer abandoned his cross-examination and called Johanna's daughter, Katie, to the stand. Burke objected that the girl was too young and had not yet received First Communion (another contradiction from her testimony at the inquiry). Nevertheless Katie was called, but merely corroborated her mother's testimony. With this, Falconer abandoned his defense strategy in frustration. Rather than continue, Falconer rose and asked the court to allow his client to change his plea. Given the prosecution's strategy and the restrictions placed on the kinds of evidence O'Brien would allow entered, it was in the best interests of his client, Falconer argued, to withdraw the pleas of not guilty to murder and instead plead guilty to manslaughter.[24]

A short discussion ensued. Justice O'Brien asserted that he did not have the power to reduce that charge, that this was a matter for the prosecutor and the Grand Jury.

> *His Lordship:* I cannot take that course in law. . . . The jury have a power to return a verdict of manslaughter, but I have no power to direct them.
>
> *Dr. Falconer:* I understand that, my Lord. I will agree to a verdict of manslaughter being returned by the jury.
>
> *His Lordship:* That can only be done by the act of the jury and apparently only with the consent of the Crown.

The Queen's team of solicitors conferred briefly, then Crown Prosecutor Ryan stood and addressed the court. Given the "great peculiarity of the case" and the "extraordinary circumstances" surrounding it, he declared his willingness to accept responsibility for sending the matter back to the Grand Jury. His Lordship concurred, stating that he saw no reason to dissent from the prosecutor's wish. He then issued a form to the jury upon which was written "Not guilty of murder, but guilty of manslaughter." The jury briefly conferred and quickly returned a verdict of guilty of manslaughter. Within the space of minutes, the trial that most thought would go on for days, if not weeks, was over. Michael Cleary was ceremoniously led back to the underground holding cell to await sentencing, still holding on tightly to his blue tweed cap. He would go to prison, but would not hang for the murder of his wife. The citizens of Clonmel would be spared not only the ordeal of seeing another Irishman swing from the gallows beside the gates of the Clonmel Gaol but also the embarrassment of a protracted trial.[25]

With the case against Michael Cleary resolved, a new jury was sworn to hear the case against the remaining prisoners. In their turn, each prisoner was brought forward to hear the charge against them and each in their turn pleaded "not guilty" of wounding and assault. Only John Dunne objected, stating he believed that he should not be charged with any offense. Justice O'Brien curtly reminded him that he was present in the Cleary cottage on Thursday night, which was sufficient reason to support the charge.

After the pleas were entered, the prosecution recalled Johanna Burke to the witness dock to repeat her testimony. William and Mary Simpson were also called to testify about what they had seen on Thursday night. After the defendants heard the evidence against them, each was allowed to examine the witness. When John Dunne was asked if he had any questions for Burke, he signaled his resignation by replying gruffly, "There was no use."[26]

Each defendant had an opportunity to make a statement in his or her behalf, but without the benefit of counsel, their own pathetic appeals did little to help their cause. Patrick Boland lamely questioned William and Mary Simpson about their testimony, asking if either of them had seen him put his hands under his daughter when others placed her over the fire or if they had heard him say that she was not a fairy. They denied they had on both counts, whereupon he accused both of them of lying. He concluded his cross-examination with the following statement:

> I had no one in the world to turn to but my daughter. Her mother and myself gave her a good trade. She was only 26 [sic] years of age, and she was a fine milliner, and able to give us a bit of money, and when her mother died she was the only one I had in the world to look to. It was not me that should ever put a finger to her.[27]

After the other prisoners had a chance to cross-examine the witnesses and make their statement, William Ahearn's solicitor moved to have all charges against his client dropped by asking for a plea of *nolle prosequi* (unwilling to pursue). In what was perhaps a surprising move, the prosecution offered no objection to the defense motion. This sudden change could be explained by the fact that William Ahearn was but one of several neighbors who attended the ritual in the Cleary cottage and but one of several who actually participated. Ahearn held the candle on Thursday night while Bridget was held over the fire, but this act was much less significant than the actions of William Simpson, who was present until dawn; of Minnie Simpson, who provided urine for the ritual when Mary Kennedy's supply ran dry; and of Thomas Smyth, David Hogan, and Tom Lehy, who acted as witnesses at the fairy trial and rendered their verdict that Bridget Cleary was, in fact, a changeling.

After Ahearn's motion was granted, the young man was dismissed from the dock with the caveat that he remain in the courtroom so the prisoners could cross-examine him. The other prisoners, observing Ahearn's success, tried to file the same motion, but without the assistance of counsel, their attempts to make the same appeal failed to win the prosecution's approval. Left to their own devices, Patrick, James, and William Kennedy each asked William Ahearn to verify whether he recalled seeing any of them carry Bridget to the fire. Ahearn responded that he remembered only Patrick taking part in the mock burning on Thursday evening. When it came his turn to question Ahearn, John Dunne jumped up and declared that it was all Cleary's doing, and the rest was a "concocted job between the parties," then began whimpering that he wanted to go home. With this final pathetic display, Judge O'Brien interceded and put a stop to the proceedings, announcing that he was prepared to address the jury.[28]

In his summary to the jury, His Lordship re-emphasized his belief that moral darkness and superstition led to the burning of Bridget Cleary and that the Catholic Church was partially responsible for perpetuating moral darkness and superstition among the peasantry. He reiterated his utter astonishment that the husband, father, and close relatives of this unfortunate young woman could so mistreat her. Nothing could better demonstrate, he asserted, the "moral darkness" in which not one but several persons existed. The depth of this moral, nay, this religious darkness, came as a surprise to those who possessed higher moral feelings and a wholesome, clear-eyed understanding of God's will. Though unsatisfied with the inadequate investigation regarding Cleary's relationship with his wife and the medicines employed to reclaim the victim's spirit from "evil praeternatural companionship," he concluded that the evidence had not proved that Cleary used fairy beliefs "as a pretext for taking his wife's life." Therefore, O'Brien could only surmise that Cleary had acted out of a belief

in "superstition or sorcery . . . entirely devoid of the ordinary feeling." This want of moral feeling, which his Honor found preva-
lent in persons of Cleary's class, was also manifest by his refusal to
attend his own father's wake. From O'Brien's perspective, the
brute inhumanity of the Irish peasant stemmed from the lingering
belief in the sorcery and superstitions of paganism, an unholy
faith tolerated, if not cultivated, by the Catholic Church, an institution that absorbed rather than banished pagan practice.

Having dispensed with Cleary and the Catholic Church, His
Lordship turned to Patrick Boland, who he observed had exhibited "unnatural conduct" toward his daughter. Upon hearing the
charge of "unnatural conduct," Boland jumped up and shouted
that he had not taken his daughter to the fire; he had put his own
bare hands under her body to protect her from the flames; that
Cleary had pushed him aside, and he was at the time "after a fit of
sickness" and in a very weak condition. Addressing Boland directly, O'Brien replied that his statement was inconsistent with
the evidence and that he found it "extraordinary" that a father
would allow his daughter to be tortured in any manner, whether
he actively participated or not. As for John Dunne, Patrick,
William, and James Kennedy, His Lordship determined they were
"more actively engaged" than they claimed, and if the jury agreed,
he did not see how the jury could "come to a conclusion in their
favor." There simply was no kind of legal excuse for what these
individuals had done or witnessed. These actions were beyond
"human comprehension," and his honor "could not conceive any
doctrine so dangerous to morality and the public peace" as the
idea that "expelling a witch from a body" should be used as an excuse to take a life.[29]

When O'Brien finished delivering his recommendations, the
jury retired to consider the verdicts against each of the seven pris-

oners. Some forty minutes later, the jury returned with their verdict: all guilty as charged, with mercy recommended for Patrick Boland, Michael Kennedy, and Mary Kennedy.

With the guilty verdicts recorded, O'Brien sentenced each in their turn:

Patrick Kennedy was the first to stand before the judge. Justice O'Brien deemed Patrick was the "most guilty" of all the prisoners, with the exception of Michael Cleary. Patrick was present both nights; he had actively participated in the "wounding," but he also assisted Cleary with the burial. For these crimes, O'Brien sentenced Patrick Kennedy to five years' penal servitude.

John Dunne was next. O'Brien found him "equally guilty" with Patrick Kennedy and deserving of the same punishment. "With you it would seem," O'Brien intoned, "the idea originated." Yet because he had not been present on Friday night and was a much older man than Patrick, the five years allotted to Kennedy "would consume the greater portion of the remainder of the life that nature has allotted to you." Three years' penal servitude.

With respect to William and James Kennedy, His Lordship found they had also actively participated, but in light of the penal servitude sentence imposed on their older brother, he "consider[ed] the law sufficiently satisfied" with a lesser penalty. Eighteen months' hard labor.

Turning to Patrick Boland, Judge O'Brien expressed disbelief and disgust at his "great misconduct in allowing his daughter's life to be taken without any remonstrance." Once again, however, age entered into His Lordship's thinking. Six months' hard labor.

Michael Kennedy was the least culpable of all the parties, barely participating in Bridget's fairy trial and having given good reason why he had been present on Thursday night (to accompany his mother after handing over his wages). As he was a rather simple and emotionally childlike man, a harsh sentence seemed unjust. Six months' hard labor.

Judge O'Brien ordered that Mary Kennedy be released, stating that "nature has decreed a sentence upon her not far distant" and he would not abridge the remainder of her life by sending her to prison. He added, however, his grave disapprobation of her conduct and yet wished to acknowledge the reparation her daughter, Johanna Burke, had made by "the evidence she has given."[30]

After their sentences were recorded, the prisoners left the court and Michael Cleary was brought forward to hear his sentence. Prior to handing down his decision, Falconer was allowed one final opportunity to seek mercy for his client. He urged the Crown to be lenient to Cleary in light of the affection the prisoner had shown for his wife. Using his Lordship's own words, Falconer lamented his client's lapse into a "state of mental and religious darkness . . . of ignorance and superstition." But he asserted that the prisoner suffered greatly following the murder and would continue to suffer for the rest of his life, especially as the true teachings of religion became clear to him. Cleary's life-long remorse would be more punishment than any court could mete out, according to Falconer. Further, he hoped His Lordship would keep in mind Cleary's predisposition to believe in fairies since his own wife and friends believed that his mother had gone off with them. In a final plea for leniency, Falconer asked the court to recall that Cleary repeatedly called both the priest and doctor to attend his wife and nourished her to the end.[31]

"Amidst a scene of painful silence," Presiding Crown Justice William O'Brien passed sentence on the last remaining defendant in the murder trial of Bridget Cleary. He pointed out to Cleary that he had come very close to having the jury find him guilty of the capital charge of murder with its mandatory penalty of hanging. For that matter, His Lordship was still not satisfied that the trial had exposed the whole truth. He found it hard to believe that someone of Cleary's "mature years" and "more than ordinary intelligence, should in the age in which we live, so entirely yield to the influence of delusion concerning the praeternatural power that would have led you, with the assistance of so many persons whom you called to your aid, to have taken the course you did." Rather than being guided by this praeternatural power in reaching his decision, O'Brien claimed to judge solely by the evidence at hand which showed unequivocally that Cleary burned his wife alive, and in doing so inflicted great cruelty upon her. His "wicked hand" sent her to another world in the very prime of her life, and because of this, O'Brien was bound to satisfy the demands of the law and public justice by administering a punishment that fit the crime. His tone indicated that justice would prevail over mercy.

A hush fell over the courtroom as Justice O'Brien announced the fate of Michael Cleary. Jurors shuffled in the box, journalists from the country's major newspapers rustled their notebooks, spectators strained for a glimpse of the prisoner. The court's clerk asked Michael Cleary to rise. From the bench, Justice O'Brien handed down the sentence. Twenty years' penal servitude.

Although the crowd expected a stiff sentence, the courtroom burst out "in a sensation" at the term of twenty years. For his part, Michael Cleary, who had wept throughout the judge's remarks, became very agitated and began wringing his hands. As the police led him away, he shouted, "I am innocent!" To the end, Cleary maintained it was not his wife he burned but a fairy. Justice O'Brien appeared to ignore the outburst and banged his gavel to the bar, ending the trial, which many had feared would drag on to the eve of Croke's Jubilee and the general parliamentary election. It was dinnertime on the evening of July 5, when an armed escort conveyed the prisoners back through the crowded streets to the Clonmel Gaol, near which "the people groaned the prisoners vehemently."[32] Following the conclusion of the Cleary trial, the next case called before the South Riding Quarter Sessions Court was that of Mrs. Minnie Fahey and the Currenstown Four, who had battled the sheriffs to avoid eviction.

As the English court rendered its verdict, the folks of Ballyvadlea rendered theirs. Sometime in the early morning hours of July 4, 1895, a burning occurred "out the mountain" in the townland of Ballyvadlea. In an act reminiscent of Whiteboy terrorism, a group of unnamed arsonists approached the Kennedy cottage and, in the dark night, set fire to the cottage's thatched roof. By morning only the mud walls stood.[33] Although the culprits were never apprehended, there was no mystery about the meaning of the fire. The Kennedy family had brought disgrace to the village, and, on the odd chance that any of them would be acquitted, people in the area wanted to make it clear that they had no wish to see any of them return. Months later the cottage was demolished. Though the Kennedy cottage was destroyed, not a window was broken, not a stone disturbed, at the Cleary cottage, even though for months thereafter it remained unoccupied. Locals stayed away from the place, perhaps showing their disgust for what had happened there, but also for their fear of the fairies.

Sometime later—according to John Holohan, a retired county councilman living in Cloneen with whom we spoke—the Ahearn house also burned down, but that had nothing to do with the Bridget Cleary incident. The Cleary cottage, by contrast, remains standing down to the present, having never been vandalized or harmed in any way except by wandering cows. It now is lost in a tangle of tree and bush growth, with its fireplace intact as a ghostly reminder of what happened on March 15, 1895, when the fairies appeared on Ballyvadlea and made international headlines.

"Fideles Venerunt"—The Faithful Came

Concurrent with the Bridget Cleary murder trial was the Irish National Federation's nominating convention. On July 4, 1895, the same day that the trial opened and the Kennedy cottage burned, INF delegates gathered in Clonmel to select candidates to run for Parliament from Tipperary's South and East districts. Although Unionists had been predicting the fall of the Liberals, the Irish Party was caught off guard in May when the Tory leader, Lord Salisbury, suddenly formed an interim cabinet and called a general election for mid-July. Stunned by the collapse of the Liberal government in London and racked with internal dissension within the Irish Parliamentary Party, INF leaders scrambled to mount a winning campaign for the general election just two weeks hence.

The *Nationalist* tried to put a brave face on a grim situation, pluckily referring to the impending election as "Ireland's Opportunity" when, in fact, those seeking Home Rule for Ireland faced an impending disaster. Arrayed against them was a formidable coalition of Liberal and Tory imperialists who sought to expand the British empire and disgruntled Parnellites who would rather cut deals with the English than allow the Church-backed INF to control the Nationalist movement. Nationalists grimly referred to members of this anti-Nationalist coalition as "coercionists," and wailed that English imperialists, aided by Parnellite defectors, were making a "desperate resort" to forge a coherent "coercionist" policy against Ireland—a policy that would coerce Ireland to remain a vassal state in Victoria's empire.

Nationalists minced no words about the need for party unity. This is not the time, they insisted, "for carping criticism, or for anything tending to disunion or dissension in the national ranks." Neither was it a time for ignorant peasants to fuel allegations that the Irish people were unfit to govern themselves. Rather, Nationalists declared, it was time for all Irishmen to subordinate all private feelings, bury old beliefs, and go to the "hustings united" in order to defeat the "many-headed common enemy" of Salisbury's coercionist coalition. Should Irishmen fail to submit to party discipline, Nationalists painted a grim picture of what lay ahead. The apostles of the "Cromwellian and Orange creed" would continue to divide and conquer and Ireland would fall "easy prey to the foe." Nationalists warned of what might happen if the "coercionist" platform prevailed:

> The allied Coercionists, while labouring to conceal their game, have spread their nets deep and wide to catch unsuspecting votes. If they succeed . . . the cloven foot will soon be shown in the suppression of public opinion and of citizens' freedom . . . and in the packing of the tribunals to wrench-up the rents at the expiration of the judicial term next year. It is the duty of every one concerned for the welfare of our country to strain every nerve, and make every sacrifice, in order to secure that Lord Salisbury gets no chance to wreck his "Hottentot" vengeance in the rack-renters' interest.

Rather than despair, editors declared that this was Ireland's opportunity "to stand for the National flag, for Home Rule, and for the total emancipation of the Irish tenantry from hereditary thralldom."[34]

An added factor for Nationalist concern was the fact that Ireland was losing electoral clout within the British empire. In 1895,

Ireland's population was still well below pre-Famine levels, whereas the population of England, Scotland, and Wales was increasing rapidly. In 1794, Ireland's population was roughly 4.4 million and soon grew to a pre-Famine high of over 7 million. In 1891, the population was approximately 4.6 million, which meant the country had virtually no net gain over the century. Conversely, England grew from 10.5 million in 1800 to 34 million in 1894, realizing a net gain of over 300 percent. Despite this devastating population loss, Ireland was forced to assume a greater share of the United Kingdom's tax burden. In 1794, the average tax in Ireland was nine shillings per head; in 1894, it was forty-nine shillings. In England, the tax burden actually fell in the same period from seventy-two shillings to sixty-nine shillings per head. Ireland was being required to contribute disproportionately to an "exorbitantly expensive and absurdly inefficient" administration that essentially kept its people impoverished and encouraged mass emigration. Such were the blessings of Ireland's "paper union" with England.[35]

In order to reverse the paralyzing effects of depopulation and set Ireland on the road to independence, the INF searched for candidates who could unite Nationalist factions. On July 5, delegates to Tipperary's nominating convention emerged from closed-door hearings to announce their choice of candidates. For the East Tipperary district, delegates gave the nod to the incumbent Member of Parliament, Thomas Joseph Condon. The nomination was seconded by Nicholas Kickham Shee, justice of the peace from Mullinahone and INF county delegate. The incumbent M.P. for South Tipperary, Frank Mandeville, brother of John Mandeville, a martyr of the 1887 Mitchelstown uprising, also received the nomination for another term. After presentation of the candidates, Captain Donellan, the convention chairman, commended each man for his moderation, good sense, and loyalty, after which both candidates stepped forward and publicly took the party pledge.

Captain Donellan took this opportunity to reiterate the need for party unity. If the Irish Party was not able to elect its own committees and settle its own affairs, then, "the Irish Party was not competent to take charge of the interests of the nation." Healthy criticism, he continued, was the soul of public life, but incessant fault-finding with leaders of the Irish Party, who were striving and struggling amid almost overwhelming difficulties to do their very best for their country, was both "ungenerous and un-Irish." In poking a bit of fun at himself and the nominating committee, Donellan recited the following verse:

> *Most men have many faults,*
> *Our committee has but two—*
> *There is nothing right they say,*
> *And nothing right they do.*

Old soldier that he was, Donellan had a high regard for discipline. Without discipline, he insisted, an army degenerates into a mob and "a political party sinks into abject insignificance" and becomes an object of scorn, derision, and contempt.[36]

Keynote speaker T. P. O'Connor elaborated still further on the theme of unity, stressing Tipperary's importance within the Nationalist movement. This would not be the first time, he said, that Tipperary set an example for other counties and, not for the first time in Irish history, took the lead in the face of "a great National emergency." Assuming the worst happened and the Coercionists won a solid victory, O'Connor declared, the question was not what type of government Ireland would face, but rather what kind of Ireland the government would face. Amid shouts and cheers, O'Connor asked, "Would it face an Ireland that was divided or would it face an Ireland that was united?"

As the delegates roared their pledge of unity, O'Connor reviewed the disastrous effects of disunity upon the Irish Parliamentary Party and the Nationalist movement from Daniel O'Connell in 1845, to Isaac Butt, and finally to the disastrous split precipitated by Parnell's affair with Kate O'Shea. O'Connor recalled that when the scandal broke in 1891, he was in the States raising money and could personally testify to its devastating effect on the Nationalist cause. Before the split, Nationalists in America could raise $35,000 in one hour, but after, "they could not get seven dollars in seven days." Dissension in Ireland meant that America shut its coffers to Ireland, thereby paralyzing the movement. To overcome this dissension, O'Connor said that the INF must lead the fractured Nationalist movement forward. The party must unite and fight for the future of Ireland; otherwise the Irish people would perish amid the "laughter and contempt of the whole civilized world."

Even as the INF delegates cheered lustily and renewed their commitment to party unity, from Dublin came news of a serious breech in the leadership of the Irish Parliamentary Party. At the monthly meeting of the party's executive committee, Parnellite Timothy M. Healy walked out of the meeting when the committee refused his demands for more control over the party's governing body. Healy's "remarkable proceeding" threatened to cripple the party on the eve of the general election.[37] More bad news came from South Tipperary, where rumors circulated that a Parnellite challenger would run against the incumbent M.P., Frank Mandeville. These were confirmed when Mr. Arnold Power, County Sub-sheriff, received an application of candidacy at the eleventh hour, which revealed the "well-concealed plot" of the "oppositionists." The standard bearer of the "revolt" came not from Clonmel, as rumor alleged, but from Cahir. He was the wealthy landowner and tenant-tormentor Count Arthur John Moore of Mooresfort, who announced his intention to run for Parliament as an "independent Independent" candidate, heading a small and "uncongruous [sic] crowd" of irreconcilable "Tory-Unionists, landlords and toady farmers, rabid Parnellites and extreme Healyites."[38]

INF leaders viewed the crafty Count as a wolf in sheep's clothing who was trying to lure unsuspecting Irishmen into believing he was an independent candidate when he was actually a closet coercionist. This ruse Nationalists were eager to expose. According to Nationalist sources, the Count falsely professed to be "nobody's darling" and a member of neither party, yet promised to win Home Rule and free Ireland by his "individual exertions" alone without the aid of party. This Parnellite "party-wrecker" was vain enough to believe he could single-handedly win Home Rule while forgetting that the people had already made their choice in Frank Mandeville. INF observers agreed that, thankfully, the people had had enough of deceptive, renegade "free lances" and saw through his "game." They wanted a united party in Parliament pledged to secure her rights.[39]

If voters were unconvinced that Moore was not their man, the *Nationalist* provided more evidence. An election report disclosed that many of the Count's supporters were Parnellites, and although the Count himself "abstained" from the Parnellite crisis in '91, he now tried to ingratiate himself with the disgraced former leader's followers. Although the Count tried to deceive voters with his disingenuous label of "independent Independent," the die was cast. Voters understood the adage: "Tell me your company and I'll tell you what you are." Certainly the Catholic electors of South Tipperary were not deceived, nor their wives, sisters, and daughters, who so sternly revolted against the low standards of morality represented by Parnell personally and his faction. Would these good people swallow their convictions in order to "gratify a reckless self-seeker's political ambitions?" No, the voters would support the unanimous choice of the true Nationalist party, Frank Mandeville.[40]

Despite such tough, dismissive talk, Nationalists worried about the strength of the Count's candidacy, especially when defectors from their ranks came forward to support him. One was Father Matt Ryan, C.C., a leading light in the Plan of Campaign and Parnell crisis, who attended the Clonmel Convention and then declared he was joining hands with Moore. Nationalists worried even more when the Count's supporters mounted an aggressive, door-to-door canvassing campaign and reports from Tipperary town indicated that many voters were responding to the Count's anti-Church, anti-INF message. The Count argued that the INF could not be trusted to govern Ireland because it could not govern its own counsels. Furthermore, he accused the INF of being run by the Church, insisting that the upcoming parliamentary election was Ireland's opportunity to smash the power of the Irish priests once and for all. As the Count pressed money and manpower into his campaign, canvassers predicted the election would be close. Rather than commit to either side, many voters decided not to vote at all. Moreover, many clergymen and INF supporters were called away from the polls to attend Croke's Jubilee in Thurles, which was scheduled for July 18, the same day as the general election. All agreed that a lower voter turnout would go against the Nationalists since Count Moore commanded a smaller but more politically active corps of urban and landowning voters.

Victory for the Nationalists depended upon the INF's ability to rouse the sleeping electoral giant from the countryside—the Irish peasant.[41]

On election eve, July 17, 1895, both sides competed for votes in the streets of Tipperary town. Count Moore made a final canvass of the town, accompanied by a group of merchants, but, according to Nationalist observers, received only limited promises of support. Those offering their support were identified as landlords and leading Parnellites who were working "in the most harmonious manner" with the Tories and the notorious Smith-Barry evictors, who had been responsible for the "Mitchelstown Massacre."[42] The Nationalists brought in Dr. Tanner, the intrepid M.P. from County Cork, to speak for Mandeville. He arrived early that morning, accompanied by Nicholas Kickham Shee and a delegation of evicted tenants from the Smith-Barry estates, to deliver a speech later that evening. The Nationalist rally opened with a torchlight parade through the streets of Tipperary town led by the Sarsfield Fife and Drum Band. A large crowd of several thousand enthusiastic Nationalists cheered "vociferously" when Dr. Tanner's carriage appeared, and together, the entire multitude marched through the town, cheering loudly for Mandeville, groaning with equal conviction for Count Moore. A huge torch was kept ablaze as the procession moved toward the town's presbytery.[43]

In the street outside the presbytery, Dr. Tanner addressed the crowd. He recalled his arrest by the English during the Smith-Barry evictions when he was briefly detained in Tipperary before "enjoying her Brittanic Majesty's hospitality" in the Clonmel Gaol. A number of his peers went to the Clonmel Gaol at that time, he recalled. Tom Condon went to the gaol (cheers), poor William O'Brien went to the gaol (cheers), and Frank Mandeville's brother (cheers) went to the gaol and was murdered there by "Balfour's crowd" (groans for Balfour). During these trying times, Dr. Tanner recalled lines penned by Charles Kickham:

> *But troth I never doubted you,*
> *Said Rory of the Hill.*

With this stirring invocation to Tipperary's sainted poet/patriot, Tanner vowed that Ireland's claims would be carried forward by men like Frank Mandeville, men who were worthy inheritors of the mantle of "Great Dan" O'Connell, Charles Kickham, James Stephens, the young Parnell, and Archbishop Thomas Croke.

Dr. Tanner insisted that he had nothing against Count Moore personally. It was a grand thing to be respectable, and, as he was certain that Count Moore was a perfectly respectable gentleman, he would say nothing against him (laughter). As a matter of fact he knew nothing about him whatever (renewed laughter), not even whether his name were Jerry Moore or Count Moore (laughter). He only knew that he himself was good enough in the "old times" to go to the Clonmel Gaol with other brave Tipperary men for Ireland (cheers) and those men who had gone to prison for Ireland had no interest in supporting the Count, whoever he was or whatever his name might be.[44] Amid the cheers from the crowd, Dr. Tanner admonished his listeners to fill every wagon and cart in the district with voters, drive them to the polls, and cast their ballots for Frank Mandeville and Home Rule for Ireland. At the conclusion of this rousing admonition, the crowds departed to their homes, villages, and farms. The hawking for votes was over; the fate of the Nationalist cause lay in the hands of the voters in Ireland and throughout the United Kingdom.

On the morning of Thursday, July 18, 1895, early returns from the outlying districts showed the voting was evenly divided between Moore and Mandeville. Count Moore's supporters were jubilant because, if this trend held up, later returns from the towns would give the Count a substantial majority. Later in the day, Nationalists arrived with cartloads of farmers from the countryside, but in Tipperary town Count Moore's supporters were so confident of victory that they built a huge bonfire opposite the courthouse, ready to be set ablaze when all the votes were counted.[45]

On this very same morning, the faithful came from across Tipperary and beyond to honor, in "a succession of joyous and magnificent scenes" unparalleled in the annals of the county's history, the Prelate who, for twenty years, ruled the province of Cashel and Emly from The Palace, Thurles. In keeping with the spirit of the celebration, the town was gaily decked out in papal banners of yellow and red set against a mass of greenery. The streets were thronged with jubilant townsfolk dressed in their festive best and visitors who trooped in by foot, train, and cart. Although the weather reports were ominous, the day held up beautifully, and genial sunshine added further brightness and warmth to the glorious scene. The vast multitude conducted itself with the greatest decorum and good order.

An hour before the auspicious proceedings commenced, his Grace of Cashel presented his jubilee gift to the town of Thurles—a splendid illuminated chime clock. In return, the town presented his Grace with a carriage drawn by the finest team of horses obtainable. A committee from the parishes of Templemore, Clonmore, and Killea expressed their love and respect for the "great Prelate, who rules the archdiocese," with another beautifully crafted carriage, presented as a token remembrance for his labors for "Faith and Fatherland." The committee commissioned Mr. Dennehy, Lower Baggot Street, Dublin, to build a beautiful brougham carriage, all of Irish manufacture. The body was made of well-seasoned Irish and American ash and pine and American whitewood with mahogany panels. The paint was dark olive green striped with crimson and black. The upholstery was done in dark green morocco, accessorized with the latest internal fittings. Side panels bore the arms and crest of the Archbishop of Cashel, both most artistically executed.[46]

Other gifts arrived throughout the day. A special train bore a magnificent illuminated address placed within a specially built casket, presented to His Grace from the townspeople of Clonmel. The address was several pages in length and illuminated by Mr. McConnell of Dublin after the manner of the ancient Irish manuscripts. The title page was surmounted by the symbol of the Holy Spirit descending over the arms of the Sovereign Pontiff, Head of the Church, beneath which was an inscription dedicated to his Grace, and beneath that was a drawing of Clonmel. The second page contained a portrait of his Grace, surrounded by the armorial bearing of the family of Croke and those of the diocese of Cashel and Emly, Clonmel and Ireland. The binding, made by Messrs. Galway, of Eustace Street, Dublin, was ornamented with Celtic patterns and studded with Irish crystals. The entire album was placed in a beautiful casket, designed by Mr. McConnell and made by Mr. Nash of William Street, Dublin, and fashioned from handsome morocco leather, inlaid with the cross of St. Patrick, and surmounted by a gilt quatrefoil, containing the arms of the diocese. The casket stood on feet of richly ornamented Irish fibulae, supplied by Mr. Edmond Johnson, Grafton Street, Dublin.[47]

Following the presentation of gifts, the day's events opened with a grand episcopal procession of Ireland's leading prelates and priests, followed by dignitaries of the Clonmel and Limerick Corporations, headed by their respective mace bearers. After them came honored members of the laity. The procession led into the

Thurles Cathedral where the canons took their places beside the Cardinal, enthroned on the Gospel side, while His Grace the Archbishop of Cashel sat opposite him on the Epistle side. The music of the Mass was magnificently rendered by the Cathedral choir. Among the many dignitaries were a veritable regiment of priests, some from as far away as Illinois, the Utah Territory, and Australia.

The Archbishop of Dublin sang High Mass, after which, Cardinal Logue, Archbishop of Armagh, delivered an impressive sermon drawn from Psalms 88:16 ("Blessed is the people that knoweth jubilation"). The theme was jubilee; the message was unity. In his opening, Cardinal Logue observed that a "wave of rejoicing" was sweeping over the archdiocese, awaking a responsive throb in every Irish Catholic home. And why? Because of the close ties that bound a religious people and a zealous and self-sacrificing bishop or priest. Yes, Cardinal Logue declared, the "union between priesthood and people . . . have their roots struck fast and deep in the divine constitution of the Church."

The Cardinal offered an historical explanation for why these roots ran so deep. For centuries the history of Ireland was one of perpetual struggle for two great principles—religious toleration and the ordinary rights of free men. After the Protestant Reformation in England, the Catholic Church in Ireland was forced to resist the most severe persecution, while the people struggled for the most basic human rights. As a result, these two great causes—religious toleration and civil liberties—became intertwined, with religion consecrating patriotism and patriots fighting for the fatherland's dominant faith. When religious bigotry fell from style, the Cardinal charged, the English continued their persecution of the people through subtler forms of "race hatred," and three centuries after the English invasion, that spirit of religious bigotry and civil repression was "not yet dead." Throughout the turbulent centuries of persecution, the priest and people stood shoulder to shoulder, and, of the many prelates who fought for faith and fatherland, the Archbishop of Cashel's name was known throughout the world. It would be hard to find a prelate, he declared,

> who has stronger claims on the esteem, affection, and gratitude of his fellow countrymen. For well nigh fifty years his life as priest and bishop has been before them; and in all those years even his enemies, if he had any, could point to nothing which would compromise his character as an Irish priest, an Irish bishop, or an Irish patriot.

Though he made mistakes and occasionally erred in judgment, the Archbishop of Cashel was ever "at the forefront when the cause of religion or the cause of country claimed his aid."[48]

With the conclusion of Cardinal Logue's remarks and benediction, the episcopal procession moved out onto the steps of the Cathedral for the presentation of addresses. Dean Kinane of Cashel read an "eloquent and powerful" address from the clergy of the archdiocese, followed by tributes from representatives of Cloyne, Thurles, the Irish Hierarchy, and Limerick. Then Thomas J. Condon, M.P., delivered the greetings of the Irish Parliamentary Party, which spoke with "one voice" in expressing their deepest gratitude and reverence for his "long and illustrious career" in the episcopate, his "imperishable services" as a great churchman, and the qualities of character that made him an "indomitable Irish Nationalist."

> Others will, no doubt, have done justice to your Grace's fruitful and indefatigable life, in its purely religious aspect, but no body of representative Irishmen could be expected to take part in the pres-

ent auspicious celebration without recalling in a spirit of deep thankfulness the foresight, courage, and devotion with which, in critical times, your Grace vindicated the true principles of that union of priests and people, which is the foundation of all healthy, moral, and political progress in Ireland, and gave a new consecration to the combined influences of religion and nationality over every generous Irish heart.[49]

Condon reviewed Croke's influence from his Young Ireland days through the anxieties, vicissitudes, and triumphs of succeeding years, then predicted, "The time has not, perhaps, yet come for estimating the full proportions of the influence which your Grace has exercised upon the history of our generation to the glory of religion and the estimable advantage of the National cause." Closing with the hope that His Grace would be spared "for many a happy year" to ennoble the struggle for National self-government, Condon prayed that His Grace would live to see the "fullness of the triumph of those great principles of ordered national freedom for which your Grace has labored with a giant's strength"—a clear reference to Fionn McCuill and his mighty son, Ossian.[50]

Others compared Archbishop Croke to a mighty warrior. This attempt to endow the Archbishop with the qualities of Ireland's mythical heroes was expressed in one of the several jubilee odes published for the occasion. The following lines, published in May 1883 under the pseudonym "Dark Rosaleen," were reprinted for the occasion:

> Our Prelate so frank and fearless,
> Our Prelate so pure and peerless,
> Poor Erin, tho' rarely tearless,
> Is wreth'd in smiles to-day,

To honour the heart that loved her,
That bore her battles' brunt,
When brave hearts were all but dying,
Who every foe defying,
Still kept her green flag flying
Full in the battle's front![51]

Like mighty warriors of old, Archbishop Croke fought for Irish independence, and in doing so, deserved the same honor due to a national hero. Through the afternoon, representatives from towns, parishioners, convents, professional organizations, and civic groups presented their addresses, until all had a chance to add their words of gratitude. Finally His Grace stepped forward amidst deafening cheers and, laboring under visible emotion, offered a few words of his own. He was gratified by the people's affection and thanked God that he had been privileged to work among a "race of people as proverbial for chivalry in the field as for their respect for every Christian observance."

For twenty long and troubled years I have sat on the throne and held the crozier of Cashel; and it is no small thing for me to be able to say publicly, and in sober truth, that during that time I have not had, as Bishop, one hour's serious trouble on the part of either priests or people; and if at times, though rarely, I had to draw the sword and smite a clerical or lay transgressor, it was universally understood that in doing so I felt more pain myself than I inflicted on the offender.[52]

Croke went on to thank the Cardinal for his kind words, priests of the archdiocese for their twenty years' support, and the people who so faithfully served and so generously contributed to the celebration. Later that evening, dignitaries and priests sat down to an enormous banquet, accompanied by still more speech-making late into the night.

In heaping praise and honor upon the head of Archbishop Croke, the people of County Tipperary and all Ireland acknowledged the formal alliance between the country's dominant religious authority and secular nationalism—an alliance that would, as Charles Kickham envisioned, lay the foundations of a modern Irish state. This union of priest and people represented the culmination of the devotional revolution of the mid-nineteenth century, which initially tightened ecclesiastical discipline, Romanized church rituals, and filled the pews with Catholic faithful. By century's end, the devotional revolution had broadened into a cultural movement that embraced all elements of society, including secular nationalism. Missing from this transformation of Irish religious, cultural, and political life, however, were the fairies. They would be excluded, driven underground, and, on their journey to modernity's Otherworld, they would take with them the last vestiges of pagan ritual and practice. Never again would there be another tragedy such as the one at Ballyvadlea.

In Thurles, the great celebration to honor the Silver Jubilee of Archbishop Croke's ordination closed with a magnificent display of fireworks that lit up the night sky. Fittingly, in Tipperary town, the victory fire of Count Moore remained cold and unlit.

The Foxes Were Running

In the final week of Jubilee month, election returns appeared alongside accounts of the Jubilee in both of Clonmel's local newspapers. On July 17, the *Chronicle* printed the first results of the parliamentary election in England and elsewhere, which to no one's surprise, gave Lord Salisbury and the Tories a substantial lead. With less than half of the districts reporting, the Salisbury government held a thirty-six-vote majority. Of the Irish districts reported, Nationalists won thirteen seats, while the Parnellites took four. Returns published on July 20 confirmed that the trend would hold. With nearly 80 percent of the votes counted, Tory Unionists led with 318 members, and Liberals had 18; Nationalists held 44 seats, while the Parnellites had won just six. In County Tipperary, all four Nationalist candidates were returned to Parliament. Official returns showed Mandeville with 1,723 votes and Moore with a surprisingly high tally of 1,222.

While the Parnellites and their "coercionist" allies were decisively beaten back, the unexpected strength of Count Moore in South Tipperary troubled Nationalists. As the electoral combat neared its end, the INF faithful bemoaned the "criminal madness" of disunion. "Will people never open their eyes as they ought to what is signified by 'divide and conquer?'" In a spirited, score-settling public statement, the INF supporters licked their wounds but also counted their blessings:

> In spite of all this, and notwithstanding all the difficulties and disadvantages placed in our way; confronted by unholy and unnatural alliances; by time-serving trimmers and by avowed traitors, by men who preferred selfish considerations to the cause of country, the National flag in Ireland has come out of the struggle triumphantly, for the backsliders were only individuals and comparatively few— the Nation has proved staunch, and strong, and faithful.

Salisbury's coalition of Conservative and Liberal Unionists controlled Parliament, but the union of priests and people sustained Ireland's "National Faith." The INF was confident that the people would remember that they had conquered before, and time would show they were not only "constant but indomitable."[53]

As Salisbury settled in at 10 Downing Street, ominous rumors emanated from London that his government planned to introduce a new Irish policy, which commenced by reducing Ireland's representation in Parliament by twenty seats. Liberal Unionist Joseph Chamberlain discussed the matter "with lucidity" and offered statistical proof that Ireland was overrepresented in the Commons. While Chamberlain threatened to cut back Irish Party seats, Gerald Balfour, brother of the former Irish Secretary Arthur Balfour, discussed state grants for assisting poor tenants in purchasing their own land, as well as other social reforms. The government's carrot-and-stick policy toward Ireland—to cut representation while offering benefits—was driven, in part, by the faithfulness of the Irish people to the Irish Party. Without this solid party loyalty, along with the threat of civil unrest, the English policy might well have been all stick and no carrot. While Unionists found it easy to sneer at the Irish elections, characterizing it as the work of "machine politics," other observers marveled at the "remarkable constancy of the island" to the Nationalist cause. The government's plan to advocate redistribution of seats was perhaps the only way to reduce the Home Rule majority in Ireland—"a result apparently, that cannot be accomplished in any other way."[54]

In a warning to the people, Nationalists predicted a return of the backward, "Hottentot" policies of the Conservative government. Should the people prove at all "restive," the government was prepared to put forth a new Crimes Act, and to gain support for it, they were prepared to orchestrate new "outrages" in the countryside. Given these troubling indicators, the *Nationalist* urged calm, declaring: "We repeat our warnings to the people to continue their present course of peacefulness, and to remember well that 'he who commits a crime gives strength to the enemy.'"[55]

As it turned out, Salisbury's third ministry was not nearly as terrible as the Nationalists feared. Salisbury appointed Gerald Balfour to carry on his brother Arthur's dual coercion/conciliation policy, which the newly appointed Gerald described quite accurately as an attempt to "kill Home Rule with kindness." Gerald supported the Land Act of 1896 to facilitate the purchase of land by tenants and, most importantly, the Local Government Act of 1898, which broadened the voting franchise to include women and ultimately transferred local government to urban, rural, and county councils under the control of Catholic Nationalists. This meant that the Grand Juries, such as the one which heard the Cleary case, long dominated by Protestant and Anglo/Irish landlords, lost their legal, fiscal, and administrative access to these now democratically elected councils, giving Irish Nationalists invaluable, responsible political experience. Such economic and political reforms temporarily deferred Home Rule agitation in Ireland and Parliament, but it remained in the minds and hearts of the Irish as a goal that British concessions could not win, nor coercion kill. From O'Connell through Parnell, Irish Catholic nationalism had developed a life of its own—independent of British policy or improved conditions in the land of Erin. After a century of dissension and discussion, the Irish Catholics had achieved a new confidence and cohesion. No longer could they be ridiculed into believing that they were incapable of self-government.[56]

As Croke's Jubilee paean wafted on and political storm clouds unexpectedly cleared, Clonmel settled back into a normal routine. Citizens complained loudly when train irregularities delayed mail service for two days. Agents of the Great Southern and Western Railway deflected public fury, claiming that the railroad was not at fault; rather the government's mail service had failed to get the morning delivery to Limerick Junction on time. Writing in defense of the Great Southern, John O'Mohoney declared, "It is only fair to place the saddle on the right horse." More irritating than delayed mail service was the announcement that the county football championship would be postponed for three weeks until train service could be restored.[57]

The harvest report was gloomy. Observers noted that the long drought in May and June was followed by unusually hot weather in July that continued into August, making prospects for the approaching harvest the worst in twenty years. English farmers were also faced with a bad harvest, but could better afford the losses. These bleak agricultural reports gave Nationalists more reason to complain about the government's failure to pass the Land Reform Bill, which would have helped tenants faced with high rental payments. Although the new Parliament was to convene on August 12, Lord Salisbury evasively planned to delay its opening until February 1896, which would be too late for Parliament to do anything about the "current crisis."[58]

There was some reason for cheer "out the mountain," where Laurence Maher, of Peafield, was reinstated to his home after a fourteen-year fight. Maher was one of the first evicted tenants to be helped after the establishment of the Land League. He never gave up hope and for fourteen years lived within sight of his old place. At the time of his eviction, the landlord racked his rent to £24, but in an agreement negotiated by Maher's solicitor, Nicholas Kickham Shee, henceforth Maher would pay but half that amount.[59]

On Friday, August 2, the faithful came to celebrate the Feast of Portiuncula at Clonmel's Franciscan Church. The Reverend T. Burke, C.C., Powerstown, said High Mass, and Professor Walshe led the choir in an "effectively rendered" presentation of sacred music. In the evening after the rosary, the Very Reverend J. H. Cooney, Guardian, preached an "eloquent and very instructive" sermon on the history and nature of the *Portiuncula Indulgence*. Crowds packed the beautiful church morning and evening, and a "large number of the faithful approached the Holy of Holies and participated in the great indulgence."[60]

Sports fans delighted in news of "Con Brennan's Plucky Ride." At 6:15 on the morning of Friday, August 2, Con Brennan left Cork city on his bicycle, a twenty-pound Raleigh path-racer, and reached Dublin at 7:30 that evening. Brennan's time of 13 hours, 15 minutes shaved an hour off the previous record for the 168-mile race. The feat was all the more astonishing due to the muddy conditions of the road, which some claimed was the fault of the government. Brennan reported that on the final sprint into Dublin, his pacing machine fell behind and rain came down in torrents. The mud was so bad that he had to get off his bike three times to wash away the weight of mud. He ate nothing past Athy, survived on "lemonade," and once had to pedal back a mile to retrieve his purse. In spite of his troubles, he pedaled into Dublin still "fresh," but as "dirty as a miner."[61]

At Limerick Junction, the Kickham Memorial Committee met to discuss plans for a memorial to honor Charles Kickham, Tipperary's revered poet/patriot. Chairman William Hurley announced that the committee had spent £70 for the handsome Celtic cross that stood on Kickham's grave in Mullinahone, and there remained over £335 in the treasurer's hands. It was decided that with these funds the committee would commission a memorial statue of the deceased patriot. Members agreed that anyone who happened to be in Dublin would "wait upon a sculptor for the purpose of procuring designs and estimates." The committee deferred the final decision on where to place the statue. Today the statue still stands in Tipperary town.[62]

As Jubilee Month wound to a close, occasional reminders of the "Tipperary Witchcraft Case" reverberated throughout the town. On July 31, the *Nationalist* reprinted a series of "interesting letters" that appeared in London newspapers following the conclusion of the Cleary trial. Public comment on the trial and sentencing began with a letter written by Andrew Lang, who decried the sentence of Michael Cleary as being too harsh. Lang labored under the erroneous assumption that the sentence was "penal servitude for life," yet argued that since Cleary sincerely believed his wife was a witch when he tortured and murdered her, the sentence was inappropriate. Lang's critique of the sentence drew a sharp response from a reader who signed his letter "Clifden." Mr. Clifden took a less sympathetic view toward the trial's outcome than Mr. Lang and, in his support of the English judicial system, reflected commonly held racial stereotypes regarding the Irish. Clifden argued that it would be dangerous, particularly in Ireland, to subscribe to Lang's "singular as well as peculiar" code of ethics that would grant mercy to Cleary because he believed his wife was a fairy. He implied that to tolerate such subtle distinctions in ethical thought would be possible "in a staid, well-ordered country like England," where reason held sway, but would be "awkward for Irishmen," adding snidely, "if there were many who could write." No, he implied, higher ethical thought would be lost on the Irish race. And worse, he continued, "Do not with one breath tell excitable Irishmen—'Thou shalt do no murder,' and with the next give them to understand that previous torture will exempt them from capital punishment." Such "vagaries" would wreak havoc with the administration of English justice in Ireland, Clifden concluded.

Richard Bagwell, foreman of the Grand Jury and Clonmel's wealthiest landlord, joined in the discussion. He stated that Michael Cleary was not a peasant in the ordinary sense of the word; rather, he was a cooper by trade, who had worked for years in Clonmel, a large market town. Furthermore, the medical evidence was "horrible, almost beyond belief;" even the country people among whom he lived had no wish to see Cleary's sentence reduced. The Suttee and Thuggee peoples of India have superstitions that involved burning, but, he noted, the English treated them as capital offenses. Rather than foster superstition, Bagwell argued that English law must bury it. Then he recited the following anecdote to illustrate how cases of this kind should be handled:

> There is a story of a very eminent judge which seems to have some indirect bearing on the case. He was trying a man for larceny, and the defence set up was kleptomania. "I suppose, my lud," said the defending counsel, "you understand what that means?" "Yes," answered the judge, "it is the disease which I am put here to cure."

An equally stern rejoinder came from a writer identified only as "B. L.," who stated flatly that the sentence must stand because "the peasantry must be taught in a plain way that superstition will not justify in the killing of anyone. Otherwise from burning witches we might soon get on to burning heretics."[63]

The president of the Irish Folk Lore Society, Edward Cloud, offered his opinion that, although some tried to blame superstition for the crime, Michael Cleary murdered his wife for baser reasons. Cloud acknowledged that "although the evidence goes to show that belief in 'changelings' exists among the Irish peasantry, and has led to inhuman acts," it appeared to him that "other and wholly base motives prompted the murder of Bridget Cleary."

He indicated that Justice O'Brien and the Grand Jury were too lenient in accepting the lesser charge of manslaughter; sentences should not be mitigated because of any "fairie defence," as some were advocating. In conclusion, he asserted that the Folklore Society Council "agrees with me that the case does not warrant action with a view to obtain mitigation of the sentences."[64]

Even the vacant Boland/Cleary cottage at Ballyvadlea became the subject of a spirited dispute. In May 1895, while the nine prisoners awaited trail, authorities received complaints from neighbors that William Simpson had taken possession of the cottage without the permission of the local Guardian Board and was escorting visitors around the place, attempting to "profit by this horrible transaction." The complaints charged that, since the tragedy, the cottage had been very much photographed and was made a kind of "peep show." To prevent this travesty, complainants requested that Simpson be relieved of the key to the door and the Guardians take possession of the cottage.[65]

To stop Simpson's sideshow, the Cashel Guardians filed suit in September against the lessee, Patrick Boland, father of the "unhappy victim of the Ballyvadlea tragedy," and William Simpson, to recover possession of the cottage in which the young wife of Michael Cleary was so cruelly "done to death." Mr. H. T. Sayers, representing the Guardians, noted that "old man Boland" was served eviction papers at the Clonmel Gaol, while William Simpson received his summons in Fethard, where he now lived. Neither appeared at the hearing. William Meldon, representing Boland, asserted that his client was unable to defend himself in court because he was serving a prison sentence, but he should not be disqualified from his leasehold for failure to appear. Sayers countered that the cottage cost the Guardians £150 so they naturally wished to protect it from damage. In the end, the court found for the Guardians. Boland, who was due for release in December, lost his lease, and William Simpson lost his budding tour business.[66]

During the proceedings, the following exchange occurred. Sayers opened his remarks by stating that he would proceed under the Cottier clause of the Deasy Act to recover possession of the cottage, which had been "rather celebrated in that part of the county." Mr. D. Scully, chairman of the Fethard Petty Sessions, joked that the Guardians could sell the cottage to Madame Tussaud's Wax Museum in London and get a heap of money for it. The playful banter continued:

> *Sayers*: She has made an offer for it already?
> *Scully*: You will get more for it in that way than you will ever get from a tenant.
> *Sayers*: (*still joking*) We are in treaty about the price to [be] paid.
> *Scully*: That was only an aside. You must prove your case now.

Though Sayers and Scully were only joking, their friendly exchange at the Petty Session was picked up by Dublin's *Freeman*, which, taking these remarks at face value, printed a story erroneously stating that negotiations were underway between the Cashel Guardians and Madame Tussaud, for possession of the Cleary cottage. Indignant citizens in Clonmel promptly responded that the statement was untrue and every member of the Cashel Guardians condemned it as falsehood. In this and all references to the "Ballyvadlea Tragedy," the good people of "rare Clonmel" wished the matter ended and not heard of again.[67]

But the matter did not die. In December 1895, at the Presentment Sessions of the barony of Middlethird, magistrates considered a claim for £50 filed on behalf of Mr. Thomas Lindsay,

County Cork, landlord of the Kennedy cottage burned at Bally-vadlea on the night of July 3–4. According to the claimant's solic-itor, Mr. Walter Nolan, Ballyvadlea was the site of "one of the most awful outrages committed in this country in the memory of living men." The incident had attracted the attention of the civi-lized world on account of the odious, frightful, and cruel injury done to a poor young woman by her own kinsmen. The house for which the landlord now asked compensation had been occupied by the Kennedy family, cousins and tormentors of the poor crea-ture who had been roasted to death in her own house. Unnamed people set fire to the cottage in order to make some feeble state-ment of communal opinion, believing the only way they could show resentment for the awful outrage that occurred in their community was to set fire to the house. But, Nolan argued, the people only considered their own feelings and neither the feel-ings nor the plump pocketbook of Mr. Lindsay, the owner of the house, who was paid rent for it, and who now sought damages from the people of Middlethird barony.

William Simpson, caretaker, testified on behalf of his em-ployer. Simpson stated that the cottage was unoccupied, and on the evening of July 3, he passed by and noticed nothing unusual. As far as he knew the door was locked. The very next morning, July 4, a very different sight greeted his eyes. Fire had destroyed the cottage; the thatched roof was still smoldering, but the walls remained standing. In assessing Mr. Lindsay's loss, William Ma-her, a farmer residing in the area, testified that the cottage could be rebuilt for £10–15. Since the Guardians were paying £150 for new cottages, he thought citizens of the barony could save money by rebuilding the cottage so Mr. Lindsay could have back his lost rental of £1 per year. A man named Mullally testified that the cottage was a "hovel" and it would be better to "level" it. The magistrates agreed on a settlement of £15, but even then rate-payers in the barony objected. Speaking for the outraged citizens of Middlethird, Scully asked: "Why should you spread this witch case over to us? We had no connection with it whatever." The magistrates agreed and ordered the levy of £15 due to Lindsay be charged upon the parish where "the thing occurred."[68]

In the fall of 1895, there were two notices to appear in local newspapers affecting those related to the tragedy at Ballyvadlea. On September 14, the *Clonmel Chronicle* reported that the Cashel Guardians Board awarded to Dr. William Crean, recently discharged chief medical officer of the Fethard dispensary, an annual pension of £45, a figure that represented a third of his former salary of £135 per annum. The notice made no mention of Dr. Crean's alcoholism but stated that the doctor suffered from "ill health."

On November 6, the *Chronicle* reported that Magistrates Evanson and Grubb heard a case against a caretaker named Simpson, who resided with his son at Ballyvadlea, near Cloneen. The elder Mr. Simpson was charged with stealing a bottle of whiskey from Mrs. Mary Fox's shop in Clonmel. The arresting officer, Sergeant Joyce, testified that he found Simpson in a lodging house drinking the stolen whiskey. Sergeant Joyce offered other testimony related to the prisoner's character. Joyce stated that he had known Simpson when he was a caretaker in Ballingeary and, at that time, Simpson was tried for obtaining goods under false pretenses, representing himself as a retired head-constable, an offense for which he was bound to good behavior for twelve months. He was also charged with stealing a magistrate's whip. Speaking in his defense, Simpson stated that he had got the whiskey "on the notion of paying for it." The magistrates were not convinced and sentenced Mr. Simpson to one month's imprisonment.

In the closing months of 1895, memories of the "Ballyvadlea Horror" began to fade and the Tipperary Hounds were out for another season. The voice of the Tipperary Hounds, Larky Grigg, reported that on Saturday, October 19, a fox was on the move at Coolmore, near Fethard, but the hounds lost it. Ballylusky was "blank" as well, but the Harriers found action on Kylnagranagh hill, near Mr. Scanlon's farm, where the hounds scared up several foxes. One sly creature set its head toward Slievenamon, and the hounds gave chase. Wheeling to the right, however, it crossed the Cloneen and Drangan road, and ran west through rough country near Rathkenny. It led the Harriers on a lively chase for another twenty minutes, then several foxes broke with it out of the Rathkenny cover. Rather than disperse, Hound Master Richard Burke decided to keep the Hounds on the trail of the wily vixen, which had eluded them for so long, and continued on. With fox in the lead and Harriers in hot pursuit, the chase continued in earnest for another half an hour, until once again, the creature slipped into the cover and was gone. Rather than pursue, the Harriers gave up and retired for the evening, leaving the bent-necked fox to run another day on Kylnagranagh hill.[69]

Afterword

As historians, we have had difficulty coming to terms with what happened to Bridget Cleary in County Tipperary, Ireland, over a hundred years ago. We have often been asked why we embarked on such a project: The case involved just another dead woman, and, in Ireland, there were plenty of those. So why concern ourselves with Bridget Cleary? We can recite how the case, when set within its particular historical moment, became significant. We have sketched an outline of the Nationalist movement in Ireland, the frustrating fight for Home Rule, and the enormously significant role that Archbishop Thomas Croke played in urging the Catholic Church into the movement. We have looked back at one of Ireland's most loved literary figures, Charles Kickham, Tipperary's most renowned poet/patriot, and described his vision of a free and independent Irish state. We have described the frustration of Irish peasants in dealing with their English overlords. We have reconstructed, through stories and fragmentary bits of testimony, a dynamics of the full-blown fairy trial that ended in Bridget Cleary's burning in the early morning hours of March 16, 1895. We have shown how all these elements of the story came together in a strange and startling climax in July 1895 with the criminal trial of the nine defendants, the Parliamentary election, and the Archbishop's Silver Jubilee. When all this is placed together, we can understand, from a new perspective, how Ireland suffered, how she struggled, and what she faced in her fight to win her freedom.

From our story, we can also see how faith in folk beliefs can affect history. Fairies remain the stuff of faith since they don't write letters, pay taxes, or grant interviews. Although they leave no records that we can scrutinize, analyze, and footnote, historians recognize their power in shaping human history. Without our noticing, they cross over the boundary between our world and theirs and alter the shape of our sternest cultural meanings, particularly in times of rapid change, as was the case in late nineteenth-century Ireland as well as in our own day. There is much evidence of a contemporary fairy revival, demonstrated by the 1997 films *Photographing Fairies* and *Fairy Tale: A True Story* and the 1999 low-budget box-office blockbuster, *The Blair Witch Project*. In late nineteenth-century Ireland, people were drawn to the fairies; in the late twentieth, after a century of bustling, brutal modernity, people still are.[1]

We have written a story about a cooper's wife who went missing in 1895 in County Tipperary, Ireland. It's a simple story that shows how simple beliefs can shape big events. One Wednesday afternoon in March, a woman went to a fairy fort on Kylnagranagh hill, where she "took a fit of tremblin'"—meaning, her spirit was taken by the fairies. In the nine days that followed, her husband and family did all they could to get her spirit back. When their time ran out, the husband burned his wife, hoping that he could reclaim her spirit and body from the Otherworld. After the story hit the presses, an ambitious prosecutor saw a way to make a name for himself, while Unionist politicians spied a chance to embarrass their arch-foe, the Archbishop of Emly and Cashel, on the eve of his Silver Jubilee. Even more, Unionists hoped to embarrass the Irish people and influence the outcome of a crucial parliamentary election that would determine the fate of Home Rule for Ireland, thus ensuring their rule of another generation.

We do not suggest that the burning of a cooper's wife at Ballyvadlea led directly to the delay of Home Rule and the continued subjection of the Irish people. What we do say is that had not so many people in Ballyvadlea, Dublin, New York, London, and around the world believed in the fairies, an ambitious prosecutor would not have used the incident to promote his career, Unionist politicians would not have exploited a woman's death to influence the election, and we would never have written this book.

Through his fifteen long years of prison servitude, Michael Cleary had plenty of time to reflect upon what he had done, and he claimed that, over time, he had changed his mind about fairies and changelings. Known as prisoner number 866, Cleary served out fifteen years of his twenty-year sentence in three different penal facilities. By all accounts, he fared as well as could be expected. Physically, he remained in good health. When first admitted, he had a bad scar on his left arm, a cut mark over his right eyebrow, three cuts on the first finger of his left hand, and a broken thumbnail on his left hand. In 1904 he broke his arm and periodically required a special ointment for a rash on his hands. Apart from these minor injuries and ailments, he remained healthy. When he entered the federal prison in December 1895, he measured 5'10" and weighed 167 pounds; when he left prison in 1910, he was a heavier man at 189 pounds.

Michael Cleary's prison records characterize his deportment as generally "good," although he was "cautioned" five times between

1896 and 1904 for "irregular" and/or for "filthy" conduct. On one occasion he assaulted another prisoner, and once "prohibited articles" were found in his cell. Cleary remained attentive to his mother, Bridget, during his imprisonment. He wrote to her forty-eight times—an average of four times a year—before her death in 1907. He learned of her death when the forty-ninth letter was returned marked "Deceased." He did not write to his former father-in-law, even though Patrick Boland, after his release from prison, wrote him once from Cloneen on Christmas in 1895.[2]

During his imprisonment, Cleary renounced his belief in fairies and the "foolish superstitions" that led to the murder. As a prisoner in good standing, Cleary was allowed to petition for early release and was eligible for parole by 1910. Beginning in 1901, Michael painfully handwrote page after page of petitions, totaling over thirty pages in all, pleading for an early release. With each appeal, he told his version of the murder, each time with more and more embellishment, and each time employing new arguments that might win sympathy with parole officials.[3]

In all his petitions, Cleary argued in so many words that he had been "on the best of terms with his wife" and that it was his relatives who convinced him that his wife was a changeling. Cleary stated that had it not been for his wife's father and relations—especially John Dunne, about whom "it was believed in the locality that [he] had knowledge in the use of herbs"—he would never have sought the aid of a "quack or Fairy Doctor." They and they alone convinced him that his wife suffered from "no ordinary illness" but from a "case of witchcraft." Dunne, in particular, told Michael that Cleary would rid Bridget of the "enchament" if the treatment that Dunne "perscribed" was carried out. Cleary insisted that his in-laws prompted him to engage in proceedings based on *their* "foolish superstition" and his own ignorance. Therefore, he became the victim of *their* "superstition of sorcery" and *their* "evil spell," although he acknowledged that he had been raised in an area (Killenaule) where such beliefs also "unfortunately prevailed." He insisted (using the third person about himself) that while in prison God had "purged [him] of such unholiness and it [was] with loathing that he look[ed] back upon his ignorance and [was] truly repentant for his crime." In 1905 he noted that because he had been taking care of his wife "night and day untill he was in a manner just as bad as [she was]. . . . his crime was committed when his mind [was] upset by trouble and want of sleep."

Beginning in 1903 Cleary tried to use physical and mental reasons to win early release. He argued that "if compelled to under go his full time [he] will be discharged at an age after such a lengthened imprisonment as will unfit him for active employment and seriously militate against the possability of his making reasonable provision against want in his old age." In 1904 after he fell from a prison roof and broke his left arm, Cleary added this injury to his list of reasons for an early release. While he maintained that his right arm had also been "seriously injured," the prison report for that year countered that the accident had been due to Cleary's negligence and was certainly not the prison's (or the warden's) fault. This was an English prison, after all. The medical officer did note, however, that Cleary spent five weeks in the hospital recovering from his injuries, but recovered "without any deformity" and was released from the hospital in "good heath." By 1907 he maintained that he was "now well advanced in years and while suffering from mental uneasiness and the toils and hardships of Prison life well nigh thirteen years have greatly aided to unfit him for worldly life which he will be compelled to face when released as he has no friends from whome he [could] expect any aid or help."

In the course of writing his petitions for early release, Michael Cleary included new facts about the case that were not brought out at trial. In 1905, Cleary told of his frustration at trying to get help from Dr. William Crean—information that might have helped his defense had it not been for the fact that his attorney Richard Crean was a relative of the doctor. Cleary stated that Dr. Crean ignored two red dispensary tickets for a home visit and he was finally obliged to obtain a written order from Edmond Cummins of Brook Hill, the district's Guardian, for Crean to attend the Clearys. Cleary also wrote that during those same few days he had asked Father Ryan to call on his wife and the cleric had administered the last rites to Bridget, implying that nothing more could be done for her. According to Cleary, Father Ryan cast aspersions on the medicine prescribed by the alcoholic Dr. Crean. This statement, we will re-member, contradicted Father Ryan's testimony that he encouraged Cleary to give the medicine to Bridget.

Cleary wrote that, after Father Ryan's departure, Patrick Boland, Mary Kennedy, and John Dunne all told him that "if he did not do what they would tell him his wife would dye [sic] in a day or two . . . that it was not a case for the Doctor at all." Based upon their advice, Cleary left early the next morning to visit "a quack doctor the name of Geainy" for herbs, which he gave his wife following directions from Dunne. From Michael's 1905 peti-tion we learn that during the first five days of Bridget's illness he actually spent as much, if not more, time contacting traditional sources of help—the Church and the medical profession—as he did going to fairy doctors. Both traditional venues failed him. His frantic efforts to obtain Dr. Crean's services would not indicate that he was abusing or planning to murder his wife. He said noth-ing to suggest that he might have been driven to despair by jeal-ousy over his wife's rumored affair because this would have done

nothing to help his appeals. For years prison officials denied parole with the stern words, "The Law must take its course."

In 1910, when he was due for parole, Cleary's petitions received more attention. In February he asked to have the three
months he "spent awaiting trial to count in my sentence [because]
it would be greatly in my favour to be released early in the summer [for] it would be easy to get employment than in a later period of the year." In April Cleary asked to be discharged "from
prison without a [probation] licence" so that he could obtain employment without "being exposed to my fellow workmen as a
man discharged from a convict prison and under police supervi-
sion." Cleary concluded this, his last petition, with the words: "I
was never before in prison and I faithfully promise if granted this
concession I will never return to prison again." On April 5, 1910,
the report of the chairman of the General Prisons Board at Dublin
Castle noted that the prisoner had no previous convictions before
the murder of his wife and the prison chaplains were "convinced
that these men's actions in the case were owing to superstition
and not malicious." Finally, on April 12, 1910, Michael Cleary
was released with an earned gratuity of a little over £17 in his
pockets. Immediately he departed for Liverpool, and on June 30
he migrated to Montreal, Canada. Although we have tried, we
could find no further records of his life there. Of the seven defendants sentenced to prison, Michael Cleary served the longest.

John Dunne, prisoner number 867, served somewhat less than
his three years. He never renounced his belief in fairies. Although
he arrived at Maryborough Prison, missing several upper and
lower teeth, with poor vision, and suffering from a hernia, prison
officials, of course, recorded his physical condition as "good."
During his term, his conduct was considered merely satisfactory,
and he stubbornly refused to learn a trade. While his official age

was listed as fifty-five in 1895, by February 1896 he was claiming in the first of five petitions that he was over sixty. All these petitions stressed that he was not at the Cleary cottage the night Bridget Cleary was killed.[4]

A year after the trial, the presiding Catholic judge, William O'Brien, changed his view of this celebrated case. For example, replying to one of Patrick Kennedy's petitions for early release, O'Brien wrote that he had concluded that "delusion and superstition" did not cause the crime; rather, Michael Cleary cynically used the superstitions of his in-laws to cover up his own "deliberate and wicked design to kill his wife." This change in O'Brien's thinking reversed the view he had when, in his instructions to the jury he implicitly attacked the Catholic Church for indulging the pagan beliefs of rural peasants. A year later, only four months before his own death, O'Brien downplayed his criticism of the Church and was more willing to believe that Michael Cleary was guilty of premeditated murder.[5]

Although O'Brien did not recommend that Patrick Kennedy receive an early release from prison, he showed considerable sympathy for the Kennedy family, whom he believed had been caught up in the husband's murderous scheme. He had less compassion for John Dunne. The "fairy expert" was not, in O'Brien's opinion, an accomplice in the murder itself, but because he "was considered to have a special knowledge in sorcery . . . he was the tool of the husband [and] was the person who put the idea of witchcraft either as a delusion or pretext for the husband's deed." In 1896, O'Brien expressed regret that the case against Michael Cleary had ended so quickly "by consent to a verdict for manslaughter" and that more was not known of the defendants' beliefs and their role in causing Bridget Cleary bodily harm. We view O'Brien's private comments with some skepticism because he facilitated, though didn't engineer, the course of that truncated trial. Since he may have been aware of his impending death in 1896, as a Catholic, O'Brien may have gravitated toward a less critical view of the Catholic Church than he had held a year earlier.[6]

As a result of O'Brien's denial, Patrick and Michael Kennedy served out their prison terms. None of the three—Dunne, Patrick, or Michael—was literate enough to write his own petition, and although Patrick Kennedy signed his name to his, the other two simply made their marks. William and James Kennedy did not appeal for early release. Neither Patrick nor Michael Kennedy was listed in good health during their prison terms. Patrick's was at best "fair" and Michael's was considered "delicate" because of his lungs, for which he underwent "special treatment" at the Clonmel Gaol. Officials, of course, did not think that his life was in any way "endangered by further confinement" in their prison system.[7]

In January 1897, Dunne made a special appeal to be released following the death of his wife Catherine (Kate), claiming he would be homeless if he stayed in prison. Dunne argued that his wife had been occupying "a house and small portion of land at the time of his conviction and it was held for him by [her] until he would be released and as he has no one now to look after it for him he will be homeless when his [term] is complete." Apparently, Dunne's fears were realized. The census of 1901 indicated that a widower John Dunne was living as a farm servant on property of James Skehan in Ballymuck, indicating that Dunne did indeed lose his home. He was finally released on October 3, 1897, with a gratuity of a little over £1. During his nearly three years in prison, Dunne corresponded four times with his wife; the fifth letter was returned bearing the notice that the addressee was "Deceased." Dunne also sent one letter to Patrick Boland, who was then living in Ballywater, near Cloneen, but received no reply.

For their involvement in the Cleary tragedy, the Kennedy family paid dearly. Their leased cottage was burned down on the eve of the trial, then leveled, which left them all homeless, although most seem to have stayed in the Clonmel/Cloneen area. Apparently Johanna Burke did not remain with her husband and children in Rathkenny. The 1901 census indicates that she was not living in Rathkenny. After the trial, she probably led a pathetic peripatetic life, disliked by her own kin because of her testimony for the Crown. Initially at least, the Royal Irish Constabulary (RIC) provided her with police protection, including lodging and expenses for her and her daughter, Katie. The county Death Registry notes that a Johanna Burke, widow of laborer, died on September 4, 1914, in a workhouse in Clonmel. The 1901 census indicates that Katie was working as a domestic servant in the Protestant household of farmer Richard Hunt in the townland of Brumsick near Clonmel.[8] We could find no record of her in the Death Registry for the Fethard District. Mary Kennedy ironically ended up as a servant living with the Resident Magistrate Colonel Evanson in Glenconnor, Clonmel, only to disappear from there by the 1901 census. We found a Mary Kennedy, widow of laborer, who died in a Clonmel workhouse on April 25, 1902, at the age of fifty-five, but if this was the aunt of Bridget Cleary she should have been sixty-two years old. Patrick and James can be found in the 1901 census working as laborers; nothing is known of the whereabouts of the other Kennedy brothers, Michael and William, by the turn of the century.[9]

As for William Simpson, the 1901 census indicates that he was thirty years old and living with his wife Minnie, aged forty, and their two daughters on the property of Paul M. Lindsay in Garrankyle, a townland near Ballyvadlea. It seemed that Simpson's role as a leading Crown witness and local tour guide did little to improve his standing with the powers that be, and, within his own community, he remained a hated "emergency" caretaker.[10]

The case apparently did little to further District Inspector Alfred Joseph Wansbrough's career, who had been implicitly censured by Crown Solicitor Michael Gleeson for unnecessarily delaying the magisterial inquiry proceedings to gather evidence about the fairies. By 1901 Wansbrough had risen to the first category of seniority list for inspectors, and by 1914 he was eighth from the top on that list.[11] He always seemed a bit off the mark, despite the description of him in 1895 as "an able young man who deserved to rise high in the Royal Irish Constabulatory." In 1916, Wansbrough was stationed in Cork during the Easter Rising and subsequent war with England. In February 1920 he retired to England without either distinguishing or disgracing himself.[12]

Father Cornelius Ryan remained a curate at the Catholic church in Drangan for his entire clerical career. After he died, on December 19, 1916, the priests and people of the parish erected a large monument in the Drangan churchyard bearing the following inscription: "His charity and zeal endeared him to the people to whom he faithfully ministered for 22 years."

The famous Ballyvadlea cottage, where the infamous fairy trial took place, was sold several times in the course of the twentieth century. It has been unoccupied for the last quarter century and is now owned by an American heir of the last occupant, presumably unrelated to the Clearys, Kennedys, and Bolands.[13]

Although the principal participants faded into poverty-ridden obscurity, the case of the missing cooper's wife remains historically significant because of its effects on Irish culture, the Nationalist movement, and the English judicial system. We have argued that the extraordinary attention paid to the "tragedy at Ballyvadlea" was in part due to the fact that the incident occurred in the thick of Nationalist organizing, Unionist maneuvering to kill Home Rule, and Archbishop Croke's Silver Jubilee, and was used by all parties to serve political ends. Because of the unusual constellation of events in early 1895, the murder of Bridget Cleary became an international sensation, but this case would be the last of its kind to be given legal standing in the British system. Thereafter, few, if any, fairy-induced murders were given the dignity of a capital-offense charge. Never again would the English sensationalize the fairies to serve their political ends in Ireland.

A year after the Cleary case, another incident arose that was in many ways remarkably similar to the tragedy at Ballyvadlea yet was handled very differently. This incident took place in Lisphelan, County Roscommon, on March 6, 1896, in the home of the "hard working and respectable" Cunningham family consisting of the father William, four sons—Michael, John, James, and Patrick—and a daughter Lizzie. They farmed extensively but also worked as bootmakers and shoemakers. James was a shoemaker as well as an artificial manure dealer. The trouble started when the entire family heard a "blast of wind" come through the door while they were saying the rosary and a voice from the loft was heard saying, "Now is your time. . . . Take care of yourself."[14]

After this blast of wind, brother James began acting strangely, displaying what the Irish newspapers called "evidences of mental affliction." On March 5 Dr. French of Ballygar came to examine him, but James refused to see the doctor and asked for a priest instead. Both the parish priest, Father Gately, and his curate, Father Mulleady, had been in "frequent" communication with him, and Mulleady paid him a long visit on March 5, and the next day it appeared that he would make a speedy recovery. But then on Friday, March 7, the curate was called again, and this time James asked him to administer the last rites. Perhaps learning something from the Cleary incident, Father Mulleady refused upon "seeing the healthy condition of the man." Father Mulleady testified that James was "labouring under some hallucination," but neither he nor Father Gately took any precautionary or preventive action even though James went to the church later in the day and prayed for an unusually long time. Like Father Ryan, both priests vehemently denied any personal knowledge that "witchcraft and fairies" played a role in the incident.[15]

A huge man weighing 238 pounds, James, like Bridget Cleary, made frequent visits to an ancient rath called "The Fairies' Fort." Because of his strange behavior and unusual interest in the fort, family members became convinced, on the evening of March 6, that "evil spirits were hovering around" their homes. As a result they decided not to sleep in their respective dwellings but to stay up until the "cock would crow." Just before midnight the family knelt together and prayed. Suddenly James jumped up and tried to choke his father, shouting that there were fairies in his throat. Other family members attempted to subdue James, but because of his great size, they were obliged to use "every instrument in the place . . . to subdue the powerful maniac." In the ensuing struggle, James was bludgeoned to death, leaving him "terribly battered, chin cut away, [and] teeth broken." Neighbors heard the screams, rushed in, and some of them helped to put an end to James. The Cunninghams, unlike Michael Cleary and the Kennedys, did not try to conceal their deadly assault. The morning after, they told the local priests and that evening informed the police, who promptly arrested the father, three sons, and daughter, as well as three neighbors.[16]

Five of the suspects were locked in a holding cell at the local barracks where they became convinced that evil spirits had followed them and that Patrick Cunningham was now possessed. In a fit of frenzy, the five men broke out of their cell and charged the six policemen on duty; reinforcements were brought in to subdue what had become a battle royal. When the Cunninghams arrived in Athone for magisterial inquiry, the battered and chained men "presented a frightful appearance." They too were jeered by a large crowd, but the Cunninghams were not finished. From their cells in the Athone prison, the entire family—including the sister who had "attacked her father, and nearly choked him *trying to draw fairies out of his throat*"—continued their "roaring," requiring a large contingent of guards to control them.[17]

In the investigation that followed, the coroner's jury found that the defendants killed James Cunningham in self-defense, despite the fact that the melee arose from their collective belief that "their house had been filled with devils and fairies, whom they felt cracking the door, and [whom] they had to hunt with holy water." In the end, Patrick Cunningham was acquitted, since it was he who was attacked, while John, Patrick, and sister Lizzie ended up in the insane asylum. Because the Cunninghams were deemed to be "sober, industrious people"[18] and because there was no political advantage to be gained, the verdicts raised more relief than outrage and because the English no longer needed another explosive, embarrassing incident. Obviously a lesson had been learned from the Cleary case. Fairies would be banned from English courtrooms and banished from the Irish countryside by declaring those who engaged in fairy practices to be insane.

Interest, however, in fairies, folklore, and the occult did not die but was transmuted into respectable, socially useful forms. By 1895, the Celtic literary revival was underway in elite cultural circles, led by Lady Gregory and future Nobel Prize–winner William Butler Yeats. This literary movement bestowed intellectual credibility to pagan beliefs and fairy folklore, while less cerebral types used fairies and Celtic folk myths to titillate Victorian pornographic tastes.[19]

Rather than diminish interest in fairies, the Cleary case fanned the public's curiosity. Following the trial, newspapers in Ireland, England, and the United States printed background stories on witchcraft and superstitions and compared them with what had happened in Ballyvadlea. Scholars discussed the technical differences between witches and fairies and capitalized on the Victorian passion for spiritualism and the occult. One American group interested in the occult, known as the Christian Endeavorers, organized a conference in Salem, Massachusetts in July 1895, to revisit sites made famous by its late seventeenth-century witch trials. Other articles appearing after the Cleary trial discussed witch trials in England—the last having taken place in 1712 at Hereford, when one Jane Wenham was convicted but was not executed; readers learned that the last execution took place in Scotland in 1722, and the last witch trial in Switzerland occurred in 1793. Under pressure from England, Ireland had passed its first statute against witchcraft in 1586 and in 1821 became one of the last countries in Europe to repeal its anti-witchcraft laws.[20]

Pursuing his fascination with witches and changelings, William Butler Yeats wrote the play *The Land of Heart's Desire*, which premiered almost a year to the day before Bridget died. The Cleary case, in fact, resembled Yeats's plot, eerily, up to a point, telling the tale of a young wife who became enchanted by the fairies, then was spirited away to the Otherworld. Laughed at and scorned by first-night urban audiences, critics described the play as an absurd melodrama and a "pretty fancy" of the young playwright Yeats.[21] Yeats went on to become a major figure in the Anglo-Irish Celtic revival, in part because he included the fairies in Ireland's literary renaissance, yet his fairies were gentrified and respectable, much as Kickham's residents of Knocknagow had been.

As gentrification progressed, new heroes and new myths emerged to replace the older, less socially useful beliefs. In their literary work, both Yeats and Kickham presented an idealized vision of the gentrified Irish peasantry—not of the most downtrodden tenant laborer. Kickham's portrayal of the "old Irishry" was based on a sentimental, romantic Catholic nationalism stemming from his vision of a stable and prosperous Irish nation of bourgeois farmers based on the "strong or snug" farmers, who, by 1881, lived on holdings over fifteen acres and comprised 56 percent of the rural hierarchy. Yeats proposed a Germanic-style ethnic brand of secular cultural nationalism based on Celtic legends written in Gaelic about a primitive Irish paradise. In the late 1890s, Yeats's view emerged to challenge the vision of Charles Kickham, which was shared by Archbishop Croke. While intellectuals and Nationalist politicians began to tout Yeats's version of Gaelic nationalism, the Irish masses remained devoted to Kickham's vision of an Irish Catholic nation rooted in the simple values of *Knocknagow*, that mythical, idealized home of a frugal people who devoted their leisure to spiritual pursuits and valued material wealth only as the basis of right living.[22]

In 1895, change was in the air throughout all Ireland; changelings were seen everywhere, among politicians, priests, poets, and pundits. As the Italian Marxist Antonio Gramsci would later say of such times, "The old is not yet dead, the new not yet born; in the interim, monsters abound." Charles Stewart Parnell, once Ireland's savior, became its Satan in the eyes of Catholic Nationalists, after he willfully split the movement in 1891. The Church, which initially was reluctant to support the Nationalists, changed its position and threw its weight behind the movement. Slowly, the Church was drawn into a movement for independence that would inevitably turn more violent in the first two decades of the twentieth century. But by supporting the Nationalists, the Church retained its centuries-old bond between people and priest.

The place of the fairies in Irish culture was also changing. Superstition and pagan practice waned as the Old Irishry, particularly the rural laborers, dwindled in size and importance. After fifty years, the devotional revolution of the Church was well entrenched, as indicated by the fact that every Sunday over 90 percent of the population attended Mass. The Church continued its war on paganism, gradually driving most of the fairies off to the Otherworld. Yeats and other Anglo-Irish revivalists gentrified those that remained. Superficial superstitions persisted in modern Ireland, but it was only a matter of time before few could or would profess belief in fairies with impunity. Fewer still dared to practice the old rituals in the open.

One of the constants in our story is the majestic mountain, Slievenamon—a sacred place to the local people. In 1995, a U.S. company, the New World Company, sought permission to test the feasibility of placing power-generating windmills on its northwest slope and the County Council approved a test station. Local residents quickly formed a group, Save Our Slievenamon (SOS), to stop construction, and forced the County Council to withdraw its approval. The determined resistance of SOS saved the mountain for future generations of hikers, poets, protesters, and, perhaps, fairies. Today the wind blows freely over the fabled mountain, as it has from time immemorial, as it did a century ago when the poet Dennis McCarthy described "The Wind of Slievenamon."

> *The magic wind from Slieve-na-mon—sometimes it*
> *was a blast*
> *Of faint enchanted bugles blown from Ireland's*
> *glorious past,*
> *How many a dream it brought of the day when*
> *Ireland's banner shone,*

And Irish cheers were mingled with the wind from
Slieve-na-mon![23]

With luck, the wind from Slievenamon will always blow freely and retain just a bit of the old magic.

Ironically, the one person about whom we have almost no information is the enigmatic Bridget Boland Cleary—the woman who set this project in motion with her furtive visits to the fairy forts on Kylnagranagh hill. In her day, people wondered why she went there; in our day, people are still wondering. While our book documents the influence of those visits on the larger culture, we still cannot answer the question definitively. No one ever will because she left so few records.

Bridget's student records from the Drangan convent school indicate that she entered school in 1871 at the age of four. This date is consistent with the birth date of February 19, 1867, recorded in the Fethard Birth Registry, which means Bridget was twenty-eight years old when she died. We now know that Bridget stayed in school on and off until 1881, when she was fourteen. Then there is the record of her marriage to Michael Cleary, on August 5, 1887, in the Drangan church. Finally, we found what we briefly hoped was her neat, clear, rather forthright signature in the Fethard District Death Registry, made on the death of her mother in February 1894, but it turns out the handwriting was the district clerk's not Bridget's.[24]

Beyond these few facts, we know nothing of Bridget Cleary personally—what she thought, or believed, or even, definitively, what she did. She left no personal records— letters, a diary, photographs—that might help us understand the role she played in the events leading up to her death. Perhaps, then, she must remain always a mystery—the missing cooper's wife who went "out the mountain" more than a century ago.

Notes

Chapter One

1. The details about the 1894 Christmas in Clonmel in the opening pages of this book come from issues of the *Nationalist* and the *Clonmel Chronicle* for the first half of January 1895. Generally when the names and specific dates of newspapers are given in the text, no footnotes are given.

2. Although they owned most of Clonmel, the Bagwells lived in Marlfield, and Richard Bagwell served as foreman of the Grand Jury that found against Michael Cleary and his wife's relatives in April, leading to their July trial for murder. For the Bagwell family's political and economic domination of Clonmel politics, see R. V. Comerford, "Tipperary Representation at Westminster, 1801–1918," in William Nolan and Thomas G. McGrath, eds., *Tipperary: History and Society. Interdisciplinary Essays on the History of an Irish County* (Dublin: Geography Publications, 1985), pp. 325–326, 330; and *The Nationalist Centenary Supplement* [*NCS*], *1890–1990*, p. 92.

3. Quarterly Report, 21 February 1887, Cloneen District. Education Correspondence, ED9 #4536, and June 1887 Report, Roll #13231, National Archives, Dublin.

4. David Fitzpatrick, "The Disappearance of the Irish Agricultural Labourer, 1841–1912," *Irish Economic and Social History* 7 (1980): 84–85. The flawed dichotomy between the "Old Irish" (pre-Cromwellian native Irish landowners and peasants) and the "Old English" or Anglo-Irish (pre-Cromwellian English landowners) was first encapsulated by William Molyneux when he published *The Case of Ireland Being Bound by Acts of Parliament in England Stated* in 1699. This distinction was later employed by Jonathan Swift and, by the end of the nineteenth century, had become a standard form of ethnocentric "race" bashing in political rhetoric between the English and the Irish over Home Rule. See Thomas E. Hachey, Joseph M. Hernon, Jr., and Lawrence H. McCaffrey, *The Irish Experience* (Englewood Cliffs, N.J.: Prentice Hall, 1989), p. 35; and Thomas P. Power, *Politics and Society in Eighteenth-Century Tipperary* (Oxford: Clarendon Press, 1993), pp. 65–75, *passim*. "Old Irishry," a variation of "Old Irish," came to apply less to Irish landowners in the course of the nineteenth century (as more Irish Catholics became landowners) and more to poor Irish tenants who embodied the oral tradition of Irish folklore. This term was also used by Nationalist politicians to bolster the concept of Celticism or Gaelicism to counter Victorian

anti-Irish stereotypes. See L. P. Curtis, *Anglo-Saxons and Celts: A Study of Anti-Irish Prejudice in Victorian England* (Bridgeport, Conn.: Conference on British Studies at the University of Bridgeport, 1968), pp. 108–116.

5. *Nationalist*, June 9, 1894.

6. Registry of Births, Marriages and Deaths, 1864–1895, Fethard District, Books 1–25, Community Care Centre, Clonmel, County Tipperary. It should be noted that Catholic/Nationalist rhetoric in the second half of the nineteenth century often asserted that the absence of infanticide in Ireland distinguished it from "'pagan' English society," where the practice was said to be much more widespread. Irish girls might "get in trouble" in large cities in England or the United States, but not in Ireland and even if they did they never became desperate enough to try to murder their children. See R. B. Comerford, *Charles J. Kickham: A Study in Irish Nationalism and Literature* (Portmarnock, Co. Dublin: Wolfhound Press, 1979), p. 202.

7. For representative examples, see stories in the *Cork Examiner*, March 29, 1895; *Nationalist*, March 30, 1895; *Daily Graphic*, April 13, 1895; *New York Times*, April 22, 1895; and Boston *Daily Globe*, May 7, 1895.

8. C. J. Boland, "The Carrick Dog," in James White, ed., *My Clonmel Scrap Book*, 3rd ed. (Clonmel: Tentmaker Publications, n.d.), pp. 317–324.

9. George Henry Bassett, *County Tipperary. One Hundred Years Ago: A Guide and Directory, 1889* (Belfast: Friar's Bush Press, 1991; reprint of 1889 edition entitled *The Book of Country Tipperary*), p. 67.

10. Boland, "The Battle of Boulick," in White, ed., *Clonmel Scrap Book*, pp. 57–59.

11. Liam de Paor, *The Peoples of Ireland: From Prehistory to Modern Times* (London: Hutchinson, 1986), pp. 148–158; Thomas E. Hachey, Joseph M. Hernon, Jr., Lawrence H. McCaffrey, *The Irish Experience* (Englewood Cliffs, N.J.: Prentice Hall, 1989), pp. 21–24; R. F. Foster, *Modern Ireland, 1600–1972* (New York: Penguin, 1989; reprint of 1988 Viking edition), pp. 80–103; J. G. Simms, "The Cromwellian Settlement of Tipperary," *Tipperary Historical Journal* (1989): 27; Bassett, *County Tipperary*, p. 71; and "Rare Clonmel," in White, ed., *Clonmel Scrap Book*, pp. 43–46 (poem quoted on p. 45). Hugh Duff (Dubh) O'Neill took over the defense of Clonmel from his uncle, the legendary Owen Roe O'Neill, who successfully commanded the army of Ulster against Protestant Reformation forces until his death in November 1649, and who in turn was the nephew of the great Hugh O'Neill, Earl of Tyrone, who had resisted the Tudor conquest of Ireland at the end of the sixteenth and beginning of the seventeenth centuries.

12. Kevin Whelan, "The Catholic Church, 1700–1900," in Nolan and McGrath, eds., *Tipperary: History and Society*, p. 243. Whelan notes that the most persistent form of violence, the "faction fight, a ritualised method of settling disputes without recourse to external authority, remained endemic in Tipperary life despite the determined opposition of the Catholic Church." Also see Paul Johnson, *Ireland: A Concise History from the Twelfth Century to the Present Day* (Chicago: Academy Publishers, 1980), p. 140; Carlo Gébler, *How to Murder a Man* (London: Abacus, 1999; reprint of Little, Brown 1998 edition), *passim*, for a historical novel about the Ribbonmen; and Alan O'Day and John Stevenson, eds., *Irish Historical Documents Since 1800* (Dublin: Gill and Macmillan, 1992), p. 74 for a chart of agrarian crimes from 1850 to 1913. See Chapter 3 below for more details about the general subculture of violence in Ireland and "Whiteboy" activity in particular.

13. Bassett, *County Tipperary*, pp. 69–121.

14. C. J. Kickham, *Knocknagow: Or, the Homes of Tipperary* (24th ed. Dublin: James Duffy, 1873) pp. 627–628. The population of County Tipperary alone dwindled from 435,553 in 1841, to 331,567 in 1851, to 249,106 in 1861, to 216,702 in 1871, and to 199,692 in 1881. By the 1890s, it had slipped to a little over 173,000. Tipperary figures are from the *New York World and American Industrial Liberator*, March 3, 1894, p. 5; *New York Irish World and American Industrial Liberator*, March 3, 1894; and Foster, *Modern Ireland*, pp. 323–324.

15. *New York Irish World and American Industrial Liberator*, November 18, 1893, p. 6; *The Nationalist Centenary Supplement [NCS] 1890–1990*, pp. 91–92; Bassett, *County Tipperary*, pp. 69–121; and Michael O'Donnell, "Lighting the Streets of Fethard, 1870–1914," *Tipperary Historical Journal* (1998): 128–132.

16. Despite all its modern bustle and hustle, it cannot be said that Clonmel was prosperous by European or American standards of the 1890s. Lacking Dublin's reputation as one of the world's literary centers at the end of the century, Clonmel shared with its northern sister city "overcrowded, rat-and-vermin infested tenements . . . [and] diets of tea, jam, and bread [which] produced unhealthy bodies. Tuberculosis was an Irish urban and rural scourge, and the infant mortality rate was appalling. In a country with little industry, few natural resources, and a low level of capital investment, the urban working class suffered from unemployment or partial employment at low wages. Poverty, hunger, disease, and filth bred alcoholism, depression, and prostitution." See Hachey et al., *Irish Experience*, pp. 141, 144. This is a description of living conditions in Dublin in the 1890s that can also be applied to Clonmel and other medium-sized Irish towns.

17. What is unusual about Irish migration is that it actually began on a large scale before the Great Famine and continued long after it. Nonetheless, the loss of 2.5 million people from disease, starvation, and migration between 1845 and 1851 was demographically catastrophic. Of these, 775,000 died and about 1.5 million emigrated—250,000 alone in 1851 compared to an estimated rate of 130,000 a year by 1841 before the Famine. Between 1845 and 1900 some 4 million Irish migrated to the United States, but 2.3 million of those came after 1860. See Bull, *Land, Politics, and Nationalism*, pp. 7, 21; James S. Donnelly, Jr., *The Land and the People of Nineteenth-Century Cork: The Rural Economy and the Land Question* (London: Routledge and Kegan Paul, 1975), pp. 85–86, 219; and Emmet Larkin, *The Historical Dimensions of Irish Catholicism* (New York: Arno Press, 1976), p. 651.

18. Since the beginning of the 1800s, English government and business interests had been foisting off on Irish landlords a primitive and ruthless brand of capitalism based on laissez-faire economic ideology. This new capitalism, rooted in parliamentary enclosure laws that drove rural masses into urban manufacturing centers, worked for English landowners but not their Irish counterparts. Landowners in Ireland had neither the dubious blessing of enclosure laws nor the capital from a burgeoning market economy to spend on eliminating the strip farming (Rundale) system, in order to consolidate their landholdings. Moreover, Irish agricultural laborers did not have the opportunity of alternative employment in urban industries, and so they were predestined to disappear as a significant class of workers during the last half of the nineteenth century—a fate hastened by massive migration and death through starvation and disease resulting from the Great Famine. As of 1850, the only notable Irish industry, by contemporary British or American standards, existed in cities in northeast Ulster. And by the 1890s the south had still not industrialized to any great degree; there literally was no place for even the remnants of the "old Irishry" to go to find work in the land of Erin. See Philip Bull, *Land, Politics, and Nationalism: A Study of the Irish Land Question* (Dublin: Gill and Macmillan, 1996), pp. 8–18; and David Fitzpatrick, "The Disappearance of the Irish Agricultural Labourer, 1841–1912," *Irish Economic and Social History* 7 (1980): 66–92.

19. Donald H. Akenson, *The Irish Education Experiment: The National System of Education in the Nineteenth Century* (London: Routledge and Kegan Paul, 1970); Patrick Power, *A History of South Tipperary* (Cork: Mercier Press, 1989) pp. 170–181; Larkin, *Historical Dimensions of Irish Catholicism*, p. 652. By the end of the century only 16.4 percent of Roman Catholics could not read or write, compared to 45.8 percent in 1861.

20. Ironically, for the quarter century after the Great Famine, things went well for the Irish tenant farmers who remained. Their numbers increased steadily through the last half of the century as the number of agricultural laborers declined. The decline in farm laborers meant larger farms, larger harvests, higher agricultural prices, stable rents, and fewer evictions throughout the

late 1850s, 1860s, and well into the 1870s. Rural cottage size and education improved, as did health and education among the peasantry. Not that Irish life was fun and games in the immediate post-Famine decades. But it was marginally better, and it was that margin that produced rising expectations among farm tenants, moving them into organized political activity over land problems not possible before the Great Famine. See Fitzpatrick, "The Disappearance of the Irish Agricultural Labourer," pp. 84–85; Hachey et al., *Irish Experience*, p. 97; and Donnelly, *The Land and the People of Nineteenth-Century Cork*, pp. 66–92, 219, Larkin, *Historical Dimensions of Irish Catholicism* (New York: Arno Press, 1976).

21. J. J. Morrissey, "The Clonmel Rowing Club," in White, ed., *Clonmel Scrap Book*, pp. 181–197.

22. Alexander Mackintosh, *From Gladstone to Lloyd George: Parliament in Peace and War* (New York: Kraus Reprint Co., 1970; reprint of 1921 Hodder and Stoughton edition), pp. 56–60; Lord Eversley, *Gladstone and Ireland: The Irish Policy of Parliament from 1850–1894* (Westport, Conn.: Greenwood Press, 1971), pp. 370–373; and L. P. Curtis, *Anglo-Saxons and Celts: A Study of Anti-Irish Prejudice in Victorian England* (Bridgeport, Conn.: Conference on British Studies at the University of Bridgeport, 1968), pp. 49–65, 101–103. According to Curtis, behind the Parliamentary rhetoric of Unionists about the Irish being "little removed from savages," living with, and as dirty as, pigs, stood "ethnologists and historians, novelists and poets, literary reviewers and cartoonists who had contributed something to that Anglo-Saxon stereotype called Paddy. . . . [and] what really killed Home Rule in 1886 and 1894 was the Anglo-Saxonist stereotype of the Irish Celt."

23. *Nationalist*, January 2, 1895.

24. Mark Tierney, *Croke of Cashel: The Life of Archbishop Thomas William Croke, 1823–1902* (Dublin: Gill and Macmillan, 1976), p. 232. Unless otherwise noted all the general biographical material about Croke in the rest of the this chapter comes from Tierney's biography.

25. Ibid., p. 7.

26. Ibid., pp. 7, 11, 13.

27. Daniel O'Connell's Catholic Association inadvertently set in motion the social land and nationalism issues, convincing many that Ireland needed more political autonomy from England. The 1829 Catholic Relief Bill did not deliver all that the Catholic Association had wanted (and O'-Connell had promised). In return for Catholic seats in Parliament and government and professional opportunities, poor Irish citizens (so-called forty-shilling voters) actually lost their voting rights, and the Irish electorate shrank from over 100,000 to a little less than 16,000. The legislation not only outlawed the Catholic Association, it also forced Irish M.P.s to take an oath of allegiance before taking office. Moreover, the expense of campaigning and then living in London meant that most Irish Catholics could not afford to serve in London. Needless to say, the terms of Catholic Emancipation were less than magnanimous and did not foster a congenial union between England and Ireland. Nonetheless, Catholic Emancipation made Daniel O'Connell the counterpart of Andrew Jackson in the same time period in the United States, a defender of modern political democracy, and, in this instance, cemented Irish and Catholic priests and peasants into what would later become a formidable sectarian force for nationalism. See Hachey et al., *Irish Experience*, pp. 62–65; Philip Bull, *Land, Politics, and Nationalism: A Study of the Irish Land Question* (Dublin: Gill and Macmillan, 1996), pp. 6–7, 25, 28, 41, 56; and Foster, *Modern Ireland*, pp. 289–302.

28. Foster, *Modern Ireland*, pp. 289–302.

29. Curtis, *Anglo-Saxons and Celts*, pp. 108–116.

30. John O'Mahony, who had fled Ireland after the abortive 1848 uprising, took over and revitalized the New York–based Robert Emmet Monument Association. A Gaelic scholar, O'Mahony admired the Fianna warriors of Irish mythology and renamed the association the Fenian Brotherhood (superseded by the Clan na Gael in 1867). It was mainly through O'Mahony's efforts after he returned to Ireland that the term *Fenian* became permanently wedded to the symbolism and rhetoric of the Irish Republican Brotherhood. See Seán Nugent, ed., *Slievenamon in*

Story and Song (Kilsheelan, Ireland: Kilkenny People, n.d.), p. 33, 110–113; and Hachey et al., *Irish Experience*, pp. 90–91, 10.

31. Tierney, *Croke*, p. 17.

32. Ibid., p. 95; Whelan, "The Catholic Church," in Nolan and McGrath, eds., *Tipperary: History and Society*, p. 243; Larkin, *Historical Dimensions of Irish Catholicism*.

33. Emphasis on discipline and ritual gave greater control over behavior, indicated by the fact that by 1900 nearly 100 percent of the "old Irishry" attended Mass every week. The Church's devotional revolution would be followed in the last quarter of the nineteenth century by a "cultural and political" revolution of which Archbishop Croke was the undisputed clerical leader. Tierney, *Croke*, p. 95.

34. *NCS*, pp. 98–99. The Catholic Church preached against what it viewed as a pagan and barbaric pattern of traditional behavior among the Irish associated with a "mixture of naturalism, sympathetic magic, attachment to ancestral ground, communal involvement, and . . . gaiety and abandon." Thus, an Archbishop in Bray issued a pronouncement in 1811 against "keening," a Gaelic way for dealing with death as "unnatural shrieks and screams, fictitious and tuneful cries at wakes, together with the savage custom of howling and bawling at funerals." See Kevin Whelan, "The Catholic Church, 1700–1900," in Nolan and McGrath, eds., *Tipperary: History and Society*, p. 243; and Foster, *Modern Ireland*, p. 338; Larkin, *Historical Dimensions*.

35. Bull, *Land, Politics, and Nationalism*, pp. 40–42; Hachey et al., *Irish Experience*, pp. 102–103.

36. Foster, *Modern Ireland*, pp. 338, note vii, 383, note vii, 384, 390–391, 394; Hachey et al., *Irish Experience*, pp. 104–105; O'Shea, *Priest, Politics and Society*, pp. 168–176.

37. de Paor, *Peoples of Ireland*, pp. 262–263.

38. Ibid., p. 263.

39. Eversley, *Gladstone and Ireland*, pp. 50–87; Hachey et al., *Irish Experience*, pp. 106–107; Bull, *Land, Politics, and Nationalism*, pp. 45–53, 60–62.

40. F. L. S. Lyons, *Charles Stewart Parnell* (New York: Oxford University Press, 1977), pp. 57–87.

41. Eversly, *Gladstone and Ireland*, pp. 366–367.

42. Lyons, *Parnell*, p. 142.

43. Ibid., pp. 608–625 (quotation at 616). The most graphic example of Parnell's erratic political course can be seen in his treatment of his own sister. Having emerged as the leader of the Land League movement, Parnell rejected Gladstone's 1881 Land Act because it did not include over 100,000 tenants in arrears on their rents. Despite warnings from the government, he continued to endorse agrarian agitation, forcing Gladstone to arrest him. While cooling his heels in jail, Parnell's sister, Anna, stepped into the vacuum and created the Ladies' Land League in March 1881 in order to ensure agitation would continue. Under Anna Parnell's leadership, women managed the Land League finances, cared for evicted tenants, and put teeth into the "No Rent" policy by encouraging tenants to pay no rent at all. In spite of their successes, the Ladies' Land League was condemned by the Church "as unworthy of a child of Mary," but surprisingly, abandoned by Parnell, who tacked off in a different direction, dumping his sister's Land League without so much as a "thanks." Upon his release from jail, Parnell accepted Gladstone's 1881 Land Act, suppressed his sister's Ladies' Land League, and established the Irish National League in October 1882. The Land League movement was short-lived under Parnell because his commitment to violent agrarian agitation proved a short-lived interval before his conversion to parliamentary Home Rule. See Lyons, *Parnell*, pp. 177–180, 267.

44. Emmet Larkin, *The Roman Catholic Church and the Creation of the Modern Irish State, 1878–1886* (Philadelphia: American Philosophical Society, 1975), pp. 13–14.

45. Ibid., p. 14.

46. Ibid., pp. 28–29.

47. Ibid., pp. 17–18.

48. Ibid., pp. 20–21.

49. Ibid., p. 21.

50. Ibid., pp. 26–27.

51. Ibid., p. 29.

52. Ibid., p. 26. As for the one who stood "higher in the estimation of the Irish race" than he, Croke did not mention anyone specifically. We assume he referred to Archbishop John MacHale, the "Lion of the Fold of Judah."

53. Ibid., p. 46.

54. Ibid., pp. 50–51.

55. Ibid., pp. 51–52.

56. Ibid., pp. 69–71.

57. Ibid., p. 71.

58. Lyons, *Parnell*, pp. 178–179 (quotations).

59. Larkin, *Roman Catholic Church and Creation*, pp. 115–116.

60. Ibid. p. 126.

61. Ibid., p. 130.

62. Ibid., p. 162.

63. The four-day period between Parnell's release on May 2 and the Phoenix Park murders led immediately to the charge by the Tories that Gladstone's policy of reconciliation with the Irish Parliamentary Party had failed since there *had* to be a connection between the Parnellites and the secret society known as the Invincibles, which had planned and carried out the murders. In January 1887, the London *Times*, apparently in collaboration with the Tories, began to publish letters trying to discredit Parnell by implicating him in the murders. When these proved to be forgeries, Parnell was acquitted in February 1890 of all the charges brought against him. However, these murders hung like the sword of Damocles over the Parnellite movement for most of the 1880s. Lyons, *Parnell*, pp. 178, 186, 205–212, 227–228, 368–378; Foster, *Modern Ireland*, pp. 189, 244, 429–430; L. P. Curtis, *Coercion and Conciliation in Ireland, 1880–1892: A Study of Conservative Unionism* (New York: New York University Press, 1968), pp. 15, 182, 279–300.

64. Alexander Mackintosh, *From Gladstone to Lloyd George: Parliament in Peace and War* (New York: Kraus, 1970; reprint of 1921 Hodder and Stoughton edition), pp. 50–55, 76–77; Larkin, *Roman Catholic Church and Creation*, p. 184; and Mark Tierney, O.S.B., "Dr. Croke, the Irish Bishops and the Parnell Crisis: 18 November 1890–21 April 1891," *Collectanea Hibernica*, no. 11 (1968): 120–121. George Errington, an Irishman and Whiggish Home Ruler, lost his seat in Parliament in 1885 and became an unofficial British envoy to the Vatican.

65. Larkin, Roman Catholic Church and Creation, p. 186.

66. Ibid., p. 187, 189.

67. Eversly, *Gladstone and Ireland*, pp. 308–310; Malcolm Pearce and Geoffrey Stewart, *British Political History, 1867–1995* (London: Routledge, 1996), pp. 120–124; and Mackintosh, *From Gladstone to Lloyd George*, pp. 42–48.

68. Eversly, *Gladstone and Ireland*, p. 324; Power, *South Tipperary*, pp. 192–194.

69. The "Mitchelstown Massacre" occurred on September 9, 1887, at the trial of O'Brien and Mandeville who had encouraged the tenants on the Kingston estate to resist eviction in violation of the Crimes Act. These shootings by the police embarrassed the Conservative government, giving the Irish Secretary Arthur Balfour the nickname "Bloody Balfour," and consolidated tenant resistance under the Plan of Campaign. A subsequent government investigation criticized the RIC officers in the areas for being in a "very bad state of discipline and morale." See L. P. Curtis, *Coercion and Conciliation in Ireland, 1880–1892: A Study of Conservative Unionism* (New York: New York University Press, 1968), pp. 197–200, 223–224, 436–441; Donnelly, *Land and People*, pp. 341–347; and "John Mandeville," in Martin O'Dwyer, ed., *A Biographical Dictionary of Tipperary* (Cashel, Co. Tipperary: Folk Village, 1999), p. 251.

70. Eversly, *Gladstone and Ireland,* p. 368; Tierney, pp. 226–230. The details of the final 1895 settlement between Smith-Barry and his tenants can be found scattered for that year in Croke's Papers, Microfilm Reel 6013, National Library, Dublin. Also see Denis G. Marnane, "Fr David Humphreys and New Tipperary," in Nolan and McGrath, eds., *Tipperary: History and Society,* pp. 370–375; Denis G. Marnane, "Land and Violence in 19th-Century Tipperary," *Tipperary Historical Journal* (1988): 81–82; Power, *South Tipperary,* p. 194 (for Croke's quotations).

71. Eversly, *Gladstone and Ireland,* pp. 324–325.

72. Lyons, *Parnell,* p. 207; and Eversley, *Gladstone and Ireland,* pp. 299–310.

73. Ibid., pp. 334–337, 458–460.

74. Tierney, *Croke,* pp. 236–237.

75. Ibid., 237; and Tierney, "Dr. Croke, the Irish Bishops and the Parnell Crisis," p. 118.

76. Tierney, *Croke,* pp. 242–244; and Tierney, "Dr. Croke, the Irish Bishops and the Parnell Crisis," pp. 142–143.

77. Tierney, *Croke,* pp. 241, 245 (last quotation).

78. Ibid., pp. 243, 245 (second quotation).

79. Ibid., pp. 246.

80. Dillon letters to Croke and to M.P. William O'Brien, and O'Brien to Croke in Croke Papers, Microfilm Reels 6012–6013, and in the John Dillon Papers for 1891–1894—both at the National Library, Dublin; and Tierney, "Dr. Croke, the Irish Bishops and the Parnell Crisis," pp. 126, 128–129, 133–135.

Chapter Two

1. "Telling Letter from a Clonmel Priest," *Nationalist,* March 20, 1895; Mark Tierney, *Croke of Cashel: The Life of Archbishop Thomas William Croke, 1823–1902* (Dublin: Gill and Macmillan, 1976), pp. 240–241; O'Donnell to Croke, January 6, 1891, Mark Tierney, O.S.B., "Dr. Croke, the Irish Bishops and the Parnell Crisis, 18 November 1890–21 April 1891," *Collectanea Hibernica,* no. 11 (1968): 129–130; and O'Donnell to Croke, February 11, 1893, Microfilm, Reel P6013, Thomas William Croke Papers (microfilm and calendar for letters), National Library, Dublin.

2. James O'Shea, *Priest, Politics and Society in Post-famine Ireland: A Study of County Tipperary, 1850–1891* (Dublin: Wolfhound Press, 1983), 170–174; and Thomas E. Hachey, Joseph M. Hernon, Jr., and Lawrence J. McCaffrey, *The Irish Experience* (Englewood Cliffs, N.J.: Prentice Hall, 1989), p. 141.

3. Discussion of the social role played by the GAA comes from authors' interview with Dr. Patrick C. Power, June 16, 1999. By the late 1880s and early 1890s, the Church and the Fenians were still at loggerheads over the GAA, each side trying to control individual clubs. In County Tipperary, both sides fought to a draw. By 1890, fourteen of the thirty GAA clubs, mainly in the northern part of the county, were under cleric control; of the county's 1,500 members, 895 belonged to Church-approved clubs. *Cork Examiner,* April 10, 22, 1895; Croke to T. W. Finn, October and November, 1892, Croke Papers, Microfilm, Reel P6013; and Tierney, *Croke,* pp. 189–204, 258–260; and George Henry Bassett, *County Tipperary. One Hundred Years Ago: A Guide and Directory, 1889* (Belfast: Friar's Bush Press, 1991; reprint of 1889 edition, entitled *The Book of Country Tipperary*), p. 97. Like the other clerical patrons of the GAA, Croke had been invited to be one *after* the organization had chosen secular leadership. Priests began to work their way into leadership positions of individual clubs, and there is no doubt that anti-Parnellites made a great effort to rejuvenate the GAA following the decline in membership created by the Parnell fiasco. On August 31, 1892, Member of Parliament William O'Brien wrote to Croke that Maurice (first name is given as William in Bassett, *County Tipperary,* p. 97) Prendergast of Clonmel, the former GAA secretary for all of Ireland, wanted

to head this anti-Parnellite effort in the south and that his fellow M.P. John Dillon believed this a good idea. He noted that such activity was *not* to be political, but then added these somewhat portentous words: "If we are to hold our guard with the young men of the country we should be able to command men physically capable of defending themselves against organized intimidation." O'Brien also informed the Archbishop that various GAA groups would be approaching him, as a long-time patron, for advice and support. See John Dillon Papers, National Library, Dublin.

4. Croke to T. W. Finn, October and November, 1892 (quotations), Croke Papers, Microfilm, Reel P6013; and L. P. Curtis, *Coercion and Conciliation in Ireland, 1880–1892: A Study of Conservative Unionism* (New York: New York University Press, 1968), pp. 410–414; and Alexander Mackintosh, *From Gladstone to Lloyd George: Parliament in Peace and War* (New York: Kraus Reprint Co., 1970; reprint of 1921 Hodder and Stoughton edition), pp. 200–211.

5. *Clonmel Chronicle*, January 5, 1895.

6. The Paris Fund consisted of political money left after Parnell's death. Most of it (£20,000) was earmarked for tenant relief. There was another £14,000 in claims against the Fund. Croke was deeply involved in the negotiations over administering the Fund—negotiations that included gaining assent from Kate Parnell to the Archbishop's proposal, as well as from the anti-Parnellites Michael Davitt, John Dillon, and William O'Brien and the Parnellites Timothy Harrington and D. Kenny. In the settlement reached at the end of 1892, Croke was to act as umpire with respect to future disputes. See Michael Davitt to Croke, November 19 and 23, December 6 and 24, 1892, Croke Papers, Reel P6013; and *Clonmel Chronicle*, January 9, 1895. Parnellite leader William Redmond, head of the Irish League's central branch, chastised anti-Parnellite Tim Healy for humiliating Parnell posthumously, imploring Healy to come forward and rescue the great man's name from allegations of dishonesty. Healy responded that he wished to put down "the domination of individuals who denied the right of criticism." The dispute between Redmond and Healy erupted long after Archbishop Croke thought he had settled the dispute over the Paris Fund in 1892. Upon learning of this embarrassing breakdown of the 1892 agreement, former Prime Minister Gladstone warned his Irish allies that Home Rule would never pass if the Parnellite/anti-Parnellite split persisted. Every Irish Nationalist, he declared, should understand that discord meant "postponement of the Irish claims," and if any man could step forward and reunite the movement, he was obligated to do so. Those bound to discord, he warned, bore a "terrible responsibility." With this, Gladstone departed for the Riviera to rest. See Tierney, *Croke*, p. 244; Tierney, "Dr. Croke, the Irish Bishops and the Parnell Crisis," pp. 111–112; and Michael Davitt to Croke, November, 19, 23, December 6 and 24, 1892, Croke Papers, Reel P6013; and *Clonmel Chronicle*, January 9, 1895.

7. John W. Boyle, "Irish Rural Laborer," in Samuel Clark and James S. Donnelly, Jr., eds., *Irish Peasants: Violence and Political Unrest, 1780–1914* (Madison: University of Wisconsin Press, 1983), pp. 277–278, 332–335.

8. *Clonmel Chronicle*, January 9, 1895. The Guardian Board made every effort to replace perishable materials, such as thatched roofs, in constructing these cottages. Rents were as low as 1 shilling a week and each cost approximately £105 to build in the 1880s. After 1892, these cottages came with an acre of land. See Boyle, "Irish Rural Laborer," in Clark and Donnelly, Jr., eds., *Irish Peasants*, pp. 332–333.

9. *Nationalist*, June 11, 1888.

10. Ibid., January 9, 1895.

11. *Clonmel Chronicle*, March 20, 1895; *Cork Examiner*, April 10, 1895.

12. *Clonmel Chronicle*, March 16, 1895.

13. Ibid., March 13, 1895.

14. Death Registry, Book 5, p. 65, no. 323, Registry of Births, Marriages, and Deaths, Community Care Centre, Clonmel, County Tipperary.

15. *Clonmel Chronicle*, March 20, 1895; *Nationalist*, March 16, 1895.

16. *Clonmel Chronicle*, March 20, 1895.

17. *Clonmel Chronicle*, March 29, 1895.

18. Ibid.; *Daily Graphic*, March 30, 1895; London *Times*, March 30, 1895; and *Cork Examiner*, March 29, 1895. The Marriage Registry for the Fethard district lists Bridget's occupation as "housekeeper" and indicates that she was living in Cloneen at the time of her marriage in August 1887.

19. Marriage Registry, 1887, p. 2, no. 4. We have corrected the ages of Bridget and Michael Cleary and the Kennedy brothers using the Registry of Births, Marriages, and Deaths in Clonmel, the Clonmel Gaol Registers, and the Penal Record of Convicts at the National Archives in Dublin. Both Bridget and Michael were two years older than reported in all previous accounts because parish records for baptisms were used instead of actual birth records. According to the Birth Registry, 1867, Book 1, p. 94, no. 486, Patrick and Bridget Boland had a child named Bridget. There is no record of this child's death or the record of the birth of another child to them named Bridget two years later, so we believe she was born on February 19, 1867. In nineteenth-century Ireland, the gap between the birth of a child and when it was baptized ranged from a few months to a few years. Births were not registered in Ireland until 1864, so for the older characters in this story, we used their police records or the 1901 Census, and only as a last resort consulted baptismal records for their approximate ages.

20. John Dunne's medical history can be found in the Penal Record of Convicts [PEN] 1897/110 in the National Archives, Dublin. His relationship to Patrick Boland and to the Kennedys can be found in Michael Cleary's Petition for early release, June 28, 1905 (no. 9109), PEN 1910/28.

21. Boyle, "Irish Rural Laborer," in Clark and Donnelly, Jr., eds., *Irish Peasants*, pp. 332–333; and *Nenagh News*, March 30, 1895.

22. Cornelius F. Ryan Deposition, April 14, 1895, Crown Files Assizes, 1895, National Archives, Dublin; London *Times*, March 30, 1895; and *Cork Examiner*, March 30, 1895. Most of the regional newspapers reported positively on the relationship between the Clearys in contrast to couples whose disputes attracted the attention of neighbors and the local police. Maria Luddy, "Women and Work in Clonmel: Evidence from the 1881 Census," *Tipperary Historical Journal* (1993): 95–101. According to Luddy's figures for Clonmel from the 1881 Census, 1,246 or 40 percent of all working women in Clonmel were domestics, while only 195 were milliners, dressmakers, or staymakers, and another 108 were shirtmakers or seamstresses. Since sewing could be done at home, more and more young women became seamstresses with minimal apprenticeships compared to those who worked for established businesses in town. There is no evidence indicating that Bridget ever worked in Clonmel for a draper, milliner, or dressmaker; rather she appears to have successfully worked on a piece basis out of her home, selling clothes in the Ballyvadlea/Cloneen area. For other information about working women in late nineteenth-century Ireland, see Mary E. Daly, "Women in the Irish Workforce from Pre-industrial to Modern Times," *Saothar* 7 (1981): 74–82.

23. *Nenagh News*, April 13, 1895; *Cork Examiner*, March 29, 1895. Most of the region's newspapers commented on the Clearys' unusual economic situation and the reasons for it. Also see Angela Bourke, *The Burning of Bridget Cleary: A True Story* (London: Pimlico, 1999), pp. 41–43, 146–147, 229 fn. 23.

24. *Cork Examiner*, March 29, 1895, p. 6; and *Nenagh News*, April 13, 1895.

25. T. G. McGrath, "Fairy Faith and Changelings: The Burning of Bridget Cleary in 1895," *Dublin Studies* 71 (Summer 1982): 183.

26. Michael J. F. McCarthy, *Five Years in Ireland, 1895–1900* (Dublin: Hodges Figgis, 1902), p. 144.

27. W. Y. Evans-Wentz, *The Fairy-Faith in Celtic Countries* (Gerrards Cross: Colin Smythe-Humanities Press, 1977; reprint of original 1911 edition), p. 24. An Irish barrister, Michael J. F.

McCarthy personally observed Irish beliefs in fairies and witches in his firsthand account, *Five Years in Ireland*, pp. 141–194.

28. Ibid., p. 70.

29. Ibid.

30. Ibid., pp. 242–243.

31. Ibid., p. 61.

32. Ibid., p. 77.

33. Ibid., pp. 75, 332–333.

34. Ibid., pp. 72–73.

35. Ibid., p. 251.

36. Ibid., pp. 244–253.

37. For confirmation and expansion of Evans-Wentz's views about the origins of fairies and their relationship to the changeling phenomenon, see Carole G. Silver, *Strange and Secret Peoples: Fairies and Victorian Consciousness* (New York: Oxford University Press, 1999), pp. 33–87.

38. Edward Walsh, "The Fairy Nurse," in William Butler Yeats, ed., *Irish Fairy and Folk Tales* (New York: Barnes & Noble, 1993), p. 69.

39. Evans-Wentz, *Fairy-Faith*, p. 71.

40. Ibid., p. 74.

41. Letitia Maclintock, "Jamie Freed and the Young Lady" in Yeats, *Irish Fairy & Folk Tales*, pp. 70–77.

42. Johanna Burke Deposition, March 25, 26, 1895; Mary Kennedy Deposition, April 5, 6, 1895, Crown Files Assizes, 1895, National Archives, Dublin.

43. Brendan Long/Gerry McCarthy Transcript (hereafter, Long Transcript), p. 52.

44. Patrick Logan, *The Old Gods: The Facts about Irish Fairies* (Belfast: Appletree Press, 1981), p. 98.

45. *Nenagh News*, March 30, 1895; *Irish Times*, April 2, 3, 1895; and Thomas Smyth Deposition, April 2, 1895, William Simpson Deposition, April 1, 1895, Crown Files Assizes, 1895, National Archives, Dublin.

46. Patrick Kennedy, "The Fairy Child," *Legends of Irish Witches and Fairies* (Dublin: Mercier Press, 1976), pp. 47–52.

47. Kennedy, "The Woman in White," *Legends*, pp. 37–38.

48. Logan, *Old Gods*, p. 112.

49. Jim McGrath of Cloneen and Patrick C. Power of Ballyneale both told the authors about the stigma attached to having tuberculosis in interviews on June 18 and 19, 1999.

50. Herbert Butler, "The Eggman and the Fairies," in R. F. Foster, ed., *The Sub-Prefect Should Have Held His Tongue and Other Essays* (London: Allen Lane and Penguin Press, 1990), p. 104.

51. Bourke, *Burning of Bridget Cleary*, pp. 85–86, 135–136.

52. Victor Anthony Walsh, "Across 'The Big Wather': Irish Community Life in Pittsburgh and Allegheny City, 1853–1885," Ph.D. dissertation, University of Pittsburgh, 1983, pp. 23–24, 42; and Owens Davies, "Urbanization and the Decline of Witchcraft: An Examination of London," *Journal of Social History* 30, no. 3 (Spring 1971): 597–617.

53. If Bridget and Simpson had been lovers, the prosecution would have had to think twice about using him as a witness against the two peasant families involved—that is, on the grounds of conflict of interest, the defense could argue he testified seeking revenge against the murderers of his lover. The prosecution also would have risked compromising its case if their relationship was revealed in the depositions or at trial.

54. *Clonmel Chronicle*, March 13, 1985; *Nationalist*, March 16, 1895; *Irish World and American Industrial Liberator*, April 13, 1895; and Registry of Deaths, Book 5, no. 323, p. 65, Community Care Centre, Clonmel, County Tipperary. James Egan, Jim McGrath of Cloneen, and Patrick C. Powers of Ballyneale, all told us that they believed Michael Cleary had been motivated out of jealousy over some anonymous lover or lovers of his wife. Interviews with authors, June 18 and 19, 1999.

55. Butler, "The Eggman and the Fairies," *Sub-Prefect*, p. 104. The most recent summary of the views of past and present ethnographers and cultural historians can be found in Silver, *Strange and Secret Peoples.*

Chapter Three

The events described in this chapter are drawn from sworn depositions and reported court testimony taken from witnesses involved in the trial resulting from the death of Bridget Cleary. English law did not require official transcripts from the magisterial inquiry or the South Riding Quarter Session Court of County Tipperary—even in capital offenses where hanging was the mandatory penalty. Therefore, the most complete record of the Cleary incident comes from handwritten depositions and from articles by newspaper reporters, some of whom doubled as court stenographers. When editors realized the magnitude of the case, correspondents from across Ireland and England flocked to Clonmel. Their accounts augment the depositions and also indicate how the case was used politically by the Church, politicians, and the British colonial government.

This account represents the authors' reconstruction of two trials—the fairy trial in the cottage at Ballyvadlea and the judicial trial conducted by the Crown. In our reconstruction, we follow the unfolding drama of the two trials, both presented in chronological order. The first is sketched from the point of view of the police, prosecutors, and judges, and describes public reaction to the case. It begins with the police investigation and culminates with the July trial of the nine defendants. The second trial takes the reader into the cottage at Ballyvadlea to witness the nine-day ordeal of Bridget Cleary, offering a rare glimpse into the proceedings of a full-blown fairy trial, which some have called the last witch burning in Western Europe.

1. By the spring of 1895, Ryan had been curate at the Drangan church for about a year and a half. In the depositions taken by Protestant justices of the peace or other Protestant representatives of the British legal system, Ryan was misidentified as the "co-adjucator," a misspelling of the word "co-adjutor," which referred at the time to a priest who was the assistant to a bishop and usually his designated successor. In this instance, Ryan was technically the assistant, a curate, to the local parish priest, Michael M'Grath. Names designating positions within in the Church hierarchy, according to Professor Emmet Larkin, an authority on nineteenth-century Catholicism in Ireland, were often confused, misused, and, in this case, also misspelled, by English authorities in Ireland.

2. *Nationalist,* January 30, 1895. The parish priest, Father M. M'Grath, was elected branch president.

3. Unless otherwise noted, most of the details of the incident in this chapter and Chapters 3, 4, and 5 come from the *original* handwritten statements of the accused or in the depositions of the crown witnesses in March, April, and May 1895. They can be found in the Crown Files Assizes 1895 at the National Archives in Dublin. These depositions were read aloud in court, and witnesses were questioned and cross-examined on the basis of them. So when we say someone "testified," we are either referring to the original statement of the accused or a deposition of a witness or the answers they gave in the legal proceedings based on these documents. Ryan gave his deposition in Fethard on April 14, 1895.

4. John Dunne Statement of the Accused, April 3, 1895; Cornelius F. Ryan Deposition, April 14, 1895; Crown Files Assizes 1895, National Archives, Dublin; Michael J. F. McCarthy, *Five Years in Ireland, 1895–1900* (Dublin: Hodges Figgis, 1902), p. 164; and *Irish Times,* April 2, 1985.

5. Carole G. Silver, *Strange and Secret Peoples: Fairies and Victorian Consciousness* (New York: Oxford University Press, 1999), pp. 60–87.

6. Patrick Kennedy, *Legends of Irish Witches and Fairies* (Dublin: Mercier Press, 1976), pp. 62–64.

7. Ibid., pp. 47–52.

8. Mark Tierney, *Croke of Cashel: The Life of Thomas William Croke, 1823–1902* (Dublin: Gill and Macmillan, 1976), p. 18.

9. Henry Glassie, ed. *Irish Folktales* (New York: Pantheon, 1985), pp. 145–146.

10. John Dunne, Statement of the Accused, April 5, 1895, Crown Files Assizes 1895, National Archives, Dublin.

11. Thomas E. Hachey, Joseph M. Hernon, Jr., and Lawrence J. McCaffrey, *The Irish Experience* (Englewood Cliffs, N.J.: Prentice Hall, 1989), p. 56; R. F. Foster, *Modern Ireland, 1600 1972* (New York: Penguin, 1989; reprint of 1988 Viking edition), pp. 294–295.

12. Clonmel Gaol Registers, No. 13, General Register, January 1, 1894–January 28, 1903, and Limerick Gaol Registers, No. 20, General Register, December 25, 1894–December 31, 1898, National Archives, Dublin.

13. R. McAnnlly, Jr., "The Police," in *Irish Wonders* (New York: Gramercy Book, 1996; reprint of 1888 Houghton Mifflin edition), pp. 30–31.

14. Ibid., p. 33.

15. For all of Egan's activities that day, see Patrick Egan Deposition, April 4, 1895, Crown Files Assizes 1895; *Irish Times*, March 27, 1895.

16. *Freeman Journal*, April 5, 1895.

17. *Clonmel Chronicle*, January 9, 1895.

18. Ibid., February 6, 1895.

19. *Nationalist*, March 16, 1895.

20. Ibid., March 20, 1895.

21. Ibid. Homilies on St. Patrick's Day departed from the Gospels (which, after all, did not include Ireland's patron saint), to stress the virtues of the only Saint to have converted an entire nation to Catholicism in his own lifetime. So important a day was this in Irish religious history, the *Nationalist* reported on March 20 that at the conclusion of Solemn Vespers on the Saturday before St. Patrick's Day, bishops and priests announced that the Church, as was traditional, had "relaxed the rigour of the Lenten times, in order to enable the Catholics of this country to celebrate the feast of their National Apostle."

22. *Boston Daily Globe*, March 18, 1895, evening edition, p. 6.

23. Ibid. The phrase "Putting Up the Shutters" comes from a chapter title used by Tierney to describe Croke's activities from 1892 to 1897. See Tierney, *Croke of Cashel*, p. 247.

24. *Nationalist*, March 16, 1895.

25. Ibid.

26. Victor Anthony Walsh, "Across 'The Big Wather': Irish Community Life in Pittsburgh and Allegheny City, 1853–1885," Ph.D. dissertation, University of Pittsburgh, 1983, pp. 13–19. According to Walsh's summary of economic literature, beneath the largely absentee English landlords were "middlemen, land agents and other supervisory personnel." Most of these "intermediate landlords" were Protestants, with a sprinkling of Catholics, and all of them held long-term leases of ninety-nine years or more based on outdated, eighteenth-century land values. This group profited by endlessly subdividing their holdings based on short-term leases. Approximately 20 percent of the leaseholders were known as "strong or snug" farmers with 21- or 31-year leases from either absentee proprietors or from rack-renting middlemen. They lived in "comparative comfort" of the type that C. J. Kickham later idealized in his novels and which are discussed in Chapter 7. They generally emulated genteel English country life; preferred marriage arranged late, rather than the customary random, early marriages; and practiced a form of primogeniture to prevent further subdivision of their holdings. The vast majority of the "old Irishry" fell into the destitute categories of "smallholders, cottiers, and laborers" before the Great Famine. Smallholders were the typical tenant farmers who had short-term leases from middlemen on one to ten acres depending on the region of the country and lived "under the relentless onus of rents and dearth of capital," which forced them to practice primitive, land-depleting

farming. The cottier was basically a "bound laborer" who rented a cabin and small potato garden from a "strong or snug" farmer at inflated rates in exchange for the labor of the entire family. Finally, there was the "unbound laborer" who held land under the conacre system, meaning only seasonal use of the land for which he had to pay inflated rents from the sale of his crops, eggs, garden products, and the family pig. Essentially an "indigent speculator," the unbound tenant laborer and his family became beggars if his crop failed because he could neither pay his rent nor feed his family. Both cottiers and unbound laborers were known as tenant laborers. Some cottiers and smallholders also held some of their land in conacre at exorbitant rents.

27. James S. Donnelly, Jr., *The Land and the People of Nineteenth-Century Cork: The Rural Economy and the Land Question* (London: Routledge & Kegan Paul, 1975), pp. 6–26; and Emmet Larkin, trans. and ed., *Alexis de Tocqueville's Journey in Ireland* (Washington, D.C.: Catholic University of America Press, 1990), pp. 14, 75–77, 95, 102, passim; and Walsh, "Across The Big Wather,'" p. 19 (last quotation).

28. L. P. Curtis, Jr., *Anglo-Saxons and Celts: A Study of Anti-Irish Prejudice in Victorian England* (Bridgeport, Conn.: Conference on British Studies at the University of Bridgeport, 1968), pp. 49–65.

29. David Fitzpatrick, "The Disappearance of the Irish Agricultural Labourer, 1841–1912," *Irish Economic and Social History* 7 (1980): 67; and Donnelly, *The Land and the People of Nineteenth-Century Cork*, p. 14.

30. Foster, *Modern Ireland*, p. 292; Hachey at al., *Irish Experience*, p. 42; Samuel Clark and James S. Donnelly, Jr., eds., *Irish Peasants: Violence and Political Unrest, 1780–1914* (Madison: University of Wisconsin Press, 1983), pp. 25–26; Maurice Bric, "The Whiteboy Movement, 1760–1780," in William Nolan and Thomas G. McGrath, eds., *Tipperary: History and Society: Interdisciplinary Essays on the History of an Irish County* (Dublin: Geography Publications, 1985), pp. 148–184; Maureen Wall, "The Whiteboys" and Joseph Lee, "The Ribbonmen"—both in T. Desmond Williams, ed., *Secret Societies in Ireland* (Dublin: Gill and Macmillan, 1973), pp. 13–35; Gael E. Christianson, "Secret Societies in Ireland, 1790–1840," *Agricultural History* 46 (July 1972): 369–384; and Carlo Gébler, *How to Murder a Man* (London: Abacus, 1999; reprint of 1998 Little, Brown and Company edition).

31. Paul E. W. Roberts, "Caravats and Shanavests," in Clark and Donnelly, *Irish Peasants: Violence and Political Unrest*, pp. 64–97.

32. Thomas P. Power, *Land, Politics and Society in Eighteenth-Century Tipperary* (Oxford: Clarendon Press, 1993), pp. 177–188; Roberts, "Caravats and Shanavests," p. 69, n. 12 (magistrate quotation); Hachey et al., *The Irish Experience*, pp. 42 (Burke quotation), 56. The bulk of the Whiteboy violence in southern County Tipperary occurred in the towns of Fethard and Clonmel. See map in Bric, "Whiteboy Movement," Nolan and McGrath, eds., *Tipperary*, pp. 164–165.

33. Foster, *Modern Ireland*, pp. 289, 293–294. Peel, Lewis, and Ribbonman quotations, pp. 320–321.

34. The dissipation of random, rural violence was evident during the Great Famine, when food riots broke out throughout Ireland with little bloodshed, perhaps because the hardest hit among the poor quickly died or became demoralized and docile. This, however, did not prevent English authorities from boasting that they "exercised great forbearance in mastering the hunger-crazed, violence-prone" crowds. By 1848–1849 the starving and diseased were too feeble to carry out mass demonstrations for food and simply resorted to furtive turnip, grain, and animal thefts. Although the lower tier of the peasant class was bound for extinction, in some areas, such as that around Slievenamon, the rural peasantry remained strong enough to disrupt the countryside until late in the century. Denis G. Marnane, "Land and Violence in 19th Century Tipperary," *Tipperary Historical Journal* (1988): 53–78; Clark and Donnelly, eds., *Irish Peasants*, pp. 25–26; and Donnelly, *Land and the People of Nineteenth Century Cork*, pp. 87–91.

35. Marnane, "Land and Violence in 19th Century Tipperary," *Tipperary Historical Journal* (1988): 78–82; and *Nationalist*, Saturday, March 16, 1895.

36. Croke Papers, Resolutions by Bishops at Maynooth, January 4, 1895, plus testimonials and letters about Croke's approaching jubilee, Microfilm Reel P6013; National Library, Dublin; and *Nationalist,* Saturday, March 16, 1895.

37. *Nenagh News,* March 30, 1895.

38. *Nationalist,* March 16, 1895.

39. L. P. Curtis, *Coercion and Conciliation in Ireland, 1880–1892: A Study of Conservative Unionism* (New York: New York University Press, 1968), p. 200; Angela Bourke, *The Burning of Bridget Cleary: A True Story,* (London: Pimlico, 1999) pp. 119–120.

40. Registry of Births, 1885–1895, Fethard District, Community Care Centre, Clonmel.

41. Burke Deposition, March 19, 1895, Crown File Assizes 1895, National Archives, Dublin.

42. *Nenagh News,* March 30, 1895.

43. Donnelly, *Land and the People of Nineteenth Century Cork,* p. 324; *Nationalist,* June 13, 1894; and Patrick C. Power, "1829 in Tipperary" in Kickham Centenary Committee, eds., *Knocknagow Remembers* (Clonmel: *Nationalist* Press, 1982), p. 40. On occasion evicted tenants became care-takers on the land from which they had been ejected. There was a significant legal difference between being a caretaker and full tenant; the former could be evicted without notice; a tenant had to be given notice and usually had six months to redeem the land after being evicted if he paid arrears and costs. So an Irish tenant who became a caretaker not only placed himself in greater legal jeopardy, but also was even more resented by the Irish as an interloper than an English caretaker because he began to function as an agent of the British government. See W. E. Vaughn, *Landlords and Tenants in Mid-Victorian Ireland* (Oxford: Clarendon Press, 1994), pp. 23, 37.

44. Simpson Depositions, March 18, April 1, 1895, Crown File Assizes 1895, National Archives, Dublin.

45. *Freeman's Journal,* March 25, 1895.

46. Burke Deposition, May 21, 1895, Crown File Assizes 1895, National Archives, Dublin.

47. Burke Deposition, March 19, 1895, Crown File Assizes 1895, National Archives, Dublin.

48. Apparently by the time of the magisterial inquiry, Johanna Burke was more compliant. At least this is how the reporter from the *Dublin Evening Mail* perceived Burke's testimony. Obviously, she was forced to comply in order to help the cause of her mother and brothers. See Bourke, *Burning of Bridget Cleary,* p. 126.

49. *Nationalist,* March 20, 1895.

50. John Dunne probably also went to the fort with Cleary and the Kennedys, but by the time he talked with authorities he was trying to distance himself from the man for whom he had served as best man back in 1887. John Dunne Statement of the Accused, April 3, 1895, Crown Files Assizes 1895. The phrase "out the mountain" was explained to authors by historian Patrick C. Power in a letter dated August 9, 1999, and in our interview with him on June 13, 1999.

51. *Clonmel Chronicle,* March 20, 1985.

52. *Nenagh News,* March 30, 1895. For a similar tour conducted with another reporter by Simpson see *Cork Examiner,* March 30, 1895.

53. Rogers Deposition, April 2, 1895, Crown File Assizes 1895, National Archives, Dublin; *Daily Graphic,* March 30, 1895, p. 20.

54. Ibid.; descriptions from coroner's inquest and magisterial inquiry.

Chapter Four

1. L. P. Curtis, Jr. *Anglo-Saxons and Celts: A Study of Anti-Irish Prejudice in Victorian England* (Bridgeport, Conn.: Conference on British Studies at the University of Bridgeport, 1968), p. 54.

2. Unless otherwise noted, all details and descriptions in this chapter are taken from our reconstruction of events based on depositions and cross-examination of witnesses, statements of the accused, prison records, newspapers, Brendan Long's trial transcript, and Rory Fitzpatrick's compilation of media coverage. Some of this material was not made public during either the magisterial inquiry or the trial. Only information that is unique to a single source will be footnoted.

3. Brendan Long/Gerry McCarthy Transcript (hereafter, Long Transcript), pp. 5–6, in authors' possession.

4. Ibid., p. 6.

5. Ibid., p. 7.

6. Ibid., pp. 7–8; *Irish Times*, March 26, 1895; *Nationalist*, March 23, 1895; *Freeman's Journal*, March 25, 1895.

7. Generally speaking, the further away from Clonmel newspapers were, the less likely they were to have correct information and more likely to equate the incident with witchcraft.

8. *Cork Examiner*, March 29, 1895; *Nenagh News*, April 13, 1895; and Wansbrough Informational Statement (ordering Ganey's arrest), March 20, 1895, Crown Files Assizes 1895, National Archives, Dublin.

9. Ganey's arrest by English authorities carried with it such a stigma that a local Cloneen resident, Jim McGrath, told us some members of this fairy doctor's immediate family and other relatives changed their names to Gahan, Gainey, Geany, and other variations of Ganey. However, those who knew them at the time refused to call them anything but Ganey and actually joked in a sing-song fashion about the "Ganeys/Gahans/Gaineys/Geany." The 1901 Census listed the spelling of his last name and that of his two children as "Geany." This British affront to a respected herbalist constituted an official assault on folk practices that was as unprecedented as the "Tipperary Witchcraft Case," as the Cleary case was officially known, proved in the annals of British legal history. Local doctors knew that such herbal mixtures as Ganey made were not harmful, and usually helpful. Patrick C. Powers, Ph.D., a County Tipperary historian, told us many stories of the "cures" that Ganey had performed which still are passed down orally from generation to generation in the area. We retell one of them later in this chapter.

10. St. John Drelincourt Seymour, *Irish Witchcraft and Demonology* (New York: Causeway Press, 1973; reprint of original 1913 edition), pp. 1–2, 6–11, 16–18, 23, 57, 85, 247–249, passim. Among other things, Seymour points out that a blending of sorcery and fairy lore was much more common in Scottish witchcraft trials than can be found in the few that occurred in Ireland and, with the exception of a fourteenth-century sorceress, Dame Alice Kyteler of Kilkenny, there is a "barrenness of Irish records on the subject of sorcery and witchcraft." In fact, belief in witchcraft seems to have been introduced in Ireland by Cromwellian and Scottish colonists in the last half of the seventeenth century and reached a peak between 1661 and 1690, only to decline precipitously after that. Seymour attributes the "comparative freedom" of Ireland from witchcraft and demonology to its physical isolation, the lack of a strong Reformation movement, and "the total absence of literature on the subject" until the beginning of the nineteenth century.

11. *Irish Times*, March 27, 1895.

12. *Cork Examiner*, March 26, 30, 1895; *Nenagh News*, March 30, 1895.

13. *Nenagh News*, April 13, 1895.

14. *Cork Examiner*, March 28, 1895.

15. *Cork Examiner*, March 19, 1895.

16. *Nationalist*, April 10, 1895.

17. *National Centenary Supplement, 1890–1990*, p. 8.

18. One such story appeared in the *Nationalist*, June 30, 1894, involving a wealthy young gentleman from the United States who was buying up land after evictions. It was predicted that this action would "unite the plucky people of Drangan once more and revive that agitation which made Drangan a hot place for grabbers and emergency men in the good old times of the Land League."

19. *Dublin Evening Mail*, March 28, 1895; *Irish Times*, March 29, 1895; *Nenagh News*, March 30, 1895. Curiously, neither of the two newspapers in Clonmel described the boycott by local priests that resulted in the surreptitious, non-Christian burial of Bridget Cleary. For the contemporary comment see, Michael J. F. McCarthy, *Five Years in Ireland, 1895–1900* (Dublin: Hodges Figgis, 1902), p. 171.

20. *Nenagh News*, March 30, 1895.

21. Ibid.; Angela Bourke, *The Burning of Bridget Cleary: A True Story* (London: Pimlico, 1999), pp. 127, 150.

22. *Cork Examiner*, March 9, 1895.

23. Penal Record of Convicts [PEN], 1910/28; and Convict Reference Files (CRF), 1910/Misc. 1619, Criminal Index Books, National Archives, Dublin National Archives, Dublin.

24. Mary Kennedy Statement of the Accused, April 5, 6, 1895, Crown Files Assizes 1895, National Archives, Dublin. Caitlin Matthews, *The Elements of the Celtic Tradition*. Rockport (Massachusetts: Element Books, 1989), pp. 5–6, 41–48; and John Dunne, "The Fenian Traditions of Sliabh-na-mban," in James Maher, ed., *Romantic Slievenamon in History, Folklore, and Song: A Tipperary Anthology* (Mullinahone, Co Tipperary: n. p., 1955), pp 62–94; and Death Registry, vol. 8, p. 72, no. 356 in Registry of Births, Marriages, and Deaths, Community Care Centre, Clonmel, County Tipperary. The Bolands had three boys born before Bridget Cleary but they do not figure in this narrative, having died or left the area before the 1895 incident that took her life.

25. Patrick Logan, *The Old Gods: The Facts About Irish Fairies* (Belfast: Appletree Press, 1981), p. 110.

26. Thomas Smyth Deposition, April 2, 1895, Crown Files Assizes 1895, National Archives, Dublin.

27. Caitlín Matthews, *The Elements of the Celtic Tradition* (Rockport, Mass.: Element Books, 1989), pp. 2–4, 11–12, 21.

28. Ibid., pp. 11–12.

29. Ibid., pp. 2–3.

30. Logan, *Old Gods*, p. 99.

31. Bourke, *Burning of Bridget Cleary*, pp. 63–64. Quotations are from Convict Reference Files (CRF), 1910/Misc 161 (hereafter, Cleary Petition), June 28, 1905, No. 9109, received by the Lord Lieutenant of Ireland, July 7, 1905, Criminal Index Books, National Archives, Dublin.

32. 1905 Cleary petition; Long Transcript, p. 52.

33. Ibid.

34. William Crean Deposition, April 5, 1895, Crown Files Assizes 1895, National Archives, Dublin; and McCarthy, *Five Years in Ireland*, p. 144.

35. William Crean Deposition, April 5, 1895, Crown Files Assizes 1895, National Archives, Dublin; and *Irish Times*, April 6, 1895.

36. Long Transcript, pp. 37–40; Magisterial Inquiry and Trial Description from Irish newspapers compiled by Rory Fitzpatrick, circa 1994 and given to authors (hereafter, Fitzpatrick Media Coverage), pp. 34–35, 44, 85–84; Thomas Smyth Deposition, April 2, 1895; Mary Kennedy Statement of the Accused, April 5, 6, 1895, Crown Files Assizes 1895, National Archives, Dublin.

37. Mary Kennedy Statement of the Accused, April 5, 6, 1895, Crown Files Assizes 1895, National Archives Dublin; Bourke, *Burning of Bridget Cleary*, p. 66.

38. Bourke, *Burning of Bridget Cleary*, p. 68.

39. 1905 Cleary petition.

40. Logan, *Old Gods*, pp. 96–99. The fairy dart was believed to be a physical object that one could hold in one's hands.

41. Ibid., pp. 90–91.

42. Ibid., pp. 94–95.

43. 1905 Cleary petition.

44. Burke Deposition, May 21, 1895, Crown Files Assizes 1895, National Archives, Dublin.

45. Patrick Kennedy, "The Changeling and His Bagpipes," *Legends of Irish Witches and Fairies* (Dublin: Mercier Press, 1976), pp. 54–56. As in the Cleary incident, a group of neighbors witnessed the exorcism.

46. For specific examples of how child changelings were treated, see Carole G. Silver, *Strange and Secret Peoples: Fairies and Victorian Consciousness* (New York: Oxford University Press, 1999), pp. 59–87.

47. Folk story told by Dr. Patrick C. Powers of Ballyneale to authors.

48. John Dunne Statement of the Accused, April 5, 1895, Crown Files Assizes 1895, National Archives, Dublin.

49. Ibid.

50. Mary Kennedy Statement of the Accused, April 5, 6, 1895, Crown Files Assizes 1895, National Archives, Dublin.

51. Logan, *Old Gods*, p. 99.

52. W. Y. Evans Wentz, *The Fairy-Faith in Celtic Countries* (Gerrards Cross: Colin Smythe Humanities Press, 1977), p. 49.

53. Fishwives had a reputation as notorious scolds. There were less than a half dozen female fishmongers in Clonmel. Michael Cleary, at least, may have been exposed to their vulgarities while working there and knew what his wife meant when she made this comment. See Patrick C. Power's letter to authors, July 26, 1999; and Maria Luddy, "Women and Work in Clonmel: Evidence from the 1881 Census," *Tipperary Historical Journal* (1993): 97.

54. William Butler Yeats, ed., *Irish Fairy and Folk Tales* (New York: Barnes and Noble reprint, 1993), pp. 221–222; and Powers to authors about meaning of "to make a hare out of a person," July 26, 1999.

55. Mary Kennedy Statement of the Accused, April 6, 1895, Patrick Boland Statement of the Accused, April 5, 1895, Crown Files Assizes 1895, National Archives, Dublin; and *Nationalist*, April 6, 1895. Boland testified that he attended the funeral, but for some reason appears to have arrived back sometime Friday morning in time to look in on his daughter, whom he found "grand," whereas the Kennedy boys came back much later. Conceivably, they simply stayed longer at the wake than he did.

Chapter Five

1. On disproportionate Protestant control of the Irish judicial system before and after the Great Famine, see Emmet Larkin, trans. and ed., *Alexis de Tocqueville's Journey in Ireland* (Washington, D.C.: Catholic University of America Press, 1990), pp. 21, 43, 101–107, 136; and Victor Anthony Walsh, "Across 'The Big Wather': Irish Community Life in Pittsburgh and Allegheny City, 1853–1885," Ph.D. dissertation, University of Pittsburgh, 1983, pp. 286–288, 343–349. For a satirical view of how justice was administered in Clonmel, see anon., "In Clonmel–The Assizes, 1830," in James White, ed., *My Clonmel Scrap Book*, 3rd ed. (Clonmel: Tentmaker Publications, n.d.), pp. 81–89.

2. Patrick C. Power, "1829 in Tipperary" in Kickham Centenary Committee, eds., *Knocknagow Remembers* (Clonmel: *The Nationalist* Press, 1982), p. 40; Power interview, June 19, 1999.

3. Unless otherwise noted, all details and descriptions in this chapter are taken from our reconstruction of events based on depositions and cross-examinations of witnesses, statements of the accused, prison records, newspapers, Brendan Long's trial transcript, and Rory Fitzpatrick's compilation of media coverage. Some of this material was not made public during either the magisterial inquiry or the trial. Only information unique to a single source will be footnoted.

4. Clonmel Gaol Registers, No. 13, January 1, 1894–January 28, 1903, National Archives, Dublin.

5. Information about the physical appearances and ages of the accused came from the following sources: Chief Secretary's Office Reports (CSORP), Ireland, Crime Branch Special (CBS), 1895, 9786/s; Convict Reference Files (CRF), Criminal Index Books, 1910/Misc. 1619; Penal Record of Convicts, 1897/110, 1910/28, National Archives, Dublin; and Registry of Births, Marriages, and Deaths, Community Care Centre, Clonmel, County Tipperary.

6. *Irish Times*, March 27 and April 2, 1895; *Cork Examiner*, March 29, 1895; and Clonmel Gaol Registers, No. 13.

7. *Cork Examiner*, March 29, 1895 (quotations); *Nenagh News*, April 13, 1895.

8. Magisterial Inquiry and Trial Transcript compiled by Gerry McCarthy, circa 1940s and given to authors by Brendan Long (hereafter, Long Transcript), p. 9.

9. *Daily Graphic*, March 30, 1895. None of the defendants or witnesses ever corroborated Simpson's assertion that Cleary "trusted" him enough to give him the key. As noted in Chapters 2 and 3, caretakers were generally disliked by tenant farmers and laborers, and Simpson's claim to be the friend of the Clearys and Kennedys comes only from him—not them.

10. *Dublin Evening Mail*, March 25, 1895; *Nationalist*, March 26, 1895.

11. Power, "1829 in Tipperary" in *Knocknagow Remembers*, p. 40; Angela Bourke, *The Burning of Bridget Cleary* (London: Pimlico, 1999), pp. 203–204; Angela Bourke, "The Burning of Bridget Cleary: Newspapers and Oral Tradition," *Tipperary Historical Journal* (1998): 117. There is a record for the death of a Johanna Burke, widow of labourer, 4 September 1914 at the Clonmel workhouse. It is not known if this is the same Johanna Burke. Clonmel Death Register, Book 32, p. 26, no. 130.

12. *Cork Examiner*, March 27, 30, 1895.

13. Minnie and William Simpson acquitted themselves well from the prosecution's point of view; they were upstanding members of the English establishment who did not believe in fairies, but could report condescendingly that their peasant neighbors did. William and Mary Simpson Depositions, April 1, 1895, Crown Files Assizes, 1895, National Archives, Dublin.

14. It should be remembered that Simpson told Burke to lie when she was first called to give a deposition on March 19 and not to mention that his wife took part in the proceedings. See Chapter 3.

15. Burke Deposition, May 21, 1895, Crown Files Assizes 1895, National Archives, Dublin. Burke was the only witness to implicate Minnie Simpson in the pagan ritual, and this fact was never brought out by the prosecution because it would have compromised the testimony of both Minnie and William Simpson. It is possible, however, that by the time Burke gave her May deposition, she deliberately tried to implicate the Simpsons in order to take attention away from her brothers' active participation on Thursday night.

16. Simpson's excuse for not interfering in the ritual can be found in Michael J. F. McCarthy, *Five Years in Ireland, 1895–1900* (Dublin: Hodges Figgis, 1902), p. 153.

17. Mary Simpson Deposition, April 2, 1895, Crown Files Assizes 1895, Crown Files Assizes 1895, National Archives, Dublin. Had the prosecution known that she had participated in the "cure," before Burke's May deposition, Mary "Minnie" Simpson probably would not have been called to testify.

18. Our reconstruction in Chapter 4 suggests that it was Michael Cleary who stopped at Drangan while returning from Fethard and requested Father Ryan's visit on Wednesday in anticipation of administering the Seven Sisters Kill or Cure potion.

19. Burke Deposition March 25, 26, 1895, Katie Burke Deposition, March 26, 1895, Mary Kennedy Statement of the Accused, April 5, 6, 1895, Crown Files Assizes 1895, Crown Files Assizes 1895, National Archives, Dublin.

20. Cathal Ó Baiull and Seán Ó Heochaidh, "The Fairy Shilling," Henry Glassie, ed. in *Irish Folktales* (New York: Pantheon, 1985), pp. 169–170.

21. *Clonmel Chronicle*, July 6, 1895; and *Cork Examiner*, April 3, 1895.

22. There were only three other references to "the people" in all the depositions gathered by Wansbrough, two of them from Mary Kennedy. After the burning Mary admonished Michael Cleary to reveal the site of the body because "the people," or the police, would eventually find the grave. In the other, she reported that Patrick Boland would not go to the police because "the people," meaning friends and family involved in the ritual, would think that he had betrayed them. These usages suggest that Mary Kennedy used the term "the people" to mean the police, authorities, family, and friends. When asked, she also adamantly denied the rumor that Bridget had been dressed up on Friday night "to go to the people," or "go to the fairies"—that is, to be taken to the Otherworld of the fairies.

23. Mary Kennedy, Statement of the Accused, April 5, 6, 1895, Crown Files Assizes 1895, National Archives, Dublin.

24. Smyth Deposition, April 2, 1895, Edward Anglim Deposition, April 5, 1895, Crown Files Assizes 1895, National Archives, Dublin. Tom Hogan was not deposed or called as a witness.

25. Smyth Deposition, April 2, 1895; *Cork Examiner*, April 3, 1895.

Chapter Six

1. Unless otherwise noted, all details and descriptions in this chapter are taken from our reconstruction of events based on depositions and cross-examinations of witnesses, statements of the accused, prison records, newspapers, Brendan Long's trial transcript, and Rory Fitzpatrick's compilation of media coverage. Some of this material was not made public during either the magisterial inquiry or the trial. Only information that is unique to a single source will be footnoted. We have also drawn upon stories and folk tales that would have been familiar to the participants.

2. Convict Reference Files (CRF), 1910/Misc. 1619, Cleary's petition, November 10, 1902, Criminal Index Books, National Archives, Dublin.

3. Peadar O Beirn, "How the Shoemaker Saved his Wife," in Henry Glassie, ed., *Irish Folktales* (New York: Pantheon, 1985), pp. 147–148.

4. *Freeman's Journal*, April 6, 1895.

5. Kate Purcell, "The Capture of Bridget Purcell" as told by T. Crofton Croker, in Glassie, *Irish Folktales*, pp. 143–145.

6. Burke Deposition, March 25, 26, 1895, Crown Files Assizes, 1895, National Archives, Dublin.

7. Burke Deposition, May 21, 1895, Crown Files Assizes, 1895, National Archives, Dublin.

8. Brendan Long/Gerry McCarthy Transcript (hereafter, Long Transcript), p. 12; *Irish Times*, March 27, 1985.

9. Burke Deposition, May 21, 1895, Crown Files Assizes, 1895, National Archives, Dublin.

10. Long Transcript, p. 12, and *Irish Times*, March 27, 1985.

11. Burke Deposition, March 25, 26, 1895, Crown Files Assizes, 1895, National Archives, Dublin.

12. Long Transcript, p. 12; *Irish Times*, March 27, 1985.

13. Ibid.

14. Burke Deposition, May 21, 1895, and Mary Kennedy, Statement of the Accused, April 5, 6, 1895, Crown Files Assizes, 1895, National Archives, Dublin.

15. Kate Burke Deposition, March 26, 1895, Crown Files Assizes, 1895, National Archives, Dublin; Long Transcript, p. 17, *Irish Times*, March 28, 1895.

16. Long Transcript, pp. 11–12.

17. Patrick Kennedy, "The Fairy Nurse," *Legends of Irish Witches and Fairies* (Dublin: Mercier Press, 1976), pp. 70–74.

18. Burke Deposition, March 25, 26, 1895, Crown Files Assizes, 1895, National Archives, Dublin.

19. James Egan, the great-grandson of Thomas Smyth, who now owns the property formally occupied by both Smyth and Thomas Hogan in 1895, told the authors in an interview on June 19, 1999, that the story about the dogs barking had been orally handed down within his family over several generations.

20. William Simpson Depositions, March 18, April 1, 1895, and Burke Deposition, May 21, Crown Files Assizes, 1895, National Archives, Dublin.

21. Burke Deposition, March 25, 26, 1895.

22. Dunne Statement of the Accused, April 6, 1895, Crown Files Assizes, 1895, National Archives, Dublin.

23. Patrick Kennedy, "The Recovered Bride," *Legends*, pp. 75–77.

24. Wansbrough Deposition, April 2, 1895, Crown Files Assizes, 1895, National Archives, Dublin.

25. Ibid.; and *Cork Examiner*, April 5, 1895.

26. Chief Secretary's Office Reports (CSORP), Ireland, April 2, 1895, telegram to Dublin Castle from the Under Secretary of State, Home Office, London, Royal Irish Constabulatory Office, 1895/6694, National Archives, Dublin.

27. *Cork Examiner*, April, 5, 1895.

28. Ibid.

29. Burke Deposition, April 4, 1895, Crown Files Assizes, 1895, National Archives, Dublin.

30. Chief Secretary's Office Reports, Ireland, 1895/6694, Gleeson to the Under Secretary, April 4, 1895, National Archives, Dublin.

31. *Clonmel Chronicle*, April 27, 1895, citing report of the Fethard Dispensary Management Committee to the Cashel Board of Guardians.

32. *Nenagh News*, March 30, 1895; Crean Deposition, April 5, 1895, Crown Files Assizes, 1895, National Archives, Dublin.

33. William Crean Deposition, April 5, 1895, Crown Files Assizes 1895, National Archives, Dublin; *Irish Times*, April 6, 1895.

34. Heffernan Deposition, April 5, 1895, Crown Files Assizes, 1895, National Archives, Dublin.

35. Ibid.

36. Edward Anglim Deposition, April 5, 1895, Crown Files Assizes, 1895, National Archives, Dublin.

37. Cleary Statement of the Accused, Deposition, April 5, 1895, Crown Files Assizes, 1895, National Archives, Dublin.

38. Long Transcript, p. 40; and Magisterial Inquiry and Trial Description from Irish newspapers compiled by Rory Fitzpatrick, circa 1994 and given to authors, p. 48.

39. *Irish Times*, April 8, 1895; Patrick Kennedy, Statement of the Accused, April 6, 1895, Crown Files Assizes, 1895, National Archives, Dublin.

40. James Kennedy Statement of the Accused, April 6, 1895, Crown Files Assizes, 1895, National Archives, Dublin; *Cork Examiner*, April 8, 1895. This appears to be the only newspaper account of Michael talking about his wife as a deceiver. However, we have quoted the original deposition and not the newspaper account, which is worded slightly differently.

41. Michael Kennedy Statement of the Accused, April 6, 1895, Crown File Assizes, 1895, National Archives, Dublin.

42. William Kennedy Statement of the Accused, April 6, 1895, Crown Files Assizes, 1895, National Archives, Dublin.

43. Ahearn Statement of the Accused, April 6, 1895, Crown Files Assizes, 1895, National Archives, Dublin.

44. *Nationalist*, April 10, 1895.

45. Patrick C. Power, "1829 in Tipperary" in Kickham Centenary Committee, eds., *Knocknagow Remembers* (Clonmel: Nationalist Press, 1982), pp. 39–40; and "The Convict of Clonmel," translated by J. J. Callanan, in Kathleen Hoagland, ed., *1000 Years of Irish Poetry* (New York: Konecky and Konecky, 1975), pp. 193–194.

46. Folk story told to authors by Dr. Patrick C. Power in an interview with authors on June 13, 1999.

Chapter Seven

1. *Clonmel Chronicle*, May 4, 1895.

2. *Nationalist*, May 15, May 20, 1895.

3. *Nationalist*, April 17, 1895.

4. Chief Secretary's Office Reports (CSORP), Ireland, Police and Crime Division (Ordinary), Crime Branch Special (CBS), 9854S, National Archives, Dublin.

5. *Cork Examiner*, April 22, 1985.

6. *United Ireland*, April 27, 1895; and CSORP, Ireland, Crime Branch Special (CBS), report #9854S, National Archives, Dublin.

7. *Clonmel Chronicle*, April 27, 1895.

8. *Clonmel Chronicle*, April 24, 1895; *Cork Examiner*, April 24, 1895. For more information about the Mitchelstown incident see above Chapter 1, note 69.

9. *Clonmel Chronicle*, May 1, 1895.

10. Ibid., April 27, 1895.

11. Based upon a complaint of the Local Government Board (LGB), Dr. Crean resigned his position as chief medical officer of the Fethard Dispensary on May 2, 1895. In September, the Cashel Guardians voted that Dr. Crean should receive an annual pension of £45, a sum that the LGB rescinded. Apparently Dr. Crean left the area following his removal. See Angela Bourke, *The Burning of Bridget Cleary* (London: Pimlico, 1999), pp. 70–71.

12. George Henry Bassett, *Bassett's Guide to Tipperary* (1889; Belfast: Friar's Bush Press, 1991), pp. 38–39.

13. Patrick C. Power, "Slievenamon in Myth and Legend," in Seán Nugent, ed., *Slievenamon in Story and Song* (Kilsheelan, Ireland: Kilkenny People, 1995), p. 13.

14. Caitlín Matthews, *The Elements of the Celtic Tradition* (Rockport, Mass.: Element Books, 1989), pp. 5–6; and John Dunne, "The Fenian Traditions of Sliabh-na-mban," in James Maher, ed., *Romantic Slievenamon in History, Folklore, and Song: A Tipperary Anthology* (Mullinahone, Tipperary: n.p., 1955), pp. 62–94.

15. Ibid., pp. 47–48.

16. Ibid., pp. 41–42.

17. Power, "Slievenamon in Myth and Legend," in Nugent, *Slievenamon in Story and Song*, p. 14.

18. Mary Condren traces the fall of the Goddess Macha to show how this ancient goddess gave way to the rising power of patriarchal tribes. See "The Curse of Macha," in *The Serpent and the Goddess: Women, Religion, and Power in Celtic Ireland* (New York: Harper and Row, 1989), pp. 30–36.

19. John Dunne, "The Fenian Traditions of Sliabh-na-mban," in Maher, *Romantic Slievenamon*, pp. 64–65.

20. Power, "Slievenamon in Myth and Legend," in Nugent, *Slievenamon in Story and Song*, pp. 13–15.

21. Mary Condren sees the story of Diarmuid and Grainne, like that of Macha, as one that presents the decline of the older matriarchal culture and the rise of the Celts. Condren, *Serpent and the Goddess*, p. 50.

22. John Dunne, "The Fenian Traditions; of Sliabh-na-mBan," in Nugent, *Slievenamon in Story and Song*, pp. 18–19.

23. Death Registry, Book 8, p. 72, no. 356 in Registry of Births, Marriages, and Deaths, Community Care Centre, Clonmel, County Tipperary. Bridget's mother died of influenza with "no medical attendant" but Bridget at her side.

24. Michael Hall, "Thomas Ryan: 'A Drangan Boy,'" in Nugent, *Slievenamon in Story and Song*, pp. 63–65.

25. *Clonmel Chronicle*, March 23, 1895.

26. *Nationalist*, March 23, 1895; *Clonmel Chronicle*, March 23, 1895.

27. *Nationalist*, March 23, 1895.

28. R. V. Comerford, *Charles J. Kickham: A Study in Irish Nationalism and Literature* (Portmarnock, County Dublin: Wolfhound Press, 1979). See Appendix Two, p. 224, for the details about why it was assumed well into the twentieth century that Kickham had been born in Mullinahone, which now annually celebrates his life and work. In fact he was probably born in the home of his maternal grandparents, either Mocklershill or, more likely, Palmershill—both townlands near Cashel in 1828.

29. Comerford, *Kickham*, p. 1317; Martin O'Dwyer, *A Bibliographical Dictionary of Tipperary* (Cashel, Tipperary: Fork Village, 1999), pp. 207–208; and Sheila Foley, unpublished biographical account of C. J. Kickham given to authors.

30. Comerford, *Kickham*, pp. 18–19.

31. Ibid., 18; and Mick Larkin and the Carraigmoclear Commemoration Committee, eds., *Battle of Carraigmoclear: Slievenamon, 1798* (Clonmel: Sureprint, 1998).

32. Thomas E. Hachey, Joseph M. Hernon, Jr., and Lawrence J. McCaffrey, *The Irish Experience* (Englewood Cliffs, N.J.: Prentice Hall, 1989), pp. 48–49; R. F. Foster, *Modern Ireland, 1600–1972* (New York: Penguin, 1989; reprint of 1988 Viking edition), p. 268, note xi.

33. Hachey et al., *Irish Experience* p. 49; Foster, *Modern Ireland*, pp. 175, note xxiii, 277–280; and James White, ed., *My Clonmel Scrap Book* (Clonmel, Tipperary: Tentmaker Publications, 3rd edition, 1995), p. 19.

34. Hachey et al., *Irish Experience*, p. 49; and Thomas Ryan, "Norton of Mullinahone: An Episode of '98," in Nugent, ed., *Slievenamon in Story and Song*, p. 93.

35. Hachey et al., *Irish Experience*, p. 49.

36. Charles J. Kickham, "Rory of the Hill," in Kathleen Hoagland, ed., *1000 Years of Irish Poetry* (New York: Konecky and Konecky: 1975), pp. 525–526.

37. Nugent, *Slievenamon in Song and Story*, p. 107.

38. Ibid., pp. 108–109.

39. Comerford, *Kickham*, pp. 21–23; Hachey et al., *Irish Experience*, pp. 90–91; and miscellaneous selections in Nugent, ed., *Slievenamon in Story and Song*, pp. 108–113.

40. For more detail, see Chapter 3, especially footnote 34.

41. Comerford, *Kickham*, p. 40.

42. Ibid., pp. 33–41.

43. Ibid., pp. 36–37.

44. William Murphy, *Charles J. Kickham, Patriot, Novelist, and Poet* (County Dublin: Carraig Books, 1976), no page numbers.

45. Miscellaneous selections, Nugent, *Slievenamon in Song and Story*, pp. 27–33, 110–113; Hachey et al., *Irish Experience*, pp. 90–91, 102; Comerford, *Kickham*, pp. 20–27, 55, 58–59. A copy

of the Fenian oath can be found in Alan O'Day and John Stevenson, eds., *Irish Historical Documents Since 1800* (Dublin: Gill and Macmillan, 1992), p. 74.

46. Comerford, *Kickham*, pp. 57–58.

47. Ibid., pp. 56–57.

48. Nugent, *Slievenamon in Song and Story*, pp. 115–120.

49. Comerford, pp. 58–59.

50. Ibid., p. 73.

51. Hachey et al., *Irish Experience*, pp. 103–104; Comerford, *Kickham*, p. 79; Nugent, *Slievenamon in Song and Story*, pp. 34–35.

52. Comerford, *Kickham*, pp. 82–83.

53. Ibid.

54. Quoted in William Murphy, *Charles J. Kickham: Patriot, Novelist, and Poet* (Blackrock, Dublin: Carraig Books, 1976 facsimile of 1903 edition), no page nos.

55. Comerford, *Kickham*, pp. 83–91; and O'Dwyer, *Bibliographical Dictionary*, p. 207.

56. Comerford, *Kickham*, p. 98.

57. Ibid., p. 101.

58. C. V. Comerford, "Why Is Kickham Remembered?" in The Centenary Committee, eds., *Knocknagow Remembers* (Clonmel, Tipperary: *Nationalist* Press, 1982), pp. 4–8.

59. *Knocknagow* is a testament to Kickham's memories of the depopulation of Ireland through deaths, evictions, and migrations that took place around Mullinahone during and immediately after the Great Famine. The area suffered the highest percentage of poor law famine relief in all of Leinster, and Mullinahone suffered a 23 percent loss of population, bringing it down to little over a thousand inhabitants. Weddings, which averaged thirty-five a year from 1840 to 1846, fell to thirteen in 1847 and nine in 1850. One nearby townland of Killahy, "which had 109 people living in 18 houses in 1841 was reduced to 20 people in 3 houses by 1851." By 1881 Mullinahone had a population of 733. This is the stuff of *Knocknagow*, whose first chapters were originally published in installments beginning on March 12, 1870, in the New York *Emerald* and subsequently in the Dublin *Shamrock*. However, both stopped carrying the series a third of the way through the novel, and it did not appear as a complete book until June 1873. See Comerford, *Kickham*, pp. 103, 197–199, and Bassett, *County Tipperary*, p. 405.

60. Charles J. Kickham, *Knocknagow: or, The Homes of Tipperary*, 24 ed. (Dublin: James Duffy, 1887 ed.), p. 9. The characters are based on real people Kickham knew in the area and some have been identified. For example, Maurice Kearney and his wife were modeled after Kickham's uncle Tom, Thomas Kickham of Clonagoose and his wife, Mary (O'Mahony) from Ballydunmore. One of Kickham's cousins, Clara Kickham, became their daughter, Mary Kearney, and another cousin, Gertrude, whom he had written about in the poem "St. John's Eve," became Grace Kiely, the daughter of a local doctor who was the only Fenian in the novel; Matt the Thrasher was based on a local athlete from Ballycullen known as Cuddihy; and Dr. Arthur O'Connor was modeled after Dr. Thomas J. Crean of Clonmel, a relative of Dr. William Crean. Phil Lahy was actually Denny Shea, a local authority on all the wrongs done Ireland, and about whom Kickham inquired while in prison. The priests were purportedly Dean MacDonnell of Cashel and Fr. Richard Cahill of Thurles. See James Maher, *Romantic Slievenamon in History, Folklore and Song: A Tipperary Anthology* (Mullinahone, Co. Tipperary: n.p., 1955), pp. 226–229. There was never a townland in Country Tipperary called Knocknagow or Cnoicín-a-ghabha, as it is known in Irish, but there is a Knickeenagow (the smiths' little hill), where Kickham's mother came from. Moreover, neither of the townlands near Cashel where Kickham may have been born (see note 28, above) have any claim to being the one and only Cnoicín-a-ghabha. In all likelihood, Kickham meant the name Knocknagow to refer to all the parishes of Mullinahone, Grangemockler, Drangan,

and Cloneen. See James Maher, "Return to Knocknagow: The Original Characters and Places," in Maher, ed. *Romantic Slievenamon*, pp. 226–229; and Comerford, *Kickham*, Appendix 2, p. 224.

61. *Knocknagow*, pp. 620–621.

62. Ibid., pp. 520–521.

63. Ibid., pp. 521, 523.

64. Willie Nolan, "Knocknagow: A Geographer's View," in Kickham Centenary Committee, *Knocknagow Remembers*, pp. 80–85.

65. Comerford, *Kickham*, pp. 197–223.

66. Ibid., pp. 157–158.

67. Ibid., pp. 160–161; and Most Rev. Thomas Morris, "Not All Melting Ruth," in Kickham Centenary Committee, eds., *Knocknagow Remembers*, pp. 68–70.

68. Comerford, *Kickham*, pp. 158.

69. Ibid., 173–174.

70. Ibid., p. 174; and Morris, "Not All Melting Ruth," p. 69. Comerford points out that, contrary to contemporary custom, the "practice of automatically receiving the remains of the Catholic dead in church had not yet been fully established in Ireland" by the 1880s. Therefore, when "a belated and peremptory request was made to have [Kickham's] coffin admitted overnight to the cathedral . . . the refusal did not amount to denial of an accepted right." The obvious political overtones of the request for an uncommon privilege was, therefore, logically turned down by Father Cantwell in the absence of Croke. It could also, however, have reflected bias against Kickham among priests in the archdiocese for his Fenian connection and anticlerical remarks.

71. Comerford, *Kickham*, pp. 172–177.

72. Ibid., p. 174.

Chapter Eight

1. Saint O'Toole was a twelfth-century Archbishop of Dublin who, upon the urging of Pope Alexander III, pressed the Irish clergy to pledge loyalty to Henry II of England in return for Henry's recognition of Rory O'Connor as the Irish high king of all unoccupied areas. See Thomas E. Hachey, Joseph M. Hernon, Jr., and Lawrence J. McCaffrey, *The Irish Experience* (Englewood Cliffs, N.J.: Prentice Hall, 1989), p. 10; *Nationalist*, June 12, 1895.

2. *Nationalist*, June 12, 1895.

3. *Nationalist*, July 6, 1895.

4. *Nationalist*, July 3, 1895. Archbishop Croke undoubtedly knew about the Cleary case, and probably wrote about it in letters, but unfortunately he destroyed most of his private correspondence from this period. See Mark Tierney, O.S.B., "A short-title calendar of the papers of Archbishop Thomas William Croke in Archbishop's House, Thurles: Part 3, 1891–1902," *Collectanea Hibernica*, no. 17 (1974–1975): 111–144.

5. Michael J. F. McCarthy, *Five Years in Ireland, 1895–1900* (Dublin: Hodges Figgis, 1902), pp. 172, 286–287; and Angela Bourke, *The Burning of Bridget Cleary* (London: Pimlico, 1999), p. 180.

6. *Nationalist*, July 6, 1895; and Henry H. Jones, April 2, 1895, Crown Files Assizes 1895, National Archives, Dublin. The American paper, the *New York Irish World and American Industrial Liberator* reported on July 27, 1895, that the weather in Clonmel had been unusually hot during June and July.

7. *Clonmel Chronicle*, July 6, 1895.

8. *Nenagh News*, July 6, 1895; Magisterial Inquiry and Trial Transcript compiled by Gerry McCarthy, circa 1940s (hereafter, Fitzpatrick Media Coverage), p. 53; Magisterial Inquiry and Trial

Transcript compiled by Gerry McCarthy, circa 1940s and given to Brendan Long (hereafter, Long Transcript), p. 46. Earlier in April the judge presiding over the Mayo Criminal Quarter Sessions also noted that crime was down in that county. In honor of there being no cases for hearing, the judge was presented with a pair of white gloves. See *Freeman's Journal*, April 2, 1895.

9. Long Transcript, p. 47.

10. Ibid., pp. 47–48.

11. Ibid., p. 44.

12. *Clonmel Chronicle*, July 6, 1895; and Fitzpatrick Media Coverage, p. 53.

13. Long Transcript, p. 53.

14. Fitzpatrick Media Coverage, p. 53; *Clonmel Chronicle*, July 6, 1895.

15. Fitzpatrick Media Coverage, p. 56; and *Nenagh News*, July 6, 1895.

16. Long Transcript, p. 51; *Clonmel Chronicle*, July 6, 1895.

17. Long Transcript, p. 49; *Clonmel Chronicle*, July 6, 1895; *Nenagh News*, July 6, 1895.

18. Fitzpatrick Media Coverage, p. 55.

19. Ibid., 56; *Nenagh News*, July 6, 1895. Burke had not previously testified about the family saying the rosary or Cleary's refusal to participate.

20. Long Transcript, p. 52; and Fitzpatrick Media Coverage, p. 57.

21. *Nenagh News*, July 6; and Long Transcript, 52.

22. Fitzpatrick Media Coverage, p. 58.

23. *Clonmel Chronicle*, July 6, 1895.

24. Ibid.

25. Fitzpatrick Media Coverage, p. 59; Long Transcript, p. 53.

26. Long Transcript, p. 54.

27. Ibid., p. 54.

28. Ibid., Fitzpatrick Media Coverage, p. 61.

29. *Clonmel Chronicle*, July 6, 1895; Fitzpatrick Media Coverage, p. 63.

30. *Clonmel Chronicle*, July 6, 1895; Fitzpatrick Media Coverage, p. 64.

31. *Clonmel Chronicle*, July 6, 1895.

32. Ibid.; Fitzpatrick Media Coverage, p. 66.

33. Long Transcript, p. 50. The report of the Crime Branch Special (CBS or Secret Police) investigation of this fire is missing from records at the National Archives in Dublin.

34. *Nationalist*, July 3, 1895.

35. James S. Donnelly, "Landlords and Tenants," in W. E. Vaughan, ed., *A New History of Ireland, 5: Ireland Under the Union, 1801–1870* (Oxford: Clarendon Press, 1898), pp. 338–343; Philip Bull, *Land, Politics, and Nationalism: A Study of the Irish Land Question* (Dublin: Gill and Macmillan, 1996), pp. 143–175; and Alan O'Day and John Stevenson, eds., *Irish Historical Documents Since 1800* (Dublin: Gill and Macmillan, 1992), pp. 73–74.

36. *Clonmel Chronicle*, July 6, 1895.

37. *Nationalist*, July 3, 1895. Healy, formerly a private secretary to Parnell, had been a thorn in the INF's side since 1891, when he established the *National Press* because he did not think that the *Freeman's Journal* was anti-Parnell enough. Even after the *Freeman* came out against Parnell, it continued to lose readers and income, especially after Healy successfully sued it for libel. Croke stepped in and insisted that the two publications amalgamate because he wanted to try to unify the Irish Parliamentary Party behind Gladstone's Home Rule Bill, but Dillon and Healy could not resolve their differences over control of the *Freeman* until 1893. See Mark Tierney, *Croke of Cashel: The Life of Archbishop Thomas William Croke, 1823–1902* (Dublin: Gill and Macmillan, 1976), pp. 248, 251–253. Through 1895, however, Dillon and Healy continued to fight one another for control of the INF and to complain to Croke and others about each other. See Dillon to William O'Brien, July 30, Au-

gust n.d., September 28, 1895, John Dillon Papers and Thomas William Croke Papers for 1891–1895 (microfilm and calendar for letters), Reel Nos. P6012–6013, National Library, Dublin.

38. *Nationalist*, July 17, 1895.

39. Ibid.

40. Ibid.

41. Ibid.

42. *Cork Examiner*, July 18, 1895. See Chapter 1, footnote 69 for more details of the Mitchelstown Massacre.

43. *Cork Examiner*, July 18, 1895.

44. Ibid.

45. *Cork Examiner*, July 20, 1895.

46. *Nationalist*, July 3, 1895.

47. *Nationalist*, July 17, 1895.

48. *Nationalist*, July 20, 1895.

49. Ibid.

50. Ibid.

51. *Nationalist*, July 17, 1895.

52. *Nationalist*, July 20, 1895.

53. *Nationalist* , July 27, 1895.

54. *Toronto World*, July 29, 1895.

55. *Nationalist*, July 27, 1895.

56. Hachey et al., *Irish Experience*, pp. 134–136; Malcolm Pearce and Geoffrey Stewart, *British Political History, 1867–1995* (London: Routledge, 1996), pp. 96–98; and R. F. Foster, *Modern Ireland, 1600–1972* (New York: Penguin, 1989; reprint of 1988 Viking edition), pp. 423–426.

57. *Nationalist*, July 24 and August 7, 1895.

58. *Nationalist*, August 7, 1895.

59. Ibid.

60. Ibid. The Portiuncula (meaning "little portion") Feast Day and Indulgence comes from the name of the small chapel within the basilica of St. Mary of the Angels, located near Assisi.

61. *Nationalist*, August 7, 1895.

62. *Clonmel Chronicle*, September 14, 1895.

63. *Nationalist*, March 20, July 31, 1895.

64. *Cork Examiner*, August 3, 1895.

65. *Nationalist*, May 15 and September 25, 1895.

66. *Nationalist*, September 25, 1895.

67. *Nationalist*, September 18, 1895.

68. *Clonmel Chronicle*, December 14, 1895.

69. *Clonmel Chronicle*, October 23, 1895.

Afterword

1. *New York Times*, December 25, 1997, February 1, 1998, October, 3, 1999; *New Yorker*, November 1, 1999. By the end of the twentieth century, witches had definitely gone mainstream with stories about covens, wiccans, and pagan communities commonplace, especially around Halloween in the United States in local newspapers and on the web. See *Missoulian* [Montana], October 21, 1999, and www.witchvox.com.

2. Convict Reference Files (CRF), Criminal Index Books, Penal Record of Convicts (PEN), 1910/28, National Archives, Dublin.

3. Ibid. All of the quotations from Cleary's appeals come from these CRF and PEN records.

4. Convict Reference Files (CRF), Criminal Index Books, Penal Record of Convicts (PEN), 1910/Misc. Dunne's files were mixed in with the CRF and PEN records for Patrick and Michael Kennedy.

5. Ibid. O'Brien's revised opinions can be found in the Dunne and Patrick Kennedy files.

6. Michael J. F. McCarthy, *Five Years in Ireland, 1895–1900* (Dublin: Hodges Figgis, 1902), pp. 461–462. McCarthy notes that Justice O'Brien died on December 5, 1896. Coincidentally, O'Brien also served as the judge in the controversial 1882 Phoenix Park murder trial. See Chapter 1, especially footnote 64.

7. Convict Reference Files (CRF), Criminal Index Books, Penal Record of Convicts (PEN), 1910/Misc. Dunne's files were mixed in with the CRF and PEN records for Patrick and Michael Kennedy.

8. Patrick C. Power, "1829 in Tipperary," in Kickham Centenary Committee, eds., *Knocknagow Remembers* (Clonmel: *Nationalist* Press, 1982), p. 40; Death Registry, Book 32, p. 26, no. 130, Community Care Centre; Irish Census, 1901, Thurles County Library; and Angela Bourke, "The Burning of Bridget Cleary: Newspapers and Oral Tradition," *Tipperary Historical Journal* (1998): 117, and Angela Bourke, *The Burning of Bridget Cleary: A True Story* (London: Pimlico, 1999), pp. 203–205.

9. Death Registry, Book 32, p. 26, no. 130, no. 25, p. 92, no. 457, Fethard District, Community Care Centre, Clonmel, County Tipperary; and Irish Census, 1901, 1911, Thurles County Library.

10. *Nationalist*, September 25, 1895.

11. *Thom's Official Directory of the United Kingdom of Great Britain and Ireland* (Dublin: Alex Thom, 1895, 1901, 1914), p. 800.

12. Michael J. F. McCarthy, *Five Years in Ireland, 1895–1900* (Dublin: Hodges Figgis, 1902), p. 167; and Bourke, *Burning of Bridget Cleary*, pp. 119–120, 227 footnote 11.

13. Authors' interview with John Holohan, June 14, 1999, Cloneen, County Tipperary.

14. *Irish Daily Independent* (Dublin), March 9, 10, 1896, pp. 5, 7; and *Cork Examiner*, March 10, 1896, p. 5; and April 16, 1986, p. 5.

15. *Irish Daily Independent* (Dublin), March 9, 1896, p. 5; *Cork Examiner*, March 10, 1895, p. 5; and McCarthy, *Five Years in Ireland*, pp. 176–177, 189.

16. *Irish Daily Independent* (Dublin), March 9, 10, 1896, pp. 5. 7; *Cork Examiner*, April 16, 1896, p. 5, and McCarthy, *Five Years in Ireland*, pp. 178–182.

17. McCarthy, *Five Years in Ireland*, pp. 183–185.

18. *Cork Examiner*, March 10, 1896, April 16, 1896; McCarthy, *Five Years in Ireland*, pp. 175–189.

19. Carole G. Silver, *Strange and Secret Peoples: Fairies and Victorian Consciousness* (New York: Oxford University Press, 1999); *New York Times*, December 25, 1997, Arts Section, pp. 1, 14, 1997, February 1, 1998, Arts Section, p. 48.

20. *Nationalist*, March 30, 1895; *Cork Examiner*, March 29, November 16, 1895; *Spectator*, April 6, 1895; *Daily Graphic*, April 13, 1895; *Regina Weekly Standard*, April 4, 1895; *New York Times*, April 22, 1895; *Boston Daily Globe*, May 2, 7, July 16,1895; *Toronto World*, August 8, 1895, and St. John Drelincourt Seymour, *Irish Witchcraft and Demonology* (New York: Causeway Press, 1973; reprint of original 1913 edition), pp. 61, 247–248. In 1944, Helen Duncan and Jane Yorke were convicted of practicing witchcraft during World War II under the 1735 Witchcraft Act. A spiritualist, Duncan predicted the sinking of a warship and officials feared she might reveal sites chosen for the D-Day landings in Normandy. Winston Churchill called the 1735 act "obsolete tomfoolery," and in 1951 replaced it with the Fraudulent Mediums Act. When Doreen Valiente, a self-proclaimed witch of the 1950s, died in Brighton, England, on September 1, 1999, her work was positively

reported in the *New York Times* as having contributed to feminism, environmentalism, and New Age views. London *Times*, January 31, February 4, 1998.

21. W. B. Yeats, *The Land of Heart's Desire*, 3rd ed. (Portland, Maine: Thomas Mosher, 1903).

22. Victor Anthony Walsh, "Across 'The Big Wather': Irish Community Life in Pittsburgh and Allegheny City, 1853–1885," Ph.D. dissertation, University of Pittsburgh, 1983, p. 80; and R. V. Comerford, *Charles J. Kickham* (County Dublin: Wolfhound Press, 1979), pp. 208–211.

23. Seán Nugent, ed., *Slievenamon in Story and Song* (Kilsheelan, Ireland: Kilkenny People, 1995), pp. 279–286, 291 (poem).

24. Registry of Births, Marriages, and Deaths, Community Care Centre, Clonmel, County Tipperary, and Infant School register, Drangan District National School, Drangan, County Tipperary. See Chapter 2, note 19.

Notes on Sources

Usually, when acknowledging their sources of information, academics name other academics, librarians, and archivists. We will, too, but first we want to thank the local people in the Clonmel/Cloneen/Mullinahone district who aided our research with their time, advice, wisdom, and patience as we trekked this eight-to-ten-mile-square area of County Tipperary, trying to come to terms with the meaning of the Bridget Cleary incident. Our physical contact with the land, especially seeing the ancient dwelling places of prehistoric Irish peoples—known as raths, hill-forts, or now, most commonly, fairy-forts—enormously enhanced our tactile understanding of what took place in Ballyvadlea in 1895. Being the first authors in over a century to see the inside of the Cleary cottage was the kind of memorable, emotion-filled event that scholars too rarely experience. For that incomparable opportunity we are deeply grateful to former County Councilman John Holohan of Cloneen, who opened the cottage to us so we could take pictures.

Our first local contact was Brendan Long, editor of the *Nationalist* in Clonmel from 1979 to 1990. He told us that even newspaper research would be difficult because, before the turn of the century, local newspaper accounts of the trial were painstakingly excised from original copies. Some undamaged newspaper runs were later found and microfilmed, but not all of them. For example, the second edition of the *Nationalist* for July 6, 1895, containing the results of the murder trial is missing from the microfilm edition, and crucial portions of the original copies of the *Clonmel Chronicle*, a publication of the Conservative and Landlord Party in the district, remain today deteriorating in the attic above the *Nationalist* editorial offices and in the building housing the Clonmel City Corporation. Even the reels for 1885–1896 of the microfilm collection in the current offices of the *Nationalist* are missing. Fortunately, we were able to purchase copies from a microfilm dealer in Dublin.

We interviewed Brendan Long at length in 1997 because in the 1950s he had attempted some of the first serious modern research into the "Tipperary Witchcraft Case." He told us that he had received a number of anonymous letters at that time warning him to "stay clear of Ballyvadlea" when he was writing a series of newspaper articles about "Famous Tipperary Trials." Later he wrote us that he had never intended in the 1950s to write about the Cleary case "because there were then quite a number of known relatives of the persons involved still living in our circulation area, a number of them in Clonmel itself."

As it turned out, Gerry McCarthy, a retired civil servant and amateur historian, had researched a number of articles of local interest for the *Nationalist* in the 1940s. In the process, he compiled a transcript of the trial made from 1895 newspaper accounts. It is Long's opinion that McCarthy thought the Cleary trial was "'no go' area" for his historical pieces and so he gave the transcript to Tommy O'Brien, editor of the *Nationalist* in the 1940s through 1953. O'Brien, in turn, thought so highly of Long's newspaper series on Tipperary trials that he gave the transcript to him in the event that it "would be of considerable use to me if at some future time a series on the Ballyvadlea case could be published." Long, who wrote such a series on the murder of Bridget Cleary for the *Nationalist* in 1989 using this transcript, told us in a July 10, 1997, letter: "Then and at all times since I had regarded this transcript as sourced in the contemporary newspaper accounts of the trial which, in accordance with the practice then and for a long time after prevailing, would have been a verbatim record."

In the early 1990s, Brendan Long had given his only copy of this same transcript to Rory Fitzpatrick, a TV producer in Belfast, for a documentary on Bridget Cleary, which never materialized. John Caden, then at RTE in Dublin, provided us with Fitzpatrick's address, and Fitzpatrick readily sent the same copy to us in the spring of 1997, along with his own reconstruction of the Magisterial Inquiry and Grand Jury trial from various Irish newspapers. He also told us about the copies of notes he took from the Crime Branch Special (Secret Police) of the Royal Irish Constabulatory documents about the burning of the Kennedy cottage and an investigation of the political activities, if any, of Patrick Boland and the Kennedy brothers. As of 1995, 1997, and again in 1999, these and other Secret Police reports connected with the Cleary investigation, in addition to the Precis of Information about Secret Societies for 1895, could no longer be located by the staff at the National Archives in Dublin and so we are grateful to Fitzpatrick for summarizing what was in some of them.

We have checked the Magisterial Inquiry and Grand Jury trial transcripts contained in Long's sole extant copy for authenticity and Fitzgerald's newspaper accounts against the existing microfilm copies of local, county, national, and international newspapers and, most importantly, against the *original* handwritten depositions taken from the defendants and crown witnesses in March, April, and May 1895. We then constructed a chronological account of the details of the last nine days of Bridget Cleary's life from all of these materials and presented them in Chapters 4, 5, 6, and 8 as both narrative and testimony. Our reconstruction of events is taken verbatim or closely paraphrased from the depositions—even though some of this material never appeared in the public testimony at the inquiry or the trial—in order to give the reader all the available facts about the incident, rather than simply the partial version that appeared in the newspapers of the time. Only by doing this did we believe that readers could make up their own minds about the various theories involving the motivations of Bridget and Michael Cleary, the Kennedy family, and their neighbors in Ballyvadlea and the surrounding area.

We believe that our reconstruction of events represents the most thorough and systematic analysis ever undertaken of the contradictions and inconsistencies in the depositions and cross-examination of all defendants and witnesses for the prosecution. This reconstruction allowed us to make a number of informed judgments about the inferior legal treatment received by the defendants, especially Michael Cleary, whose frantic efforts to bring a priest and doctor to the aid of his wife were not revealed in detail until a decade later when he petitioned for early release from prison. Our reconstruction suggests that Michael's defense attorney covered up his alcoholic doctor brother's inadequate performance of his medical duties when attending Bridget Cleary and that the prosecution deliberately chose to ignore the participation of caretaker Simpson and his wife in the pagan cure. Using Simpson as the star Crown witness without revealing that his wife had played a significant role in the Thursday night ritual made him an even more hated emergencyman among the Kennedys and Bolands. And if he was romantically involved with Bridget herself, his testimony against these families and Michael Cleary was even more suspect. These are only a few of the hitherto untold and very complex legal aspects of the Bridget Cleary story revealed here for the first time.

Of all the theories of what happened to Bridget Cleary that are discussed in chapter 2, we ruled out only one: *that this was a case of domestic abuse, so common in Ireland at the time.* Obviously, some criminals resorted to fairy beliefs to cover up questionable or illegal activities at the end of the nineteenth century in Ireland. In this instance, however, there is simply no evidence in police or prison records or from those who knew the couple and testified that Michael had verbally or physically abused his wife before the nine-day period that resulted in her death. To highlight the difference between the Bridget Cleary case and "typical" incidents of wife abuse involving gross assertions of patriarchal power having nothing to do with fairy beliefs, we cite a few of them in Chapter 4. Some ended in murder, but most did not.

Spousal abuse based on arbitrary male authority was a serious problem at the end of the nineteenth century in Ireland, but to narrow the significance of Bridget's Cleary murder to this single explanation panders to a politically correct trend at the end of the twentieth century to write about women as victims. Most important, it ignores a basic legal fact of the matter—namely, that authorities did not prosecute the case as one of abuse that ended in premeditated murder by the husband. They prosecuted, instead, an entire family for participating in a pagan ritual that resulted in homicide that may well have been unpremeditated and unintended because the defendants believed in the power of fairies to create changelings. We argue that the true power exercised in the Cleary incident was the power of fairy beliefs, which, at a critical juncture of Bridget's illness, overrode the individual power of the men in her life, and the collective power of the state, religion, and medicine. We do not claim originality with this interpretation. E. F. Benson applied it to the Cleary incident in an 1895 article and Carole G. Silver updates and expands on power relationships associated with fairies and changelings her 1999 book, *Strange and Secret Peoples: Fairies and Victorian Consciousness.* We can only hope that we have been able to integrate the importance of fairies and folklore with the political, socioeconomic, and religious events of 1895 in Ireland for those in the twenty-first century reading about this late-nineteenth-century family and national tragedy.

We are grateful to Brendan Long, therefore, for permitting us to use his trial transcript in our historical reconstruction process, and for suggesting that we talk with John Holohan, a farmer and county councilman for twenty-five years from Cloneen, whose father had attended the local National School and knew Bridget Cleary. He proved to be most generous with his time and family knowledge about the Cleary and Kennedy families of Ballyvadlea both times that we met with him in 1997 and 1999. He not only showed us the long-unoccupied Cleary cottage, but actually obtained a key to it so that we could photograph the interior. As we drove him around, John Holohan pointed out the exact location where the police found her half-buried, half-clad body, where her unmarked grave was in the Cloneen cemetery, where some of the hill- or ring-forts in the area were located, and the birthplace of the fairy doctor Denis Ganey in the Katylea area. Mr. Holohan also showed us foundations of both the Kennedy and Ahearn cottages in Ballyvadlea. Some of our fondest memories of him are of times spent drinking in local pubs, meeting his friends, and finally celebrating his retirement as a city councilman in June 1999.

Jim McGrath, a pub owner in Cloneen, stopped us one day as we were walking around Bridget's initial burial site at the junction of the low road to Cloneen and the one leading to the Cleary cottage. He denied the entire Ballyvadlea fairy story. He emphatically said that Bridget has been burned at all, indicating instead that she had suffered from tuberculosis. He intimated that Michael stayed away too long working as a cooper in various towns in the area and may have been jealous of his wife's activities in his absence, but that each time he returned her condition had deteriorated. Finally, she simply died from the disease that took so many Irish lives, but which carried the same stigma that cancer did early in the twentieth century. The fairy story was made up by the family to avoid the embarrassment of having to admit Bridget succumbed to tuberculosis. Jim McGrath also pointed out where he thought Bridget had been born (on the low road near the Kennedy cottage) and where Skehan's gate had been on the low road. Additionally, he pointed out something that had not been clear to us from reading the 1901 census records for the Kylatlea area. After the incident many relatives of the fairy doctor Denis Ganey apparently changed their names to Gahan or Gainey, but those who knew them refused to call them any differently and actually joked in a sing-song fashion about the Ganeys/Gahans/Gaineys. Most importantly he put us on to James Egan on whose property two hill-forts still exist.

James Egan is a Cloneen farmer and local history buff who is the great-grandson of Thomas Smyth, one of the witnesses at the magisterial inquiry and trial. He now occupies the property that Smyth and David Hogan, another witness in the legal proceedings, once owned. After futilely hiking the hills around Ballyvadlea in search of ring-forts, we finally followed Jim McGrath's advice and called on James Egan unexpectedly one day. His property in Garrankyle is contiguous to the property which faces on the "low road" where Skehan's gate is still located, and he confirmed that, according to oral tradition, tenant laborers and farmers considered it a fairy place at the end of the nineteenth century.

James Egan's property is about a mile and a half by back road from the Cleary cottage, and it does still contain two very unusual side-by-side, so-called double hill-forts with the well area still very defined. He selflessly took the time to trek with us and explained historical details about the two on his property and the whereabouts of others in the area. From James Egan we learned that the actual fairy-fort Bridget Cleary had visited on Kylnagranagh was "knocked" (leveled) several years ago by another Cloneen farmer. (This at least assured us we had been hiking the right area.) He also showed us a survey map indicating the exact size and location of the fairy forts on Kylnagranagh—the larger of which (2.5 acres) on the far side of the hill that Bridget frequented. Back in 1895 Hogan's and Smyth's properties had been side by side and within easy walking distance of the Cleary place. James Egan told us that his great-grandfather heard dogs barking all over the area "like during lambing season" on the night and morning that Bridget was murdered and buried. When Smyth went out to check his own lambs he told his wife that he saw a light on at the Cleary's. This information led us to speculate that the dogs had smelled the burning flesh and reacted to Michael Cleary and Pat Kennedy as they dragged Bridget's body down the road to bury it. Since Smyth had visited the Clearys on the afternoon and evening of the March 15, James Egan said that his great-grandmother had expressed relief that her husband had returned from the ill-fated cottage before the murder took place, leading us to believe that local residents at the time feared what might happen as Bridget's relatives sought to determine, as best they knew how, whether she was a changeling possessed by the fairies.

James Egan stressed to us that he also did not believe the fairy explanation of Bridget's death. Instead, he and several others subscribed to the idea that Michael killed her out of jealousy because he suspected that she was unfaithful during his long absences working as a cooper in Clonmel. Cleary then simply used the fairy changeling story to avoid prosecution for murder. There is legitimate concern among the current residents of Cloneen that the Bridget Cleary incident not be sensationalized as it had been in 1895 to make the community look "like ignorant people were disgracing" it again at the end of this century. This justifiable local concern is one of the reasons that we have gone out of our way to place the entire affair in the historical context of the time, rather than simply describe it as a "scandalous and backward catastrophe," in the words of one local resident, or make it into an intellectual abstraction based on late-twentieth-century postmodern theories. The historical and contemporary people of the Clonmel/Cloneen/Mullinahone area of County Tipperary deserve better than this.

At the beginning of our second trip to Clonmel in 1999 we by chance wandered into the Tipperary S. R. County Museum on Parnell Street, just at it was in the process of moving to a new facility. There Robert Holland, Curator, provided us with pictures, and Bob Withers gave us the names and phone numbers of several regional historians, folklorists, and poets, including Margaret ("Peg") Rossiter, member of the Clonmel Historical Society, and two local school teacher/historians, Michael Ahern in Clonmel and Patrick C. Power (Ph.D., National University, Ireland) in Ballyneale; a poet and folklorist from Carrick-on-Suir, Michael Coady; and Joe Kenny, head of the Historical Society in Fethard. In turn, through conversations with these individuals, we learned about the local primary school teacher in Cloneen, "Shay" Ahessy, in whose school the records for the last quarter of the nineteenth century are still kept. The records for the boys are all there from 1873, but until 1885, girls from Cloneen and Ballyvadlea did not attend this second oldest National School in Ireland. Instead, they went to the convent school in Drangan. Mr. Ahessy located the Infant Register for this school, which clearly indicates that Bridget Boland began to attend school on May 26, 1871, at the age of four, confirming our discovery that she was actually born on February 19, 1867—two years before others writing about her have asserted. Bridget only attended twenty days of classes that first year because she did not begin classes until the third term. School records indicate that she went to this school until June 30, 1881, but that her days in class diminished dramatically in 1880 and 1881, dwindling to only thirty in her final year. Her last full year of attendance was 1879, when, in addition to the standard reading, spelling, writing, arithmetic, grammar, geography, and needlework, she took optional classes in singing, drawing, and learning to use a sewing machine. However, she was "struck off" the admissions list three times apparently for lack of payment of school fees. In 1875 and again in 1877 she was readmitted within a month. In 1881 she was "struck off" again and never officially readmitted, although the nuns at this convent school continued to officially grade her performance in various classes through June 1879.

From Mr. Withers we also learned about John Ryan, who owns the used book and furniture store in Clonmel where we purchased a few out-of-print publications; about Father Tony Lamb, the current Cloneen parish priest; and about Sheila Foley, the head of the Charles Kickham Museum and the annual Kickham celebration in Mullinahone. In addition to showing us Kickham memorabilia, Sheila Foley and her husband Denis, a historian of one of the oldest co-ops in Ireland located in Mullinahone, graciously invited us to their home and showed us a 1918 silent movie version of Kickham's novel *Knocknagow*, directed by Fred O'Donovan, a member of the Film Company of Ireland, founded in 1916. The film, adapted for the screen by Mrs. N. F. Patton and shot on location in the valleys and mountains of Tipperary where Kickham had set his novel, premiered at the Phibsboro Cinema in Dublin on May 13, 1918. Viewing it gave us a vivid sense of the dress, customs, and class divisions of the period, and we are grateful to the Foleys and to the Irish National Film Archive for information about the film, which was deposited there by the film historian Liam O'Leary, whose book *Cinema Ireland, 1896–1980* is an invaluable resource on early Irish films. With the help of Rose Holohan and Meave O'Brien at the Community Care Centre on Western Road in Clonmel, we researched the Registry of Births, Deaths, and Marriages and found out that previous studies had not stated the correct ages of some of the principal characters, using baptismal dates from Church records, instead of registered birth dates. In nineteenth-century Ireland, the gap between the birth of a child and when it was baptized ranged from a few months to a few years.

The several hours we spent at the Hearns Hotel in Clonmel talking with Margaret (Peg) Rossiter were particularly rewarding. She gave us a sense of the isolation of townlands like Ballyvadlea in the late nineteenth century until the bicycle "changed everything," and the influence of the Quakers in Clonmel until the Grubb family and others converted to the Episcopal Church of Ireland. She said that the entire region remained a "gray, dispirited" place through the Second World War, suffering from severe class divisions and a politics characterized by "mad idealists" rather than practical problem solvers. This was a carryover from the previously violent history of County Tipperary and Clonmel, although the city did not become excessively involved in either the 1916 Rising or later revolutionary activity leading to independence. Peg Rossiter also underscored the stigma on Bridget Cleary for not having children—barrenness at that time always being considered the fault of the wife. In addition, we discussed with her lingering superstitions among the Irish and new forms of superstitions elsewhere in the world at the end of the twentieth century. We agreed that the veneer of civilization is still very fragile.

Two local schoolteachers—Michael Ahern of Clonmel and Patrick C. Power of Ballyneale—both of whom have published extensively about the area, gave us the benefit of their knowledge of records and history. Michael Ahern generously gave us a copy of George Henry Bassett's out-of-print guide and directory for County Tipperary for 1889. With Patrick Power we walked the mountain Slievenamon and sat on Suí Finn with him gazing down on the Anner valley below after he performed a pagan ritual that drove away the drizzle and clouds. Coming down he sang us Irish songs and we later drank a "special brew" and ate rhubarb pie with him and his wife Pauline as he told us historical and fairy stories about the mountain and the area. His vast knowledge of the fairy and folk history of the area is not only truly enlightening but also immensely entertaining. His explanations of the meaning of the term *pishoges* and the early mythological stories associated with "Other People" and Slievenamon and Finn McCuill were invaluable.

Additionally, Dr. Power clarified how the complicated hierarchical British system of justice operated in practice, as opposed to what it looked like on paper, and how prejudiced against the Irish most of the propertied justices of the peace and magistrates were at the end of the nineteenth century. Among other things, we learned from him that the Resident Magistrates (R.M.'s) evolved in the 1830s from the so-called Stipendary Magistrates, who had been brought in and paid to handle controversial cases. Thus, "he smells of a magistrate" was a common term of opprobrium among the Irish. Rather than the abusive colonial system the English often imposed on "natives" in other parts of the United Kingdom, Patrick Power said the British treated the Irish "as poor relations . . . from the outback." The English apparently did not refer to the Irish as "colonials," and so the use of the term "colonial system" with reference to Ireland so common today in academic circles is actually incorrect. He also told us some of the stories for which the fairy doctor Denis Ganey is still known in the area—over one hundred years after he was arrested in the Cleary case. Dr. Powers pointed out, however, that Ganey was probably not well-known in Clonmel before he was arrested. We had assumed that the poor Irish in Clonmel would have utilized Ganey's "cures," but Dr. Powers thinks not. Instead, in Clonmel he was considered, by rich and poor alike, a "local" from the country and disdained as someone who lived "out the mountain." Lastly, but very importantly, Dr. Powers told us that John Holohan might be able to get us inside the Cleary cottage for the pictures which appear in this book.

Mary Giunan-Darmody, Librarian at the County Library in Thurles, very patiently helped us use the materials there, often pointing out new, helpful sources. Dr. Philomena (Phil) Connolly at the National Archives guided us through the complicated procedure involved in using Irish jail and convict prison records. The general staff at the both the National Archives and National Library in Dublin and at the Public Library in Clonmel were especially helpful, as was the Most Reverend Dermot Clifford, D.D., Archbishop of Cashel and Emly, who gave us permission to look at the Thomas Croke papers at the National Library. He also asked Archivist Father Christopher O'Dwyer, President of St. Patrick's College in Thurles, to double-check Croke's records there for more information than is on the microfilm version of his papers. Father O'Dwyer located for us the picture of Archbishop Thomas William Croke and other members of the Church hierarchy taken during his 1895 Silver Jubilee.

Before we left the United States to finish our research in Ireland, both Emmet Larkin, Professor of History at the University of Chicago, and Margaret MacCurtain, recently retired as Senior Lecturer from University College Dublin, advised us as to sources and contacts. Our conversation with Larkin after he gave a graduate seminar at Ohio University's Contemporary History Institute in May 1999 answered many of our questions about the "devotional revolution" in Ireland after the Great Famine. Cliarán Toland, then a law student at Trinity College conducted valuable preliminary legal research for us in 1997 at the recommendation of Trinity Law Professor Ivana Bacik. Angie Kindig, Assistant Archivist at Notre Dame Library, photocopied some letters to Croke for us and Gayle Fischer and Dean Kotlowski conducted microfilm research on Irish newspapers when they were history Ph.D. graduate students at Indiana University, Bloomington. Bonnie Hagerman, a Ph.D. student in the Contemporary History Institute program at Ohio University researched articles and books for this project.

Finally, several women friends volunteered to represent the "general reader" for the manuscript, reading it more than once in some cases. Particularly helpful were the detailed content and stylistic comments by Elaine Reuben. Moureen Coulter, Alden Waitt, Terry Anderson, Carolyn Carpenter, and Alice Yeates also read and commented on various versions of the book. Anderson also conducted research with us in Ireland. Although the fairies plagued us from time to time with PC/MAC computer incompatibility problems, we thank them, above all others, for making this story possible and hope that we have finally given them their just due for the time that they appeared on Ballyvadlea.

Joan Hoff and Marian Yeates
Big Sky, Montana, January 2000

Bibliography

Primary Sources

Census, 1901, 1910, Thurles County Library.

Chief Secretary's Office Reports (CSORP), Ireland, Police and Crime Division (Ordinary), National Archives, Dublin.

Clonmel Gaol Registers, No. 13, General Register, January 1, 1894–January 28, 1903, National Archives, Dublin.

Convict Prisons and Depots, 1850–1914, National Archives, Dublin.

Convict Reference Files (CRF), Criminal Index Books, National Archives, Dublin.

Crown Files Assizes, 1895, National Archives, Dublin.

CSORP, Ireland, Crime Branch Special (CBS), National Archives, Dublin.

Thomas William Croke Papers (microfilm and calendar for letters), National Library, Dublin.

Thomas William Croke Calendar Letters, Hesburgh Library, University of Notre Dame Archives, South Bend, Ind.

John Dillon Papers, National Library, Dublin.

Fairy Tale: A True Story. 1997 film directed by Charles Sturridge.

Griffith's Valuations, 1850, Barony Middlethird, Thurles County Library.

Hearth Records, Clonmel Public Library.

Knocknagow, 1918 silent movie.

Limerick Gaol Registers, No. 20, General Register, December 25, 1894–December 31, 1898, National Archives, Dublin.

Magisterial Inquiry and Trial Transcript compiled by Gerry McCarthy, circa 1940s and given to authors by Brendan Long [cited as Long Transcript].

Magisterial Inquiry and Trial Description from Irish newspapers compiled by Rory Fitzpatrick, circa 1994 and given to authors [cited as Fitzpatrick Media Coverage].

Penal Record of Convicts (PEN), National Archives, Dublin.

Penal Servitude Files (on computer), National Archives, Dublin.

Photographing Fairies. 1997 film directed by Nick Willing.

Registry of Births, Marriages, and Deaths, Community Care Centre, Clonmel, County Tipperary.

RTE (Radio Erin) documentary on Bridget Cleary, 1995.

Thom's Official Directory of the United Kingdom of Great Britain and Ireland (Dublin: Alex Thom., 1893–1914), National Archives, Dublin.

Newspapers in England, Ireland, and the United States

Boston Globe
Clonmel Chronicle, Tipperary and Waterford Advertiser
Cork Examiner
Daily Graphic, London
Dublin Daily Express
Freeman's Journal
Irish Daily Independent, Dublin
Irish Times, Dublin
Times, London
Nationalist and Tipperary Advertiser, Clonmel
Nenagh News
New York Irish World and American Industrial Liberator
Punch or the London Charivari
Regina Leader
The Spectator
Toronto World
United Ireland

Secondary Sources

Articles

Amos, Keith. "James Kiely–Clonmel's Forgotten Fenian." *Tipperary Historical Journal* (1989): 35–37.

Bartlett, Thomas. "An Account of the Whiteboys from the 1790s." *Tipperary Historical Journal* (1991): 140–147.

Benson, E. F. "The Recent 'Witch-Burning' at Clonmel." *The Nineteenth Century*. No. 220 (June 1895): 1053–1058.

Bourke, Angela. "Reading a Woman's Death: Colonial Text and Oral Tradition in Nineteenth-Century Ireland. *Feminist Studies* 21 (Fall 1995): 553–586.

––––––. "The Virtual Reality of Irish Fairy Legend. *Éire-Ireland* 31, nos. 1–2 (Spring–Summer 1996): 7–25.

––––––. "The Burning of Bridget Cleary: Newspapers and Oral Tradition." *Tipperary Historical Journal* (1998): 112–127.

Bourke, Joanna. "'The Best of All Home Rulers': The Economic Power of Women in Ireland, 1880–1914." *Irish Economic and Social History* (1991): 34–47.

Butler, Hubert. "The Eggman and the Fairies." In R. F. Foster, ed. *The Sub-Prefect Should Have Held His Tongue and Other Essays.* Penguin Press, 1990, pp. 102–112.

Christianson, Gael E. "Secret Societies in Ireland, 1790–1840." *Agricultural History* 46 (July 1972): 369–384.

Condren, Mary. "Sacrifice and Political Legitimation: The Production of a Gendered Social Order." *Journal of Women's History* 6, no. 4, 7, no. 1 (Winter/Spring 1995): 160–189.

Davies, Owens. "Urbanization and the Decline of Witchcraft: An Examination of London." *Journal of Social History* 30, no. 3 (Spring 1971): 597–617.

Daly, Mary E. "Women in the Irish workforce from pre-industrial to modern times." *Saothar* 7 (1981): 74–82.

Delaney, Edward. "The Famine from Cashel to Kilfeacle." *Tipperary Historical Journal* (1995): 81–82.

Downing, Taylor. "The Film Company of Ireland." *Sight and Sound* 49, no. 1 (Winter 1979–1980): 42–45.

Dunne, John. "The Fenian Traditions of Sliabh-na-mban." *Transactions of the Kilkenny Archaeological Society* 1, part 3 (1851): 333–362.

Fitzpatrick, David. "The Disappearance of the Irish Agricultural Labourer, 1841–1912." *Irish Economic and Social History* 7 (1980): 66–92.

Galvin, Patrick. "The Last Burning," in *Three Plays. Threshold,* Lyric Players Theatre 27 (Spring 1976): 7–58.

Graham, B. J., and Susan Hood. "Town-Tenant Protest in Late Nineteenth-And Early Twentieth-Century Ireland." *Irish Economic and Social History* (1994): 39–57.

Kickham, Charles J. "Rory of the Hill." In Kathleen Hoagland, ed. *1000 Years of Irish Poetry.* New York: Konecky & Konecky: 1975, pp. 525–526.

Luddy, Maria. "Women and Work in Clonmel: Evidence from the 1881 Census." *Tipperary Historical Journal* (1993): 95–101.

MacCárthaigh, Tadhg. "Memories of the Famine from the Irish Folklore Commission." *Tipperary Historical Journal* (1996): 43–46.

Marnane, Denis G. "Land and Violence in 19th-Century Tipperary." *Tipperary Historical Journal* (1988): 53–91.

McAnnlly, R., Jr. "The Police," *Irish Wonders.* New York: Gramercy Books, 1996; reprint of original 1888 Houghton Mifflin edition.

McGrath, T. G. "Fairy Faith and Changelings: The Burning of Bridget Cleary in 1895." *Dublin. Studies* 71 (Summer 1982): 178–184.

———. "The Famine in South Tipperary—Part One." *Tipperary Historical Journal* (1996): 1–35.

Murphy, Clare C. "North Tipperary in the Year of the Fenian Rising—Part 1." *Tipperary Historical Journal* (1995): 108–115.

The National Centenary Supplement, 1890–1990.

Ni Mhainnín, Cáit. "The Famine Around Slievenamon." *Tipperary Historical Journal* (1995): 84.

Ó Cléirigh, Nellie Beary. "Glimpses of South Tipperary During the Great Famine." *Tipperary Historical Journal* (1993): 76–81.

O'Donnell, Michael. "Lighting the Streets of Fethard, 1870–1914." *Tipperary Historical Journal* (1998): 128–132.

O'Donnell, Seán. "Some Aspects of the Famine in Clonmel." *Tipperary Historical Journal* (1998): 76–157.

Ó Gráda, Cormac. "The Heights of Clonmel Prisoners 1845–9: Some Dietary Implications." *Irish Economic and Social History* (1991): 24–33.

———. "The Wages of a Fethard Farmer, 1880–1905." *Tipperary Historical Journal* (1994): 67–72.

Power, Patrick C. "1829 in Tipperary." In Kickham Centenary Committee, eds. *Knocknagow Remembers.* Clonmel, Co. Tipperary: Nationalist Press, 1982, pp. 37–40.

Simms, J. G. "The Cromwellian Settlement of Tipperary." *Tipperary Historical Journal* (1989): 27–33.

Tierney, Mark, O.S.B. "Dr. Croke, the Irish Bishops and the Parnell Crisis. 18 November 1890–21 April 1891." *Collectanea Hibernica*, no. 11 (1968): 111–148.

_____. "A Short-Title Calendar of the Papers of Archbishop Thomas William Croke in Archbishop's House, Thurles: Part I, 1841–1885." *Collectanea Hibernica*, no. 13 (1970): 100–138.

_____. "A Short-Title Calendar of the Papers of Archbishop Thomas William Croke in Archbishop's House, Thurles: Part 2: 1886–1890." *Collectanea Hibernica*, no. 16 (1973): 97–124.

_____. "A Short-Title Calendar of the Papers of Archbishop Thomas William Croke in Archbishop's House, Thurles: Part 3, 1891–1902." *Collectanea Hibernica*, no. 17 (1974–1975): 111–144.

Vance, R. N. C. "Text and Tradition: Robert Emmet's Speech from the Dock." *Irish Studies* 71, no. 282 (Summer 1982): 185–191.

Books

Akenson, Donald H. *The Irish Education Experiment: The National System of Education in the Nineteenth Century.* London: Routledge and Kegan Paul, 1970.

Bassett, George Henry. *County Tipperary. One Hundred Years Ago: A Guide and Directory, 1889.* Belfast: Friar's Bush Press, 1991; reprint of 1889 edition, entitled, *The Book of Country Tipperary.*

Bourke, Angela. *The Burning of Bridget Cleary: A True Story.* London: Pimlico, 1999.

Boyce, D. G. *The Irish Question and British Politics, 1868–1986.* New York: St. Martin's Press, 1988.

Bull, Philip. *Land, Politics, and Nationalism: A Study of the Irish Land Question.* Dublin: Gill and Macmillan, 1996.

Clark, Samuel, and James S. Donnelly, Jr., eds. *Irish Peasants: Violence and Political Unrest, 1780–1914.* Madison: University of Wisconsin Press, 1983.

Colls, Robert, and Philip Dodd. *Englishness: Politics and Culture, 1880–1920.* London: Croom Helm, 1986.

Comerford, R. V. *Charles J. Kickham: A Study in Irish Nationalism and Literature.* Portmarnock, County Dublin: Wolfhound Press, 1979.

Condren, Mary. *The Serpent and the Goddess: Women, Religion, and Power of Celtic Ireland.* New York: Harper and Row, 1989.

Curtis, L. Perry, Jr. *Coercion and Conciliation in Ireland, 1880–1892: A Study of Conservative Unionism.* New York: New York University Press, 1963.

_____. *Anglo-Saxons and Celts: A Study of Anti-Irish Prejudice in Victorian England.* Bridgeport, Conn.: Conference on British Studies at the University of Bridgeport, 1968.

de Paor, Liam. *The Peoples of Ireland: From Prehistory to Modern Times.* London: Hutchinson, 1986.

Donnelly, James S., Jr. *The Land and the People of Nineteenth-Century Cork: The Rural Economy and the Land Question.* London: Routledge and Kegan Paul, 1975.

Ellmann, Richard. *Oscar Wilde.* London: Penguin Books, 1988; reprint of 1987 Hamish Hamilton edition.

Eversley, Lord. *Gladstone and Ireland: The Irish Policy of Parliament from 1850–1894.* Westport, Conn.: Greenwood Press, Publishers, 1971.

Foley, Sheila. Biographical account of C. J. Kickham, manuscript given to authors.

Foster, R. F. *Modern Ireland, 1600–1972.* New York: Penguin, 1989; reprint of 1988 Viking edition.

Gébler, Carlo. *How to Murder a Man.* London: Abacus, 1999; reprint of 1998 Little, Brown and Company edition.

_____. *The Cure: A Novel* (Boston: Little, Brown and Company, 1996).

Glassie, Henry, ed. *Irish Folktales.* New York: Pantheon Books, 1985.

Hachey, Thomas E., Joseph M. Hernon, Jr., and Lawrence J. McCaffrey. *The Irish Experience.* Englewood Cliffs, N.J.: Prentice Hall, 1989.

Hoagland, Kathleen, ed. *1000 Years of Irish Poetry.* New York: Konecky and Konecky, 1975.

Holzapfel, Rudi, compiler. *Tipperariana: Being Notes, Pointers, & Current Market Prices of Tipperary Books for Scholar and Collector.* Fethard, Co. Tipperary: Fethard Historical Society, 1997.

Johnson, Paul. *Ireland: A Concise History from the Twelfth Century to the Present Day.* Chicago: Academy Publishers, 1980.

Kennedy, Patrick. *Legends of Irish Witches and Fairies.* Dublin: Mercier Press, 1976.

Kickham, Charles J. *Knocknagow: or, The Homes of Tipperary*, 24th ed. Dublin: James Duffy, 1873.

Kickham Centenary Committee, eds., *Knocknagow Remembers.* Clonmel, Co. Tipperary: Nationalist Press, 1982.

Larkin, Emmet. *The Roman Catholic Church and the Creation of the Modern Irish State, 1878–1886.* Philadelphia: American Philosophical Society, 1975.

_____. *The Historical Dimensions of Irish Catholicism.* New York: Arno Press, 1976.

_____. *The Roman Catholic Church in Ireland and the Fall of Parnell, 1888–1891.* Liverpool: Liverpool University Press, 1979.

_____. *The Consolidation of the Roman Catholic Church in Ireland, 1860–1870.* Chapel Hill: University of North Carolina Press, 1987.

_____. trans. and ed. *Alexis de Tocqueville's Journey in Ireland.* Washington, D.C.: Catholic University of America Press, 1990.

_____. *The Roman Catholic Church and the Emergence of the Modern Irish Political System, 1874–1878.* Washington, D.C.: Catholic University of America Press, 1996.

Larkin, Mick, and the Carraigmoclear Commemoration Committee, eds. *Battle of Carraigmoclear: Slievenamon, 1798.* Clonmel: Sureprint, 1992.

Logan, Patrick. *The Old Gods: The Facts About Irish Fairies.* Belfast: Appletree Press, 1981.

McCarthy, Michael J. F. *Five Years in Ireland, 1895–1900.* Dublin: Hodges Figgis, 1902.

McCormack, Jerusha, ed. *Wilde: The Irishman.* New Haven, Conn.: Yale University Press, 1998.

Mackintosh, Alexander. *From Gladstone to Lloyd George: Parliament in Peace and War.* New York: Kraus Reprint Co., 1970; reprint of 1921 Hodder and Soughton edition.

Maher, James, ed. *Romantic Slievenamon in History, Folklore, and Song: A Tipperary Anthology.* Mullinahone, Co. Tipperary: n.p., 1955.

Matthews, Caitlín. *The Elements of the Celtic Tradition.* Rockport, Mass.: Element Books, 1989.

Marriot, J. A. R., Sir. *Modern England, 1885–1945: A History of My Own Times.* 4th ed. London: Methuen, 1948.

Murphy, Gerald. *Duanaire Finn* [Poem-Book of Finn]. Vol. 3. Dublin: Irish Text Society, 1953.

Murphy, William. *Charles J. Kickham, Patriot, Novelist, and Poet.* Blackrock, Co. Dublin: Carraig Books, 1976, facsimile of 1903 edition.

Nolan, William, and Thomas G. McGrath, eds. *Tipperary: History and Society. Interdisciplinary Essays on the History of an Irish County.* Dublin: Geography Publications, 1985.

Nugent, Seán, ed. *Slievenamon in Story and Song.* Kilsheelan, Ireland: Kilkenny People, 1995.

O'Day, Alan, and John Stevenson, eds. *Irish Historical Documents Since 1800.* Dublin: Gill and Macmillan, 1992.

O'Dwyer, Martin, ed. *A Biographical Dictionary of Tipperary.* Cashel. Co. Tipperary: Folk Village, 1999.

O'Leary, Liam. *Cinema Ireland, 1896–1980.* Dublin: National Library of Ireland, 1990.

O'Shea, James. *Priest, Politics and Society in Post-famine Ireland: A Study of County Tipperary, 1850–1891.* Dublin: Wolfhound Press, 1983.

Paseta, Senia. *Before the Revolution: Nationalism, Social Change, and Ireland's Catholic Elite, 1879–1922.* Cork: Cork University Press, 1999.

Pearce, Malcolm and Geoffrey Stewart. *British Political History, 1867–1995.* London: Routledge, 1996.

Power, Patrick C. *A History of South Tipperary.* Cork: Mercier Press, 1989.

Power, Thomas P. *Land, Politics and Society in Eighteenth-Century Tipperary.* Oxford: Clarendon Press, 1993.

Sawyer, Roger. *"We Are but Women": Women in Ireland's History.* London: Routledge, 1993.

Seymour, St. John Drelincourt. *Irish Witchcraft and Demonology.* New York: Causeway Press, 1973; reprint of original 1913 edition.

Sidky, H. *Witchcraft, Lycanthropy, Drugs, and Disease: An Anthropological Study of the European Witch-Hunts.* New York: Peter Lang, 1997.

Silver, Carole G. *Strange and Secret Peoples: Fairies and Victorian Consciousness.* New York: Oxford University Press, 1999.

Tierney, Mark. *Croke of Cashel: The Life of Archbishop Thomas William Croke, 1823–1902.* Dublin: Gill and Macmillan, 1976.

Walsh, Victor Anthony. "Across 'The Big Wather': Irish Community Life in Pittsburgh and Allegheny City, 1853–1885." Ph.D. dissertation, University of Pittsburgh, 1983.

White, James, ed. *My Clonmel Scrap Book.* Clonmel, Co. Tipperary: Tentmaker Publications, 3rd ed., 1995.

Williams, Desmond T., ed. *Secret Societies in Ireland.* Dublin: Gill and Macmillan, 1973.

Yeats, W. B. *The Land of Heart's Desire.* 3rd ed. Portland, Maine: Thomas B. Mosher, 1903.

_____, ed. *Irish Fairy and Folk Tales.* New York: Barnes and Noble Books reprint, 1993.

Note: Articles in edited collections of essays have not been cited separately from the books in which they appear.

Index